AF579977

THE EXPERIMENTER'S CHALLENGE

THE EXPERIMENTER'S CHALLENGE

Methods and Issues in Psychological Research

John Jung
California State University Long Beach

Macmillan Publishing Co., Inc.,
New York

Collier Macmillan Publishers
London

Printed in the United States of America.

Macmillan Publishing Co., Inc.
866 Third Avenue, New York, New York 10022

Collier Macmillan Canada, Inc.

ISBN 0-02-361510-9

Printing: 1 2 3 4 5 6 7 8   Year: 2 3 4 5 6 7 8 9

To Jeffrey,
A Challenge and a Dilemma,
But Also a Father's Pride and Joy

PREFACE

The Experimenter's Challenge is an introduction to research method and design for undergraduate majors in psychology and related fields. The experimental method plays a central role in the testing of theories, discovery of new empirical evidence, and furthering our understanding of the nature of the causes and underlying processes of behavior. This approach represents a powerful alternative to common sense, intuition, and other less rigorous traditional avenues to knowledge.

Although the challenge to the experimenter is substantial, the basic logic underlying experimentation is rather simple and straightforward although there are often difficult decisions involved in the actual implementation of experiments. The first part of the book presents the basic concepts and methods of experimental psychology while the second part deals extensively with the major issues and dilemmas confronting the experimenter such as demand characteristics, experimenter bias, sources of subjects, deception, debriefing, and social responsibility. It is not enough that the student learn only the technical aspects of research, especially since the majority of undergraduate psychology majors will not continue as active researchers in their careers, but it is essential that all students are informed and educated about the limitations as well as the strengths of experimental evidence so that they can critically interpret the significance of the vast literature of research findings. By presenting this type of balanced introduction to experimental method, *The Experimenter's Challenge* is somewhat unique among existing texts in this field.

Experience with teaching research methods courses for several years had led the author to believe firmly that the most important goals include teaching students to be independent and able to develop their own research ideas, starting with the search of relevant literature, critical evaluation of past studies, formulation of hypotheses, design and conduct of appropriate controlled experiments, the interpretation of results, and the preparation of formal laboratory reports. To achieve such independence calls for more than memorization of definitions and procedures. Throughout the book, emphasis is placed on the development of such independence. Since critical thinking and judgment about each part of the research process is essential, the book is aimed toward understanding and application rather than rote learning of concepts and methods. Recommended exercises are provided at the end of each chapter in Part I to further the mastery of the material.

No formal statistical material is included although sufficient conceptual material dealing with the logical aspects of statistical thinking is provided in enough detail to enable the student to proceed with the design and execution of experiments. In some universities and colleges, students will have already taken or will be concurrently taking statistics courses. Inclusion of similar material here would be redundant and perhaps even confusing since statistical notation varies widely among different textbooks.

Helpful suggestions and criticism has come from numerous individuals. I wish to thank two former students, Darryl Beale and Keith Colman, for their insightful criticisms and careful reading of Part I. The comments from my friends, David S. Holmes of the University of Kansas and Irwin Silverman of York University, especially on Part II, provided much valuable guidance in improving the manuscript. Finally, acknowledgment and thanks are offered to Benton J. Underwood and Donald T. Campbell, truly masters of methodology, who provided me, like so many other students at Northwestern University, with their inspirational teaching and exceptional expertise on research methodology.

J. J.

CONTENTS

THE EXPERIMENTER'S CHALLENGE

PART I

THE EXPERIMENTER'S METHODS

CHAPTER 1

On the Similarity of Everyday Thinking and Experimental Logic

Chapter at a Glance

Although it may surprise you, you already think like an experimenter when you deal with daily problem-solving situations. You are not yet familiar with all the technical terminology and jargon psychological researchers use when they conduct experiments, but this fact should not intimidate you. You can easily learn this new vocabulary. We should add, however, that you probably inconsistently apply your basic knowledge of the underlying logic of experimentation. Our emotional feelings and personal involvement in specific situations can sometimes block and distort our reasoning processes. In this first chapter, we examine some common situations that illustrate the similarity between your everyday thinking and the type of logic involved in the psychological experiment, which serves as a background for the more formal discussion of this methodology to follow.

Throughout our lives, we strive to understand the events and phenomena we experience and observe. We want to know "why" various occurrences take place. We formulate the answers in terms of "causes" and "effects"; we assume that events are not random happenings but that a determinism exists wherein one class of events–causes–precede another class of events–effects–in regular or lawful patterns. Both the layperson and the scientist, although the precision and objectivity of their methods differ, are concerned with the discovery of these relationships of causes and effects. While philosophers of science may challenge the validity of the concept of causality in a strict literal sense because it may not be possible to provide formal proof, the ideas of "causes" and "effects" are very much alive in ordinary as well as scientific usage. In the present discussion, we will continue to use these terms in a general sense without worrying about the reservations of philosophers.

In his thought-provoking book, *Zen and the Art of Motorcycle Maintenance*, Robert Pirsig (1974) draws a similar parallel between everyday and experimental logic when he suggests that a motorcycle mechanic informally conducts scientific experiments when generating hypotheses about what is wrong with malfunctioning bikes. He might honk the horn to determine if the battery is defective or not, but he must also exercise care in not drawing faulty conclusions from this "experiment." He can not logically conclude that the entire electrical system is functioning merely because the horn honks, since the horn is not part of the total electrical system which makes the motorcycle run.

Even if the mechanic can determine that the entire electrical system is operative, there is still no guarantee that the motorcycle will work because other systems may be defective. Thus, as Pirsig points out, "by asking the right questions and choosing the right tests and drawing the right conclusions, the mechanic works his way down the echelons of the motorcycle hierarchy until he has found the exact specific cause or causes of the engine failure, and then he changes them so that they no longer cause the failure."

Although the typical motorcycle mechanic may have never received formal instruction in experimentation, the mechanic must be able to think and reason in ways that strongly parallel those of the professional research scientist. Some conception or theory about the factors which are involved in motorcycle operation helps the mechanic formulate testable hypotheses about the source of the breakdown. A series of "experiments" may be necessary, with the outcomes of earlier manipulations determining the choice of factors to test in subsequent "experiments."

AN EXAMPLE: TELEVISION AND CHILDREN'S AGGRESSION

We can illustrate some of the aspects of the experimental approach just described by examining the question, "Is there a causal relationship between viewing aggression on television and aggressive behavior in children?" Based on a variety of past knowledge, observation, and past experience, the layperson may formulate some hypotheses or guesses as to the possible association between television viewing and children's aggression. We know, for example, that in general, children learn much from the observation of modelled behavior; thus we may suspect that the viewing of television may similarly eventually influence the actual behaviors of children. Since children observe much aggression when they watch the typical television dramas, we might predict that there should be greater aggressiveness among those children who watch the more aggressive programs. In other words, we want to explain or determine some of the causes of the individual differences in the amount of aggressive behavior we find among children. If one of these causes or determinants involves the viewing of aggressive programs on television, this factor should have been greater for the children who are more aggressive.

A variety of ways might be used to collect evidence to test our hypotheses. The most direct method might be assumed to yield the most accurate information, but it might prove inconvenient as well as unacceptable to the children and their parents if we sat in their living rooms to monitor their television viewing and followed the children around their neighborhood to measure their degree of aggression. Obviously, we would have to rely on less direct methods such as surveys or interviews of children, parents, and other relevant persons. Other problems arise here such as the question of the honesty, accuracy, and cooperativeness of the participants. Our study might prove obtrusive and therefore cause people to act differently from their normal patterns because they are either curious, anxious, or merely distracted by our presence. Even the knowledge about the purpose of the observations may bias the behavior of some individuals, depending on their personal values and beliefs.

In some situations it is possible to use unobtrusive methods of measurement so that the participants do not realize they are being observed, or at least know the true purpose or hypothesis of the study. Thus, one could make reasonable inferences about which programs were selected by different families if one could attach a metering device to the television sets which recorded the programs selected. This would be an imperfect method, however, since we may not know who, if anyone, actually watched the programs, although the sets were on. If we do not obtain permission to make these measurements from the families, ethical problems arise, such as the invasion of privacy. We will discuss such issues more thoroughly in a later chapter.

Uncontrolled versus Controlled Methods of Observation

In all of these brief descriptions of possible research methods, we have employed *uncontrolled* observations under naturalistic conditions. The type and amount of television viewing and the extent of aggressive behavior have been observed under fairly normal circumstances without any attempt by the investigator to introduce other factors that might alter any of the behaviors. These types of studies are termed *naturalistic* studies since they involve the measurement of behavioral phenomena as they occur in real life. In contrast, experiments entail *controlled* observations wherein behavior is compared under conditions the investigator systematically varies. The experimenter "manipulates" the factors hypothesized or assumed to have an effect on the behavior under study so that different groups, otherwise equivalent, are treated differentially with regard to the factor under investigation. For example, aggression may be inhibited to some extent because of fear of criticism and disapproval. However, if an individual is part of a group rather than alone, aggressive tendencies may be less inhibited.

In light of these assumptions, one might predict that how subjects view aggressive television programs–in groups or on an individual basis–might affect the extent to which such viewing may lead to aggressive behavior. In a controlled experiment, groups differing only with respect to this factor would be compared, and any overall differences in aggression would be attributed to the influence of the type of viewing conditions. Other factors such as the *amount* of viewing, which might ordinarily affect level of aggression, could not be responsible for the differences between groups in *this* experiment since this factor was controlled or equated for the different viewing groups. Evidence obtained from experiments provides explanatory power since it enables us to support or refute our hypotheses about the role of specific factors we may think influence behavior.

The Nature of Correlation

In dealing with our question about the influence of television on children's aggression, what are the advantages and disadvantages of uncontrolled versus controlled observational methods? First, consider the evidence from a naturalistic observation in which we do not manipulate or control any variables. We would end up with two sets of measures, one on each aspect of the children's behavior. If the two variables, television viewing of aggression and aggressive behavior, tend to increase (or decrease) together so that when more aggressive viewing occurs, more aggressive behavior also occurs, we speak of a *positive correlation*, as shown in Figure 1-1 (A). A *negative*, or inverse *correlation*, where an increase in one variable is associated with a decrease in the other, is shown in Figure 1-1 (B) where higher levels of aggressive viewing are associated with lower amounts of aggressive behavior. Finally, Figure 1-1 (C) depicts a situation where no correlation exists between the two factors, and any level of one factor is equally likely to be found with a given level of the second factor. In contrast, when the correlation is high (positive or negative), we can reasonably predict a person's score on one variable, given information about the score on the other variable.

Suppose we did conduct a naturalistic study on this topic and found a high positive correlation showing a link between aggressive behavior and the viewing of aggressive programs. Does this finding represent convincing evidence that one variable, type of program viewed, exerts a causal influence on the other variable, children's behavior? An alternative explanation for this same data might be that those children who are

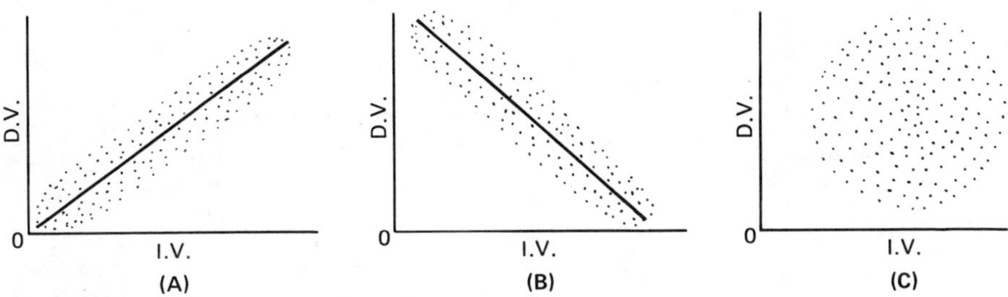

FIGURE 1-1. Three types of possible correlations between two variables, such as the amount of television viewing in children and their levels of aggressive behavior. In A, there is a positive correlation such that the higher the television viewing, the greater the aggression. In B, there is an inverse or negative relationship such that the higher the television viewing, the less the aggressive behavior. Finally, in C there is zero or no correlation between the two variables.

already more aggressive tend to find aggressive programs more enjoyable and exciting than less aggressive children who prefer nonaggressive programs. These rival explanations of the same relationship are diagrammed in the top half of Figure 1–2. The arrows indicate the two possible directions of causality.

Even if the results had been the opposite—that is, an inverse or negative correlation, with the less aggressive children watching aggressive programs to a greater extent—the problem of how to interpret any causal relationship would remain. On the one hand, such a correlation would be consistent with a theory of catharsis, which suggests that the viewing of aggression actually should reduce aggressive behavior because it provides a vicarious and safe means of releasing aggressive feelings. A rival explanation for the same inverse relationship, however, might be that nonaggressive children have a greater need for fantasy about aggression and power in order to compensate for their inability to assert themselves in real life, so they watch more of the aggressive television programs.

As long as we are dealing with uncontrolled observations, the evidence must be interpreted cautiously since it does not enable us to choose between competing explanations that fit the same data. Although any two causally-related factors will also highly correlate with each other, the opposite conclusion does not follow. High correlations may exist between two factors that have no causal relationship.

Another problem complicating the interpretation of correlations is the possibility of other "third factors," which we may be unaware of when we are comparing two specific factors or behaviors of interest. Thus, if we find that amount of viewing of aggressive television and amount of aggressive behavior are positively correlated, a direct causal relationship may still not exist between them because some undetected third factor—such as parental values—may really be the basic underlying cause of the extent to which children both watch aggressive programs

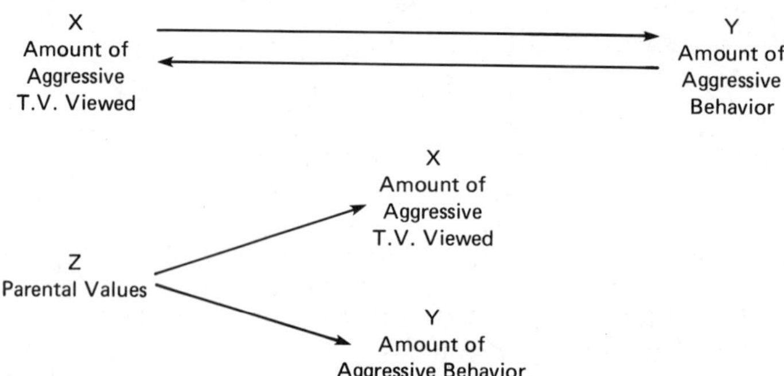

FIGURE 1–2. Several different explanations of a correlation between X and Y.

and the extent to which they act aggressively, as illustrated in the bottom half of Figure 1–2. In other words, even if no direct causal link exists between the amount of aggressive program viewing and aggressive behavior, one may still obtain a high correlation between the two dimensions because the third variable, in this case parental values, is the fundamental cause of both of these aspects of the children's behavior.

In this example then, correlational evidence is inadequate for causal inferences since it does not enable us to assume that the children who differ in the amounts of aggressive program viewing or aggressive behavior are equivalent in other important respects, such as parental values. In contrast, the use of controlled observation, such as the experiment, does allow us to examine the effect of amount of aggressive viewing since the experimenter can control this factor. The experimenter can create groups that are equal in all respects other than the extent to which they are allowed to watch aggressive programs during the experiment. After a period of such differential viewing, the experimenter can compare the groups with respect to aggressive behavior. Any differences would then be attributed to the influence of the two types of content viewed since it was the only difference the two groups encountered during the experiment.

Although the present discussion emphasizes the strengths of controlled experiments as a distinct advantage over correlational or uncontrolled evidence, we might not have fertile ideas and hypotheses about psychological phenomena and behavior to test with our experiments without the initial observation of correlations. The interplay between the two types of evidence is a necessary aspect of the total research endeavor.

Finding a Cause, Given an Effect

The basic logic underlying the psychological experiment is quite simple, as claimed earlier, and similar to the processes by which we try to solve everyday problems. The other day my pocket penlight failed to work. I probably could have fixed it by replacing both the battery and the bulb, but that may have been unnecessarily extravagant since only one component may have been defective. So I could have arbitrarily first selected to replace one part and then observed the outcome. If the penlight then worked, I would know that the replaced part had been the faulty one. If the penlight still failed, I would then try replacing the other part, remembering to replace the original first part to ensure that I could identify the effect of my second replacement. The penlight should now work, if the defect was limited to either the bulb or the battery. If the penlight still fails, I would then suspect that both parts were defective and resort to changing both at the same time. Now, unless other parts of my penlight are defective, it should work.

Finding an Effect, Given a Cause

In other situations, we "work backward" in that we want to determine what effects, if any, some suspected cause might produce. We need only introduce the "cause" and then stand back and observe its "effect." If we wish to achieve a particular effect, the task is more difficult and resembles the proverbial search for the "needle in the haystack." We might take a series of suspected causes and test them one-by-one to see if we can produce the desired effect. Of course, we might have some guides for our search based on past knowledge so that we do not engage in a random search.

Suppose, for example, I am cooking beef stroganoff but it just isn't coming out right. I "know" how it should taste, but for some reason I have been unable to produce that taste. Maybe if I just added a little bit of this or a touch of that! Suppose it tasted too flat; what might I try to add? I probably would not try corn starch, but I might try some type of spice. By comparing the taste of the dish before and after the addition of the spice, I could reach some conclusion about the "causal" effect of this ingredient. I would have to be careful not to introduce too many changes at the same time. If I tossed in five different spices at once, the taste would surely change, but how could I identify which spices made the difference? Or if I added one spice and also lowered the cooking temperature and obtained a difference in taste, could I determine the contribution of each change?

Both of these ordinary examples illustrate the use of a type of systematic substitution-and-comparison process to identify the causes of certain effects or the effects of certain causes. Similarly, in performing psychological experiments, one hopes to answer questions of psychological interest with an analogous—although more formalized—set of procedures. For example, suppose we notice that the employees of one company are more productive than those of a rival. What is the "cause" of this "effect"? The successful company has younger supervisors; should we conclude that this difference causes the differential productivity? Other important factors might be the fact that the pay scales, work environment, and employer–employee harmony differ between the two companies. Any or all of these factors might account for the differences in productivity. Ideally we might try to create a situation where the only ingredient that differed between the two companies was the age of the supervisors, if we hope to draw sound conclusions about the effect of that specific cause. As we shall see later, this strategy is the essence of the logic of true experiments.

As an example of the reverse situation wherein we wish to determine the effects of some assumed causal factor, consider the assessment of the influence of segregated schools on learning. At first glance, one might think that a comparison of achievement between segregated and unsegregated schools would answer this question. However, as Stephan (1978) has pointed out, these two types of schools also vary in a number of other dimensions which may also causally influence learning. Segregated and desegregated schools differ in racial composition of the student body, but also in socioeconomic levels, quality of teachers, equality of facilities, student–faculty ratios, racial attitudes of students, and so forth. Any or all of these factors may contribute to differences in achievement.

This type of situation is also a good example of an emotionally-charged one about which many people lack objectivity in their reasoning. They fail to analyze the situation as thoroughly as they can. Their emotions may have already helped them make their appraisals, so they are selective in their information processing, noticing only the positive evidence that supports their position while ignoring or discounting contrary information. Faced with a logically-analogous problem, such as the beef stroganoff example where emotions are not as strong, a person may readily notice that if you add five spices at once you cannot conclude that the taste difference is due entirely to only one of the additions. Yet, the same person may fail to notice that conclusions are equivocal when several factors vary at the same time for a controversial situation such as school desegregation.

This example is a complex issue and one where it may be too difficult or socially unacceptable to conduct true experiments in which only one factor—such as racial composition of schools—is varied while all other factors are equated or controlled. It should be noted, however, that unless such studies are done, interpretations of this kind of correlational evidence are equivocal.

In these everyday examples, we have tried to show how comparisons are made and conclusions are drawn, sometimes on weak grounds, when differences are observed under varying circumstances. The challenge involves finding ways to rule out alternative explanations so that an unambiguous conclusion can be made. In experimental research, as we shall soon see, the basic logic calls for systematic observation under conditions which allow us to evaluate each factor without the concurrent covariation of other factors. In this fashion we hope to exclude rival interpretations about the causes of the observed effects.

THEORY AND ITS RELATIONSHIP TO EXPERIMENTS

The real-life observations are a necessary first step in the process of inquiry since they provide us with detailed descriptions of the actual nature of the phenomenon or behavior to be explained. Based on the pattern of evidence obtained, we may develop an explanation or theory. Theories vary widely in amount of detail and formality, but they are basically a set of abstract statements that explain or account for a set of facts or observations. Equity theory, for example, deals with the idea that fairness or justice is important to most people in that they think rewards received should be in proportion to the amount of work or effort expended. This theory could be applied to diverse areas such as worker motivation, exchange of gifts, and attitudes about criminal justice.

A useful theory must be testable or capable of disproof. Some theories, although abstract explanations of behavior, are circular in the sense that you can never disprove them. The notion that suicides are caused by a "death wish," for example, would be difficult to test unless we could find a method of measuring the presence of this factor prior to the actual behavior. Then we could compare persons differing in the amount of this factor and see if our prediction of more suicides among those with this tendency is confirmed. In short, testable theories permit the derivation of implications or hypotheses of the sort, "If x, then y," which can be evaluated in experiments, as shown in Figure 1-3. If predictions are confirmed, the theory is more credible, but if negative results are obtained, doubt is aroused which may eventually lead us to revise or reject the theory.

In other words, theories serve as guides which direct the course of research. For example, if we create an inequitable situation, we should expect people to attempt to restore or achieve equity, according to the equity theory. Thus it has been predicted and found (Adams & Rosenbaum, 1962) that feelings of inequity can lead to lowered work output

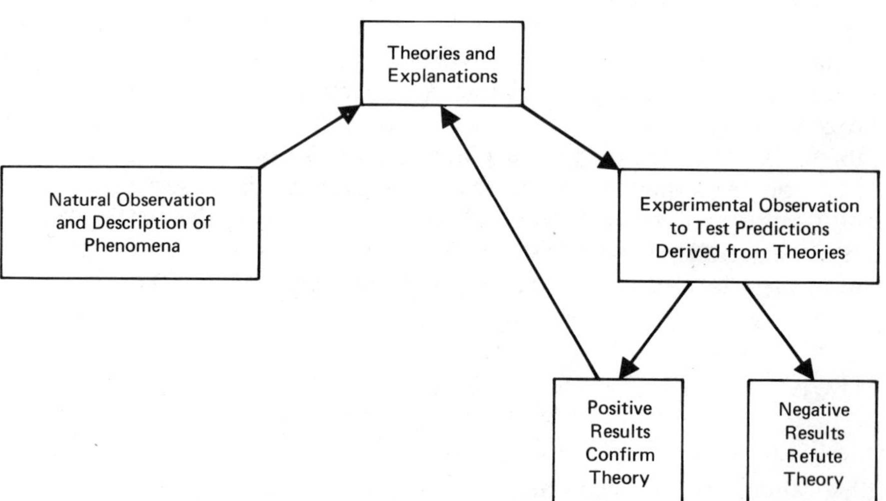

FIGURE 1-3. The relationship between natural observation, theory, and experiments and their outcomes in the research process.

in a laboratory situation because this reaction is a means by which a balance or equity can be established. In our ordinary common examples of cooking and penlight repair, our theoretical assumptions are more implicit or informal. We have some general knowledge about cooking and electrical circuits, which might loosely be termed theories, and they affect our choice of variables to test. We don't just toss any ingredient into our beef stroganoff any more than we adopt a random choice of procedures for remedying our inoperative penlight.

Theories help us organize disparate phenomena under a smaller set of principles or laws. Thus, equity theory might be applicable to the behavior of underpaid workers as well as to victims of racial or sexual discrimination since all of them may experience feelings of inequity. Although these diverse situations contain many important differences as well, it may be useful at times to focus on the commonalities they share.

Theories also contain implications which can be subjected to experimental evaluation in subsequent research. For example, suppose a worker got "overpaid" in the sense that a greater reward was provided than expected. According to equity theory, this situation still involves inequity, and the worker should attempt to restore equity. Adams and Rosenbaum (1962) predicted and found that piece-rate workers who were overpaid *reduced* the quantity of pieces produced but at the same time improved the quality in order to produce equity.

OTHER RESEARCH EXAMPLES

Finding the Causes of Obesity

The research of Stanley Schachter and his associates (Schachter, 1967; Schachter, 1971) illustrates the use of theory to both explain some known behavior and also to point out the direction to search for additional evidence that will either further support or refute the theory. Schachter's theory is concerned with identifying some of the factors involved in obesity. Common sense might tell us that overweight persons simply eat more than do normal-weight persons. In fact, some debate remains (Wooley, Wooley, & Dyrenworth, 1979) on this point, especially since accurate eating records are difficult to obtain. But, for the sake of argument, even granting that overweight persons eat more, we might still ask why this is so.

Using Strunkard and Koch's (1964) observation that normal-weight persons show a greater correspondence between self-reports of hunger states and actual stomach contractions (measured by having volunteers swallow gastric balloons) than do overweight persons, Schachter theorized that normal-weight persons may be primarily influenced in their eating by internal need states related to food deficits, whereas the eating of obese persons could be influenced by a variety of other factors external to the individual. Such external cues include the sight, smell, or taste of food as well as the eating behavior of other persons in one's presence. Perhaps the internal cues, being physiological, are more basic, and if they were the only factors, a person should stop eating when signalled by internal cues that the food deficit has been eliminated. External cues, however, are independent of bodily states, and their availability depends on the environment.

Introspection and personal experience as well as observation and discussion with our friends and acquaintances can certainly confirm the fact that people often eat when they do not "feel hungry." The food may just look and smell so appetizing or taste so delicious that we just can not resist the temptation, especially if we see other people gorging themselves.

However, this type of evidence, while suggestive, is not conclusive or objective. Other theories might also account for the differences in eating. For example, a genetic theory might hold that an inherited disposition may be the main basis for weight differences. We need evidence that aligns with the predictions of our theory—evidence that rival theories can not reconcile.

Schachter and his associates made a number of predictions and devised experiments to provide the desired evidence or data. In one study (Schachter, Goldman, Gordon, 1968), the internal cues were manipulated by the experimenters in a cleverly-disguised manner so that half of the participants had full and the other half had empty stomachs at the outset of the session. Since the study was allegedly concerned with the assessment of taste, it was possible to ask participants to skip the meal just prior to the experiment without arousing suspicion. Then half of them were "preloaded" or fed roast-beef sandwiches while the other half were not. They were next asked to taste and judge several flavors of crackers for 15 minutes. A count was made of the number of crackers consumed for each group, half of which were obese and half of which were of normal weight.

Schachter's theory, recall, assumes that the level of the internal cues will affect the amount of eating of the normal weighted, but not that of the obese. It would be predicted, then, that fewer crackers would be eaten by normal-weight subjects with stomachs full of roast-beef sandwiches than by subjects with empty stomachs. In contrast, this internal factor should make little difference for the obese who are assumed to be affected more by external factors. The findings, shown in Figure 1-4, generally upheld this prediction and supported the theory.

Other procedures aimed at testing this theory have also yielded positive results. In another study conducted just prior to dinner time, Schachter and Gross (1968) attempted to provide direct evidence that

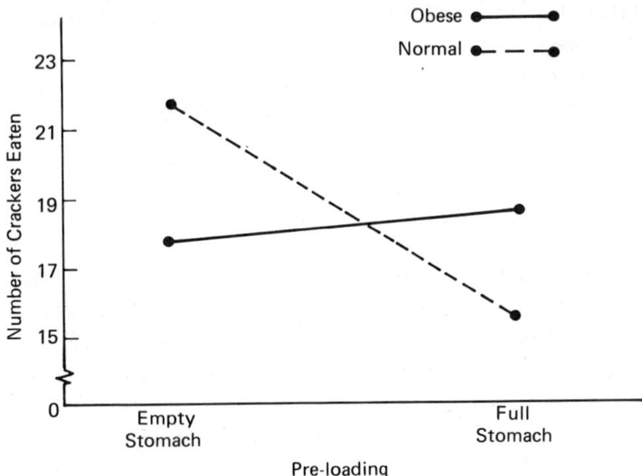

FIGURE 1-4. Effects of preloading on the eating behavior of normal and obese subjects in experiment by Schachter, Goldman, and Gross (1968). Source: "Cognitive Effects on Bodily Functioning: Studies of Obesity and Eating," by S. Schachter, in *Neurophysiology and Emotion,* by D. C. Glass (Ed.), New York: Rockefeller University Press, 1967. Copyright 1967 by Rockefeller University Press. Reprinted by permission.

external cues differentially affected normal and obese persons. This study was also described as a taste-discrimination study and took place in a room without windows, so that outside light cues were not available to help participants judge the time of day. They also were asked to remove their watches at the outset so that the experimenter could apply electrode paste to their arms to permit the taking of psychophysiological recordings without discoloring their watches. The true purpose of this step, however, was to enable Schachter to surreptitiously alter the time on the clocks in the room backward or forward by about 30 minutes without the participants' knowledge. The experimenters thus took into account the fact that we are socially conditioned to eat at certain times, thus the external cue of a clock might affect the hunger experienced by the participants. Later hours should be associated with greater hunger than earlier hours, at least for obese persons who are more strongly affected by external cues.

During a rest break, the experimenter invited the participants to help themselves to crackers if they wished. The number eaten by the obese was greater when the fake clock time was closer to the typical dinner hour. This effect did not occur for the normal weighted who presumably are governed by their true internal state of hunger.

Numerous subsequent studies have been done to further refine the theory. Our intent here is not to present all of the findings but to illustrate the interrelationship between theory and experiment. Both are essential parts of the research process. The explanation or theory that accounts for existing evidence is a tentative formulation, always subject to scrutiny and reevaluation in the light of new evidence. The implications of a theory lead to hypotheses which can be tested by the collection of new data from well-designed experiments.

Finding the Effects of Human Crowding

As an example of the interplay between theory and experiment when we are given the cause and wish to predict and understand the effects, let us examine the factor of crowded living space. Social critics have been concerned about the possible adverse effects of crowding on the quality of life. Our large and crowded urban areas have high rates of crime, mental illness, alienation, and other societal ills. But are these phenomena the consequences of overcrowded living conditions?

Undoubtedly these social problems exist in our big cities, but it is difficult to prove conclusively that a direct causal link exists because the researcher has no control over events and must passively observe the natural occurrences. Higher crime and the other problems of the big cities might be due to poorer socioeconomic conditions, greater opportunities for such activities, the ethnic mix of the population, and so forth, than to the fact that living conditions are more crowded in big cities than in small towns. The problems of interpretation are analogous to those involved in our earlier example of segregated and desegregated schools.

In order to gain more precision over inferences, the researcher may turn instead to experiments that enable better identification and control over factors which may affect behavior. In the case of the issue of crowding, a more objective definition is needed. Whereas crowding refers to subjective feelings (Stokols, 1972), the term density is more objective and can be defined in terms of the number of square feet available to each person.

What might we expect the effects of high density to be? According to theories from fields such as psychology, ethology and anthropology, organisms have a need for a certain amount of personal space (Sommer, 1969), territory (Lorenz, 1965), or privacy (Altman, 1975). Invasion or threat to this territory is stressful and can evoke defensive and protective behaviors.

Although the laboratory experiment is artificial and does not resemble the real situations one may hope to understand, it does offer a valuable method for providing definite answers about the effects of specific factors the researcher may suspect are important in the real situation but can not directly prove. As an example of a laboratory test of the stressful and disruptive effects of high density on task performance, we can examine an experiment by Freedman, Klevansky, and Ehrlich (1971) in which high-school students were asked to do tasks involving reasoning and memory in rooms of varying size so that density could be manipulated. Despite differences in density, students performed equally, thus no evidence was obtained that density affects performance.

Although many studies of humans have failed to produce dramatic effects of density, studies of lower species have not. Calhoun (1962), in a classic report of the "behavioral sink," showed that as crowding conditions among rats increased, a number of adverse effects on fertility, mortality, aggression, and sexual deviancy occurred. Perhaps important factors distinguishing humans and lower species account for the lack of similar effects. On the other hand, the laboratory experiments with humans are of relatively mild and short duration.

Other aspects of human experiences with high density also make it difficult to generalize about the adverse effects of density on humans. All of us, on occasion, have found that high density or crowding can be quite pleasurable and enjoyable. Imagine how dull a party would be with only ten people in a large room, or how strange it would be to attend a football game in a huge stadium with only 1,000 spectators. In these cases, we would probably regard *low* density as undesirable. On the other hand, we can all live without bumper-to-bumper freeway congestion. In short, the tolerable or beneficial density level may vary with the situation.

Freedman (1975) noted the importance of considering both the positive and negative effects of density and devised a theory to incorporate both effects. Density is to be regarded as an intensifier of the prevailing mood in a situation. If there is a positive mood, such as a party, the more the merrier; but if there is a negative mood, as with an angry mob, high density might prove disastrous.

One experiment (Freedman, Heshka, & Levy, 1975) tested this formulation by requiring college students to deliver a short speech which was prepared for them. An audience arbitrarily gave half of them positive evaluations while providing negative feedback to the other half. Density was also varied by conducting the session in either a large or small room. As predicted, high density enhanced the existing mood experienced by the students. High density led to more positive experiences coming from those with positive evaluations while it was associated with more negative reactions for those with negative feedback.

This sample of experiments on the effects of crowding illustrates a number of important points about the relationship between theory and experiments. Theories do have limits as to their generalizability. Formulations about animal behavior may not apply to similar forms of behavior among humans. Thus, sexual behavior, aggression, reactions to

TABLE 1-1. Ratings of Group and Session as a Function of Density and Pleasantness.

	Pleasant Condition		Unpleasant Condition	
	Low Density	*High Density*	*Low Density*	*High Density*
Liked other people	2.01	2.22	2.10	1.92
Would participate again	2.38	2.74	2.48	2.21
Learning experience	2.01	2.30	1.70	1.48
Lively	1.26	1.65	1.65	1.22
Liked other speeches	4.50	4.61	3.79	3.63
Be with same people again	2.36	2.54	2.47	2.46

Note: On all scales a higher number is more positive.
Source: From *"Crowding and Behavior"* by J. L. Freedman, San Francisco: Freeman, 1975. Copyright 1975 by W. H. Freeman and Company. Reprinted by permission.

crowding, among others, may differ significantly because of the role of human values, ethics, and morals.

One or a few experiments with "negative" findings that fail to support a theoretical prediction do not "disprove" the theory. The experiment itself may have been poorly conceived or the execution may have been inadequate. However, if additional experiments continue to generate negative or unsupportive results, doubt is cast on the validity of the theory and we begin to lose confidence in it. As with the studies of crowding on human performance, we then try to either revise or modify the theory so that it can incorporate or explain as much of the new evidence as possible. If someone else proposes a different theory that seems to account for a greater amount of the known evidence, we may abandon our former theory in favor of the more powerful one which, in turn, will also be subjected to the same scrutiny over the future.

In summary, we have examined two specific areas which have each generated a number of experiments. Whether we are trying to unravel the causes of a known effect, such as obesity and overeating, or identifying some of the effects of a known or assumed cause, such as crowding and population density, the experimenter is faced with the challenge of gathering information or data, using methods that permit unambiguous and conclusive inferences. Nature's secrets are not always readily uncovered and the experimenter must use ingenuity and skill in devising methods for discovering evidence that furthers our understanding and explanations of psychological phenomena and processes.

In Part I of this book, we will discuss the major aspects of the primary method of the experimenter. The emphasis will be on the logic of experimental procedures and assumptions rather than on a cookbook description of methods. The goal of Part II is to call your attention to some of the limitations of the experimental method and approach, especially those experiments using human subjects and/or those with implications for the quality of human life due to the potential applications of the research findings. Some of the issues raised are methodological and deal with limitations of the experimental method as a means of studying human behavior, while other issues are of an ethical nature and deal with potential misuses of experimental research. Both of these types of issues are often overlooked when the primary focus of the education of psychology students is on "how to do research" while other matters such as the "what," "who," and "why" of research is ignored. Taken as a whole, it should be clear that they present an imposing challenge to the experimenter!

SUMMARY

A great deal of similarity exists between the basic logic of experimental research and the way we think when we try to solve a variety of ordinary problems we face everyday. Whether we are trying to identify some of the causes of an effect or starting from the opposite direction, we engage in some type of systematic search for comparative evidence. In the cooking example, we compare the taste before and after we add certain spices. In the penlight example, we keep everything constant while we change one part, such as the battery, so that we can compare the outcome before and after the substitution. If that procedure fails to fix the problem, we then keep the same battery while we compare the effect of using different bulbs.

Theories or conceptions about the underlying process help guide research. These formulations are tentative explanations of the evidence existing at any given point in time about some behavioral phenomenon. We evaluate or test the theory by making predictions that are logically derived from it. Experiments are a special type of observation in which one can draw more conclusive inferences about the effects of factors which are systematically compared under conditions where no other factors are allowed to vary simultaneously. Results from experiments can support a theory or cast doubt on its validity. When negative findings accumulate from a number of experiments, a once adequate theory must be revised to accommodate the new and larger body of information or be rejected in favor of a more adequate theory.

Several examples of specific research topics, such as experiments and theory on the causes of obesity and the effects of crowding, illustrated the interplay between theory and experiments in the enterprise of psychological research.

REFERENCES

Adams, J. S., and Rosenbaum, W. B. The relationship of worker productivity to cognitive dissonance about wage inequities. *Journal of Applied Psychology*, 1962, *46*, 161-164.

Altman, I. *The environment and social behavior: Privacy, personal space, territory, crowding*. Monterey, Calif.: Brooks-Cole, 1975.

Calhoun, J. Population density and social pathology. *Scientific American*, 1962, *206*, 139-148.

Freedman, J. L. *Crowding and behavior*. San Francisco: Freeman, 1975.

Freedman, J. L., Heshka, S., and Levy, A. Crowding as an intensifier of pleasantness and unpleasantness. In J. L. Freedman, *Crowding and behavior*. San Francisco: Freeman, 1975.

Freedman, J. L., Klevansky, S., and Ehrlich, P. The effect of crowding on human task performance. *Journal of Applied Social Psychology*, 1971, *1*, 7-25.

Lorenz, K. *On aggression*. New York: Harcourt, 1966.

Pirsig, R. M. *Zen and the art of motorcycle maintenance*. New York: Morrow, 1974.

Schachter, S. Cognitive effects on bodily functioning: Studies of obesity and eating. In D. C. Glass (Ed.), *Neurophysiology and emotion*. New York: Rockefeller University Press, 1967.

Schachter, S. Some extraordinary facts about obese humans and rats. *American Psychologist*, 1971, *26*, 129-144.

Schachter, S., Goldman, R., and Gordon, A. Effects of fear, food deprivation, and obesity on eating. *Journal of Personality and Social Psychology*, 1968, *10*, 91-97.

Schachter, S., and Gross, L. Manipulated time and eating behavior. *Journal of Personality and Social Psychology*, 1968, *10*, 98-106.

Sommer, R. *Personal space: The behavioral basis of design*. Englewood Cliffs, N.J.: Prentice-Hall, 1969.

Stephan, W. G. School desegregation: An evaluation of predictions made in Brown versus Board of Education. *Psychological Bulletin*, 1978, *85*, 217-238.

Stokols, D. On the distinction between density and crowding: Some implications for future research. *Psychological Review*, 1972, *79*, 275-277.

Strunkard, A. J., and Koch, C. The interpretation of gastric motility, I. Apparatus bias in the reports of hunger by obese persons. *Archives of General Psychiatry*, 1964, *11*, 74-82.

Wooley, S. C., Wooley, O. W., and Dyrenforth, S. R. Theoretical, practical, and social issues in behavioral treatments of obesity. *Journal of Applied Behavior Analysis*, 1979, *12*, 3-25.

LEARNING ACTIVITIES

1. Choose two factors or behaviors, such as amount of television viewing of aggression and the viewers' own levels of aggressive behavior. Make a set of observations on both behaviors in a sample of at least 30 individuals.

Other examples might be:
grade-point average and amount of study
amount of eating and level of anxiety
talkativeness and time of day
age and reaction time
In order to make observations readily, you can restrict yourself to behaviors that can readily be observed in public or obtained by self-report from individuals. For example, it may prove difficult to determine the relationship between the amounts of extramarital sex and the amount of underreported income on tax returns.

2. Present the results of your observations with the use of graphs, as illustrated in Figure 1-1, plotting one behavior or factor in varying degrees along the horizontal dimension and the other along the vertical dimension of the graph. For each individual observed, place a "dot" on the graph at the point where that person's two scores, one on each of the two factors, intersect. From this so-called "scatterplot," how would you *describe* the relationship between your variables.
3. Assuming that some type of relationship is found, how would you *explain* the basis for it? Thus, in the example of television viewing and aggressive behavior, suppose we found a positive correlation. One possible explanation is that the difference in amount of viewing is the, or at least one of the, causes of the differences in aggressive behavior. (If your observations suggest no clear relationship, it would still be useful to formulate explanations for some of the *possible* relationships that might have been obtained.)

CHAPTER 2

Independent and Dependent Variables

Chapter at a Glance

Every experiment involves at least one *independent* and one *dependent variable*. These technical terms used by experimenters often confuse students. It may help to think that the independent variable corresponds to the causal factor which produces changes or differences on the behavior of interest—the dependent variable. The independent variable precedes the dependent variable in a temporal aspect, as diagrammed in Figure 2-1. We can also see that internal states and processes of the organism must intervene between the independent and dependent variables. These internal states include such abstractions as learning, motivation, emotion, and personality variables. At the theoretical or explanatory level, we must consider the nature of these internal states and processes in order to predict and understand the kinds of effects various independent variables might have on the dependent variables being observed in experiments.

In this chapter, we primarily focus on a thorough discussion of the nature of independent and dependent variables. We also examine the importance of operational definitions for both types of variables, and discuss some of the factors that must be considered in choosing the levels or different values of the independent variable to be used in an experiment. Similarly, we examine some of the issues involved in choosing the types and numbers of dependent variables to be employed. Finally, we raise the issues of the reliability and validity of dependent variables, two important but often neglected problems in experimental research. The topic of construct validity is closely related to our theoretical assumptions about the nature of the internal processes of the individual which operate between the antecedent independent variables of our experiments and the consequent dependent variables.

INDEPENDENT VARIABLES

The factors the experimenter wishes to systematically manipulate or vary in an experiment are commonly referred to as the *independent variables*. Other common terms for these factors are antecedents, causes, and determinants; these terms all imply that they are potential correlates of some aspect of behavior. There are two or more levels for each such dimension; hence, they are termed "variables." All experiments must have at least one independent variable and typically have two or three. In most of our discussion of the basic logic of experiments we will restrict our examples to situations with only one independent variable to simplify our discussion. Increasing the number of independent variables, however, does not alter the basic logic.

Table 2-1 shows a sample of some typical independent variables which fall into different categories; environmental, task or stimulus, and sub-

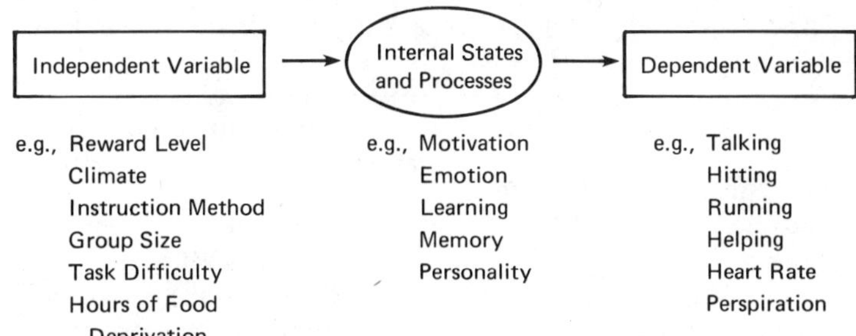

FIGURE 2-1. The temporal relationship between the independent variable and the dependent variable in an experiment, with the former as the antecedent of the latter. A number of internal states and processes within the individual organism mediate between the independent and dependent variable.

ject. *Environmental variables,* such as the type of setting, temperature, or time of day, are factors that are external to the subject under observation. They deal primarily with the context, physical or psychological, in which the behavior occurs. *Task* or *stimulus variables* are not always present in a formal sense as experiments do not always involve a specific laboratory activity. Examples of this category include difficulty of task, type of task or stimulus materials, variations in instructions, and consequences of task performance. Experiments involving sensation, perception, learning, memory, and cognition are areas where some type of task is always provided by the experimenter, such as judging brightness of stimuli or solving concept-identification problems. In social psychology, tasks are sometimes, but not always, necessary. For example, situations are often devised to see if a person will render aid to another under various conditions or whether one's liking of others depends on how similar to oneself one perceives them.

Subject variables are a special type of independent variable differing from the others in that, strictly speaking, they are not under the experimenter's control. Subject variables are dimensions along which the research participants or "subjects" vary—age, sex, personality, ability, motivation, and so forth. Hence, we might also refer to them as individual difference variables. Other variables might be special designations like juvenile delinquents, exceptional children, honor students, wife beaters, alcoholics, blue-collar workers, ethnic minorities, or sports fans. Subjects already hold the features that distinguish them from other individuals prior to their serving in any experiment. In contrast, if we wanted to study the effects of large vs. small print—a task variable—on reading speed, the experimenter can exercise control by deciding which subjects will receive large or small print.

Subject variables are complicated in that persons who differ on one dimension may also differ on other dimensions as well. People who are

TABLE 2-1. Major Categories of Independent and Dependent Variables.

Independent Variables	Dependent Variables
Environmental or Situational	Behavior
Physical	Verbal
Social	Nonverbal
Task or Stimulus	Physiological Reactions
Instructions	Subjective Experience
Apparatus, Equipment	Thoughts
Stimulus Materials	Feelings
Subject	Emotions
Age	Moods
Sex	Attitudes
Ethnicity	
Physical Attributes	
Personality	
Abilities	

taller are generally heavier as well. If we were to compare tall and short persons on some behavior and found a difference, would we be correct in attributing the difference to the height difference or to the correlated difference in weight? Similarly, in the general population higher intelligence is displayed among the middle than the lower socioeconomic classes. How do we explain this difference when socioeconomic classes differ in numerous ways such as size of family, ethnic background, and so on?

If we find that physically attractive persons are more successful than average-looking persons, we still have to explain how that happens. Is it because physically attractive persons have superior intelligence or is it because they tend to get preferential treatment from society?

The sequence of causality is ambiguous for subject variables. Alcoholics, for example, have a high divorce rate. But one might argue that alcoholics may generally be older than nonalcoholics since the ill effects of chronic alcohol abuse usually take years to produce serious adverse consequences. Suppose one still found more divorce among alcoholics when you compared them with nonalcoholics of the same age? One would still have to determine which factor was the cause and which the effect. Did alcoholism precipitate divorce or vice versa? The situation is complicated by the fact that both sequences do occur in real life. Usually, however, it is argued that alcoholism is the cause of divorce.

Most importantly, subject variables are not under the strict control of the experimenter as are other categories of independent variables. Some psychologists prefer the term, correlational study, rather than experiment when all of the variables are nonmanipulable. One must be especially cautious in making causal inferences when subgroups on some subject variable show differences since there are numerous ways of interpreting such findings. Groups that differ on one subject dimension may also differ on other yet unidentified subject variables. Among young children, for example, taller children would be older than shorter ones if we compared them across the entire height range. If we failed to recognize this obvious fact, we could end up with some ridiculous conclusions such as "tall children are smarter" which would not hold true if we equated for age.

Direct and Indirect Independent Variables

Independent variables, such as time of day or sex of subjects, are direct and easily defined. In contrast, a factor such as anxiety is less direct and harder to reach consensus on its measurement. A typical procedure for instilling different levels of anxiety in experiments has been to prepare instructions that presumably generate different levels of tension. We could tell one group of subjects that the test they were about to receive was merely for practice, while we instruct another group that the test will measure their intelligence.

Assuming for the moment that the instructions are credible, how can we be sure that anxiety was created at all in the intended group or that it was *not* induced in the other group? Can we be sure that the *difference* in anxiety between the groups is adequate for our purposes? We can not be as confident that our indirectly-defined variable of anxiety is valid as we could if we varied the ethnicity of the subjects and thus directly observed the variable.

A one-to-one correspondence does not exist between the defining procedures and the induced consequences in the subjects for indirectly defined independent variables. While we might be sure that 12 hours of food deprivation was twice as much time as six hours, we can not assume that the resulting hunger level is also twice as great. It is more likely that hunger will reach a peak after a given number of hours of deprivation so that additional deprivation time will have diminishing added impact on hunger.

Another complicating problem is that some factors, such as anxiety, may exist both as a subject variable and as an environmental variable. Individuals differ in their chronic disposition or personality so that we speak of low or high anxious *traits,* whereas situations differ in their capacity to generate momentary *states* of stress and anxiety. Whereas the *trait* of anxiety can be varied by selecting persons who score differently on a paper-and-pencil personality test, the *state* of anxiety would be manipulated by variations in the experimental context, task, or instructions. Which of these different ways of identifying and varying anxiety really measures true anxiety?

Operational Definitions

Problems like those just described have led to reliance on the use of operational definitions of variables and concepts. A description of the set of operations or measurement procedures one uses constitutes the *operational definition* of that concept. This approach is advantageous in that it improves communication since the precisely-stated operations can be repeated by other researchers. Unlike colloquial and dictionary definitions, which are often vague or abstract, the operational definition is a model of clarity and precision.

Let us return to our example of the experiment showing that frustration can cause aggression. Suppose a friend did not accept your conclusion. He might begin cross-examining you with the challenge, "What do you mean by frustration?" "That's easy," you smugly reply. "I told one group that they were failing on the achievement task I gave them while I told the other group they were doing fine." Your friend counters with, "Oh, I hardly call that 'frustration'." He adds, "frustration is what you feel—like fatigue or anger." So what really is frustration and can we reach any agreement on it?

Now another student who overheard your debate jumps into the fray. This student accepts your definition of frustration because he can "relate to it," having flunked many a midterm! But he never becomes aggressive at all, so he claims, and questions your definition of aggression. You reply that in your study, aggression was measured by the extent to which a subject administered a painful shock to another subject in an adjacent room (actually, the other subject was an accomplice of the experimenter and never actually received any shocks). In other words, some type of response that implies physical pain or harm is your definition of aggression.

Your adversary denies ever resorting to physical harm to others when he has been frustrated, but he does admit, upon questioning, that he has, on occasion, used foul language, curses, and sarcasm when frustrated. Could it be argued that these behaviors are aggressive in nature even though not physical?

We have all been in numerous heated and lengthy discussions with other people in situations similar to the one above. Due to the use of the *same* verbal terms by people who are actually referring to *different* concepts, confusion and controversy often result.

Eventually, in many cases, terms become clarified and spelled out in more detail (define your terms!). When this point is reached, the combatants often decide that they actually don't disagree after all ("Oh, if that's what you mean by X, then I agree with you").

A parallel situation occurs in the process of psychological experimentation. Investigators using the same terms, such as intelligence, anxiety, conflict, and so forth, may be using different methods of measurement or definition. Some, but not all, controversies about results of experiments involve confusion created by the same terms referring to different concepts or processes by different investigators.

One approach toward minimizing misunderstanding of this sort is *operationalism* which equates the meaning of constructs with the procedures used to measure or define the concept. Thus, an operational definition of intelligence might be "intelligence is what intelligence tests measure." Not very satisfying, is it? On the other hand, an everyday definition of intelligence might be "know-how" or "what it takes to get ahead in the world." Is that any better? Webster's New World dictionary offers "the ability to learn or understand from experience; ability to acquire and retain knowledge; mental ability." But "ability" is a potential and may or may not be converted into actual achievements or performance of intelligent behavior. The psychologist relies on observed behavior as a basis for making inferences about the amount of mental ability.

The disadvantage of operational definitions, interestingly enough, is a feature that might also be considered a strength. Precise concepts are too narrow and may lack comparability with other operational definitions of the same concept. The kinds of mental ability that enable some to benefit from academic tasks may enable one to get along very well in our type of society, but it may be of little adaptive value in the jungle. Intelligence, as measured by present intelligence tests, emphasizes verbal ability, thus it is not surprising that this type of definition of intelligence correlates with academic achievement. Would this type of intelligence, however, be predictive of social skills or social intelligence, which involves the ability to know how to get along with other people?

Even when an operational definition is proposed for a psychological variable or construct, there is no guarantee that it is valid. For instance, one could use speed of running a mile as an invalid but nevertheless "operational" definition of intelligence. Of course, this example is rather exaggerated. By "valid" we imply that some abstract conception is generally accepted as what intelligence means. Researchers try to develop tests, essentially small samples of behavior, that are predictive of differences in intelligence. The widely used Stanford Binet intelligence test is accepted as a valid index of intelligence because its measures of a large number of students give good predictions of their relative academic achievement. A valid measure need not have face validity or sound plausible, but it must reflect the underlying process for which it is proposed. The conception of intelligence, as generally held in our society, is an ability that should be related to academic success. If there is a positive correlation between our psychological test of intelligence and the criterion of academic success, we feel we have adequately measured this construct of intelligence with a valid procedure.

Manipulation Checks

We cannot assume that groups treated differently or receiving different levels of an independent variable will in fact be different. For example, if we tried to manipulate anxiety levels by using different types of criticism for performance on a task, how can we be sure that our procedures have induced appreciably different levels of anxiety? If we did not succeed, and our experiment showed no differential performance for our different groups, we would end up erroneously concluding that anxiety differences made no impact on performance. Even if performance differences did occur for groups we assumed differed in anxiety, it is conceivable that such differences could have occurred for some other reason even if our manipulation failed to generate differences in anxiety. We cannot assume that the intended independent variable, anxiety, was present in varying amounts for different groups merely on the basis that their performance differed in the predicted direction.

We need some type of independent verification of the anxiety levels of the different groups to ensure that they are different. In the present example, we could resort to the use of psychophysiological indices, such as the galvanic skin response (GSR) which indicates emotional arousal. Another possibility might be the use of verbal self-reports from the subjects regarding their feeling states. Finally, observers who were "blind" or uninformed on how the different groups were treated could make unbiased ratings.

It is customary to allow subjects to ask for clarification of instructions prior to any experiment. Sometimes this procedure can help avoid misunderstandings and enable the experimenter to identify the weakness of the intended manipulations when they are embodied in instructions. In contrast, many independent variables involve subtle environmental variations the experimenter obviously cannot ask subjects about prior to the experiment. Suppose we wanted to see if a person would make more errors on a learning task if another person was in the room and whether or not the sex of the other person affected errors made. Can we be sure that the subjects even noticed the presence of another person and, if so, paid any attention to the person's sex? If the subjects were preoccupied with the task, they may have been unaware of the other person. Or suppose that although the experimenter intended that the other person be a source of distraction, the subjects perceived them as rivals or competitors and increased their learning scores rather than performed less well. In short, procedures designed for one purpose may have a different and unexpected impact on the subjects themselves. Manipulation checks that determine, if possible, how subjects perceive or react to various procedures are most useful.

Choosing the Levels of Independent Variables

Whether we choose two, three, or more levels of an independent variable, we can avoid certain problems if we can identify the normal range of the dimension. For example, if we want to see how the size of one's dinner affects ability to solve algebra problems after dinner, we know from past experience what constitutes relatively larger- and small-sized dinners. We would not, for example, compare a one-ounce serving to a 20-pound serving. We might also wish to "explore" the dimension and choose points that cover the entire dimension in approximately equal intervals, if possible. This procedure would give us the most complete picture of the effects of our independent variable. In contrast, if we chose only two different levels of values and they were both close together and at either one end or the other of the dimension, we would have little faith that our results would generalize widely.

The practical problem is that we do not always know the nature or range of variations for the dimensions we wish to assess. If we have developed a new drug and wish to assess its effect on pain tolerance, how do we know what is a high and what is a low end of the dosage to use? In this case, we might err on the low side, just in case harmful effects result, and gradually over a series of trial-and-error approximations, arrive at an estimate of the size of the range. In other situations where a body of research has been established, we might examine a number of past experiments and use their procedures as a guide to determining what are reasonable values of the independent variable to use.

If we err and compare only values of the independent variable toward the high end, we may find that no effect seems to appear when in fact there is an influence over a wider range. We have encountered a "ceiling effect" in which further increases in the independent variable cannot produce more change in the dependent variable. If, for example, we offered money to runners, we would find that larger rewards up to some point would increase speed. Beyond that point, greater incentives would prove ineffective because there is a physical limit to how fast a person can run.

Conversely, a "floor effect" occurs when the manipulation of the independent variable fails to produce further decreases because all groups are already near rock bottom. Failure to sample levels of the independent variable that are sufficiently separated might lead to the erroneous conclusion that the independent variable had no effect in this situation as well. Both the ceiling and the floor effects illustrate the need to use levels of the independent variable that represent the whole dimension to allow proper detection of the influence of that factor.

There is widespread tendency to refer to different levels of an independent variable in relative terms like, low, medium, and high. Within a given experiment, no serious problem will occur unless one is using only very low or very high absolute levels. However, if one is not specific about the absolute values of the independent variable when comparing different studies, changes can arise. In one experiment, low, medium,and high deprivation might refer to 2, 4, and 6 hours, whereas the same labels might apply to 4, 6, and 8 in another and possibly lead to contradictory conclusions about the effects of 6 hours since it is the medium value in one study and the high value in the other.

Unfortunately, many independent variables have no objectively quantifiable referents. The method of inducing frustration in different experiments may differ on qualitative aspects so that it is difficult to know if the meaning of high, medium, and low frustration in one experiment equals the meaning in another study. It is probably safer to assume that they are not comparable.

DEPENDENT VARIABLES

The aspect of behavior being measured in relation to variations in the amount of the independent variable is termed the *dependent variable.* It is assumed that differences in the independent variable are the causes of the variations in the dependent variable. For example, we varied the number of hours of instruction provided to students, we could see if that variation bore any relationship to the amount of material learned. Other examples of categories of dependent variables are shown in Table 2.1

Functional Relationships

A number of possible types of relationships between the independent and dependent variables may occur in experiments, as shown in Figure 2–2. It is customary to refer to graphs as "figures" and to use the horizontal baseline or X-axis to represent increasing amounts or levels of the independent variable as one moves from left to right. The dependent variable or behavior measure is usually represented along the vertical or Y-axis of figures, with values often, but not always, increasing as one goes from the bottom to the top. The manner in which the dependent variable changes in relation to changes in the independent variable is called a functional relationship.

In the idealized or smooth curves depicted in Figure 2-2, we see that when no effect of the independent variable occurs, the function or curve in panel (a) (often a straight line) is horizontal, indicating that the level of the dependent variable is the same at all levels of the independent variable (the exact height of the line depends on other factors, but this is unimportant for the present discussion). A curve that rises from the lower left to the upper right shows that as the independent variable increases so does the dependent variable, as shown in Figure 2-2b. This same type of linear relationship in the reverse direction (Fig. 2-2c) is termed an inverse relationship since the greater the independent variable, the lower the dependent variable. Finally, there may be a nonmonotonic function relating the independent and dependent variables in which there is some reversal. The curve either increases to a peak before declining or it starts at a high level and then declines to a bottom before reversing upward again as the independent variable increases in magnitude (see Fig. 2-2d).

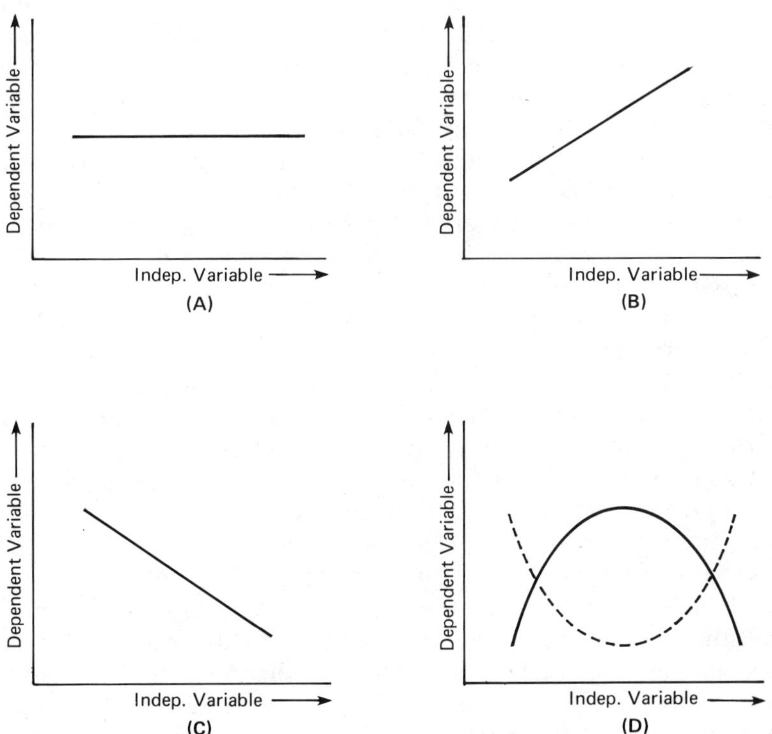

FIGURE 2-2. The basic types of functional relationships between an independent variable and a dependent variable: (a) no effect, (b) positive or increasing effect, (c) negative or inverse effect, (d) nonmonotonic effect, first increasing to a peak and then decreasing or vice versa.

It should be noted that whereas any experiment can be done with only two levels or values of the independent variable being manipulated, it is necessary to include at least three levels if one is to detect a non-monotonic relationship. If one uses only two levels, the results will fail to disclose any existing nonmonotonic function and show instead a monotonic or straight-line function such as in Figures 2–2a, b, and c.

Choosing Among Operational Definitions

A number of different ways may exist for measuring a particular behavior of interest. If frustration is assumed to cause aggression, how do we measure aggression? Do we use a physical response such as hitting, a verbal response such as abusive language, a nonverbal response such as an obscene gesture, or some indirect or subtle method of retaliation? Different investigators working on the same problems may adopt different operational definitions of the same dependent variable. Since the effects of an independent variable on "aggression" may vary with the specific operational definition used in different studies, we must be careful when comparing results from apparently similar studies and take into consideration the different ways in which the same concept is operationally defined by different experimenters.

A large body of research has been performed to identify the factors affecting human memory: the type of material, the temporal presentation rate, the amount of material, and so forth. However, the method in which memory is measured can make a difference in the effects of some factors. The basic methods used for the most part are: free recall, recognition, and relearning. Free recall of a list of words allows the words to be remembered in any sequence, whereas recognition tests of memory involve the subject trying to pick out the material originally presented out of a set of alternatives. Relearning defines memory in terms of the amount of time saved when the material is relearned in comparison to the original time needed for learning. The more that is remembered, the less relearning time should be needed.

All of these methods are accepted procedures for defining memory, but it should be obvious that results obtained with them may not always agree. High similarity of words may aid free recall but can hinder recognition. Is one method more valid than the others? The answer depends in part, on the intended use of the results. If we intend to generalize the findings to other learning situations, the degree of similarity between the specific methods and the situation where one wishes to apply the results is important. The recognition test more closely resembles situations like multiple-choice examinations or the identification of suspects in a police lineup whereas the free-recall test somewhat parallels an essay test. Perhaps no single correct method for measuring a concept like memory exists because of the variety of memory situations.

Levels of Analysis

A different issue deals with the appropriate level of analysis in measuring the effects of an independent variable. Should we give more importance to overt behavior, covert physiological responses, verbal report, or biochemical reactions? All of these levels exist simultaneously in a given behavior. A person who smokes a cigarette is engaging in observable behavior which can have subjective consequences of pleasurable taste which can be verbally reported. At the same time, nicotine is producing changes on psychophysiological functions such as heart rate and respiration as well as altering blood alkalinity and catecholamine levels. Is one of these levels more basic or more useful for investigation?

Again, there are no simple answers. Different researchers are interested in different aspects of a phenomenon and may find other aspects of little value to their purposes. One could argue that one should measure as many dependent variables as possible, but this position is unrealistic and usually unpersuasive. When multiple measures are consistent in their relationship to the independent variable, investigators are apt to feel they wasted a lot of effort and expense in collecting and analyzing all of that data. On the other hand, discrepant conclusions based on different dependent variables can be quite interesting.

Nesbitt (1972), for example, noted the paradox among smokers in that they report subjective experiences of relaxation when smoking but the pharmacological effect of nicotine is stimulating. Or alcohol, which is a nervous-system depressant, often has a disinhibitory effect on behavior. Reliance on only one level of analysis would be misleading.

In his studies of reactions to stressful films, Lazarus (1966) found that for *some,* but not all, subjects there was a correspondence between subjective verbal reports of stress and psychophysiological indicants of stress which were measured concurrently. Evidence concerning personality differences was examined and revealed that subjects who failed to show this correlation tended to cope with problems by denial strategies. It was hardly surprising, then, that they reported less stress than their bodily responses displayed. A similar situation exists in lie detection. The assumption is that the verbal response of the liar will be contradicted by the less distortable reactions of the autonomic nervous system.

Multiple Dependent Variables

There is value in having several dependent variables, whether at the same or different levels of analysis. Many psychological outcomes are broadly defined—aggression, memory, social interaction, altruism, perception, and so forth—so that it is overly simplistic to think that they can be captured by one or a few narrow sets of operations. A good example of the use of multiple measures is the set of categories developed by Bales (1980) for use in measuring group interaction. The Interaction Process Analysis, summarized in Table 2-2, contains 12 specific types of interpersonal responses each member of a group might make during inter-

TABLE 2-2. The System of Categories Used in Interaction Process Analysis. Brackets and Arrows Indicate Categories that Are Related to Each Other. From Bales (1980).

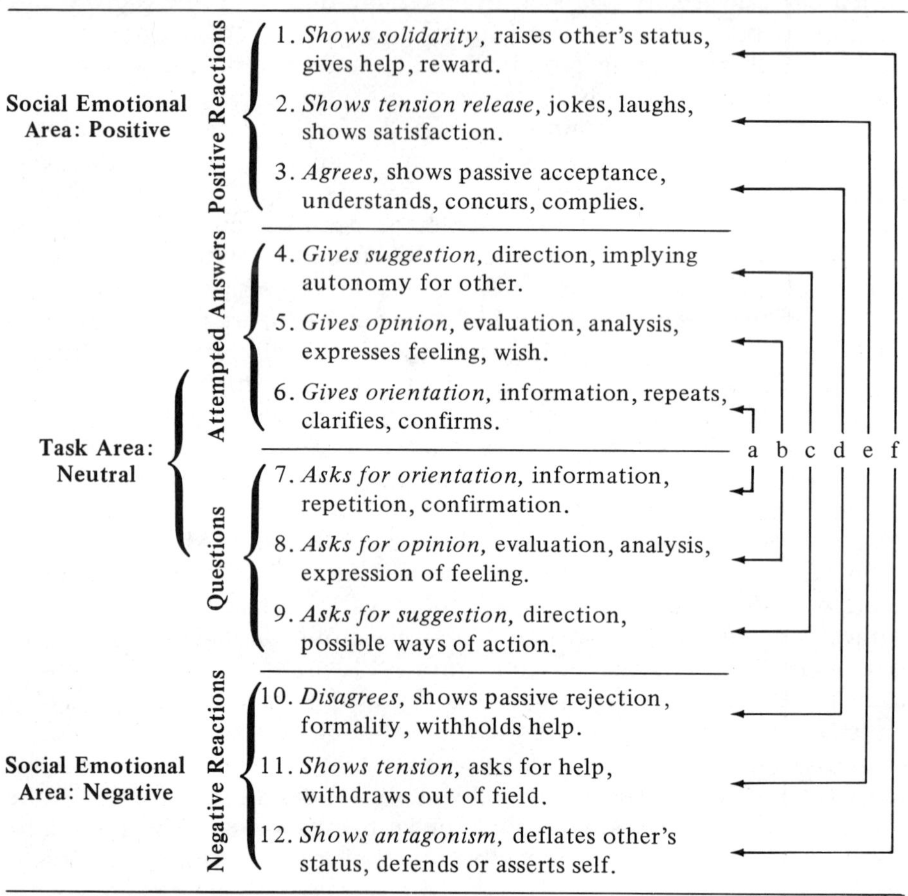

Area	Group	Category	Related
Social Emotional Area: Positive	Positive Reactions	1. *Shows solidarity,* raises other's status, gives help, reward.	f
		2. *Shows tension release,* jokes, laughs, shows satisfaction.	e
		3. *Agrees,* shows passive acceptance, understands, concurs, complies.	d
Task Area: Neutral	Attempted Answers	4. *Gives suggestion,* direction, implying autonomy for other.	c
		5. *Gives opinion,* evaluation, analysis, expresses feeling, wish.	b
		6. *Gives orientation,* information, repeats, clarifies, confirms.	a
	Questions	7. *Asks for orientation,* information, repetition, confirmation.	a
		8. *Asks for opinion,* evaluation, analysis, expression of feeling.	b
		9. *Asks for suggestion,* direction, possible ways of action.	c
Social Emotional Area: Negative	Negative Reactions	10. *Disagrees,* shows passive rejection, formality, withholds help.	d
		11. *Shows tension,* asks for help, withdraws out of field.	e
		12. *Shows antagonism,* deflates other's status, defends or asserts self.	f

Source: "Interaction Process Analysis," by R. F. Bales. Reprinted by permission of the University of Chicago Press.

Key

a Problems of Orientation
b Problems of Evaluation
c Problems of Control
d Problems of Decision
e Problems of Tension Reduction
f Problems of Reintegration

action. Use of this set of categories provides a more detailed and accurate picture of behavior than any single measure could. Contrast this method with a hypothetical dimension of "interaction" which was unidimensional and varied only from low to high. With this dimension we would watch a group interaction and rate each person somewhere on this scale from low to high as to how much that person showed "interaction." We would obviously miss a lot of information if we used this approach instead of multiple measures such as those developed by Bales.

Another example of the use of several dependent variables in the same study was the Freedman et al. (1975) study cited in Chapter 1 which dealt with the effects of crowding and stress.

Reliability and Validity of Dependent Variables

Whether we use one or a dozen dependent variables in an experiment, they must meet the criteria of *reliability* and *validity*. In its simplest form, reliability refers to repeatability or stability of the measure used to define a given behavior under the same conditions on different occasions. If we find that X causes one effect on one occasion, it is of little value if the next time we look under similar conditions X now leads to a different effect. In practice, however, experimenters may not check over separate occasions under identical conditions to make sure that obtained effects are reliable but merely proceed on the implicit assumption that they are.

As Epstein (1979, 1980) has noted, the experiment as it is normally conducted is a single-occasion event, so that temporal reliability is never empirically assessed. The results observed in one experiment may disagree with those obtained in a similar experiment simply due to low reliability of the behavior in question. Just as you would not expect your grade based on one exam during the semester to be the same on other exams in the same course, nor should the behavior observed on a single occasion in an experiment necessarily be an accurate indication of the person's typical behavior.

Epstein (1979) demonstrated the low reliability of a wide variety of behavior ranging from physiological indices to objective indices of social behavior to self-ratings of emotions by taking repeated measures with the same subjects over several weeks. Reliability was assessed by correlating the scores on any one day with those obtained on the next day. As shown in Figure 2–3, the reliability coefficient (a higher score indicates higher reliability) increases as one uses the average of scores from a *larger* number of separate pairs of consecutive occasions or days for observation. The maximal value of 1.0 occurs if the scores on two occasions are identical, and while this level is never achieved, it was possible to obtain very high (.8–.9) levels in some cases when

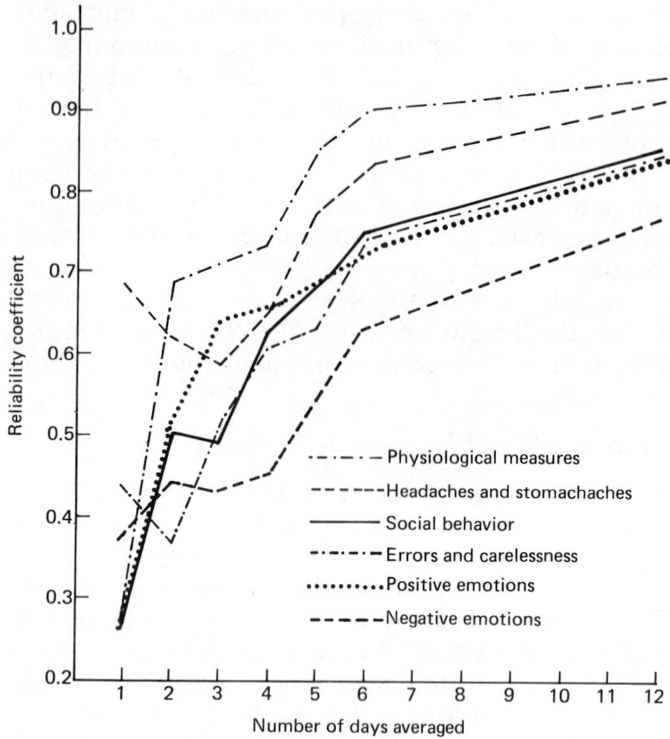

FIGURE 2-3. Reliability coefficients for several dependent variables as a function of the number of pairs of consecutive days. (The data consisted of daily self-ratings of positive and negative emotions recorded in the classroom; of measures of heart-rate mean and range; of records of discrete objective events of social significance, such as number of social letters written and received; and of objective behavioral events recorded by the instructor, such as number of erasures and omissions made in filling out the answer sheets, number of minutes late to class, and number of times a Number 2 pencil was forgotten. (From "The stability of behavior: II. Implications for psychological research." by S. Epstein, *American Psychologist,* 1980, *35,* 790-806. Copyright 1980 by the American Psychological Association. Reprinted by permission.)

observations were based on six or more separate days. The situation exemplified in most experiments, however, uses only one occasion and, as Figure 2-3 shows, the reliability or agreement of just one day of observation with the next day's observations shows the lowest value.

Experimenters, when they are concerned about reliability, tend to rely on a different type of reliability, *interobserver agreement* on a single occasion, when attempting to measure certain types of subjectively defined responses. For example, the assessment of some factor's influence on hostility or helpfulness may involve the concurrent use of several independent observers to rate the subject's behavior along these dimensions. High agreement among observers would be accepted as evidence that the dependent variable could be reliably measured, at least on the single occasion when ratings were made.

Reliability can be diminished by inadequate sampling of responses assumed to reflect the behavior of interest. What specific responses do we look at if we are assessing jealousy and its determinants? If different observers focus on different types of responses so that one observer makes ratings based on nonverbal reactions while another observer relies on verbal responses of persons in jealousy-arousing situations, the reliability or interobserver agreement of the two sets of measurements will be less than perfect.

Another basis for lowered reliability is the fact that no two situations are ever exactly the same. The conditions under which we obtained our first set of measures will vary somewhat when we make a second set, thus producing a reduction in reliability. Finally, it is also possible that observations taken on two different occasions, especially if the interval is long, may have low reliability because the person changes over time.

Despite these problems, the actual procedures for determining reliability are relatively simple and straightforward in comparison to the assessment of *validity*. Most authors readily agree on a verbal definition of validity as a matter of whether or not one is measuring what one intends to measure. In other words, is the specific dependent variable used by the investigator actually a reflection of the assumed underlying psychological process? In some cases it is not an easy question to answer because there may be many underlying causes of the specific response we use as our dependent variable. In addition, a given psychological process or construct can generate numerous responses other than the one we are recording so that no single response can adequately reflect the operation of the underlying processes.

As an example, consider the phenomenon of anger. Suppose we wanted to compare two methods for reducing anger. We first set up a contrived laboratory task in which subjects are scolded by the experimenter after they fail on some insoluble math puzzles. Assume that our subjects experience anger. At this point, they receive one of two different treatments which may reduce their anger. The specific techniques are unimportant for this example, but for sake of illustration, let us say that one group is asked to engage in light exercise while the other group is asked to read comic books for the same amount of time.

What can we use as a dependent variable or measure of the amount of anger each subject has after these different experiences? Self-report is direct but it may not be sensitive or it may be distorted to avoid a confrontation. Observers might be asked to watch the subjects and rate their anger levels. Indirect measures might be used such as measuring how much hostility they show toward the experimenter's assistant after the experiment. In short, a variety of different methods can be devised, but how can we be sure that any of them are "valid" reflections of the underlying levels of anger instilled in the subjects?

In essence, we need to compare angry *and nonangry* subjects and identify some of the ways in which they differ under these two conditions: facial expression, posture, social behavior, verbal behavior, and so on. Any response system on which differences are obtained under conditions known or assumed to produce anger vs. nonanger may be regarded as a valid index to use in *other* research settings where we have no idea beforehand whether or not the subjects are angry. Using the previously-validated index as our dependent variable, we infer how much anger may exist in a new situation on the basis of scores on this response system.

As a second example, suppose we want to measure the effects of two teaching methods on the creativity of artists. "Creativity" is an abstraction and not something we can directly observe, but presumably those artists who have "it" will produce more creative works than those who do not.

Our problem now is finding some aspect of artists' behavior we can measure that we feel reflects differences in artistic creativity. We might ask each artist to produce a sample of work and ask a panel of art experts to judge the creativeness of each work. Certainly on the surface, at least, this approach seems to have merit. In contrast, other aspects of the works which could be measured, even with high reliability, such as the speed of work, the number of works, or the enthusiasm of the artist, do not seem to satisfy our intuitive sense of the meaning of creativity.

Artistic merit, however, can be highly subjective since "beauty may lie in the eye of the beholder." Different judges may use different criteria and standards in reaching their verdicts. In essence, they may be employing different operational definitions to assess creativity, although many experts would claim that they used some ineffable and elusive sense of aesthetics in making their judgments. Although we might hope that a more objective statement of the process were possible, in this type of situation we usually yield to the evaluations of the experts which are accepted by society as the valid or best indices.

The same issues arise in research dealing with other constructs which are postulated to intervene between the incoming stimuli and the behavior or responses produced by individuals. Intelligence, motivation, extraversion, altruism, and so forth refer to abilities and processes within the organism that can not be directly observed, although in everyday life most of us assume the existence of such constructs. A person with high intelligence should do better in school than one with lesser intelligence. Someone with greater motivation should work harder than someone with lesser motivation, and so forth.

Although this type of thinking is adequate in everyday situations, the researcher needs more precise definitions of the kinds of behavioral differences predicted to be associated with varying levels of a given construct. Do we use self-report descriptions, actual resistance-to-temptation in a behavioral situation, testimony of friends, or physiological reactions to a lie detector, for example, to measure "honesty"? How valid is each of these different types of dependent variables as a measure of this construct?

Although investigators are aware of the issue of validity, often simple or easy-to-obtain measures are objectively defined, readily quantified and accepted without further evidence to be valid measures. Proof that a given operational definition is valid calls for a comparison of scores on it for groups which differ on some already established or accepted measure of that construct. Thus, groups of known liars and truth-tellers could be compared to make sure they also differ in their scores on any new procedures for assessing honesty.

It should not be inferred that any one measure of a construct is valid while all others are not because most constructs are too broad in scope for a single operational definition to capture their full essence. As pointed out earlier, this can be confusing and can create conflicting conclusions. Yet, as Cook and Campbell (1979, p. 62–63) observed, there are some benefits to this situation because:

> This is fortunate because propositions about constructs are more reliable if they have been successfully tested, not only across many overlapping operational representations of a single definition of a construct, but also across representations of many overlapping definitions of the *same* construct. Think how much utility there is in knowing that for many propositions about aggression it is irrelevant whether or not one defines aggression to include "intent to harm," for the same relationships hold with or without the inclusion of intent.

By having multiple methods and multiple operational definitions of a construct, we increase the likelihood that the total body of research will capture the phenomenon of interest and disclose laws and principles which have generalizability. One can see if new procedures for defining a construct produce effects similar to those obtained with already established and accepted procedures. Such accord would validate the new approach.

Precision of Measurement

When most people think of the process of measurement, they think of using some numerical scale or index to describe some properties of whatever they wish to measure. Common examples might be the measurement of physical length or time. In the case of length, we could determine that one object is 10 inches long while another is 20 inches long. The difference, 10 units, is exactly the same whether we are comparing 30 and 40-inch lengths or 200 and 210-inch lengths. The types of objects being measured are unimportant since we are interested only in their "length". Furthermore, a score of zero, which reflects a total absence of the dimension, exists for the concept of length so that we can conclude that a 20-inch length is twice as long as one of 10 inches.

In contrast to the foregoing example, generally much less precision is possible when we try to measure many independent and dependent variables of psychological interest. The lowest level, known as the *nominal* scale of measurement, entails subcategories of a qualitative nature. An example of an independent variable of this type might be religious affiliation or type of reading material. Dependent variables at this level can be illustrated by different types of foods preferred, such as protein, carbohydrate, or fat, the type of hobbies different individuals engage in, or variations in political preferences.

The different subcategories in each example reflect different kinds of stimuli or responses, but there is no implication that the subcategories on any of these dimensions vary in amount or degree. Usually no numerical values are assigned to the different subcategories, except for the purposes of coding data for convenience or for processing by computer. Thus, males may be coded as "1" while females may be coded as "2" but the latter is not "twice as much" of some dimension as is the former subgroup. The assignment of the number codes is highly arbitrary and could just as readily have been assigned in the reverse sequence, with males as "2" and females as "1."

The next level of precision, the *ordinal* level, provides more information about the subgroupings since they vary in amount or degree along some dimension. Size designations such as small, medium, and large, for example, convey information about the relative magnitudes of the different values of this type of independent variable. Variations in task difficulty, such as easy, moderate, or difficult, could also represent an independent variable of an ordinal level. On the dependent variable side, we could examine the degree of physiological arousal, the amount of physical effort expended, or the degree of aesthetic appeal experienced.

Although ordinal measurements tell us how different values stand relative to each other, we can not say exactly how much they differ on an absolute basis. The difference between the small and medium values is not necessarily the same magnitude as the distance between medium and large. Subjective ratings of aesthetic appeal such as "very much" may differ from "somewhat" by a different degree than "somewhat" exceeds "very little."

The *interval* level measurement scale is a step above the ordinal level and contains units assumed to be equal throughout the scale. Thus a person with an intelligence test score of 130 exceeds the person with 120 by 10 points and this difference is comparable to the 10-point difference between persons with scores of 100 and 110, or 115 and 125.

However, it can not be accurately claimed that a person with an intelligence score of 200 is "twice as smart" as someone who scores only 100. For although we may sometimes disparagingly comment that someone has "no intelligence at all," the charge is not literally true. Furthermore, even if someone took an intelligence test and received a score of zero, it would be erroneous to conclude that this individual was totally lacking the intelligence.

Only with the *ratio* scale of measurement, where the value 0 actually refers to an absence of some dimension, can we make valid proportional comparisons, as in the above example. Variables meeting this condition are relatively rare in psychological research and usually involve physical properties such as weight, length, width, depth, and time. These dimensions are all independent variables which can be manipulated by the experimenter, but only time can be regarded as a behavior or dependent variable, as when we measure how long a response requires.

Problems arise in psychology because researchers sometimes assume, at least implicitly, that the variables and constructs they are studying have the properties of ratio scales. This confusion occurs largely because numbers are convenient to use in defining variables. Thus we might operationally define the independent variable of stress by having judges rate several situations on some numerical scale such as: 5=very high, 4=high, 3=moderate, 2=low, 1=very low. When we measure dependent variables such as retention, we might similarly rate the accuracy of recall or count the number of correctly-recalled items. In either case, the numbers themselves represent a ratio scale but the underlying psychological variables of stress and memory usually do not. We must be careful not to equate the mathematical properties of our number system with the abstract psychological dimensions we are measuring with it.

SUMMARY

Every experiment must have at least one independent variable, the factor that is manipulated or controlled by the experimenter so that different amounts or types of the factor can be presented to different groups. Every experiment must also have at least one dependent variable,which is the aspect of behavior assumed to be affected by the independent variable.

Operational definitions are precise statements of the procedures or operations used to measure abstract concepts including independent and dependent variables. A given concept may be defined by different investigators by different sets of procedures, which can be confusing if this situation is not realized. There is no single "correct" set of operations for most concepts; by using a variety of methods, we hope to converge on the common feature represented by an abstract psychological construct.

It is important to conduct manipulation checks by which we obtain independent appraisals of the extent to which our procedures for creating variations in the independent variables are effective. Subjects may not detect or react to these variations in the manner intended by the experimenter; unless these manipulation checks are made, we may draw erroneous conclusions about the effects of the independent variable.

Dependent variables exist at a number of levels: physiological, biochemical, behavioral, and experiential. Most human research focuses on the latter two but it can sometimes be useful to include several. Within a given level, it is also worthwhile to include more than one dependent variable since the pattern among them may be important.

Two important yet often overlooked issues dealing with dependent variables are those of reliability and validity. Reliability is concerned with the repeatability of results on different occasions. If reliability is low, the data are not very useful since we would have widely divergent findings on two different times.

Validity is a more complex matter dealing with the extent to which the dependent variable being used is a true reflection of the underlying process or phenomenon it is supposedly measuring. A number of alternative measures, rather than only one, can be valid. Thus if we want to measure variations in aggression, what type of behavior adequately reflects this construct? Do we use self-report, verbal sarcasm or swearing, or physical responses such as hitting others? On the surface, any of these measures might seem plausible, but without further evidence it is risky to assume that any specific dependent variable is a valid index of some construct. It is necessary to actually compare scores on the proposed dependent variable between groups known by some existing, accepted criterion of aggression to differ in this tendency. With this empirical process, we have greater confidence that the new dependent variable is a valid measure of aggression because persons who differ in aggression according to already-established criteria also show differences on it as well.

REFERENCES

Bales, R. F. *Interaction process analysis*. Chicago: University of Chicago Press, 1980.

Cook, T. D., and Campbell, D. T. *Quasi-experimentation: Design and analysis issues for field settings*. Chicago: Rand McNally, 1979.

Epstein, S. The stability of behavior: I. On predicting most of the people much of the time. *Journal of Personality and Social Psychology*, 1979, *37*, 1097-1126.

Epstein, S. The stability of behavior: II. Implications for psychological research. *American Psychologist*, 1980, *35*, 790-806.

Freedman, J. L., Heshka, S., and Levy, A. Crowding as an intensifier of pleasantness and unpleasantness. In J. L. Freedman, *Crowding and behavior*. San Francisco: Freeman, 1975.

Lazarus, R. S. *Psychological stress and the coping process*. New York: McGraw-Hill, 1966.

Nesbitt, P. D. Chronic smoking and emotionality. *Journal of Applied Social Psychology*, 1972, *2*, 197-196.

LEARNING ACTIVITIES

1. Using the categories in Table 2-1, name three examples of independent variables and three examples of dependent variables.
2. For each example provided above, devise an operational definition. Without disclosing your definitions, ask another student to provide operational definitions of the same terms. Then compare your operational definitions with those of the other student and try to reconcile disagreements, if any.
3. In everyday interaction, we often use terms whose meanings we seemingly readily agree upon although we may actually hold somewhat different interpretations. How would you operationally define terms such as:
   a difference of opinion
   unreasonable risk
   tender loving care
   an ounce of prevention
   higher than a kite
4. Referring back to an activity at the end of Chapter 1 in which you made observations of some aspects of behavior for a sample of individuals, how can you determine if your measurements are reliable? If you can contact the same set of individuals again, determine the degree of reliability of one of your measures. If you can not identify or locate the original group, arrange to make observations of a new sample you will be able to observe twice. Do not indicate to the individual *in advance* the exact purpose of your second set of observations.
5. Assuming that your observations are reliable, how can you determine if you have a valid measure of what you intend to measure? Can you think of an independent index that is already well-established as a measure of this factor? If so, how would you use it to assess the validity of your new procedures for measuring it?

CHAPTER 3

Experimental Designs and Controls

Chapter at a Glance

The concept of an experiment is confusing because the term is often misused in everyday situations to refer to any innovation or modification of existing procedures. Thus a teacher or a school is said to be doing an "experiment" if a new teaching method is adopted. A corporation is claiming the use of an "experimental" system of more flexible scheduling of work hours. Professional sports leagues are "experimenting" with novel procedures and rule changes to improve the games and increase spectator appeal.

While any *attempt* to improve some existing situation can be considered as praiseworthy, it must be cautioned that in many cases it is another and often more complex matter to *evaluate* the actual impact of these changes in an objective manner. Most of these modifications are not true experiments in the sense that the scientific researcher uses the term "experiment." A true experiment involves controlled manipulation of factors which permits one to compare outcomes with *and* without the innovation. Usually X, the changed factor or independent variable, is not controlled in everyday innovations but is introduced across-the-board as a wholesale change into the existing system. Although comparisons are sometimes made between performance before and after X is introduced, as we shall see later, other factors that have nothing to do with X at all can be responsible for these behavioral changes. Before we can accept the conclusion that the specific change, X, was responsible for the observed behavior change, we must be able to rule out the chance that these suspected alternative causes may have produced the change in behavior.

INTERNAL AND EXTERNAL VALIDITY

An experiment that enables us to reach such firm conclusions about the effects of some assumed causal factor(s), represented as the independent variable(s), has *internal validity*. We feel confident that no other factors could have led to the results of the experiment. In a later chapter we will discuss *external validity* in detail, but briefly describing this concept here will help clarify the concept of internal validity.

External validity refers to the degree to which the results of a specific experiment can be generalized to other situations, persons, occasions, and so forth. When we conduct an experiment, we almost always implicitly or explicitly assume that the results can be applied beyond the specific individuals and types of individuals who serve as subjects. Similarly, we hope the results can be extended to some other types of settings or situations, particularly those of the real world. We also hope that the results are not limited to the particular time the experiment was conducted but will hold up over a longer time period.

In one sense, internal and external validity are reciprocally related to a large extent. In order to gain analytical precision so that we can make inferences about causality, we design experiments with highly controlled but somewhat artificial conditions to optimize internal validity. At the same time, this procedure inevitably restricts external validity of that particular experiment since a given phenomenon may be altered under circumstances different than those present in any specific experiment. On the other hand, if internal validity is *low* so that the results are inconclusive, external validity becomes an irrelevant issue.

In this chapter we will first examine the sources or factors that act as threats to the internal validity of situations we will call "nonexperiments." Although they are often termed "experiments" in everyday usage, they are not true experiments. We will point out the limitations of these research designs before proceeding to a discussion of control procedures which are a key aspect of valid or true experiments. We will show that these controls enable one to establish internal validity by allowing one to exclude the possibility that the results could be due to rival or alternative factors other than those assumed by the experimenter.

THREATS TO INTERNAL VALIDITY

A number of factors represent alternative explanations for observed effects which may be mistakenly attributed to the influence of a variable assumed to be the causal mechanism. Campbell and Stanley (1963) summarized the major threats to internal validity of experiments, as listed in Table 3-1. We will describe them briefly before illustrating them with examples of various situations which are sometimes loosely referred to as "experiments" but, lacking adequate control procedures, would more accurately be labelled "nonexperiments."

First, the factor termed *history* refers to any other factor occurring concurrently with X, the factor assumed to be responsible for some effect on behavior. Suppose we are measuring attitude change as a function of a classroom communication about the need for taking care of one's health. We would be mistaken if we obtained a large change in attitude in the direction of the message and attributed it to the communication if during the course of the study a large-scale epidemic of some illness occurred or a mass-media campaign aimed at improving health practices was instituted. These other factors, rather than or in addition to the factor we thought was producing the attitude change, operate simultaneously with the assumed factor and threathen to invalidate any conclusions.

A second threat is *maturation* or the process of growth and change over time which takes place concurrently with the operation of any other factors assumed to affect behavior. Both history and maturation are stronger threats for studies involving longer time periods. Even if the treatment factor, X, had no effect on behavior, some changes due to maturation may occur which we may mistakenly assign to X.

A third threat to internal validity is *testing*. Behavior can change on subsequent tests simply due to the increased sophistication and familiarity the subject gains from more experience with being tested. Even if a treatment factor, administered between different testings, has no effect at all, some changes will result from the practice effect of repeated testing which may be assumed to stem from the treatment factor.

Instrument change is a fourth source of threat to internal validity. If the apparatus or equipment used to obtain measurements over the course of the experiment becomes unreliable in its operation, changes between successive measurements may appear even though X had no influence at all. Unless one was aware that such instrument impairment existed, one might mistakenly draw the inference that these differences were due to the influence of X.

A fifth source of error in drawing conclusions in some designs, *regression effects*, is statistical in nature. Measurement, it must be recognized, is not highly reliable in psychology and thus is imperfect. Measurement should be seen as an estimate of some hypothetical true value. If second measurements of the same individuals are made at a later time, they will usually produce varying readings simply due to chance factors.

How does measurement theory affect the conclusions drawn from pre- and posttest design comparisons? Statistical theory assumes that retest scores for extremely high or low initial scores will tend to fall back toward the middle of the range of scores. In effect, we are dealing with the law of averages, so that retest scores will be expected to change for individuals with extremely high or low scores, *even* if the individuals did not change themselves.

The significance of this phenomenon of *regression toward the mean*, as it is called, is that persons with extreme scores on the pretest will *appear* to be affected by some event, X, which falls between the pre- and posttest because their scores on the posttest will shift or regress toward the mean. This statistical shift will occur even if the intervening event has no true influence but the investigator may erroneously think that the change due to the statistical regression effect was really due to the impact of X.

Selection is a sixth threat to internal validity. If the subjects assigned to different treatment conditions are unequal at the outset, these initial differences can affect the kinds of results obtained. Allowing subjects to choose for themselves which treatment to receive would represent a similar problem in interpretation. These biases might either add to any differences stemming from the treatment variable or they might even counteract and mask any effects of the treatments.

Seventh, when differential experimental *mortality* or attrition of subjects occurs—that is, initially equal groups become unequal when individuals drop out of the experiment under different treatments—conclusions about the effects of the treatment variable are invalidated.

Are you now a bit discouraged and wondering if one can conduct a sound experiment at all? Certainly all of the threats to internal validity are serious and it would be nice to be able to eliminate them. While we may be able to prevent selection and mortality, we can not reduce to zero factors such as history or maturation which are inevitable. However, we can devise control procedures to "hold constant" these factors and prevent them from jeopardizing inferences about treatment factors. This is done with a control group that is otherwise equal to the experimental group receiving the treatment variable except for this one difference. In this way, both groups are equated for history, maturation, testing, and instrumentation so that any difference in their behavior must be due to other factors, such as the independent variable, X. We no longer need to actually measure these extraneous factors because, now controlled, they no longer threaten internal validity.

NONEXPERIMENTAL DESIGNS

Posttest Only

One type of nonexperiment—the posttest-only design shown in Table 3-1—which arises frequently occurs when evidence is recorded about some behavior immediately after a dramatic and usually unexpected event or change takes place. Partly due to the unplanned nature of the event, X, no data exist about the level of that behavior existing prior to the sudden event. For example, suppose a manufacturer announces that a particular model of automobile has been found defective and will be recalled. A survey is then made of 10,000 randomly-selected owners (who know about the recall notice) about their degree of satisfaction with their automobile; and 70 per cent are "dissatisfied." To what extent has the recall notice contributed to the level of owner dissatisfaction? Certainly no automobile yet has made 100 per cent of its owners happy, and we can safely assume that some portion of the 70 per cent of dissatisfied owners were already disgruntled before they learned of the recall. For all we know, this particular car may be so poor that about 70 per cent of the owners were already dissatisfied prior to learning of the recall plan. Without a measure of their sentiment prior to the event, it is somewhat risky to interpret the impact of the recall notice on the owners' attitudes toward their cars.

In extreme cases one can make reasonable inferences from posttest only designs even though no pretest comparison data exist. Attitudes of Americans toward Iran were extremely negative following the 1979 taking of hostages at the American Embassy in Teheran. Since this event was largely unanticipated, it is unlikely that attitudinal measures toward Iran were taken prior to the event; thus pre- and postcomparisons are not possible. It is reasonable to assume, however, that much, if not all, of the negative attitude was generated by this one dramatic event.

Generally, however, we must be cautious in accepting these "one-shot" studies, which only have measures of one group following some event, since we can not rule out the possibility that factors other than the specific event caused the observed scores. Without some knowledge of the pre-event scores, it is impossible to know whether the postevent scores reflect an increase, decrease, or no change. Even with the addition of pretest scores, unless we can compare the changes of the group exposed to the event with a comparable group that did not encounter the event, we can not be confident that all or much of the change was due to the specific event rather than to other concurrent events we may not have noticed.

In real-life situations, we usually lack these added types of information and are left with situations like the posttest-only comparison which, at best, is only suggestive evidence about causal relationships. It is not a true experiment and should be regarded only as uncontrolled natural observation which can lead us to hypotheses that must be more adequately evaluated under proper experiments.

Pre- and Posttest

This design, diagrammed in Table 3–1, extends the posttest-only design by the inclusion of information about the level of behavior that existed prior to the factor under study. Referring back to the automobile-recall example, suppose we had surveyed a random sample of owners about their satisfaction with their car prior to the recall campaign. Comparison of this data with that obtained from the identical sample after notification of the defect permits a somewhat firmer basis from which to draw a conclusion about the effect of this event.

Nonetheless, the hazards of this design jeopardize the validity of conclusions one can make. For example, the procedure of repeated testing itself can alter the results. *Sensitization* of the respondents can occur during the pretest; they can become more aware or interested in the factor that will be introduced to them. Thus, a pretest of attitudes toward different ethnic groups may alert subjects to pay attention to

TABLE 3-1. Diagram of Common Nonexperimental Designs and the Presence or Absence of the Major Threats to Internal Validity in Each Situation. The treatment is designated as "X," pretests as O_1, posttests as O_2. If only posttests are used, they are represented by O.

Type of Design	History	Maturation	Testing	Instrumentation	Statistical Regression	Selection	Mortality
One Group, Posttest Only X O	Yes	Yes	Yes	Yes	Does Not Apply	No	No
One Group, Pre- and Posttest Design O_1 X O_2	Yes	Yes	Yes	Yes	Yes	Yes	Yes
Two Groups, Nonrandom Posttest Only X O - - - - - - - O	No	No	No	No	Does Not Apply	No	No
Two Groups, Nonrandom Pre- and Posttest O_1 X O_2 - - - - - - - - - - O_1 O_2	No	No	No	No	Yes	No	No

the content of a subsequent lecture or film dealing with racial prejudice—a film they might have paid less attention to without the pretest sensitization. If subsequent measures on the posttest revealed large changes in attitudes in comparison to the pretest scores, one might erroneously conclude that all of the change was due to the lecture or film content, *per se*.

Another serious problem threathening the validity of conclusions drawn from the pre- and posttest design is the possibility that concurrent factors other than the assumed factor are responsible for all or at least some of the pre- and posttest changes. For example, suppose a pre- and posttest comparison of the knowledge of psychology was made for students enrolled in my Introductory Psychology course showed a whopping 250 per cent increase. Can I rest assured that all of this gain resulted from being in my class? Suppose that during the semester, unknown to me, an excellent course on psychology was broadcast on public television. These programs featured outstanding and eminent scholars discussing their own theories and research. And with their dazzling visual graphics and spectacular animation, these programs were not only educational but highly entertaining. Let us also suppose that most of my students watched the series regularly over the semester, although many of them cut my classes.

In this example, much, if not all, of the students' gains in knowledge were due to the "other" factor operating concurrently with my lectures. My unawareness of the existence of this rival factor (or my vanity) would lead me to erroneously conclude that all of the pre- and posttest gains were due to my teaching skill.

Another alternative explanation for my students' improvement over the entire semester might be increased motivation and maturity as they became acclimated to the more demanding academic environment of college compared to their recent high school experience. This factor alone could produce some gains in course attendance, study habits, and test scores over the semester.

Two Groups Nonrandom (*Ex post facto*)

Another type of naturalistic comparison that resembles the true experiment is one in which two nonrandomly created groups are involved, as illustrated in Table 3–1. In this paradigm also referred to as the *ex post facto* design, a comparison is made between a group that has experienced one type of situation and a group that has not. It is important to note that a high degree of selectivity is involved in determining the group an individual belongs to since often each subject must choose whether or not to participate in a specific experience. For example, comparisons between boys who are or are not Boy Scouts or between sorority and nonsorority members involves subgroupings which are essentially self-selective and voluntary. In many other cases, although selectivity is still evident, the individuals are less in control; for example, when ability or financial resources are major determinants—doctors vs. nondoctors, or professional athletes vs. non athletes. But in all cases we are dealing with comparisons of naturalistically formed or intact groups. Unlike groups that were created by the experimenter for research purposes, these existing groups probably differ in ways other than the one we are focussing on.

When comparisons are made between existing groups, the research goal is often to draw some conclusion about the factor that distinguishes the groups behaviorally. For example, arguments exist that Boy-Scout training builds better citizens since so many former Scouts seem to do well in later life, and that participation in sororities provides social benefits such as greater popularity. While there may be some merit to these conclusions, one cannot make these definitive statements simply because the factor on which the subgroupings are compared is usually not the only factor distinguishing them. Boy Scouts and sorority members differ from their counterparts on other dimensions, such as social-class background, personality, and attitudes, prior to joining these affiliations. Thus these other dimensions may be responsible for some of the subsequent differences generally attributed to the experience of belonging to Boy Scouts or sororities.

Posttest Only. Another situation that involves a comparison of two nonrandom groups includes only a posttest, as diagrammed in Table 3–1. For example, comparisons have frequently been made of children who grow up in father-absent homes with those who have their fathers present at home. In general, it seems that when no father is present in the home, serious psychological problems occur for the children, leading to the inference that the father plays an important role in their psychological development. Without rejecting this interpretation totally, it must also be noted that father-absent and father-present families differ in numerous *other* respects such as social class, number of children, and psychological adjustment of the mother (Lamb, 1979).

If we restrict ourselves to cases of father absence involving divorce or desertion, it could be argued that the kinds of persons who are likely to leave their families may differ from those who, for whatever reason, decide to stay. They may already have had different effects on their children even before they leave the home so that all of the differences between children of father-absent and father-present homes may not result from this factor of separation alone.

If it were possible to obtain some information about the characteristics or behavior of the two groups prior to time when the groups are being compared, we might be able to resolve this question. Many times, however, it is not possible to go backward in time to obtain "pretest" measures of what subjects were like prior to some experience.

Pre- and Posttest. An example of a comparison of two nonrandom groups in which both pre- and postmeasures are available (See Table 3–1) is a controversial study by Armor, Polich, and Stambul (1978). Alcoholics receiving treatment were compared with a group of alcoholics of similar age and socioeconomic background over a six-month period. The remission or recovery rate, as measured by reduction in drinking and drinking problems, was greater for the group receiving treatment. One might conclude then that the treatment program was effective, but one might first ask why the nontreated group did not receive treatment. Were they more seriously impaired than the individuals who were treated? If so, it would not be surprising that greater improvement occurred in the "treated" group, but not specifically because the treatment itself was so effective. Or if they were equal in the severity of their problem, could it be that those with more positive attitudes opted for treatment whereas those with negative views rejected treatment? If so, could it be that as long as attitudes were positive, a variety of treatments could have been effective, and not only the one used in this study?

In short, we can reasonably assume that the groups differed from each other in ways other than whether or not they underwent treatment. Some of these other factors, rather than the treatment itself, may be important determinants of the improved condition of the treated group. To the extent that the inclusion of the pretest allows us to conclude that the two groups were equal on some factors assumed to affect drinking levels–such as severity of problem, motivation for improvement, age, sex, and so on–this type of design is an improvement over the comparison of nonequivalent groups where only a posttest is possible. The groups possibly still differ on some important factor we are unaware of, so this design must still be used cautiously.

EXPERIMENTAL DESIGNS

Now that we have a good idea of some designs that are confused with experiments but do not permit sound conclusions, we can discuss the nature of experimental designs. It should be obvious that the outstanding advantage of experiments is that they enable us to reach sound conclusions. Just how this goal can be achieved with experiments, but not with nonexperiments, is the subject of the following discussion on the topic of control we touched on earlier.

Control is not a specific procedure but a variety of methods. The essence of control procedures is that they involve the creation of conditions or circumstances whereby one can rule out specific alternative factors that can account for differences between two groups until only one factor is left. For example, if we wish to conclude that the state of health of a group of rats that receives vitamin A for four weeks is due to the vitamins, we also need a comparable group that does not receive them *but* is otherwise treated identically. The *difference* in the health of the two groups tells us if the vitamins are effective. Without the control group (which received no vitamin), a critic could argue that some other process or factor like maturation, during the four weeks of vitamin-A treatment was responsible for the condition of the treated rats at the end of the month. These other explanations are "ruled out" by the inclusion of the control group; since the vitamins are the only difference between the two groups, it can be concluded that any group differences are due to the vitamins.

Control by Equating

The most positive procedure for ruling out the possible influence of some unwanted factor on performance is to equate all treatment groups or conditions on that factor. The test room, the time of day, the experimental assistant, and so on, are examples of variables that could be equated for groups otherwise treated differently. If we obtain differences in performance as a function of the independent variable, we can rest assured that any factor equated for all groups could not be a confounding factor.

The specific factors held constant by equating them depend on the nature of the independent variable. If we wish to assess the effect of group size on social interaction, we might wish to equate all groups on ethnicity or sex, but we would probably not bother holding all sessions on the same floor of the building as long as the rooms were of the same size and furnishings.

It is impossible, however, to identify all of the factors on which groups should be equated. Even if we could, it would be impossible, or at least highly impractical, to achieve. One tries to hold groups constant on the factors obviously important to control by equation, and relies on another method—control by randomization—to control for all other factors.

Control by Randomization

According to the laws of statistics, when a random method is used to assign subjects to different groups, a greater likelihood exists that the groups are equal in all respects other than any procedures used to treat them differently during the course of the experiment. Thus the age, sex, intelligence, ability, personality, and other characteristics of each group generally should be equivalent for all groups formed in this manner. It must be emphasized that no direct measurement is needed to check the validity of these assumptions because the concept of randomness implies that equality should exist. In actual fact, especially with small samples, these assumptions may not be completely accurate. Yet unless we actually made measurements on these dimensions, we could not actually know that the assumptions were invalid in a specific situation.

Randomization is achieved by a variety of methods such as the use of statistically-computed tables called random-number tables, and the tossing of fair coins or dice. Any method allotting each individual an equal chance of being assigned to each of the groups is considered random. This method is advantageous in that it permits us to assume that the groups are *more or less* equal on any conceivable dimension, without the necessity of actual measurement to confirm this assumption. In actual fact, some error or lack of exact equality will exist, but generally these errors will be quite small and inconsequential in their effect on behavior in the experiment relative to the assumed effect of the independent variable.

Control by randomization does not mean that a given factor is equated or literally held constant or invariant. Actually, the factor is allowed to fluctuate or vary, but the extent of such variation within each group is assumed to be equal for all groups. Thus, random assignment allows us to assume that the average height of subjects in one group is equal to that in other groups. The groups are equal in the average height of subjects, but within each group the height of subjects varies in a manner reflective of the actual variation in the general population from which the samples are randomly chosen.

Control by Balancing

A special type of procedure known as counterbalancing is used to prevent factors that cannot literally be eliminated or held constant from reducing the internal validity of an experiment. We will discuss this technique more fully in Chapter 5 in conjunction with the topic of using the same subjects in all of the different treatment conditions of an experiment. For our purposes here, we need only to understand counterbalancing as a means of equating the influence of some unwanted factor evenly across the levels of our independent variable so that we can draw sound inferences about the effect of the latter variable.

One general type of situation calling for this type of control is when two or more stimuli varying along some dimension, such as attractiveness or tastiness, are presented simultaneously for the subject to evaluate. They must be presented in some spatial arrangement. To keep the example simple, suppose we want to compare reactions to two stimuli that vary in size, large and small. If we presented the large one on the left side of the display and the small one on the right on every test and for every subject, it is conceivable that many subjects may have a position preference or bias favoring those objects placed on one side rather than the other, especially if the discrimination is a difficult one and there is no clearcut preference based on the properties of the stimuli, *per se*. Counterbalancing in this case would call for the placement of each stimulus size equally often on the left and right sides so that spatial position could be ruled out as an explanation if subjects consistently preferred a given stimulus size.

One might argue that the problem could be solved by presenting the two stimuli successively, rather than at the same time, directly in front of the subject so that position bias can not operate. While this strategy solves one problem, it raises another potential source of contamination, a temporal bias. Successive presentation requires that one stimulus be shown first, followed by the next, and so on. There are biases known as primacy and recency effects, referring to the fact that the first or the last stimulus, respectively, to be encountered may have more influence strictly because of its temporal location rather than to any inherent features of the stimulus itself. Since we want to identify the effects of the stimuli, we wish to avoid the potential rival influence due to the temporal factor. Again, counterbalancing is used so that each stimulus size occurs equally often in each temporal location. Combining the performance scores for each stimulus summed over the two different temporal locations enables us to draw some conclusions about the effect of the stimulus-size variable without concern that the effects are due to the influence of temporal position instead.

Spatial or temporal location need not affect behavior in every situation; in fact, these factors often have no influence in experiments employing counterbalancing. Use of counterbalancing where unnecessary does not hurt, whereas failure to counterbalance when it is needed can be disastrous. Although more work is called for in planning an experiment using counterbalancing, one can at least rest assured that the factor balanced across the levels of the independent variable of interest will not threaten the internal validity of the experiment.

The Zero-Control Condition

Although all experiments must contain some degree of variation in the types or levels of treatment it is not absolutely necessary to include a zero-control condition, which receives a "zero" amount of the independent variable. Inclusion of such a condition, however, can add invaluable information and affect the kinds of conclusions one makes from a study. Nevertheless, it is quite common to find studies that do not bother to include the zero control.

If one is interested, for example, in comparing two teaching methods, A and B, one does not usually employ a zero control that receives no instruction. It is adequate to use two groups, one taught with method A and one with method B. Suppose, however, that both methods were not very sound and while the students learned some material, they formed such a negative attitude toward learning from both methods that they were hostile toward the subject matter. If they had to take a second or advanced course in the same subject matter, might a third group that received "zero instruction" initially fare better in the advanced course? In other words, without a zero-control condition, one can only determine the *relative performance* of two or more groups, which does not tell if all groups were doing well or poorly by some *absolute* criteria.

Take the following example in which a comparison is made of the impact of two amounts of positive verbal comments given as reinforcement for learning. Suppose a small advantage is found with the larger amount of positive comments, but that either amount of verbal response is *superior* to a "no-verbal-comment" or "zero control" group as shown in Fig. 3-1(A). Or make the opposite assumption: suppose the positive-comment group, receiving a larger amount of comments, is superior, but both comment groups are *inferior* to the noncomment zero control, as shown in Figure 3-1(B) (Perhaps the comments were distracting and thus interfered with performance.) A third possibility is that the large amount of positive-comment group is best, followed by the no-comment group, with the lowest performance occurring for the small amount of positive-comment group, as represented in Figure 3-1(C).

Other outcomes are possible, but these three are sufficiently varied to give an idea of the wide range of possible outcomes. Now suppose the study was conducted *without* a zero-control condition. Examine Figures 3-1 (A), (B), and (C) visually, and in your mind, blank out the data for the zero-control condition. You will discover that the results appear to be very similar in all three cases, with the large amount of positive comments producing better performance than the small amount.

Obviously the interpretation of the superiority of the large amount of positive-comment condition is vastly altered by knowledge of what level of performance is produced by the zero-control group, which received no comments. Without this control, we can still draw some valid conclusions. With the inclusion of this condition, we gain a perspective of the total picture and more insight as to the actual processes occurring.

As a second example, suppose we wanted to assess the effects of a

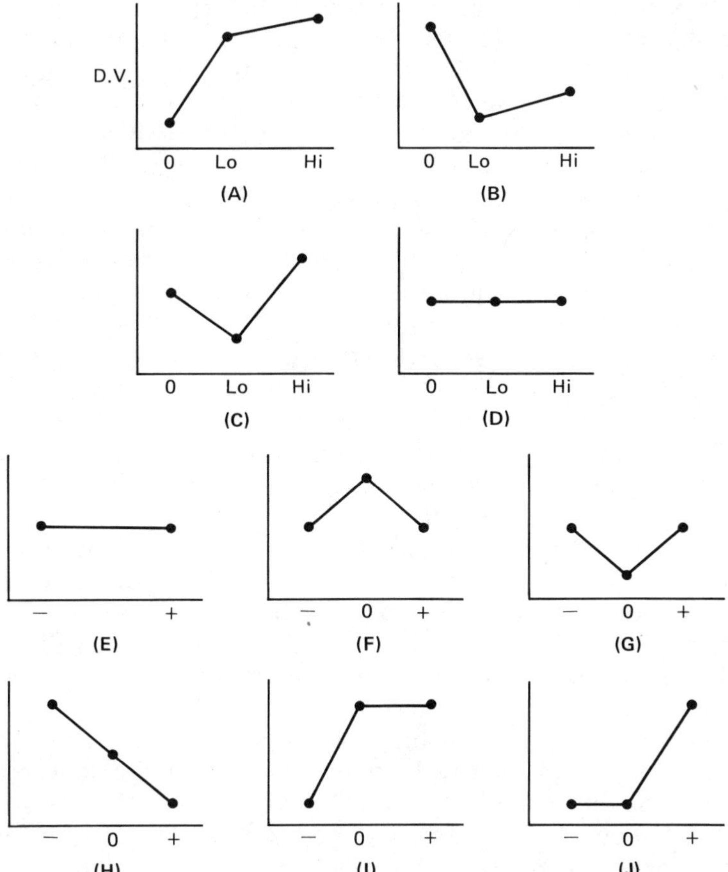

FIGURE 3-1. Some selected outcomes when a zero control group is included for comparison with at least two other levels of the independent variable. Panels A–D deal with a zero control which is at one end of the dimension (in this example, the low end) while Panels E–J deal with a zero control which falls in the middle of the range of values of the independent variable under examination. (See text for explanation.)

pay raise on productivity of employees. By comparing a group that gets a 5 per cent increase with a control group that receives no raise, we might find that productivity improved by 8 per cent. By including a zero-control group, we can clearly conclude that some raise is better than no raise. But suppose that a zero-control group had not been included, as in a situation where we merely want to compare several levels of pay raises. Suppose that the results show that productivity increases to a higher degree with a 10 per cent than with a 5 per cent raise. Can we conclude that all of the productivity gains were due to pay raises? Suppose that during the time the study was conducted the company changed managers or introduced better equipment. It is conceivable that these nonsalary changes may have contributed to the gains in productivity. Had we included a zero raise control condition, we could determine how much of the gain was due to salary increases and how much of it was due to other changes that took place coincidentally. Only the gains above and beyond those made by the zero-control group can be attributed to the salary increases.

In the foregoing examples, the performance of the zero control has been located at the low end of the scale with the other levels above it (in principle, it could be just the opposite, zero control at the "top," with other conditions involving lower levels).

In some experiments, we may choose to compare two levels of a variable that bracket the zero level, such as an increase or a decrease in temperature as compared with no change. Presumably the zero-control level falls intermediate to the other levels of the independent variable in these situations. Let us examine what might happen if the zero-control condition is omitted in these situations.

If, as in Figure 3–1(E), no effect of the higher and lower levels occurs, one would conclude that there was no effect. But as Figure 3–1 (F & G) shows, the zero condition may have led to a much higher *or* lower response level than either the greater-than-zero or less-than-zero levels. In these two cases, we would fail to realize how effective our independent variable really was.

Problems of interpretation may also arise without the zero control when differences are obtained between the above-and-below zero levels of the independent variable, as shown in Figure 3–1 (H, I, J). Although we can safely conclude that an effect occurs, there are at least three different possible refinements to this conclusion we could choose among if we had included the zero-control condition. First in (H), perhaps the above-zero level improved performance above zero while the below-zero condition reduced it relative to the zero level, more or less the same extent.

Secondly, the *same* difference between the above- and below-zero levels might reflect the fact that the zero level is equal to the above zero group performance, meaning that the above zero level was unable to increase performance and all of the difference stemmed from the tendency of the below-zero treatment to lower performance relative to both of the other conditions, as in Figure 3–1 (I).

Thirdly, the *same* obtained difference between the above- and below-zero levels could stem from a situation in which the above-zero level raised performance from that of the zero level whereas the below-zero level was unable to produce any differences from that of the zero-level condition.

Other outcomes are possible, but these examples should suffice to show the added value of a zero-control condition. Without it, a comparison between the above- and below-zero conditions showing superior performance of the above-zero treatment could reflect either of the situations (H), (I), or (J) in Figure 3–1.

Multiple Controls

In our discussion of control, the use of the term "control group" may have implied that only one group is possible in an experiment. But one can have as many control groups as needed to answer the questions of interest.

Recall the earlier example in which the effect of vitamin A on the health of animals was studied. Suppose that instead of vitamin A the experimental group received multiple-vitamin pills while the control group received similar-appearing pills that contained no vitamins. Suppose the multiple-vitamin group was superior to the no-vitamin group. If we only wish to know if *some* vitamins versus no vitamins makes any difference, we have an adequate experiment. On the other hand, we may have reason to suspect that certain behaviors or abilities may be benefited by only certain vitamins but not by others. Use of only two groups, one of which receives a multiple-vitamin treatment, is rather imprecise to establish *this* conclusion.

We might now wish to have more than two groups: a single no-vitamin group and a separate group for each type of vitamin, A, B, C, D, and so forth, which we think has the potential to affect the behavior we are observing. By using several groups, we are breaking down the several components the multiple-vitamin group received to determine which elements are beneficial and which are superfluous or even detrimental. Thus, it might turn out that only the group receiving vitamin C was different, with all of the other vitamin groups being no better than the no-vitamin control group. All of the different vitamin groups might be viewed as "control groups" in a sense because they help us narrow down the factors responsible for the difference between the multiple-vitamin group and the no-vitamin group. Thus, the determination of what constitutes adequate control procedures depends in large part on the kinds of questions we are raising.

Control Group of "Normals"

Researchers perennially fail to use a control group of "normals" in studies purporting to show some process or characteristic unique to a special population such as criminals, rapists, child abusers, alcoholics, and so forth. In the first place, the definition of "normal" varies somewhat depending on the group under study. If we are interested in the effects of a drug on institutionalized persons, the control group is typically noninstitutionalized persons. If we want to measure characteristics of private-school students, then the reference comparison is public-school students. "Normal," then, is a relative term defined somewhat by the type of problem under investigation, rather than an absolute or universal definition.

Sometimes we obtain results that seem so logical that we overlook the need for a normal control. If juvenile delinquents are found to watch 20 hours of violence on television each week, we may fail to check that nondelinquents watch much less. If we conclude that a causal relationship exists between the amount of violence viewed and the degree of delinquency, we must include evidence demonstrating that the nondelinquents, in contrast, watch substantially smaller amounts of violence.

Even when a normal control is included and results show that the groups differ from each other, we should not conclude that the specific classification is the unique category with these traits. Thus, alcoholics score higher on psychopathic-deviancy scales than do nonalcoholics. Yet it is possible that other psychiatric inmates also share a similar propensity for this characteristic. If so, it would appear that these tendencies are not unique to alcoholism but are more a reflection of institutionalization or of a general disposition associated with psychopathology.

Placebo and Expectancy Controls

Power of suggestion refers to the possibility that a person's beliefs or expectations about the effects of some experience may make the person act in accord with those anticipated consequences, even if that experience has no "real" effect. If a subject is a firm believer in hypnosis, we might use some procedure we allege is a hypnotic method and find that it will be highly effective. If we give someone a pill we claim will increase alertness, our assertion will occur if the person believes us, even if the pill contains no pharmacological agent known to influence alertness.

Precautions are usually taken in situations where the treatment under examination may involve expectancy effects. A control condition in which the subjects are given the same expectations as the experimental group is included so that the only difference between the two groups is the treatment itself. The expectancy control group does not eliminate or even reduce the expectancy but provides a baseline level of performance against which one can compare that of the treated experimental group to see if any differences occur above and beyond the influence of expectancies.

The classic situation involving the need for control of expectancies is the drug study. It is insufficient to include a no-drug group as a control because even if the drug under study were ineffectual, a difference between groups might exist because of the expectations formed by the experimental group. A "placebo" or pill, which is harmless but otherwise looks the same as that given to the experimental group, is administered to the control group to rule out the possibility that group differences are due to expectations.

INTERNAL VALIDITY AND CONFOUNDING

Ideally an experiment should enable us to attribute differences in behavior that occur between groups receiving different treatments to the influence of the independent variable. As we noted earlier, when this situation exists, the experiment is said to have internal validity. All other factors are ruled out as possible rival explanations because either they are assumed to be equal or they are made equal for all groups. In contrast, if the obtained results could possibly be due to some other factor that has covaried, unintentionally of course, with the independent variable, the experiment is said to be *confounded.*

Confounding does not permit unequivocal interpretation and thus renders any experiment in which it exists virtually useless. Table 3–2 illustrates the situation in which confounding exists. The experimenter intended to manipulate or vary one independent variable, A, giving level A_1 to one group and level A_2 to another equivalent group. Suppose instead of equating both groups on some other factor, B, either by holding the level of B fixed or constant throughout or by allowing B to vary but equally so for groups receiving A_1 and A_2, our researcher unwittingly allows the A_1 and A_2 groups to not only differ on the level of the A factor, but also on the level of the B factor. Thus, in Table 3–2, we see that confounding occurs if A_1 was administered in combination

TABLE 3–2. A Comparison of the Effects of A_1 vs. A_2 Can Be Made While Holding B Constant at B_1 (left column) or at B_2 (right column). If B is allowed to vary at both of its levels equally often with A_1 and A_2, a comparison of the entire top row can be made with entire bottom row. Confounding, as indicated by the arrows connecting diagonally located cells, involves the comparison of A_1 vs. A_2 under conditions where another variable, B, is also being varied rather than held constant or equal; i.e., A_1B_1 vs. A_2B_2 or A_1B_2 vs. A_2B_1.

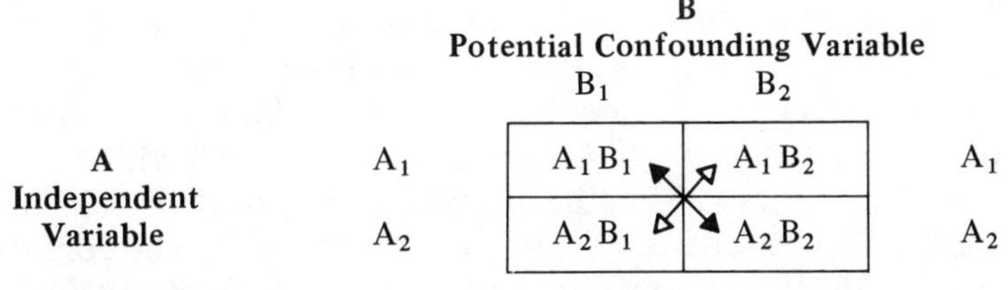

		B Potential Confounding Variable B_1	B_2	
A Independent Variable	A_1	A_1B_1	A_1B_2	A_1
	A_2	A_2B_1	A_2B_2	A_2

with conditions where the B factor was always B_1, whereas the A_2 level was always given in conjunction with B_2. Another confounded comparison would involve conditions $A_1 B_2$ versus $A_2 B_1$.

A specific example of confounding might be the comparison of the effects of size of reward, large or small, on running speed in rats. We have two levels of one factor like A. If, however, the rewards also vary in palatability, with the small reward being tastier and the large reward being less pleasing to the palate, we have confounded our comparison of the A factor by failing to equate them on the B factor, palatability.

We cannot determine how reward size, A_1 versus A_2, affects performance because some or all of the differences may be due to the influence of the concurrent variation of the B factor of palatability. To anticipate your questions, we should acknowledge that both factors can have an influence and as we will discuss later in Chapter 6, experiments can be designed to evaluate the joint effect of more than one factor. The critical point in this example, however, is that we can not evaluate the effect of even one factor if it is confounded by another one. In the examples presented earlier about counterbalancing, we can think of the temporal and spatial factors as potential confounding variables which would have prevented valid conclusions about the effects of the independent variable if they had not been counterbalanced to control their influence.

Another example of confounding might be a study in which room illumination is varied to assess its effect on assembly line work productivity. We might predict that higher illumination would enhance performance due to better visibility, but suppose that the higher illumination was uncomfortably warm in comparison with the lower level of illumination. Thus, the two illumination conditions vary not only in level of light but also in degree of temperature. If the temperature differences interfered with performance such that higher temperature reduced productivity due to discomfort, we could even obtain apparently paradoxical results of *poorer* performance under the condition assumed to yield better work. Our original thinking about the benefits of illumination on visibility may have been plausible, but due to the confounding factor of temperature, which has an opposite effect, we end up with confusing results unless we can discover the confounding factor.

Sometimes confounding factors are not identified until many years later and often by other investigators who are attempting to reconcile conflicting results from a set of experiments on a given topic. The incompatible results lead to more careful reexamination of prior studies which may suggest that *possible* confounding factors existed in some of the past studies. Then, it is still necessary to repeat or replicate these studies with and without the suspected confound to support or refute the hypothesis that such confounds did exist in prior studies.

It is, of course, possible for a confounding factor to produce results that are actually *similar* to those expected for the independent variable. If there is in fact no real influence of the independent variable, the investigator may still mistakenly conclude there is an effect due to it when the effect is really due to the confounding factor. Such a confound may be more difficult to detect than one whose effect is opposite to or different from the one expected for the independent variable. Using our room illumination example again, suppose for the sake of argument that the type of work is actually unaffected by variations in room illumination although the hypothesis stated that higher illumination would increase productivity. Suppose further that the high illumination treatment was administered by a highly enthusiastic supervisor to a group of employees whereas the low illumination treatment was used in conjunction with an apathetic supervisor. Suppose the gains in productivity after the initiation of the room illumination change were greater for the group of employees working under high illumination. If, as assumed in this example, room illumination was really not a factor, then all of the differences were due to the greater motivation generated by the more energetic supervisor.

In this example, room illumination, the independent variable, was confounded by the difference in the personality of the supervisors. The confounding factor was the true cause of the differences in work productivity, but since the direction of the differences is consonant with those predicted for the independent variable, it is less likely that the investigator may realize that his study is confounded.

Confounding and Subject Variables

Studies that examine the effects of subject variables such as age, sex, personality, and so forth, are unique in that they could be viewed as inevitably confounded. When the independent variable is a subject variable, it is impossible to manipulate or control it in the same sense that one can control other categories of independent variables, such as environment or task factors. Thus, in the preceding example, room illumination can be varied for different groups otherwise generally assumed to be equal in all other respects. Suspected confounding variables such as room temperature can be equated to permit an unequivocal determination of the effect of room illumination. In contrast, when a subject variable such as sex is involved, it is not reasonably possible to match groups on every respect except for their sex. Males and females obviously differ in their physical attributes, but also in social values which foster sex differences in personality and norms of appropriate behavior. If sex differences are found on some behavior, it is not clear how much of the difference is due to sex difference, *per se,* or to some other correlated differences.

Similarly, we may compare ethnic groups on some task and obtain differences, but are they due to genetic or environmental factors? Ethnic groups differ in their biological attributes, education levels, economic resources, and social status, to name a few factors. Or if we compare persons of differing ages on some behavior, are the differences due to age, or to other factors that also distinguish different age groups, such as amount of income, education level, marital status, number of children, and so forth?

As with all studies suspected to involve confounding factors, we must take precautions to eliminate rival explanations. With subject variables, attempts are frequently made to equate groups on factors that are obviously correlated with the independent variable. If we want to compare the effects of a training program on two different ethnic groups, we would make sure that both groups were equal in the number of years of schooling since this relevant factor is known to often be higher for some ethnic groups than for others. If we want to examine the effect of exercise on the mental health of single versus married persons, we might equate the two groups on age since this factor is probably lower for the single than for the married status in the overall population.

One cannot foresee all of the possible factors correlated with subject variables that might jeopardize the soundness of conclusions drawn from comparisons on such dimensions. It becomes time-consuming and impractical to equate groups on too many factors. It is always possible that we overlook and fail to consider some important correlated factor that should be equated when comparing groups on some subject dimension. One must always be cautious in interpreting the meaning of differences on subject variables since there is always the possibility that the primary cause is some factor unknown to us. Thus, if we find first-borns to be more anxious than later-borns, how do we explain this correlation? First- and later-borns differ in other ways: parents are younger when their first-born children arrive, parents occupy a greater percentage of the time of the first-borns' socialization, first-borns are given more responsibility, especially in helping socialize later born siblings, and so on. Any or all of these factors may be involved in producing anxiety differences as a function of birth order.

Confounding vs. Lack of Generalizability

A common problem students have in understanding the concept of confounding is confusing it with the issue of generalizability. When we try to take a finding about an independent variable obtained in one context and predict or conclude that the same effect holds true in another context, we are making generalizations which may or may not be valid. Additional experiments could be conducted to see if the effect of an independent variable applies to other stimuli, other environments, or other types of subjects, and so forth.

If our finding with males is not applicable to females, there is no generalizability across sex, but this does not mean that there is a confounding in our original findings, that, for example, alcohol leads to more aggression than Pepsi does when males are tested. Yet, when my students are asked to evaluate published experiments or to concoct fictional experiments containing what they think is a confounding variable, their examples often suggest that they equate confounding with lack of generalizability. Thus, if an experiment reported that females were more persuasible than males, some students would conclude that it was *confounded* because it was based only on college students. The criticism being raised, however, deals with the question of generalizability and has no bearing at all on the matter of confounding. In this example, confounding would exist in each of the following situations:

Males and females differed appreciably in age

Different types or amounts of persuasive content were used for males and females

Males were tested in the morning while females were tested at night

Characteristics of the person who presented the persuasive communications differed considerably for the males and females

SUMMARY

A number of nonexperimental designs were described that involve attempts to infer the effects of some treatment factor on behavior. However, these designs are not true experiments and any interpretations based on them are suspect because a number of rival explanations have not been eliminated by the comparisons involved. Many such nonexperiments occur frequently in naturalistic settings everyday. Behavior that is observed after some event is presumed to have been "caused" by that event. Although there may actually be such a causal relationship in many such comparisons, it is possible that other uncontrolled factors, such as the mere passage of time, may have created the observed behavior. Another common situation involves comparing pre- and post-event behavior. There is a strong tendency to assume that any changes over time are due to the intervening event, but it is possible that other intervening events are responsible for the behavioral changes.

Comparison of existing groups that differ in some respect–such as prior participation in athletics vs. a lack of such experience–often leads observers to attribute other differences between the groups to the influence of the distinguishing feature on which the groups were contrasted. Here, as in the other examples of nonexperimental designs, we have no assurance that there are no other factors that also differ between the groups or that such other factors may not be the real causes of differences between the groups. Thus, the physical and psychological characteristics of those who choose to participate in athletics are probably quite different from those who do not. It may be these initial differences, rather than the factor of athletic participation *per se,* that is responsible for any other observed differences between the groups.

In contrast to the nonexperiment, the true experiment is a design capable of permitting sound conclusions about the effects of factors administered to different groups of subjects. The experimenter has greater control over the situation and creates situations where comparisons can be made between groups that differ in only one respect, thus affording firmer conclusions about the effects of that single factor. A sound experiment is said to have internal validity when it allows us to make comparisons that permit valid conclusions about the effects of the independent variable.

On the other hand, experiments may be poorly designed and involve confounding variables that jeopardize the validity of conclusions. A confounded experiment is one in which one or more other variables covary with the independent variable so that it is inconclusive as to which treatment difference between groups is responsible for any group differences. For example, an experiment to test the effects of a large vs. small reward on learning is confounded if the large reward was tastier than the small reward. The two dimensions, size and taste, are confounded with each other since one value on one dimension is always associated with the same value of the other dimension. If the large and tasty-reward group performs better, is it due to the size or the taste difference?

REFERENCES

Armor, D. J., Polich, J. M., and Stambul, H. B. *Alcoholism and treatment.* New York: Wiley, 1978.

Campbell, D. T., and Stanley, J. C. *Experimental and quasi-experimental designs for research.* Chicago: Rand McNally, 1963.

Lamb, M. E. Paternal influences and the father's role: A personal perspective. *American Psychologist,* 1979, **34**, 938-943.

LEARNING ACTIVITIES

1. For each of the briefly described studies below, identify the type of nonexperimental design it most closely resembles:

a. A trend over the last decade shows decreasing Scholastic Aptitude Test scores among high school students.
b. After the election of the new governor, there has been a 50 per cent increase in the crime level in this state.
c. The percentage of youth who smoke has declined after a recent mass-media campaign about the dangers of smoking.
d. The average income of college graduates is far above that of people of the same age who did not go to college.
e. Students who drink alcohol have lower grades than nondrinkers.
f. Greater air pollution in big cities leads to more suicides.

2. For each of the fictitious studies described above, propose at least two different explanations or interpretations of the findings.

   Is it possible, at the hypothetical level at least, to design a controlled experiment that could provide evidence that would help you choose between alternative explanations for any of the above relationships?

3. Design a hypothetical experiment that contains a confounding variable in addition to the independent variable. Try to be subtle or at least suggest a confounding that is plausible in the sense that a careful investigator might still overlook and commit this error. Present your design to other students without informing them as to the nature of the confound and ask them to try to identify it. Then tell them what you regard to be the confounding factor and see if they concur. If your conception of confounding turns out to be wrong, try to identify what concept is really represented by the situation you thought involved confounding.

4. A researcher believes that depressed people improve their mood more than happy people if they watch a humorous movie. At a local theater he gives a short test to identify depressed movie-goers just before they watch a comedy. As soon as they leave at the end of the movie, he gives another test of mood and finds their mood has improved dramatically. Would you accept his claim that his experiment supports his hypothesis? If not, how could you change the study to improve it?

5. The director of a large airport wants to see how the amount of sleep obtained each night by air traffic controllers affects their accuracy. For a month he orders one group of trainees to go to bed at 10 P.M. and awaken at 6 A.M., while another equivalent group of trainees goes to bed at the same time but is allowed to sleep until 9 A.M. before getting up.

   To test his trainees, he gave them a simulated air control task right after they got up and dressed. He figured that some errors would occur but did not see any problems doing the study since it did not involve real flights. The number of "errors" made by trainees was recorded and showed that the group with 11 hours of sleep was poorer. Apparently too much sleep impairs performance on this type of vigilance task.

   Do you agree or do you see a rival explanation? If so, design another experiment to control for any problems you see with the described experiment.

6. Young children were more helpful after watching a television program in which a dog was helped by a boy compared to other children who watched a similar story in which a boy merely played with a dog. It was concluded that the modelled helping was responsible for the real-life aid given by the children. A critic

argued that the children who watched the boy help the dog were more emotionally aroused, and that it was this factor, rather than modelling, that was important in affecting their own helpfulness. How can you modify the experiment to evaluate this view?

Between-Subjects Design and the Logic of Statistical Analysis

CHAPTER 4

Chapter at a Glance

One of the many important decisions facing any experimenter at the outset of any research is whether to use different groups of subjects for each of the different treatment conditions in the experiment or to administer all of the treatments to the same group of subjects. The first design, known as the *between-groups design*, involves the risk that the subjects assigned to the different groups are not equal, on the average, in some important ways related to the behavior under investigation. If such an inequality among groups did exist, one could not attribute all of the differences in behavior among the different treatments to the influence of the independent variable, since it would obviously be confounded with any variables on which the different groups differed at the outset of the experiment. The researcher could not determine what effect, if any, the independent variable produced.

The second design, known as the *within-groups design*, will be discussed in further detail in the next chapter. One can, in principle at least, avoid the problem that different groups of subjects may be unequal in some respect since, by definition, the same group of subjects is used throughout the experiment and receives all of the treatment conditions. The within-groups design, however, may be susceptible to other problems we will discuss in the next chapter.

For the moment, let us examine the main strategy used by researchers to minimize the threat that different groups used in the between-groups design might start out unequal in some important respect and jeopardize the internal validity of the experiment. We will describe two methods, *random groups* and *matched groups*, followed by an overview of basic statistical concepts and the logic of statistical inference which is used to interpret data from experiments.

RANDOMIZED GROUPS

We previously described the use of randomization as a method of assigning subjects to different groups that receive different treatments during an experiment. This method supposedly ensures that these groups will not, on the average, differ among themselves on *any* respect other than that of the independent variable, which is deliberately varied for different groups. This simple supposition is sometimes difficult to fully appreciate or accept. Students often wonder if any group differences in the results of an experiment attributed to the independent variable might actually be due to the possibility that, despite randomization procedures, the groups might have been unequal at the outset on some factor that affects the behavior being observed. Thus, perhaps one group had a higher overall intelligence than another group which is why the former learned better, and not because it was taught by a better method. Or perhaps the group that was helpful to strangers differed from the less helpful group due to altruistic personality factors, rather than the fact that the more helpful group had a chance to observe helpful models during the experiment.

In one sense, these kinds of doubts are not totally unreasonable. Although randomization leads us to *assume* that all groups formed by such procedures are equal, the groups may *possibly* differ on some factor, especially with small-sized samples. On the other hand, the randomization procedure is advantageous in that this possibility is low, and researchers can calculate the actual probability of mistakenly concluding that any differences obtained between groups is due to the independent variable. Moreover, the real benefit of randomization to create different groups is that we need not bother checking each group to make sure they are equal on any number of variables. We merely assume that any inequalities among groups will be very small, especially compared to the effect we expect the independent variable to exert on differences among different treatment groups.

In addition to the use of randomization to *assign* subjects to different groups, it is important to *test* or "run" the subjects in an unbiased sequence. For example, one would not test all of the subjects in one group before starting on the second group because the experimenter's interest might change over time; the equipment could change gradually over time; and other environmental variations might develop. One needs a method such as randomization to determine the test sequence for the subjects. Although the term "random" is used when referring to this design, in actual practice the procedure is not strictly random. Subjects are usually assigned to and tested in "blocks" which might contain one subject for each experimental condition. Thus, if there are three different treatments, one subject would be assigned to and tested in each condition before the second subject for any treatment would be tested. Randomization would still be used within each block of three subjects to determine which condition each subject was assigned to and the order in which the three different treatments would be tested. This procedure, known as *randomized blocks*, also ensures that the experimenter will have equal numbers of subjects in each condition at the end of the experiment, whereas a pure random procedure might, by chance, lead to unequal-sized groups.

Problem of Dropouts

Thus far we have been discussing the methods for establishing equality of groups at the outset of an experiment. Although this goal may be achieved, during the course of the experiments, some types of differential mortality rates or dropout of subjects for the different treatments may occur. An extreme example of this attrition factor would be an experiment testing the effects of low versus high levels of shock as punishment for bar pressing by rats. Suppose the shock for the high level turned out to be so high that a few rats got electrocuted. In addition to the ethical problems of this experiment, it is obvious that the results for the high-shock group would be based on a highly selective group of survivors, while the results for the low-shock group would be based on the total original sample. In other words, by the end of the experiment, the two groups no longer consist of equal random samples.

Even if the *amount* of dropout in terms of the percentage of subjects leaving each group was equal, a *qualitative* difference in the types of individuals who drop out of different treatment conditions could occur. For example, suppose we start out with equivalent groups of subjects who are required to watch films about sports or cooking every day for a week. Even if the percentage of subjects who failed to return to each session of the experiment were equal for the two types of films, the kinds of subjects who drop out (as well as those who remain) are probably no longer random samples.

Either type of dropout, quantitative or qualitative, that happens at a differential rate for different treatments, seriously threatens the internal validity of the experiment. Any conclusions about the effects of the independent variable, which would be based on differences in the performance of the two groups, might reflect the confounding created by the fact that the two groups no longer consist of equivalent groups of subjects. On the other hand, if the amount of dropout is relatively small and no qualitative differences exist between the groups in terms of the characteristics of the persons who drop out, the experiment may still be sound.

MATCHED GROUPS

An alternative to randomization is the use of matching to assign subjects to different groups. For each subject in the experimental group, we ensure that a subject who is highly similar on the *matching variable* is assigned to the control group. The *matching variable* is a factor one has good reason to assume is related to the behavior under investigation. For example, if we wanted to study the effects of fear on problem-solving, we might decide to match the fear and no-fear groups on some measure of intelligence we think is connected with the ability to solve problems.

After matching we would end up with two groups of subjects, and each subject would have a counterpart of comparable intelligence in the other group. Matching involves a lot of work since it may require that we first obtain measurements of all subjects on the matching variable. If we are fortunate, the matching-variable information may already exist as part of some record files collected for some other purpose we have access to.

When we must start from scratch and gather the matching variable data just prior to the experiment, another problem known as sensitization often arises. If, for example, we wanted to study the effect of the race of the communicator on acceptance of information about child discipline, we might want to match groups on their racial attitudes. Matching would help us guarantee that the groups were equivalent overall in their racial attitudes so that we can be more confident that our results reflect the effects of the race of the communicator and not the possibility that the different groups may have been unequal at the outset in their racial attitudes.

In order to match the subjects, we have to administer a pretest to determine their racial attitudes. Unfortunately this procedure may activate or sensitize awareness of subjects about the purpose of the study. They may realize that some aspect of prejudice is being assessed and may try to avoid giving the impression that they are biased, especially if they are prejudiced. This sensitization may prevent our study from reaching an accurate conclusion.

Matching should only be employed on factors known or highly believed to be correlated with the dependent variable or behavior one is measuring. One reason we trouble to ensure that the groups are equal on this matching variable is to avoid a confounded experiment. Any differences between groups could be due to either the independent variable or to the inequality between groups on the variable that was not matched between groups.

It would be useless to match groups on a factor that was unrelated to the behavior under observation. For example, in the study on the effect of race of communicator on information acceptance, there would appear to be no value in matching groups on height since we usually do not think this characteristic affects one's reactions toward persons of different races. It is not important, then, for the groups to be equal in height in this study, whereas it may be quite useful to match subjects on height in, for example, a study of basketball ability among high-school males.

Once we have matched groups, the member of each matched pair assigned to each treatment should be selected using a random procedure. We otherwise run the risk that some bias might occur, thus the two treatment groups would remain unequal. For example, the first member of each pair who reports to the experiment might turn out to be more motivated than the other one.

As an example of the advantages of matched groups, consider an experiment on the effect of stress on problem solving. We decide to match groups on some measure of anxiety since we suspect this factor should be related to reactions to stress. A comparison of the problem-solving scores of each matched pair of subjects gives us an estimate of the influence of two levels of stress without the concern that the observed differences might really have been due to one member of the pair being more anxious than the other. Since one member of each pair works the problems under high stress while the other member works under low stress, we get a clearer picture of the influence of stress without the influence of anxiety differences, which could conceivably also affect performance. The total set of scores based on differences of members of pairs is less variable than if matching did not occur, since matching serves to control one important source of variation in performance on this task—anxiety levels.

In contrast, in the random-groups design we must depend on the comparison of the mean performance for each of the two groups that received the two stress levels to obtain a measure of the effect of the treatment variable. If, in examining the influence of stress, we tried to create pairs of subjects, one from each group, on an arbitrary basis, such as comparing the first subject in the high-stress group with the first in the low stress group, members of such pairs might also differ in anxiety as well as level of stress. Unlike the matched groups, anxiety is not controlled for any given pair of subjects, but only when each treatment group is compared as a whole with the other one. As a consequence, there is greater variability of performance among the subjects in a random-groups design than among the difference of scores for matched pairs of subjects in the matched-groups design. The importance of this difference will become clearer after we discuss the logic of statistical inferences about experiments later in this chapter.

Limitations

Nonetheless some inherent difficulties exist in interpreting studies using matched groups. For example, comparing child abusers and nonabusers might reveal some interesting differences in their attitudes toward children. But another important determinant of attitudes toward children—socioeconomic class—may also differ for child abusers and nonabusers. It becomes difficult to determine if the attitudes are due to the socioeconomic class. If one matched on this factor so that it was equal for both the abusers and nonabusers, one could more confidently interpret the obtained differences between abusers and nonabusers.

A critic might still note that the two groups differ on yet other factors such as age, which itself may determine attitudes toward children. Now it would seem necessary to match the abusers and nonabusers on age as well as socioeconomic level. With a little imagination, one can see that many other factors might differ between the groups. Must groups be matched on every variable? Obviously this goal is impossible. Usually the few factors matched are those for which the investigator has the strongest evidence that they may jeopardize the interpretation of the results. Even when these potential confounding factors are matched, one must cautiously interpret individual differences since one can never identify all the ways two or more groups can differ.

ANALYSIS OF DATA

After an experiment is completed and we have obtained the scores on the dependent variable from all subjects, how do we reach conclusions about the differential effect of the independent variable on the experimental and control groups? Table 4–1 displays a set of fictitious scores for each group on the dependent variable. These vary somewhat in each group, reflecting individual differences among subjects in their characteristics and reactions to the treatment.

We might first rearrange or group the data in each group so we can visually picture the relationship of the two groups as well as of the nature of the scores within each group.

TABLE 4–1. Hypothetical Results for an Experiment Showing the Frequency of Each Group of Scores for the Experimental and Control Groups.

Score	Experimental Group Frequency	Control Group Frequency
96–100	1	
91–95	6	
86–90	4	
81–85	9	
76–80	12	2
71–75	14	5
66–70	20	5
61–65	15	8
56–60	10	6
51–55	6	10
46–50	8	13
41–45	5	17
36–40	2	11
31–35		9
26–30		6
21–25		7
16–20		3
11–15		3
6–10		
1–5		

Each of the scores or larger subgroupings of scores will have occurred with different frequency. Using this *frequency distribution*, we could plot a graph, as illustrated in Figure 4-1, to show how often each score or subgrouping of scores occurred for both groups. This *frequency polygon* is a convenient rearrangement of the data which helps us visualize the influence of the independent variable.

Central Tendency

Although the scores vary considerably in each group, we could conveniently summarize the typical score or measure of central tendency of the distribution in each group with a single number. An index like

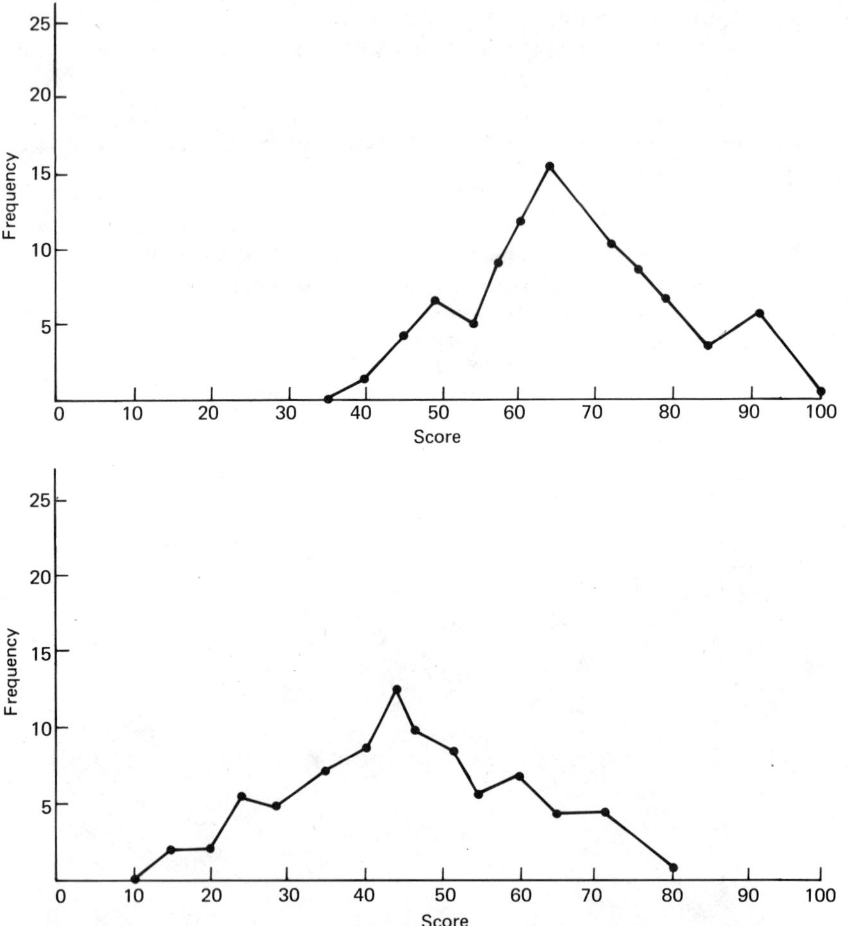

FIGURE 4-1. Graphs depicting performance scores for data of hypothetical experiment in Table 4-1.

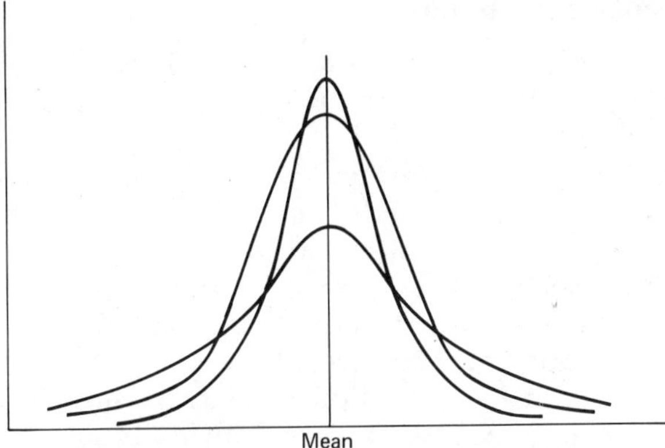

FIGURE 4-2. Three hypothetical normal frequency distributions of scores which differ in the amount of variability but have the same mean score.

the *mean* is often used for this purpose. It is simply the arithmetic average calculated by taking the sum of the scores in each group and dividing it by the total number of scores. Remember that the mean score is just a convenient way of describing the overall performance of a group. Use of the mean is more appropriate when most of the scores deviate very little from the mean, but it can be a misleading score when many scores are extremely different. Unfortunately, an examination of only the mean score of a group alone can tell us nothing about the extent to which the individual scores vary from it, and a different index is used to describe variability.

Variability

As shown in Figure 4–2, even though the mean of the three hypothetical frequency polygons is identical, the variability is quite different. One quick measure of variability is the *range*, which refers to the distance between the highest and lowest score in a distribution. A more precise measure of variability, the *standard deviation*, is derived from measures based on the degree of deviation or difference of each score from the overall mean score of the distribution. The magnitude of this index is higher in proportion to the amount of variability. If all of the scores were identical, the standard deviation would actually be zero, reflecting the fact that each score would have no deviation from the mean of the identical scores.

Another index of variability, appropriately called the *variance*, is closely related to the standard deviation since it is the squared value of the standard deviation. It is also based on the extent to which each score in a set differs from the overall mean of the total set of scores.

Normal Frequency Distribution

Although the number of cases in this example is rather small, the shape of the frequency distributions for each group approximates that of the so-called *normal frequency distribution* (the term "normal" is not a value judgment) which is theoretically based on infinite or very large numbers of cases. As shown in Figure 4–3, it is a symmetrical, bell-shaped curve with precise mathematical properties, making it very useful for many sciences. Even though psychologists deal with much smaller numbers of cases or subjects in their experiments, they find it useful to assume that the characteristics or behaviors being studied approximate the normal distribution so that its mathematical properties can be used to aid the researchers in drawing conclusions.

In the normal distribution curve, precise mathematical relationships exist between the standard deviation and the mean. Figure 4–3 shows that approximately two-thirds of the scores or cases in a normal distribution fall between the values corresponding to the scores one standard deviation above and below the mean. If we go out from the mean in both directions by two standard deviations, we have included 95 per cent of the cases, and if we go out three standard deviations we have included 99 per cent of the cases. These properties of the normal curve hold important advantages for researchers, which will soon become evident when we discuss the logic of drawing conclusions from experiments by use of statistical inference procedures.

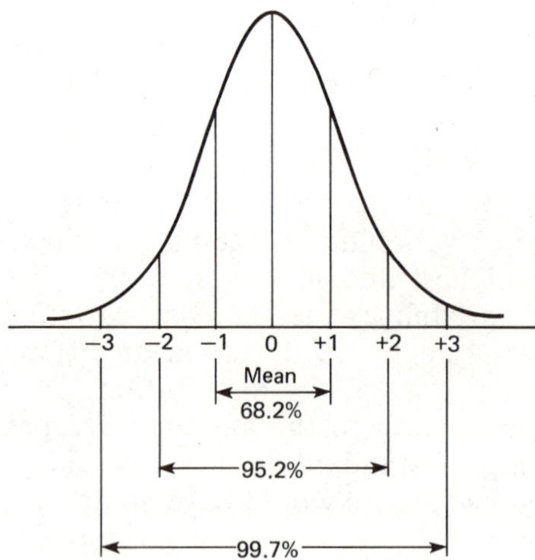

FIGURE 4-3. The normal frequency distribution; indicating the percentage of cases falling ± 1, ± 2, ± 3 standard deviations from the mean score.

Samples and Populations

Experimenters are rarely able to test every member of the total *population* and are restricted by practical considerations to the observation of a small *sample* or subset of the total set. Population indicates the members of any specified group, such as children, criminals, Cub Scouts, PTA members, or chess players. The definition is arbitrary, depending on the interests of the researcher.

Samples vary in size, ranging from one to a number that might fall just short of being equal to the population size. In practice, psychological experiments use samples of about 10 in some types of topic areas upward to about 50 or 100 in other types.

Although only samples, or smaller subsets, are actually studied, the researcher strives to make conclusions about the population or total set. One can intuitively see how faulty conclusions might arise with this procedure. If we use only 25 subjects in our experimental group and another 25 in our control group, why should we feel confident that any differences obtained with our two samples would be valid for a much larger population, such as college students in general? In fact, *if* we were to repeat our experiment and use two new samples of 25 each, it would be highly unlikely for us to obtain the exact results we obtained in our first experiment. How can we hope that the observed difference between the samples in an experiment is close to or identical to the true or population difference that would exist if the experimental and control treatments were administered to the total population?

Statistical methods exist that allow us to draw inferences about populations based on observed evidence taken from samples. However, our inferences can *not* be absolute but must remain *probabilistic* or subject to errors of chance, as illustrated in the following example.

Suppose we had the fact that the true or population difference in the height of the average American male and female was 7 inches. Instead of measuring the entire population of American adults, however, suppose we took a small random sample of 100 males and 100 females and recorded their heights. By chance, we might end up with two samples with a difference of 7 inches, in favor of the male, but the difference could possibly have been 6, 8, or even in favor of the *female*. These fluctuations in our samples from the true population mean (which we have declared to be known as 7 inches) are termed *sampling errors*. Based on statistical theories, the probability of any size of deviation from the population—or hypothesized value of 7 inches—can be computed, using the scores from samples that approximate the shape of the normal frequency distribution.

The samples must be obtained using some random or unbiased technique. If we simply used the first groups we happened to find, we might end up comparing male jockeys against women basketball players, each of which is obviously totally unrepresentative of the total populations of men or women.

In contrast to this example, we usually do not know what the true or population value is for the behaviors we are studying. If we did, we would not bother doing the experiment! After we have done our experiment and obtained our mean score for the experimental and control groups, we must decide whether or not the obtained mean difference between these groups warrants a conclusion that the independent variable is effective. Even if it has *no effect* whatsoever, and the true difference between the means of the groups is theoretically zero, we must remember that our experiment has only compared two samples of subjects. Due to chance or sampling error, our obtained experimental data may suggest a treatment effect because of the difference in the mean scores of the two groups. We need some method of quantitatively stating how likely a difference would have occurred even if no true population difference existed between the two groups. Intuitively, we might feel that small mean differences between groups are more likely to occur by chance than large ones when no true or population difference exists, but we need a more precise method.

Sampling Distribution of Differences Between Groups

If we were to conduct an infinite number of repetitions of our experiment with an independent variable that had no real effect on the difference between the experimental and control groups, we would obtain a frequency distribution of differences between the two groups that resembled the normal curve, as shown in Figure 4-4. Although sometimes the experimental group would have a higher mean than the control group, the opposite would be true equally often. The large differences are less frequent or probable than the small ones. This larger *sampling distribution of differences* would have an overall mean difference of zero, reflecting the true lack of difference. As with all normal distributions, it is possible to specify the percentage of the time the observed mean would fall between specific distances above and below the mean.

Fortunately, no one need actually conduct the infinite number of experimental repetitions described above since one can use the means and standard deviations from the samples tested in any single experiment to statistically *estimate* the likelihood or probability that differences of various sizes between the means of two groups can occur, if there is no real difference. The mean difference obtained in an experiment can be evaluated in terms of its likelihood of being a chance deviation from "no difference."

Now that we have outlined the basic statistical concepts and prin-

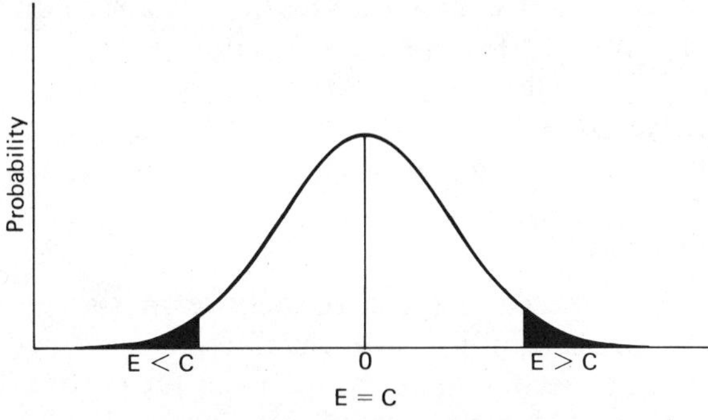

FIGURE 4-4. A sampling distribution of differences between the means of the experimental and control groups where there is no difference between them. Due to sampling error, there is a chance that an experiment will still show a difference between groups. The probability of such a difference occurring in favor of either group is smaller, as the observed difference increases in size. In contrast, small differences are higher in probability.

Rejection regions (the two shaded areas at each end of the curve) indicate the sizes of differences between groups which would be statistically significant or considered unlikely to occur by chance and lead to rejection of the null hypothesis.

ciples underlying the summarization of data obtained in experiments and the problem of making inferences about the effects of independent variables based on observations of samples, we can consider the basic logic of statistical decision making. No knowledge of statistics is assumed in order to illustrate how the experimenter uses results of experiments as an aid to decision making. The student who has already taken a statistics course may wish to skip this material.

Null Hypothesis

First, a conservative approach is adopted in which it is *assumed* that the independent variable has *no* effect. This statistical approach, known as the *null hypothesis*, is exactly opposite to the approach we took when we devised our *experimental hypothesis*, namely the prediction that the independent variable would in fact have a differential influence. One advantage of the statistical approach is that it can be mathematically evaluated, whereas no precise method of directly proving the validity of the experimental hypothesis exists. In effect, we adopt an extremely skeptical perspective and tentatively attribute any group differences in the experiment to chance fluctuations due to sampling error from the true hypothetical situation of no difference or no effect of the independent variable. However, if the obtained group difference is rather large, we are more impressed and apt to be persuaded that it is not a chance error but rather a reflection of a true difference due to the effect of the independent variable. As pointed out earlier, statistical formulas exist that enable the determination of the probability with which differences of a given size or greater can occur between two groups by chance, even when the true difference is zero.

Statistical Significance

A rule-of-thumb for researchers is to believe in the experimental hypothesis and "reject the null hypothesis," as it is termed, if the size of the obtained difference between groups is so great that it or larger differences could exist by chance only five times out of 100. More conservative researchers may insist on differences so great that they can only occur by chance one time out of 100. This cut-off is somewhat arbitrary; after all, six or seven times out of 100 is also rather rare. Nonetheless, researchers will call a study with a difference of 2 times out of 100 "statistically significant," and accept that the independent variable was effective; yet a 7-times-out-of-100 difference in a study will be considered nonsignificant and attributed to chance fluctuation from the assumed lack of difference between groups. In short, the mystical line between success and failure, significance and nonsignificance, is more an arbitrary convention than a natural law.

Type I and II Errors

One should note that errors can be made when making statistical inferences. Figure 4–5 shows that two of the four possible outcomes on decision making involve "errors." Assume that the difference between two groups treated differently is actually zero. By chance alone, we

TABLE 4–2. The Four Possible Situations That Can Occur When the Experimenter Makes a Conclusion About the Presence or Absence of a Difference Between the Experimental and Control Groups. Two outcomes involve correct decisions and there are also two that involve error.

		True Situation	
		No Difference	*Difference Exists*
Experimenter's Conclusion	*Yes, A Difference Exists*	Type I Error	Correct Decision
	No, the Difference is Small and Probably due to Chance	Correct Decision	Type II Error

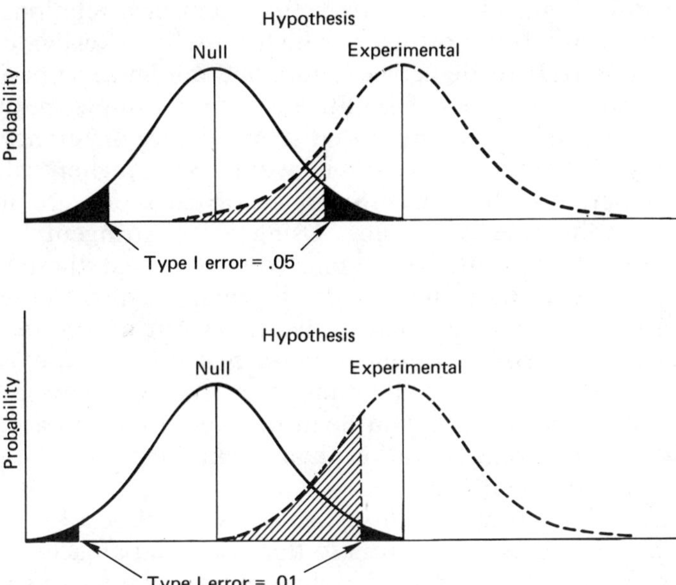

FIGURE 4-5. There is a reciprocal relationship between the size of Type I and Type II errors. In both portions of the illustration, we have the same size of mean difference between groups which we evaluate against the null hypothesis. In the top panel, we set the probability of a Type I error (solid shading) at .05 while we adopt a more stringent criterion in the bottom panel by holding Type I errors (solid shading) at .01. Notice the probability of a Type II error (diagonal striped areas) is smaller in the top panel where we risk more Type I error but it is larger in the bottom panel where we risk a lower Type I error.

could end with two samples yielding a difference so large that it or larger differences could occur by chance only four times out of 100. The convention adopted by researchers, as noted earlier, would be to conclude that the treatment was effective since the groups are really different. Most of the time (96, to be precise *in this example*), we would be right but the possibility of error for the other 4 per cent of times remains. When we erroneously conclude that there is a true effect of the independent variable that produced real differences between the groups—when there actually is no effect—it is termed a *Type-I error*. In the mind of the experimenter, this serious error parallels the situation where the little boy cried "Wolf" too often and lost his credibility.

The other type of statistical error falls in the opposite direction and involves the failure to conclude a true difference exists when one does. In other words, this *Type-II error* exists when the overly cautious researcher examines the findings and attributes the differences to the role of chance when they are really due to the influence of the independent variable.

As shown in Figure 4–5, an interesting reciprocal relationship exists between these two types of errors which puts the investigator in a sort of bind. If one tries to be very cautious and minimize Type-I errors by requiring a stringent level of significance—for example, requiring that the group difference be so great that it or a larger difference occur by chance only one time in 100—there would be a higher risk of Type II errors where true effects are not recognized but are mistakenly attributed to the role of chance. Using a less stringent level of significance, say 5 per cent, where one concludes that the independent variable is effective if a difference greater than or equal to the obtained difference could occur as much as five times out of 100, would obviously increase the error of concluding a real difference existed when there was none from one to five times per 100. On the other hand, we would reduce Type-II errors and be more likely to detect actual effects of the independent variable rather than assign them to chance with this looser criterion for significance.

The task confronting the investigator is to choose a significance level that balances these two errors so that each is at an acceptable level. Type-I errors are generally considered more serious since one is claiming that a real effect exists for an independent variable when it is so small that it is highly likely to have stemmed from chance alone. Ideally, one might wish that such errors were reduced to zero, but one must remember that such extreme conservatism would mean a large increase in Type-II errors whereby we would fail to recognize many true effects of independent variables because we would mistakenly attribute them to chance.

The use of precise cutoff points is arbitrary, but as long as one understands that, like any other decision-making situation, a line has to be drawn somewhere, one will not attach any magical properties to a specific level whether it be 5 or 1 per cent. Figure 4–5 illustrates the location of the critical area containing differences which exceed the chance level (.01 or .05) selected by the experimenter to test the null hypothesis that the experimental and control groups are equal.

Again, *statistical* significance is *not* the same matter as practical or theoretical significance. Rather, it is simply a statement of the probability of occurrence of a difference of a given magnitude or greater; whether or not this degree of difference created by the independent variable is otherwise important depends on many other factors. If one type of gasoline produces five more miles per gallon, and the difference is statistically significant, this gasoline may not be worthwhile if it costs ten times as much as the less productive fuel.

Another important issue regarding the meaning of significant differences is the extent to which such "positive results" prove the theory or hypothesis held by the investigator. Significant results enable us to reject the null hypothesis of no difference; however, these results do not prove that the correct explanation of the underlying processes for the difference is the one proposed by the experimenter. If we give a reward to one group and withhold it from another and obtain significantly better performance from the rewarded group, did the reward make the subjects feel more alert, more motivated, or more eager to please us? A statistically-significant difference may still be compatible with several different theoretical explanations. Even confounding variables unknown to the experimenter can produce statistically-significant results which, unfortunately, will be misinterpreted as evidence of the effect of the independent variable.

Negative Results

When an experiment yields nonsignificant or "negative" results, we should not conclude that the experimental hypothesis is necessarily "wrong" or lacking in merit. It may be that the specific conditions of the experiment yielded differences so small that it was more prudent to attribute them to chance. A revision of the experiment in its design, better control and execution of the procedures, use of a wider range of variation in the levels of independent variable, use of more sensitive dependent variables, and other improvements might provide "positive results."

When an experimenter fails to find significant difference, it is not equivalent to "proving the null hypothesis" of no difference due to the treatment variable. The logic of experimental decision making holds that nonsignificant differences are merely inconclusive and that one can never "prove" that there is no effect of a treatment.

However, the failure to obtain significant results may also indicate erroneous predictions. The theoretical interpretation we used may have been invalid, leading us to formulate untenable experimental hypotheses about the effects of specific factors. We might hesitate to abandon our theory on the basis of a single experiment with nonsignificant results, but if subsequent experiments produce further lack of supporting evidence for our predictions, we should go back and rethink our original explanations and consider the possibility that a different formulation may be more valid.

This back-to-the-drawing-board strategy is even more important if we not only fail to obtain evidence that our independent variable affects behavior in a given direction, but that it actually yields significant differences in the *opposite* direction. Thus, if we predict that rewarding children with praise should lead to better learning than the use of candy rewards, we are not only predicting that a difference will occur but we are also arguing that the difference will be in favor of a specific condition. In other types of experiments where we have no theoretical basis for prediction, we may compare two or more treatments just to see if any differences exist, but we can not predict which conditions will yield the best performance.

In our example, if our findings not only fail to confirm our directional hypothesis but actually show a significant difference in the opposite direction so that the use of candy produces better learning than the use of praise, the theoretical basis for our original prediction apparently needs reexamination. These "negative" results are negative only with respect to the original hypothesis but could be regarded as quite positive in relation to some other theory that could account for such an outcome.

Statistical Tests

Now that we have explained the logic of statistical hypothesis testing, we can proceed with some discussion of the nature of the statistical tests which are actually computed. The most commonly used tests are the t and the F statistics. We will not consider their formulas or the actual computation here but will examine the underlying logic.

At the outset of the experiment, we start with two groups we assume to be equal overall. Within each group, however, some variability exists among individuals due to ability, personality, motivation, and so forth. Since this *within-group* variation is constant or equal for both groups, it does not contribute to any obtained *between-groups* difference which may be produced by the only factor different between the groups, namely the independent variable. Sources of variation within each group are present as a constant factor and do not create any of the difference *between* groups.

Take the case where no true effect or difference results from the independent variable. The only source of variation in scores among groups will be those that marked the beginning of the experiment. The variation *within* each group will equal the variation *between* each group.

We can create a ratio:

$$\frac{\text{Between-Group Variance}}{\text{Within-Group Variance}}$$

which will be equal to 1.0 when the two factors are equal in magnitude, as will be the case when the independent variable has no effect; that is, no difference exists between the experimental and control groups.

In contrast, when we have an effective independent variable, more variation will occur between the means of the different groups so that the factor in the numerator of our ratio becomes larger relative to the denominator. Thus, the ratio exceeds 1.0. (The exact relationship between the size of the mean difference between groups and the numerical value of the statistical ratio depends on other factors, such as sample size and variability of the scores). Statistical tables have been computed that indicate the probability of various ratio sizes. Greater between-group differences yield higher ratios which are in turn *less* likely to occur by chance or represent *greater* statistical significance. The researcher can use these statistical ratios to determine whether or not the null hypothesis can be rejected on the basis of the degree of difference obtained between groups in the experiment relative to the variation of scores within each group.

Influence of Within-Group Variability

For a given magnitude of difference between the experimental and control groups, it will be evaluated as greater in statistical significance when the within-group variability is smaller. Another way of expressing this relationship is to note that for a given-sized numerator in our statistical ratio above, the ratio will increase as the denominator representing within-group variability decreases. Using our earlier example about sex differences in height of 7 inches, we would find this same absolute size of difference more impressive or significant in a statistical sense if the height variability within the samples of men and women was small than if it was large.

Reducing Within-Group Variability

The importance of this relationship for researchers is that it is important to find ways to reduce or minimize the within-group variation as much as possible. A given sized effect is more likely to be interpreted as a refutation of the null hypothesis that the independent variable has no effect if the variability of scores due to individual differences of the subjects within each group is reduced.

Standardization of testing procedures, equipment, and instructions to uniformity for all subjects is one method of reducing variability among subjects' performance. If some subjects are treated cordially while others are treated rudely, this factor may add to whatever effect the independent variable has on behavior. The elimination of extraneous and unintentional factors by holding them constant helps us identify any effect of the independent variable because it reduces the variability among subjects in each group due to these extraneous factors.

A major source of variability, of course, is the fact of preexperimental individual differences existing among subjects along numerous dimensions, some of which may affect their behavior in the experiment. Matching of groups on some subject variable is one way to reduce this variability when it is used to control the likelihood that such subject variables affect differences between treatment groups. In the next chapter, we discuss in more detail the use of a research design that reduces variability due to individual differences through the repeated use of the same subjects in all of the experimental treatments, rather than using different subjects in each treatment condition.

Sample Size

An important consideration for any experimenter is the number of subjects to use for each treatment condition. Such an obvious problem unfortunately has no readily available answer. On the one hand, it would be wasteful to use "too many" subjects since unnecessary time, effort, and expense would be involved. But if one uses "too few" subjects, there is a greater likelihood that the small samples might be unequal at the outset in ways other than the independent variable of interest to the investigator. Variables that might have an effect on behavior would fail to be detected and the null hypothesis would be accepted. The obvious perfect solution would seem to be to use just as many subjects as are needed, no more and no less!

Part of the problem is that the question is either incomplete or inappropriate. How many subjects are needed? For what purpose? The answer seems to be, "to get significant results." This is not a surprising answer since journal editors rarely publish research with nonsignificant results. If this is the primary concern, then one needs only to use very large samples of subjects. At some point, unless there is absolutely no difference between different treatments, a "nonsignificant" difference with a smaller sample will suddenly become "statistically significant" with a large enough sample. Statistical formulas exist that can even tell you exactly how many subjects are needed to make a given difference between two groups attain significance, depending on the degree of variability of performance within each of the groups.

However, if we have to resort to this strategy to obtain significant results, we may have achieved a hollow triumph. The size of the effect must be rather small and trivial if we have to use very large samples to achieve statistical significance. We would have benefitted more by using a moderate-sized sample even though the results showed no significant difference between groups because we would realize that the effect of the independent variable was small.

Notice that the terms used to describe sample size in this discussion have been relative terms, like very large, moderate, or small, rather than absolute numbers like 20, 50, or 100. Unfortunately the situation is too complicated to have absolute answers. Even the type of problem under investigation seems to be a factor in determining what size of sample is considered adequate. In psychophysics, for example, where there is little variability among subjects in comparison to the effects of the independent variables, and the same subjects are tested on a large number of repeated occasions, sample sizes of less than 5 or 6 are not unusual. In contrast, experiments in social psychology, where there are larger individual differences among subjects in their responses to the kinds of situations used in that area of psychology, and subjects are observed only once or a few times, sample sizes generally run between 15 and 25.

In actual practice, most investigators seem to follow tradition or precedents set by earlier experiments in a specific area. Such a process may not be the most scientific or objective method, but it seems to be generally accepted. If we view the experiment as a technique for gathering data to aid decisions, we would recognize that we are faced with a consideration of costs relative to benefits. Using more subjects costs more time, effort, and money. Will the addition of more subjects in a given experiment provide more benefits to justify the expense? If we use the number of subjects typically used by past researchers on a topic and fail to achieve significant differences, it may not be worthwhile to greatly increase the sample size merely so that significant differences will be reached, because the treatment variable is probably a weak one.

SUMMARY

One of the main experimental designs is the between-groups design in which a different group of subjects is used for each of the different treatment conditions. These groups must be equal, on the average, in all respects except for the fact that they will receive different levels of the independent variable during the experiment.

The use of random assignment so that each subject has an equal chance of being assigned to each of the groups does not directly ensure all groups are equal. However, the principle of randomization allows one to safely assume that the groups should be virtually equal or that differences will be rather small. In contrast, the using of matching procedures aims at a direct equation of different treatment groups. The experimenter uses prior information or pretest scores from each subject to guide the assignment of subjects to ensure that the groups are in fact equal on the matching variable. It is time-consuming and cumbersome to match on more than one or two variables; furthermore, the matching variable must be a factor believed to be correlated with performance on the dependent variable under investigation. The precision of matching is particularly desirable with very small samples, but generally when larger samples are used, randomization procedures for subject assignment is preferred.

After an experiment is completed, the researcher must combine the individual or raw scores from each subject. It is commonplace to use some measure of central tendency, such as the mean score, to represent the overall level of performance of each group. An index of individual differences for the subjects within each group can be provided with the standard deviation. If the scores vary in their relative frequencies in accordance with properties of a statistical frequency distribution known as the normal curve, the researcher can draw precise inferences about the probability that the obtained difference in mean scores between different treatment conditions could be obtained if the independent variable had no effect. This approach is used because any experiment can deal only with observations based on samples or small portions of individuals who represent larger groups called populations. By chance alone, one might end up with two samples that are already different initially, so that the observed performance differences between groups are not really due to the influence of the independent variable. Fortunately, the use of inferential statistics allows researchers to determine how likely the results of the experiment are "real" or merely due to chance. For example, all things being equal, larger differences between groups would be more likely to be real or less likely to be due to chance.

Two types of errors can occur when making decisions about the effects of a treatment: Type I, where one mistakenly concludes that a difference exists when it is really due to chance; and Type II, where one fails to conclude a true difference exists and assumes that the observed difference is small enough to be due to chance. As one type of error is reduced, the other type is increased so that the researcher is in a quandary and must decide how to keep both errors as small as possible.

Significant or positive results may not prove that the specific experimental hypothesis is valid; nonsignificant or negative results can not be taken as proof that there is a lack of difference due to the independent variable in the population, but show only that the experiment was inconclusive.

The logic of statistical tests relies on a comparison of the difference between treatment groups relative to the amount of variability within each group. Methods of reducing the variability within groups are desirable because a given sized difference between groups is more likely to be judged significant or not due to chance if the variability within groups is small than if it is large.

LEARNING ACTIVITIES

1. The use of randomization methods to assign subjects to different groups is assumed to create groups that are more or less equal most of the time. By

chance, however, large differences in the characteristics of subjects may exist between groups created by randomization. As an exercise, obtain the following information from the first 50 students you encounter in the library or cafeteria: name, sex, approximate grade point average, height in inches, and approximate weight. Place this information on a separate card for each student. Shuffle your deck of cards thoroughly. Now, using some random procedure, such as a Table of Random Numbers (which can be found in the back of many statistics textbooks or by flipping a coin), sort the deck into two piles to create two different groups of 25 subjects each. In actual practice, we would *assume* equality of groups on all dimensions, on the average, and would not bother to actually check the validity of the assumption.

Since we have information on several dimensions for each student, you can determine the percentage of males and females in each group. Use any of the other variables for which you have data and plot a frequency distribution showing how often each score occurs as well as the mean score in each group. Each student in the class should do this assignment independently of the other class members.

Then, for each student in the class, obtain the difference between the means of their two groups on a given variable. Describe the sizes of these differences and make a graph showing the relative frequency with which each difference size occurs over the whole class.

2. Think of some type of problem where it might be worthwhile to use matched groups with one of the variables you have measured. Using your deck of cards again, form two groups that are matched on one of the variables for which you have information. Do you expect these matched groups to be also equal on the remaining variables? Why or why not? Check your predictions.
3. Evaluate the statements below after reading this brief description of a hypothetical experiment. Do not be "picky" but make reasonable assumptions where details are not spelled out.

   An investigator wanted to assess the effects of caffeine on reading speed. By luck, he was teaching two sections of introductory psychology, each of which conveniently had a total of 50 students, half male and half female. After flipping a coin, he chose his first class and offered each student a 6 oz. cup of coffee and asked them to drink it for "scientific purposes." Two minutes after the last drop was consumed by a student, he or she was tested for the speed of reading with a list of 100 easily pronounced nonsense syllables.

   Later that day, the second class was tested with the same list in the same manner except that, unknown to the students, their coffee was decaffeinated.

   Are the following statements basically true or false? Explain

   a. Experiment is not sound since reading speed can not be measured validly with nonsense materials.
   b. The independent variable is confounded. (If "true," identify the confound).
   c. Motivation or intelligence should be stronger determinants of reading speed; the experiment is therefore invalid for this reason.
   d. Not everyone likes coffee but everyone had to drink it so the experiment can not be a valid test of the hypothesis.
   e. The hotness of the drink, not the caffeine level, may have caused any differences between the two groups' scores.

f. It is adequate to use a coin toss to decide which group gets the coffee.
g. The students' expectancies about caffeine, rather than the substance itself, may have caused any observed effects.
h. The same list should not have been used for both groups.
i. Reading speed may differ at different hours of the day so that the experiment is inconclusive.

CHAPTER 5

Within-Subjects Design

Chapter at a Glance

The within-subjects or repeated-measures design is an alternative to the independent or between-subjects design discussed in the previous chapter. In this paradigm, each subject is tested under all of the different treatment conditions to be compared. A number of what may be somewhat obvious advantages exist with this procedure. First, unlike the case for the independent-groups design, the researcher need not worry that the subjects who receive different treatments were initially unequal on some unknown factor. Since the same subjects are employed at all treatment levels in the within-groups design, all subjects were equal at the outset of the experiment. An additional practical advantage of this design is that it is more economical, since fewer different individuals are needed when the same subjects repeatedly serve in all the treatments.

When we use the same subjects in the different treatments, they are said to "serve as their own controls," which refers to the fact that subject variables such as age, sex, personality, and so forth are held constant or fixed over the course of the experiment for all of the treatments. Since these factors are held constant and can not affect differences in performance for different treatments, one can more easily identify any influence of the independent variable. The within-subjects design is essentially the perfect example of matched groups. Given that the same subjects are used for all treatments, we have ensured that the subjects for each treatment condition are matched.

The differences in performance observed under different treatments will stem entirely from the influence of the treatments themselves, without any distortion that might occur with a between-subjects design, in which the different groups, created by randomization, may be slightly unequal.

One benefit gained by the added control the within-subjects design ensures is that a difference in performance of a given magnitude between treatments is more likely to be judged statistically significant. As stated in Chapter 4, a treatment difference of a given size is less likely to be due to chance when the variability of performance among subjects for different treatments is small. By using the identical subjects in all treatments, the within-subjects design is able to achieve less variability among subjects in their performance than is possible with the between-subjects design.

One might wonder why researchers might not prefer the within-subjects design in view of this advantage. In some situations, offsetting problems do arise with the use of this design, as when one does not want the subjects to discover the purpose of the study or know what other treatments are being compared, as this knowledge might alter their behavior.

For example, suppose subjects in a control group solved math problems at their own pace while the experimental group was rewarded with praise. Since neither group knows what the treatment was for the other group, most likely they could not identify the purpose of the study or even recognize what the independent variable was. In contrast, the use of a within-subjects design here would likely enable the subjects to figure out the purpose of the study since they would be exposed to all levels of the independent variable.

In the remainder of this chapter, we will go into further detail on the major problem threatening the internal validity of within-groups designs, temporal effects, and describe the technique of counterbalancing which is used to offset this liability.

Finally, we will discuss the relative merits of the within-subjects and the between-subjects design. We will examine factors that may lead to different types of outcomes for the same variables when tested under the two different types of designs.

Temporal Effects

The use of the within-subjects design is preferred precisely because we can be sure that the subjects receiving each treatment are identical. However, this condition is upheld for relatively stable or fixed characteristics such as sex, age, race, personality traits, and so on, but not for short-term temporary states such as fatigue warmup, motivation, and familiarity with the test situation. These factors may change over the course of the experiment and be highly unequal at different points in time.

In short, whenever subjects are tested under two or more treatment conditions, certain cumulative temporal effects inevitably occur. Factors that help improve performance over the course of the experiment include warmup, practice effects, and learning-to-learn, whereby repeated contact with new situations allows the subject to become more familiar with the task and how to deal with it. On the other hand, other factors may also exist that offset or reduce performance quality, such as fatigue or boredom which may set in if the sessions are too difficult or too easy. Excessively long sessions may also contribute to these negative factors.

In either case, these temporal effects accumulate in proportion to the length of the testing, although not necessarily in an even or linear relationship with time. As Figure 5–1 shows, a *linear* relationship involves an increase of constant amount of these temporal influences on performance for each additional task, whereas a *nonlinear* relationship involves a varying amount of added influence for each additional task. Two examples are shown in Figure 5–1, one where each successive task has a greater effect and one where each successive task has less effect.

The existence of either type of situation creates problems for the use of the within-subjects design. We want to make conclusions about the

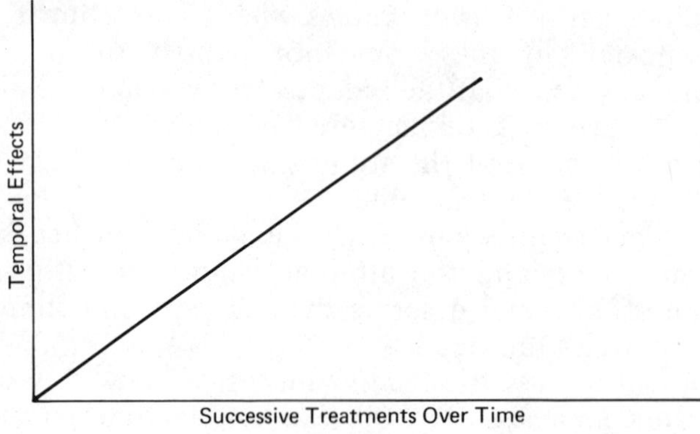

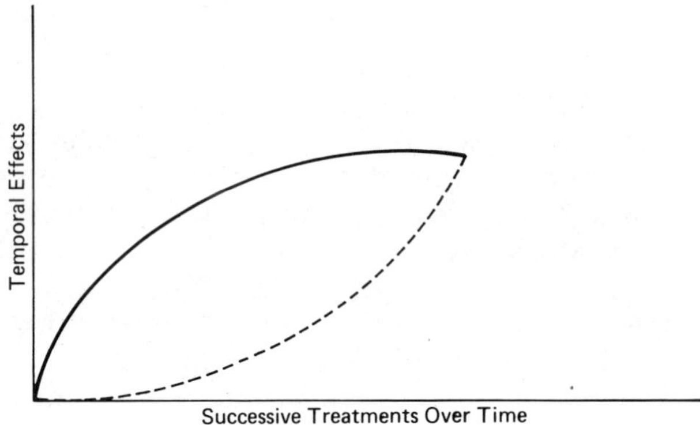

FIGURE 5-1. Temporal effects over successive treatment conditions in a within-subjects design may be linear (top panel) or nonlinear (bottom panel), with either increasing or decreasing rates.

effects of the treatments but since the influence of the temporal factors falls unequally over successive treatments, we are unable to feel very confident with our inferences. We can never eliminate these temporal effects, but if they are linear we can perhaps devise some procedure for spreading their influence more evenly across all treatments so that we can still conclude about the relative effect of different treatments.

COUNTERBALANCING

Instead of using only one sequence for administering the various treatments, a procedure known as *counterbalancing* is used in which the treatments are presented in more than one serial order. This technique is designed to ensure that the temporal effects influence each of the treatments to the same degree. If a constant factor is added to each treatment, it is still possible to make comparative judgments of the effects of the different treatment conditions.

We will simplify our discussion by restricting the analysis to a problem where only two levels of a treatment are being compared. Suppose we want to compare the visibility of road signs printed in black against backgrounds of either white or yellow. We could make a small number of different signs, for example ten, indicating various traffic situations and print them against either white or yellow backgrounds of the same size. Then we could test subjects under standard procedures, first with the white background and then with the yellow background. Suppose our hypothetical study reveals that subjects are more accurate with the signs containing the yellow background. Can we safely conclude that yellow backgrounds make traffic signs more visible?

A critic might argue that temporal effects, such as warmup, and favored recognition of the second set of signs may have occurred simply because they were presented later and not because of their yellow background.

One implication of this criticism, of course, is that if the opposite order of the backgrounds had been used, better visual recognition would have occurred with the white background. In other words, if the background color is not a factor affecting visibility, whereas the ordinal position the color occurs in is critical, we end up with the wrong conclusion!

Between-Groups Counterbalancing

If we are concerned with the possibility that temporal effects may exist, the solution involves using both sequences, yellow-white and white-yellow, one for each of two different subgroups of subjects. Then we would combine the performance of all subjects for the signs with the yellow background and compare it with that obtained for all subjects when the signs are shown with the white background. This technique of counterbalancing does not *eliminate* temporal effects. It does, however, ensure that they fall more or less equally over each of the treatment levels so that they do not contribute more to the performance of some treatments than they do to others.

Table 5–1 presents some hypothetical data for the visibility of the signs, as measured by the percentage of the signs recognized during the one-second exposure time each was presented.

As seen in the top section of Table 5–1, regardless of the background color, recognition was higher by 10 per cent when a given color was presented second than when it was in the first set. There is no difference

TABLE 5-1. Hypothetical Scores for Two Test Conditions Given in Counterbalanced Sequence. (Top half illustrates situation where independent variable has no effect while bottom half deals with situation where one treatment level is better than the other.)

I. When I.V. has No Effect and Temporal Effect = 10 Units

	Test: *First*	Test: *Second*	*Net diff.*
Order 1 *Yellow-White*	*Yellow* 70	*White* 80	+10
Order 2 *White-Yellow*	*White* 70	*Yellow* 80	+10
			x̄ = 10

II. When I.V. has An Effect of 20 Units and Temporal Effect = 10 Units

	Test: *First*	Test: *Second*	*Net diff.*
Order 1	*Before* Sunset 90	*After* Sunset 80	+10
Order 2	*After* Sunset 70	*Before* Sunset 100	+30
			x̄ = 20

in visibility between the two backgrounds at any time. When all of the data are included so that we combine the results of the first and second presentation sets together, we can see that recognition is equal, being 75 per cent for both colors. Had we failed to counterbalance, we would have concluded that one color, whichever one we just happened to present second, yielded a 10 per cent greater visibility.

It is equally important to counterbalance temporal effects when they contribute *negative* effects on performance. If fatigue leads to poorer performance on a second task, it would be invalid to draw conclusions about the effects of the independent variable if the tasks were always given in the same sequence. Use of some type of counterbalancing is needed to make it possible to determine the relative influence of the different levels of the independent variable on behavior.

Now suppose that we have a situation where the two levels of treatment variable do in fact affect performance, aside from any temporal effects. For example, we might be comparing one type of sign, say black letters on a white background, just before and just after sunset. We make up two sets of signs of equal difficulty so each subject can be tested twice, once before and once after sunset. Assume that the signs are more visible prior to sunset, with a superiority of 20 per cent. As the bottom half of Table 5–1 shows, when the first test that is given is conducted before sunset, 90 per cent are correct as compared to only 70 per cent when the first test is given after sunset. A superiority of the same size, 20 per cent, also occurs for the pre sunset test over the after sunset test when both are administered as the second test.

However, two different estimates of the effects of before vs. after sunset visibility are obtained for each of the two subgroups. There is only a 10 per cent superiority of the before-sunset test when it is the first test because warmup effects boost the performance of the after-sunset test by 10 per cent. In contrast, there is a 30 per cent superiority of the before-sunset test when it is the second test condition because it gains 10 per cent due to the benefits of warmup and practice effects. Either estimate, 10 or 30 per cent, taken alone is misleading because of the temporal effects which either mask or enhance, respectively, the true effects of the independent variable. A combination of both estimates of the effect of the independent variable, 10 and 30, yields a mean value of 20, which is what we find when we compared before and after sunset test scores at any given point in the test sequence.

It must be noted that in these simple examples the logic of the use of counterbalancing can be clearly demonstrated. In the actual conduct of research, experimenters rarely make explicit checks on the validity of counterbalancing procedures for the particular problem they are investigating. Assumptions may be made that the temporal effects are linear but usually no direct check is made.

Within-Groups Counterbalancing

Another version of counterbalancing involves the administration of all tasks to *all* subjects. In the case of two tasks, they would be given first in one order, A, B, followed immediately by the opposite order, B, A. This procedure of within-groups counterbalancing can be symbolized as an ABBA to distinguish it from the between-groups procedure described above in which one half of the subjects get an AB sequence whereas the other half get a BA order.

Whereas the comparison of the first A and first B involves greater temporal effects on B, the opposite is true for the second comparison of A and B. Therefore to obtain a balanced assessment of the performance under A and B, a combination of the scores under the two A exposures is contrasted to the scores of the two combined B exposures.

TABLE 5-2. Hypothetical Example of the Use of Counterbalancing with an ABBA Sequence Within Subjects with a Linear Temporal Effect. (Top half shows example where the effect of A is 10 points lower than that of B while bottom example has an equal effect of A and B.)

1. When Independent Variable has An Effect

Order of Tasks	1	2	3	4
	A	B	B	A
Temporal Effects	0	10	20	30
Independent Variable Effect	60	70	70	60
(A = 60; B = 70)				
Observed Scores	60	80	90	90
Mean for A = 60 + 90/2 = 75				
Mean for B = 80 + 90/2 = 85				
Difference = 10				

2. When Independent Variable has No Effect

Order of Tasks	1	2	3	4
	A	B	B	A
Temporal Effects	0	10	20	30
Independent Variable Effect	60	60	60	60
(A = B = 60)				
Observed Scores	60	70	80	90
Mean for A = 60 + 90/2 = 75				
Mean for B = 70 + 80/2 = 75				
Difference = 0				

Table 5-2 illustrates how the use of ABBA within-groups counterbalancing spreads the temporal effects evenly over both treatments to preserve the true effect of the variable, even if it has no effect.

Use of Equivalent Tasks

In some experiments the subject has to perform a task that cannot be performed again by the same subject under different treatment conditions in the within-subjects design. For example, an experiment on the effects of two types of reinforcement on memory requiring that the same group of subjects be tested on the two types of reinforcement under counterbalanced orders obviously cannot use the same set of materials for memorization under both conditions. All subjects will show better performance on the second test condition simply because they are receiving additional exposure to the same material.

It is common to create two equal difficulty lists or passages of memory material and assign them in counterbalanced sequence so that each passage is used equally often under each level of the independent variable. Failure to counterbalance the order of the sets of materials would result in a confounding between the independent variable and the sets of material, even though it was assumed that the materials were of equal difficulty. It is always possible that the two sets still differed in some important respect despite our attempts to equate them. Use of counterbalancing is desirable in this situation, even though it may have been unnecessary, because it logically excludes the possibility that confounding could occur from differences in difficulty of the two sets of material to be memorized.

More Than Two Treatments

The same basic principles apply if counterbalancing is used when more than two different treatments or conditions exist. Of course, as the number of treatments increases, the number of different sequences increases. For three treatments, A, B, and C, for example, we have six unique sequences, ABC, ACB, BAC, BCA, CAB, and CBA. If we add one more treatment to reach a total of four, the number of different sequences mushrooms to 24. In general, counterbalancing is rarely used for more than four different treatments because it is cumbersome to deal with the many different sequences of the different treatments involved with counterbalanced designs.

An added problem may exist if the amount of the temporal effects is not constant or equal between successive conditions of the experiment. If the gain (or loss) from temporal effects differs in magnitude when one goes from the first to the second treatment compared to going from the second to the third treatment, counterbalancing the order of the treatments will not be valid.

An example shown in Table 5–3 illustrates the situation when each successive stage of the experiment adds a diminishing amount of gain due to practice. Assume that treatment A is really 10 points better than treatment B, which in turn is 10 points better than treatment C. A within-groups counterbalanced sequence is used so that all subjects receive the three tasks twice in an ABCCBA sequence.

As Table 5–3 shows, the comparison of performances under the three treatments shows that the difference between each successive treatment is 10 units, when the temporal effect is linear. In contrast, there is no larger difference (17.5) between A and B performance than that obtained between B and C (13.0) when there is a nonlinear temporal effect.

Which Design Is Preferable: Between- or Within-Subjects Design

For some types of problems, there is no compelling reason why one design is preferable, thus the choice is arbitrary. Let us briefly review

TABLE 5–3. Hypothetical Scores to Illustrate the Use of Within-group Counterbalancing for Three Treatment Levels with Either a Linear Temporal Effect (top portion) or a Nonlinear Temporal Effect (bottom portion). The true effects of the three treatment conditions are A = 45, B = 35, C = 25 so that there are 10 points between each consecutive treatment level. Results with counterbalancing agree with this degree of treatment effect only when the temporal effects of counterbalancing are linear.

1. Linear Temporal Effect

Order of Tasks	1	2	3	4	5	6
	A	B	C	C	B	A
Task Effect	45	35	25	25	35	45
Linear Temporal Effect	8	7	6	5	4	3
Observed Score	53	42	31	30	39	48

$\text{Mean}_A = 53 + 48/2 = 50.5$ A vs. B = 10
$\text{Mean}_B = 42 + 39/2 = 40.5$ B vs. C = 10
$\text{Mean}_C = 31 + 30/2 = 30.5$ A vs. C = 20

2. Nonlinear Temporal Effect

Order of Tasks	1	2	3	4	5	6
	A	B	C	C	B	A
Task Effect	45	35	25	25	35	45
Nonlinear Temporal Effect	32	16	8	4	2	1
Observed Score	77	51	33	29	37	46

$\text{Mean}_A = 77 + 46/2 = 61.5$ A vs. B = 17.5
$\text{Mean}_B = 51 + 37/2 = 44.0$ B vs. C = 13.0
$\text{Mean}_C = 33 + 29/2 = 31.0$ A vs. C = 30.5

some important factors about different designs. Randomization is perhaps the simplest to employ since it involves relatively little preplanning, but there is a price for such convenience—the relatively larger number of subjects needed to justify the assumption that the randomly-created groups are equal. Furthermore, the variability among the subjects within each group is higher than what can be achieved through procedures like matching. Such high variability requires that the effect of the treatment variable be rather strong before it can be detected when comparing the performance between different groups.

Although matching calls for more preliminary work, such as gathering of background information or the administration and scoring of pretests, this procedure is reassuring when the sample sizes are small, say, less than 10. The danger of the pretests is that, for some types of situations, they may act to sensitize the subjects to the purpose or nature of the experiment and thus distort their behavior. If we wish to study incidental learning by measuring the extent to which a person can recall material without receiving explicit instruction to learn, it may be useful to match on learning ability. However, if we used a learning pretest to obtain measures for matching, the procedure may alert the subject to the possibility that subsequent tests will be given on other parts of the experimental sessions.

Counterbalancing also entails much planning prior to the experiment so that the various sequences can be prepared. The procedure has the advantage of needing fewer subjects. Furthermore, since the same subjects are used in all treatments, no question arises about the equality of the subjects who receive each treatment.

Use of the same subjects in the counterbalanced design also reduces variability of performance due to individual differences so that it provides a more sensitive method for detecting differences between different groups.

It is worth noting that some types of problems require the use of different sequences but do *not* involve counterbalancing, as in cases where one is interested in the effects of sequences of events. Thus, does it matter whether one learned French before Spanish? The main question here is not whether or not one language is easier than the other, but whether one sequence for learning both languages is easier. Sequence is now an independent variable since it differs for two groups, one receiving the French-Spanish order while the other receives the Spanish-French sequence. In this type of problem, only a between-subjects design can be employed.

Returning to situations where one has the option of choosing either a between- or within-subjects design, other important factors may need to be considered aside from those cited above, such as the number of subjects required or sensitivity of the design to detect effects.

An Experimental Comparison. If two different experiments examined the same independent variables, using exactly the same levels for comparison and following identical procedures except for the fact that one study used a between-subjects design while the other one used a within-subjects design, would one not expect similar findings about the effect of the independent variable? Grice (1966) argues that although this assumption seems to be generally held, there is good reason to doubt its validity. Uncritical acceptance of this assumption, for example, has led many researchers to prefer the within-subjects design over the between-subjects design because it appears to be equivalent to it but also offers the advantage of greater sensitivity to detecting experimental effects since there is reduced variability due to individual differences when the same subjects are used in all treatment conditions.

Grice challenged this assumption on the grounds that subjects may react differently to one treatment if they have already been exposed to some of the other treatment conditions. All too frequently, the researcher who uses the within-subjects design makes the assumption that exposure to one treatment does not affect response to other treatments but this assumption is rarely tested directly. An example of the nonequivalence of the two designs under similar circumstances is a study by Grice and Hunter (1964) who compared the reaction time to two intensities of a signal. When a within-subjects design was used the effect of this factor was five times as great as it was when the same intensities were compared using a between- or independent-subjects design. Apparently, the contrast between the high and low intensities is an important factor on response. Only the within-subjects design procedure allows subjects to experience both intensities; subjects in the between-subjects design encounter only one or the other levels, so the contrast or context effects among the set of stimuli can influence only the within-subjects design study.

The fact that the within-subjects design automatically allows contrast or context effects to occur has led some (Poulton, 1973) to recommend that this design be avoided, if possible. Although counterbalancing is used so that the sequence in which the treatments are received is not a source of confounding with the independent variable, it may not be sufficient to prevent differential carryover effects for different sequences of the treatments. A group that received a drug first, followed by the placebo control condition, may have carryover effects from the first treatment which should not exist for the group with the opposite sequence of placebo treatment followed by the drug treatment.

Another problem is that counterbalancing may not prevent practice effects from creating difficulties of interpretation if some of the treatments have different effects at varying levels of practice. A study involving two levels of task difficulty in a counterbalanced design might allow the gains due to practice effects to benefit the high-difficulty task more than it helps the low-difficulty task if performance on the latter task is virtually perfect at the outset. There is more room for practice effects to contribute to improvement if the task if difficult to begin with.

External Validity as a Criterion. A totally different consideration suggests that one type of design should be preferred for some types of questions. Suppose one wants to determine whether a communication from a high- or low-credibility person is more persuasive. Greenwald (1978) suggested that in this type of situation, it is more realistic for people to be exposed to persuasive messages from communicators with all degrees of credibility. Therefore, the external validity or generalizability of a laboratory study on this topic would be higher with a within- rather than a between-subjects design.

In other situations the same need for external validity might dictate the use of a between-subjects design. Thus, a study of the effectiveness of two markedly different types of punishment for children used by mothers would call for a between-subjects design since most children receive one type of punishment rather than a counterbalanced sequence of a variety of techniques from their mothers. On the other hand, for children whose mother and father used both of the markedly different punishment techniques, it would be more externally valid to use a within-subjects design to compare the effectiveness of the two techniques.

Although external validity may not be the major consideration in the design of experiments, it should be examined since one ultimately hopes to apply the findings of most experiments to other situations.

Confusing Interpretations of One Design with the Other. An important but often overlooked issue associated with the two types of experimental designs is the tendency for results obtained with one design to be interpreted as if they were obtained with the other design. Suppose an investigator placed subjects in both high- and low-anxiety situations, using counterbalanced orders for two subgroups, and finds that high anxiety provoking situations lead to better performance. A generalization might be made that high anxiety is associated with better performance.

Note, however, that this conclusion was based on a within-subjects design where each subject was compared in two different situations. This type of study is not equivalent to a between-subjects version of the same issue, especially when the independent variable is a subject variable that involves a comparison of persons who differ in their levels of anxiety. Here we are comparing different groups of subjects who have stable differences in the personality trait known as anxiety. We should not automatically assume that persons who differ in the *trait* of anxiety will necessarily differ in the same way that a given group of subjects reacted to two different *situations* differing in their anxiety-evoking ability.

The between- and the within-subjects versions of this topic are quite different types of studies. Nonetheless, often a conclusion such as "anxiety is correlated with better performance," derived from a study using one type of design, is interpreted as equivalent to demonstrating the effect with the other type of design. In some cases it may turn out that the same conclusion is reached for studies using either type of design, but it is also possible for quite different conclusions to be reached under the two designs. The point to remember is that we should not assume that the two designs are equivalent and should pay attention to the methodology used for obtaining the results.

Buck (1980) has discussed this problem in the context of the relationship between emotional expression and inner experience of emotions. What is the relationship between smiling or frowning, for example, and the individual's inner feelings? Can the outer expression "cause" or alter the inner experience, as implied in a popular song that encourages us to "put on a happy face," or is the outer expression primarily a reflection or effect of an already existing inner state?

Investigators of this question have usually used a within-subjects design to compare the inner emotional feelings of the same subjects under different treatment conditions; the subjects assumed different posed facial expressions specified by the experimenter's instructions, which avoided terms referring to emotions to hide the true purpose of the study. While there has been some evidence (Laird, 1974) to suggest that a smile-like expression is more likely to produce positive affective states than a frown-like expression, one should not transform this conclusion into the between-subjects design equivalent of this question. The between-subjects equivalent asserts that people who tend to express more emotion also experience more emotion than those individuals who express less emotion. The between-subjects version may or may not be true; in order to determine its validity, one must conduct a between-subjects study. Instead, as Buck pointed out, investigators fail to notice the significance of this distinction and have often interpreted the results from the within-subjects design as if they constituted support for the between-subjects design version of the question.

SUMMARY

The within-subjects design involves the repeated use of the same subjects so that each subject receives all of the different treatment conditions. This procedure ensures that the subjects receiving each treatment are not unequal in ability, personality, or other background factors at the outset of the experiment. Furthermore, since we have essentially matched sets of subjects in this design, less variability in performance will occur among the treatments due to individual differences among the subjects in each treatment condition. We will be better able to detect a given sized effect of an independent variable since it will be greater in statistical significance. Finally, this design is economical in terms of the number of subjects needed.

A potential problem with this design is the possibility that short-term temporal effects such as warmup, fatigue, and learning-to-learn develop over the course of the experiment. If all treatments are given to all subjects in the same temporal sequence, these temporal factors will be confounded with the independent variable and the results will be invalid. Counterbalancing is a procedure, not for eliminating the temporal effects, but for redistributing them so that they affect all treatments evenly over all subjects combined. Thus, one could present two treatments in one sequence for half of the subjects, and in the reverse sequence for the other half.

Counterbalancing can only be used if one can reasonably assume that there is no long-lasting or specific carryover of effects from one treatment to the next. One could not, for example, compare two levels of reward on problem solving with the use of counterbalancing if the same problem was used for both reward levels.

Another limit to counterbalancing is more practical in nature. As the number of different treatments increases, the number of different sequences possible increases at a faster rate. With five treatments, there are 120 different sequences, thus counterbalancing is rarely used for more than three or four treatments.

For some types of problems, no compelling reason exists why one type of design should be preferred over another. Randomization is easiest but involves greater variability of subjects and thus requires larger samples to provide stable estimates of the effects of the independent variable. Some special problems do require the use of a particular design. If one wants to compare different sequences to see which is more effective, one must use a within-subjects design.

While there is greater statistical advantage to use of within-subjects design due to the higher sensitivity gained by the lower individual variation among subjects, other factors must be considered. A given independent variable may not produce the same reactions among subjects under the between- and within-subjects designs. When subjects encounter more than one treatment, the contrast among them may alter the subjects' reactions so that they are not comparable to those that would be obtained with the between-groups design wherein each subject undergoes only one treatment.

External validity must be considered when choosing an appropriate design. Do subjects tend to encounter events in the real world in analogues of between- or within-groups designs? We should choose the type of design which best corresponds to the way in which the different treatments are usually encountered in natural circumstances if we hope to generalize from the laboratory to the real world.

The effect of a treatment obtained with one experimental design may or may not be the same with a different design. Failure to recognize this point may lead one to mistakenly assume that the results with between- and within-subjects designs on the same treatments should be equivalent. A direct test of this assumption would be desirable.

REFERENCES

Buck, R. Nonverbal behavior and the theory of emotion: The facial feedback hypothesis. *Journal of Personality and Social Psychology,* 1980, *38*, 811–824.

Greenwald, A. G. Within-subjects designs: To use or not to use. *Psychological Bulletin,* 1976, *83*, 314–320.

Grice, G. R. Dependence of empirical laws upon the source of experimental variation. *Psychological Bulletin,* 1966, *66*, 488–498.
Grice, G. R., and Hunter, J. J. Stimulus intensity effects depend upon the type of experimental design. *Psychological Review,* 1964, *71*, 247–256.
Laird, J. D. Self-attribution of emotion: The effects of expressive behavior on the quality of emotional experience. *Journal of Personality and Social Psychology,* 1974, *29*, 475–486.
Poulton, E. C. Unwanted range effects from using within-subjects experimental designs. *Psychological Bulletin,* 1973, *80*, 113–121.

LEARNING ACTIVITIES

1. Think of a research question you believe can be studied with a within-subjects design. Using three different levels of one independent variable, identify the specific sequences of the three treatments necessary for complete counterbalancing.
   Aside from the need for fewer subjects with the within-subjects design, what other differences can you see between the use of the within-subjects and between-subjects design for this specific research problem?
2. Think of a specific research problem in which the use of counterbalancing is unacceptable. Explain the reasons for your decision.
3. "Taste will tell," state many people who believe that their sensitivity can enable them to discriminate between rival colas, cigarettes, beers, and so forth. Does this type of situation require a within-subjects design or can it also be studied with a between-subjects design?
4. If "practice makes perfect," the experienced drinker or smoker should show better discriminability in detecting differences in tastes of alcoholic beverages or cigarettes. Does this question call for a within-subjects or a between-subjects design? Can you think of ways in which an experiment involving aspects of *both* types of designs could be done on this research question?

CHAPTER 6

Factorial Designs

Chapter at a Glance

The most widely used experimental design, the factorial design, differs from the designs described thus far because it includes two or more independent variables. Many of the principles we have discussed in connection with simpler experiments with only one independent variable are also valid for the factorial design. We still want to determine the extent to which the observed effects of the independent variables are larger than those one would expect by chance. In addition to being more efficient—since several independent variables can be manipulated simultaneously in a single factorial experiment—it is also possible to compare the relative effects of each variable at each of the levels of other independent variables to determine the extent to which findings can be generalized. As we shall see shortly, the opportunity to assess the degree of this so-called interaction between two or more independent variables is one of the primary reasons for conducting factorial experiments.

After describing the major features of the factorial type of research design, we will present more details about its advantages. We will then describe how the effect of each independent variable or main effect, as well as the interaction effect, is determined in a factorial design with two independent variables. Several specific illustrations of research containing interactive relationships will be presented so that the importance and implications of interactions among independent variables can be more fully appreciated.

BASIC NOTATION

The basic arrangement of the factorial design is illustrated in Figure 6–1 which shows the combinations of conditions that exist for an experiment involving two independent variables, each being varied at two different levels. This design, commonly referred to as 2 X 2 design, is only one of a number of possible factorial designs. The fact that there are

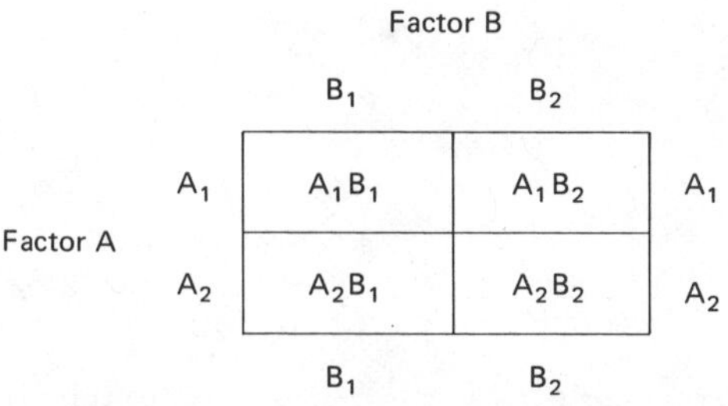

FIGURE 6–1. A diagram with the four different combinations of treatment for a factorial experiment with two levels of two independent variables.

two independent variables is represented by the presence of two different numbers in the notation while the actual numerical values reflect the number of levels used for each independent variable. Thus a 2 X 3 X 4 design refers to a study with three independent variables, one with two levels, one with three levels, and one with four levels. The total number of unique combinations of variables can be determined easily by multiplying all of the numbers in the notation. Thus, a 2 X 2 design has four different treatment combinations. As shown in Figure 6–2 in the case of the 2 X 3 X 4 design, there are 24 different treatment conditions stemming from the possible combinations of the different levels of the three independent variables. For example, an experiment on the effects of two levels of reward, three types of instruction, and four different subjects involves the 24 unique combinations of treatments depicted in Figure 6–2.

In theory, there is no limit to the number of independent variables or levels of same that could be used in an experiment. In practice, however, rarely more than three different independent variables exist in a single experiment. In addition, most often less than four or five levels of any given independent variable exist since it is possible to sample most dimensions adequately with this number of levels. One reason for such limits is the fact that the number of different treatment conditions increases rapidly as one adds more levels of independent variables or more independent variables, so that the experiment becomes costly in terms of time and effort without much additional return in informa-

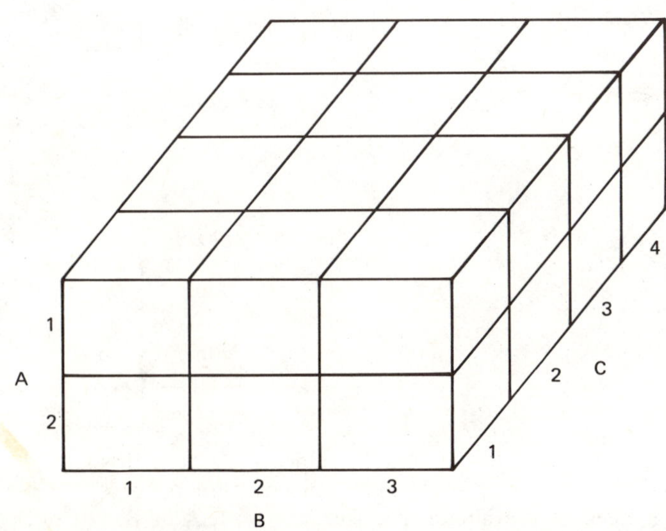

FIGURE 6–2. A diagram illustrating a 2 X 3 X 4 factorial design with a total of 24 different combinations of the three independent variables, A, B, and C, with two, three, and four levels, respectively.

tion. Furthermore, the results can become very difficult to analyze and interpret when there are more than three independent variables.

Advantages

The use of factorial designs involves a number of advantages. First, there is an economy of effort if one can examine the effects of several independent variables in the same experiment rather than conducting separate studies for each. Suppose we wanted to use 20 subjects in both a between- and independent-groups design to examine the effects of two levels of variable A in one experiment and then similarly examine the effects of two levels of variable B in another study. A total of 80 different subjects would be needed, as Figure 6–3(a) illustrates.

If we could use a 2 X 2 design, like that illustrated in Table 6–2(b), where two independent variables were varied simultaneously to create four different treatment combinations, we could use half the subjects we would need if conducting two separate experiments and still have 20 subjects at each of the two levels of both independent variables. How does this all come about? How can we use only a total of 40 subjects but still come up with comparisons that seem to involve 80 different subjects?

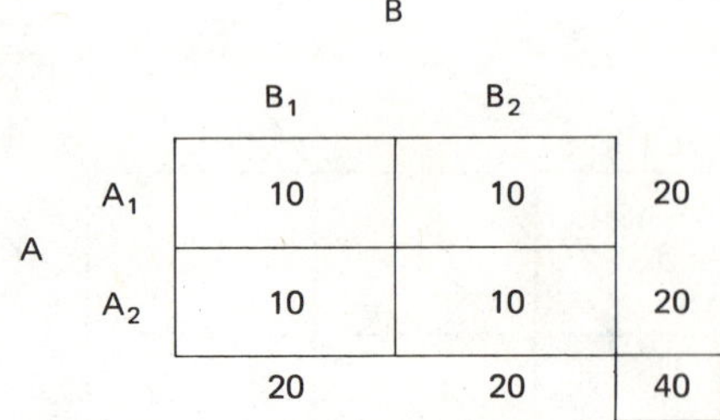

FIGURE 6–3. Top panel shows that 40 subjects are needed when 20 subjects are assigned to each of the two levels when only one independent variable is used. A total of 80 is needed to evaluate the effects of both A or B. Bottom panel shows how 20 subjects, as above, can be available to evaluate both A and B in the factorial design, but with a total of only 40 subjects.

The secret is to use each subject twice, in a sense, when making comparisons of the data. Each subject's data can be counted twice since it can be used in assessing the two levels of each of the two independent variables. Thus, a subject in the $A_1 B_1$ combination contributes data to the A_1 vs. A_2 comparison as well as to the B_1 vs B_2 comparison.

Main Effects

The influence of the *main effect* of each of the two or more independent variables of a factorial experiment is determined by comparing the performance of all subjects who received each level of a given factor with that of subjects who received the other levels of that variable. Thus in Table 6–1, one would combine the scores for subjects in groups $A_1 B_1$ with those in group $A_1 B_2$ (top row) to determine the overall effect of A_1. The fact that the two groups differed in the level of the B factor is ignored for this purpose. Similarly, one would evaluate the effect of A_2 by combining scores of the groups $A_2 B_1$ and $A_2 B_2$ (bottom row), again ignoring the fact that the two groups differed in the level of the B factor. A comparison of the A_1 and A_2 subgroupings provides a measure of the effect of the A variable.

A similar comparison of Groups A_1B_1 and A_2B_1 (left column) with groups A_1B_2 and A_2B_2 (right column) provides an index of the influence of the B factor. Thus, in assessing each of the main effects, it is necessary to combine subgroups that received a given level of one factor but were treated quite differently on the other factor. Consequently, if the main effect of a given factor is significant, we know that the effect probably exists over all levels of the other factors, although not necessarily to the same extent at all levels.

Interaction Effects

A more precise measure of the relative influence of one factor at different levels of the other factors involves the concept of *interaction*, which was briefly described in Chapter 4. We want to know if a factor has an overall main effect, but we also want to know how the magnitude of its effect might vary at other levels of other factors. Thus, if A_1 is superior to A_2 when the B factor is at a specific level, can we assume that it is also superior when a different level of the B factor is involved? If the effect is similar, our generalization is safe. In contrast, if the effect of the A factor is present at one level of the B factor but is either absent or different at another level of the B factor, our generalizability is very low. This situation involves an interaction between the A and B factors. When the effect of one factor is different for various levels of a second factor, an interaction occurs between the two variables. Higher-order interactions can also exist when there are more than two independent variables, but we will limit our discussion to situations where we have only two factors.

The factorial design gives us some direct evidence on the generalizability of results by providing a direct test of the presence or absence of interaction. In contrast, generalizations are often made about effects of variables when no direct evidence exists. The assumption is made that a variable shown to have an effect in one situation will have a similar effect over a variety of other situations; only when concrete evidence arises that challenges this assumption is it usually ever questioned.

Although there are statistical methods of evaluating the extent to which an interaction exists (is statistically significant or unlikely due to chance), we will limit the present discussion to a graphical and logical description of the nature of interactions between variables in the factorial design, with actual examples to follow shortly. Figure 6–4 provides some examples of widely different outcomes that might possibly occur in a 2 X 2 design. The two levels of one factor, arbitrarily chosen as A in this example, are placed along the horizontal baseline of the graphs, while the two levels of the other factor are represented by the two lines in each graph. The height above the baseline along the vertical ordinate of the graphs represents the amount of performance on the dependent variable.

If we remember that the *lack* of interaction between two variables means that the effect (or lack of) of one independent variable is exactly the same at all observed levels of the other independent variable, we should expect the two lines on the graph indicating that relationship to involve parallel lines. In other words, the difference (or lack of it) between B_1 and B_2 should be the same for both A_1 and A_2, as illustrated by the situations a, b, c, and d in Figure 6–4.

A number of different outcomes can occur with the 2 X 2 design where there is no interaction effect:

1. neither A nor B factors have any effect (Fig. 6–4a);
2. one factor, but not the other, has an effect which is the same at both levels of the other factor (Fig. 6–4b; 6–4c);
3. both A and B have an effect and they are the same at both levels of the other factor (Fig. 6–4d).

When an interaction *does* exist, there are also a variety of situations where it occurs:

1. neither A nor B factors have any *overall* main effects because each has an opposite effect at the two levels of the other factor (Fig. 6–4h);
2. one factor, but not the other, has an effect that differs for each level of the other factor (Fig. 6–4f; 6–4g);

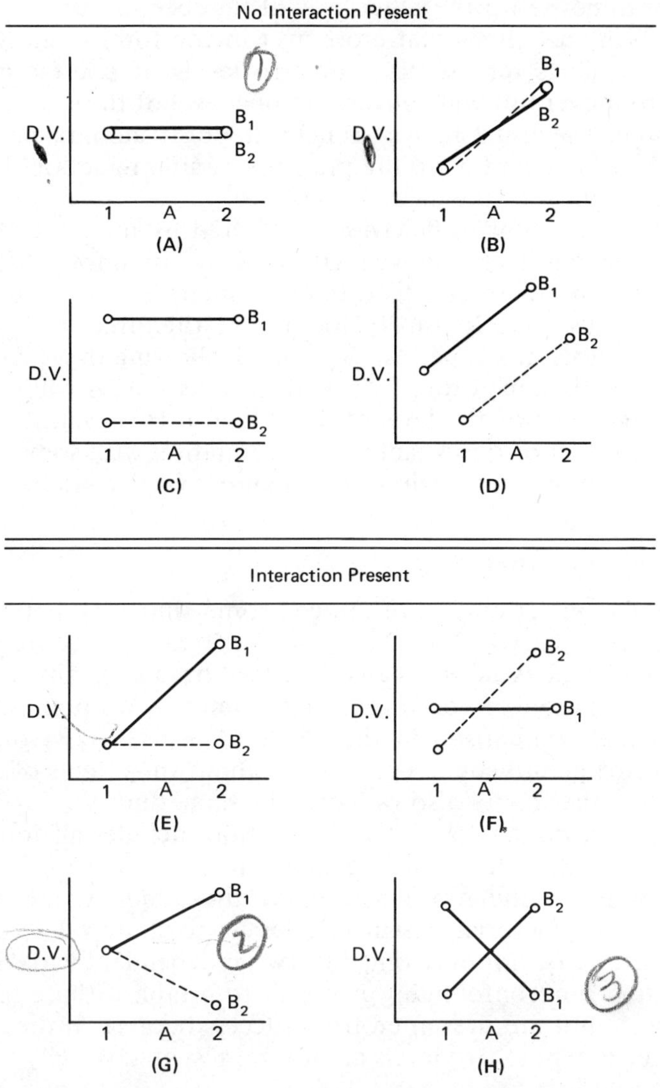

FIGURE 6–4. Some possible outcomes of a 2 X 2 factorial experiment. Top half shows four situations without interactions, while bottom half shows four situations with interactions.

3. both A and B have an effect, but it differs in magnitude for each level of the other factor (Fig. 6–4e).

A graph of the results of a factorial design will yield lines that are *not* parallel when an interaction exists. In some cases, such as where the effects of one variable at one level of the other variable are completely reversed or opposite for the other level of the second variable, the graph will actually involve lines that cross over in the form of an X. In other instances, the lines representing the two levels of one factor will not actually cross over but will converge at one level of the second independent variable. The visual analysis is helpful, but it should be emphasized that the final judgment as to the presence of an interaction depends on a statistical analysis of the data.

Most important human behavior is affected by numerous factors, so it is not surprising if interactive relationships exist among different factors in the nature of their effect. In experiments such interactions may not exist because one is usually looking at the effect of a very small number of factors at a time. An experiment showing that factor A does not interact with some other factor, B, tells us that A will have a similar effect regardless of the level of the B factor. However, if we were to examine the effect of the A factor in combination with some other variable such as factor C, we might discover an interactive relationship.

Relationship to Confounding

The reflective reader may have noticed some similarity between Table 6–1 (see page 131), which outlines the four treatment combinations of a 2 X 2 factorial design and Table 3–2 (see page 65), which contained a visual explanation of confounded experiments. We pointed out that either diagonal comparison in that table (A_1B_1 vs. A_2B_2 or A_1B_2 vs. A_2B_1) did not permit sound conclusions about the effects of either factor since the other factor also varied at the same time.

The factorial design for a 2 X 2 situation includes all four possible combinations rather than just one of the diagonal pairs of the four possible treatment combinations of the two independent variables. In essence, then, the factorial design enables us to draw valid conclusions about the effect of not only one, but two independent variables, A and B. In contrast, in confounding we wish to establish the effect of one factor, say A, but are prevented from success because of the confounding variable, B, whose two levels are not represented equally often at all levels of A as it is in the factorial design.

One should not be misled by the preceding comparison and conclude that confounding can not occur with a factorial design. On the contrary, just as the one independent variable in a one-factor experiment may be confounded by a second extraneous factor, any of the two or more independent variables in a factorial design may also be confounded by yet another factor. Thus, in Fig. 6–3 we see an example of a 2 X 2 factorial design containing two independent variables, A and B. A third factor, C, is confounded with the A factor since all levels of C do not occur equally often at all levels of A. Consequently, any per-

TABLE 6–1. Illustrative Example of Confounding by a Third Factor, C, in a Factorial Design with Two Independent Variables, A and B. The four cells containing Xs represent the combinations of two levels of A with two levels of B included in the design. Unfortunately the variable A is confounded by the variable C since A_1 is always combined with C_1 while A_2 is always combined with C_2. A valid factorial experiment involving only A and B as treatments requires that the level of C be constant.

C_1

B	*A* 1	*A* 2
1	X	
2	X	

C_2

B	*A* 1	*A* 2
1		X
2		X

formance differences between the two levels of A could really be due to the variation in the confounded factor, C.

An example of a factorial experiment with two independent variables, one of which was confounded with a third unintended variable, can be found in a study by Horowitz (1968). After subjects completed a simple task, they were or were not given a choice of participating in an alleged "second experiment," that was really part of one experiment. The second experimenter was reportedly in great need either because of his own shortcomings (he was falling behind schedule) or because of circumstances beyond his control (his professor was leaving town).

We will not explain the full rationale behind the study because our purpose is to illustrate confounding in a factorial design. It should be clear that this experiment is a 2 X 2 factorial design. Unfortunately, in addition, the experimenter whose predicament was beyond his own control was also described as independent and competent while the experimenter who was to blame for his own plight was also depicted as dependent and inadequate. Thus, there is a confounding between the traits attributed to the experimenter and the extent to which the experimenter was responsible for his problem; it is thus impossible to know how much each factor affected the evaluations subjects were asked to make about the second experimenter.

What should have been done? If the traits attributed to the experimenter had been varied equally often for the two types of causes for the experimenter's need for subjects, we would have a factorial design with three independent variables and no confounding variable. As it was designed, however, the study did not permit unequivocal evaluation of the effect of the cause of the experimenter's need for subjects, since this variable was confounded by the traits associated with each experimenter.

Specific Examples of Interaction

We have already encountered several examples of published research involving interactions. For example, in Chapter 1, it was reported that Schachter and Gross (1968) had examined the influence of two fake clock times, one ahead and one behind the actual time, on eating behavior. They predicted, based on theoretical assumptions discussed in Chapter 1, that the extent to which this factor, clock time, would affect eating would differ depending on the individual's weight. Specifically, it was found that overweight persons were influenced by this external temporal cue so that they ate more for the later clock time. In contrast, eating of the normal-weighted subjects, who presumably are more affected by internal or bodily cues of hunger, was not influenced by the different clock readings. Thus, an interaction occurred between the clock times and the two categories of subjects classified on the basis of weight.

A second example of an interaction was also presented in Chapter 1. Freedman, Heshka, and Levy (1975), you may recall, were interested in the effects of density on mood. They theorized that the prevailing mood was a second important factor in determining the effect of density. They felt that there may be no universal effect of density, but that it serves to intensify the existing mood. Here again we are dealing with an interaction between two variables. The effect of one factor, density, differs depending on the level to which the other factor, prevailing mood, is involved. In this example, the effect of density is actually opposite in the two situations studied, an initial positive vs. an initial negative mood. All interactions, however, do not require that "opposite" effects occur. It may be, as in the Schachter and Gross study, that one variable has no effect at one level of the other variable while it has a strong effect at the other level of the other factor. As long as the effects of one factor are "different" for the various levels of the other factor, we are dealing with interactions.

A final example of an interaction can be found in a study by Zanna and Pack (1975) who were interested in the social-influence process whereby one person's attitudes may affect those of another individual. One important factor seems to be the attractiveness of the potentially influential person, since many people may conform to the views of attractive persons more than they might to those of less attractive individuals. We want to obtain the approval and liking of the attractive persons, and conforming to their views may be one approach to achieve this goal.

Zanna and Pack used female college students as subjects in an impression-formation task where they were presented information about a male student and asked to form an evaluation. Half of the females were informed that the male was attractive as well as "available" since he had no girlfriend, whereas the other half learned that he was not attractive and also not available since he did have a girlfriend.

In addition, the subjects received other information including a description of the male's personal conception of the "ideal" woman. Two extreme conceptions were devised, one rather traditional and the other somewhat liberated. Half of the females with the attractive male received the traditional ideal while the other half were told that the male held the liberated ideal. The same procedure was used for the females who heard the description with the unattractive male, creating a 2 × 2 factorial design with two levels of male partner attractiveness and two types of male partner conception of his "ideal" woman.

The logic of this procedure was to see to what extent the females' own conception of themselves might be affected by attractiveness of the male partners and by the two types of ideal-woman conception attributed to the males. The researchers presumed that the females would more likely shift their views toward those held by the attractive male, but would less likely do so if he was unattractive.

Earlier in the semester the females had completed some scales in a different study that assessed their self-conceptions. The female subjects completed these same scales again at this point in this unrelated experiment, presumably to provide information that would be given to the male later. A comparison of each subject's scores on the same tests provided a measure of the extent to which the females changed their self-presentation about themselves toward the type of ideal woman held by one of the males.

Zanna and Pack predicted an interaction between the two independent variables—that is, that the level of male attractiveness would alter the extent to which the two male conceptions of the ideal woman would affect the females' tendency to change their self-conceptions. As shown in Table 6–2, the results were supported and showed that the male's ideal woman conception made little difference on the change in self-presentation of the females when the male was unattractive and unavailable. However, when the male was attractive and available, large shifts in self-presentation occurred in the females toward the conception of the ideal woman allegedly held by the male.

We should consider what would have happened to our conclusions if we had conducted two separate experiments that would not have enabled us to detect the interaction found by Zanna and Pack. Suppose in one experiment, we compared the effect of attractive and unattractive males on the females' change in self-presentation *without* analyzing any change caused by the male's ideal woman conception. We would conclude that the male's attractiveness had no effect since an

TABLE 6-2. Mean Change in Self-Presentation on the Sex Role Stereotypic Traits.[a]

	Partner's Stereotypic View of Women	
Partner's Desirability	*Untraditional*	*Traditional*
High desirability	5.05	−2.35
Low desirability	.60	.60

[a]Note—N equals 20 per condition. Positive scores indicate changes in self-presentation in the untraditional direction: negative scores in the traditional direction.
Source: From "On the Self-fulfilling Nature of Apparent Sex Differences in Behavior," by M. P. Zanna and S. J. Pack, *Journal of Experimental Social Psychology*, 1975, *II*, 583–591. Copyright 1975 by Academic Press. Reprinted by permission.

equal lack of change in self-presentation occurred in the two subgroups of females. For the unattractive male group, however, this lack of change would be real and caused by the failure of the unattractive male to influence the females. In contrast, two large but opposite factors influence females presented with an attractive male that cancel each other out when all of the group data are combined for the traditional and liberated views of the attractive male's "ideal" woman.

Similarly, if we ignored the level of male attractiveness and conducted an experiment that compared self-presentation change only as a function of the two conceptions of the ideal woman, we would obtain an intermediate, misleading effect. This effect would obscure the fact that there was a large effect of this factor for the attractive males and absolutely no effect of it for the unattractive males.

Some Implications

Neither of the conclusions about the main effects of each independent variable accurately reflect the actual effects when the two variables interact. In this example, where an interaction has already been identified, we can easily identify this problem. However, when we do not yet know which factors interact with a particular independent variable, the results of different experiments (that study the effects of that specific variable) can be quite confusing and discrepant. A set of experiments that focus on the influence of a given independent variable on a specific phenomenon usually differ widely in the procedures, apparatus, test setting, and so forth. Any of these uncontrolled factors might, unknown to the investigator, interact with the independent variable under investigation.

For example, Jenkins (1979), in a discussion of research methods on human memory, pointed out that four major categories of variables are involved in any single experiment: type of subjects, orienting tasks such as instructions, type of materials to be remembered, and criterial tasks by which memory is measured. If one compared a set of experiments dealing with essentially the same research question, it is quite possible that they would differ in at least one of these four dimensions. Thus, if one wanted to see how memory for two different types of materials differed, some studies might examine this question with college students while others might use high school students. Or one subset of studies on this topic might use a recall test while another used recognition tests as the criterion of memory.

If no interactions occurred among these different categories of independent variables, these variations among studies would create no problem. However, when interactions do exist, some confusing and conflicting patterns of results may be obtained. If, for example, the effect of the type of materials on memory interacts—that is, is different, depending on the type of subjects, the type of instructions, or the type of criterial task—a number of conflicting findings will arise among the total set of studies dealing with the independent variable, type of material. Hopefully, we would eventually suspect the existence of such interactions and employ factorial designs which examined two or more of these factors simultaneously to test for the presence of interactions.

Assumptions about the processes underlying a specific phenomenon may make it more plausible to expect that certain variables have interactive relationships with an independent variable. Thus, spoken versus written instructions may be equal in effectiveness for adults, but not for young children. The rationale for predicting this interaction would be the fact that young children may not be proficient in reading ability. We do not have to wait until conflicting results arise before we suspect or search for interactions; theories may imply that certain variables interact, and we may then design experiments to test the validity of such predictions as a means of gathering support for the theories from which they are derived.

Failure to find significant differences due to the independent variable being studied may occur for a variety of reasons. The existence of an undetected or unrecognized interacting factor is a strong possibility. In any experiment, some types of individual difference factors or subject variables such as age, sex, personality, ability, and so on, may exist, and these may have an interactive effect with the independent variable under investigation. Consequently, we may observe no overall effect of our treatment if it affects different subgroups of subjects in opposite patterns that cancel each other out. For example, if group size tends to increase motivation for extroverts but reduce it for introverts, our study may show that group size has no overall effect.

If we could only have known at the outset of an experiment what we suspect after we analyzed our data, we would never fail to confirm all of our hypotheses. Alas, our foresight is never as sharp as our hindsight. We can, however, sometimes reanalyze our data by subgrouping subjects along certain dimensions if enough subjects of each type exist. We could compare the performance of males versus females quite readily. If we had other data about the subjects, such as their grade point average or some personality test scores, we could try to reanalyze or break down our data by creating, so to speak, additional "independent variables" to see if the effect of the original independent variable varied, depending on the level of one of these subject variables. Hopefully, our choice of subject variables to compare would be guided by some logical basis, such as a theory about the topic being studied, since one can not examine every conceivable variable. We might discover some evidence that suggests a particular subject variable interacts with the treatment variable and may have masked the effect of the treatment. We would still need to repeat the experiment to double check on our speculation. We could include the suspected subject variable as an explicit planned independent variable and predict that it would interact with the treatment variable, or if we were not particularly interested in the interaction, we might simply eliminate this variable or hold it constant by using only one type of subject from that dimension and predict that the treatment variable would now be stronger.

SUMMARY

Most psychological experiments include more than one independent variable. The use of the factorial design allows the examination of the influence of two or more independent variables within the same experiment. All unique combinations created by combining the levels of each independent variable with every other independent variable are used in this design. Thus, if we have two independent variables, one with two levels and the other with three levels, we have a 2 × 3 factorial design which contains 6 possible different combinations of the two treatment variables. An example might be a study of sex differences in performing three types of learning tasks.

A comparison of all subgroups that receive one level of one independent variable can be contrasted with those subgroups tested at each of the other levels to provide a measure of the so-called main effect of that factor. Thus, in the example, one could determine the main effect of sex by combining scores over all three types of tasks separately for each sex and then comparing them, ignoring for the moment that different tasks were involved. The main effect of the other independent variable, type of problem, would be measured by combining the scores of all subjects who took each task, regardless of their sex.

In addition to providing evidence on the overall effects of each independent variable separately, the factorial design permits a measure of the interaction of the independent variables. An interaction means that the magnitude of the effect of one independent variable is not the same at all levels of the other independent variable. Males might be better than females for one type of problem while females might be superior on another type. When there is no interaction, there is greater generalizability of the findings about each variable since one knows that one variable has a similar effect at all of the levels of the other independent variable.

REFERENCES

Freedman, J. L., Heshka, S., and Levy, A. Crowding as an intensifier of pleasantness and unpleasantness. In J. L. Freedman, *Crowding and behavior*. San Francisco: Freeman, 1975.

Horowitz, I. A. Effect of choice and locus of dependence on helping behavior. *Journal of Personality and Social Psychology*, 1968, *8*, 373-376.

Jenkins, J. J. Four points to remember: A tetrahedral model of memory. In L. S. Cermak and F. I. M. Craik (eds.), *Levels of processing in human memory*. Hillsdale, N. J.: Lawrence Erlbaum Associates, 1979.

Schachter, S., and Gross, L. Manipulated time and eating behavior. *Journal of Personality and Social Psychology*, 1968, *10*, 98-106.

Zanna, M. P., and Pack, S. J. On the self-fulfilling nature of apparent sex differences in behavior. *Journal of Experimental Social Psychology*, 1975, *11*, 583-591.

LEARNING ACTIVITIES

1. Using any of the hypothetical experiments you designed at the end of previous chapters, convert it into a factorial experiment by adding one new independent variable.
2. How many levels are there for each of your independent variables? How can your experimental design be described in notation that indicates the number of variables and the number of levels of each variable?
3. Can you formulate any predictions about the main effect of each independent variable and the nature of any expected interaction effect? If so, briefly explain your rationale in arriving at these predictions.
4. Make a graph showing the approximate pattern of the results you have predicted in visual form. Place the dependent variable along the vertical axis of your graph and the levels of one of your independent variables along the horizontal axis. Use different curves within the graph to represent the different levels of the second independent variable.

CHAPTER 7

Interrelationships Among Experiments

Chapter at a Glance

In our discussion of the nature of psychological experiments thus far, we have focused on the logic and mechanics of conducting *individual* experiments. Of course in practice one must consider the interrelationship between two or more experiments and their outcomes. When similar experiments conducted by different investigators lead to basic agreement, greater confidence can be placed in the reliability and generality of the findings. When different experiments conflict in their implications and results, or when different theoretical explanations are proposed to account for the same basic set of findings, the researcher must design and conduct additional experiments to help resolve the impasse. In many instances, conflicts in the results of a set of studies arise because complex interactions exist among several factors, and these interactions affect the phenomenon under examination. The suspicion that certain factors may interact can be directly examined through the use of factorial design experiments, as we saw in the preceding chapter.

This chapter provides some selective examples that illustrate some of the patterns existing among experiments, and show how periodic conflict, discrepancy, or gaps in the body of existing knowledge call forth new research aimed specifically at providing evidence to help resolve these problems. No standard or uniform formula for the genesis of new research exists, and the examples cited in this chapter illustrate some of this diversity of factors and conditions that stimulate investigators to conduct and design new experiments. Sometimes the reasons will even appear emotional and subjective rather than "scientific" in a cold detached sense of the word. Curiosity, ego-involvement, or even rivalry with other researchers are some of the real motives for research. As the great cognitive psychologist, Edward Chace Tolman (1959) noted, the important thing in doing research is to have fun!

RESOLVING CONFLICTING EVIDENCE

New experiments are often designed to provide evidence that may support explanations reconciling conflicting experiments in the research literature dealing with a particular problem. An example of this motivation can be found in a study by Matthews, Scheier, Brunson, and Carducci (1980) dealing with the effect of predictable and unpredictable patterns of aversive stimulation on the experience of negative physical symptoms such as shortness of breath, ringing ears, watery eyes, sweaty hands, flushed face, and stiff muscles.

Some research (e.g. Weidner & Matthews, 1978) reported that, in a laboratory situation, subjective reports of unpleasant physical reactions followed unpredictable sequences of noise bursts. Perhaps predictable aversive stimuli generate less stress because one can brace oneself for the onslaught. A different possibility, suggested by Matthews et al., is that attention to stimuli wanes more rapidly for predictable than for unpredictable stimuli, which in turn results in less perceived stress for the predictable patterns. However, other experiments, such as a series conducted by Glass and Singer (1972) fail to show any difference in psychophysiological responses that reflect stress as a function of the degree of predictability of noxious noise bursts.

How can one account for the discrepant findings about the effects of predictability of the stimulation? Matthews et al. conjectured that other factors differing between the two sets of studies might act to offset the effect of the predictability factor. Suppose some factor that prevented the decline of attention for the predictable pattern was present in studies showing no effect of predictability level. For example, high-intensity stimuli may be so compelling that attention does not decrease for the predictable pattern. Another factor may be the duration of the test session; very long sessions may lead subjects to pay less and equal attention to both predictable and unpredictable stimuli. Matthews et al. suggested that this situation may have existed in the Glass and Singer experiment, which failed to show an effect of predictability level, since they used a relatively long session. At the end of the session, neither level of noise predictability produced stress reactions exceeding those of a control group that was not exposed to any noise.

Despite the plausibility of this analysis, Matthews et al. realized theirs was a *post hoc* or after-the-fact explanation. Still other explanations could also account for the discrepant findings. They conducted several experiments to provide direct evidence for their attentional explanation. In one study, subjects were assigned arithmetic problems to work while they received background four-second noise bursts in either a predictable or unpredictable pattern. Subjects were also required to depress a button whenever an auditory signal was presented periodically during the session. This second task provided a way to measure how attentive the subjects were to the two tasks. The researchers assumed that less attention to the stressful noises would allow faster button-press reaction. If, as hypothesized, predictable stimuli require less attention, one should eventually expect better reaction time to the button-press task for the group receiving predictable noise, especially as the session progressed toward the end. At the start of the session, however, attention should be high and equal for both predictability levels. In other words, interaction between the two factors in this experiment, predictability level of the noise and the stage of practice in the session, should occur.

The results of the experiment shown in Figure 7–1 supported the predictions, with faster reaction time for the predictable stimuli de-

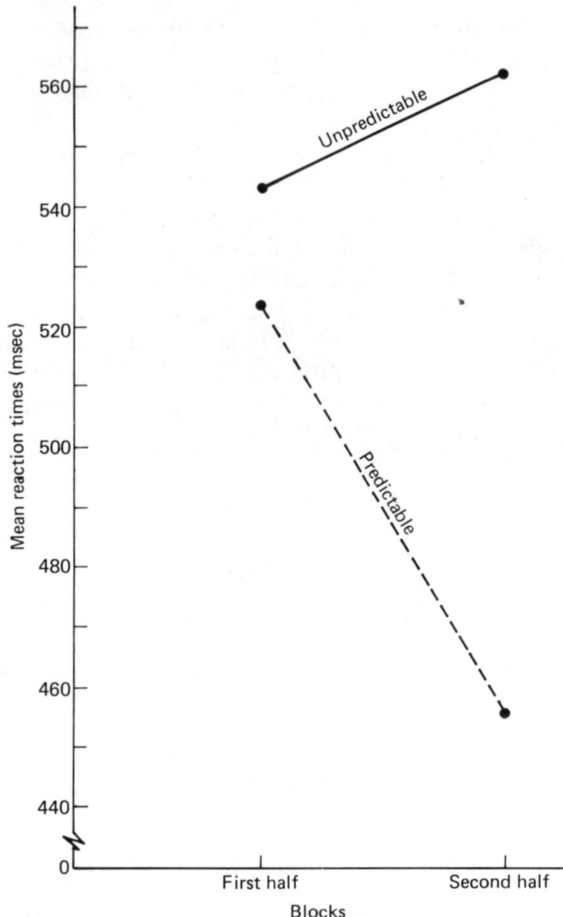

FIGURE 7-1. Mean reaction time as a function of predictability and blocks of trials. (From: Matthews, K. A., Scheier, M. F., Brunson, B. I., and Carducci, B. Attention, unpredictability, and reports of physical symptoms: Eliminating the benefits of predictability. *J. Personality and Social Psych.,* 1980, 38, 525-537. © 1980 by the American Psychological Association. Reprinted by permission.)

veloping by the second half of the test session. Matthews et al. also determined the number of subjects who actually showed decreased reaction time between the first and second half of the session. All but two of those receiving predictable stimuli showed the improved reaction time, whereas only one-third of those receiving unpredictable stimuli improved, and the rest actually increased their reaction time.

This analysis of changes over time within individual subjects is more convincing evidence for the processes assumed to affect individuals over the test session. We have less confidence in our interpretation of the underlying processes if we rely solely on differences in the mean scores of groups that received different treatments. A few extreme scores can unduly affect the group means, and misleading conclusions can be formed about the effect of the treatment variable. More seriously, the same direction of differences between means from different groups might really be due to some process other than the one postulated. One best use direct evidence, if possible, that the hypothesized process shows a relationship with the observed behavior. In this case, Matthews et al.'s finding that most of the individuals actually showed improved reaction time in the predictable stimulus group—but not in the unpredictable stimulus group—correlates with the lower stress found there.

Better evidence would be a finding that subjects who showed the least stress also showed the least attention to the predictable stress stimuli, as measured by improved reaction times to the auditory signals. As Underwood (1975) has argued, theoretical formulations can be evaluated in this fashion by checking to see if individual differences among subjects with respect to the postulated process also show a strong relationship with the behavior supposedly affected by that process.

In the case of the Matthews et al. experiment, no attempt was made to determine if subjects' levels of stress correlated with their amount of attention, as it should have; but their demonstration that the subjects show declines in attention only in the predictable stimulus group lends some credence to the hypothesis that this postulated process does occur. However, one could still argue that the reduced stress in the predictable group is conceivably due to some process other than a decline of attention. Furthermore, even if one shows that subjects who pay less attention to the signals are also the ones who show less stress so that we can feel safer that our theoretical account is correct, some other process may really be the cause. On the other hand, we can be sure that our theory is *wrong,* according to Underwood, if we find an *absence* of a relationship between individual differences in behavior and in the process assumed to be responsible for that behavior.

Returning to the Matthews et al. study, one other approach was used to test their explanation. What would happen, they asked, if the assumed loss of attention to predictable stimuli was prevented. By equating attention to the two levels of predictability, this factor should no longer have any differential effect on stress, and thus performance should be equivalent regardless of predictability level.

Matthews et al. tested this hypothesis in another experiment by instructing half of the subjects at each predictability level to concentrate on the noise bursts; the other subjects received no special instruction. The researchers predicted that the reduction of adverse physical symptoms with predictable stimuli would disappear when subjects were forced to attend to the stimuli. The prediction was upheld, lending further support to the researchers' theory about the basis for the lowered stress found when the adversive stimuli occur in a predictable pattern.

THEORY DEVELOPMENT AND TESTING

In a series of closely interrelated experiments, Stanley Schachter and his associates proposed and tested an intriguing analysis of the determinants of heavy or addictive cigarette smoking. As most experienced smokers are well aware, the urge to smoke is rapidly developed with increased experience. The active pharmacological ingredient in cigarettes, nicotine, is a central nervous system stimulant. When there is a prolonged absence of smoking, the addicted smoker suffers withdrawal reactions and begins to crave cigarettes. According to Schachter et al.'s model, the addiction to nicotine requires the smoker to continue a high level of smoking in order to maintain a comfortable nicotine level in the body.

Nicotine is gradually eliminated from the body as it undergoes detoxification by the liver in a fashion similar to the way in which it rids the body of alcohol. One can infer the level of body nicotine by measuring the alkalinity or pH levels of urine samples. Past studies indicate that when the pH level of the body is normally balanced, the body loses nicotine at a rate of about 7 per cent. However, factors that increase the alkalinity level seem to reduce the loss of nicotine to a one per cent level, while conditions of low alkaline (or acidic) pH levels dramatically increase the rate of nicotine loss to about 36 per cent.

With this background information, one can see why Schachter et al. developed the hypothesis that variations in alkalinity might affect the number of cigarettes that a smoker consumed. If the smoker's chemical state was on the alkaline side so that little nicotine is lost, the physical need to smoke should not be as great as in the case of an acidic state which is associated with rapid loss of nicotine.

Schachter conducted an experiment in which one group received sodium bicarbonate pills prior to the test so that high alkalinity would

TABLE 7–1. Daily Number of Cigarettes Smoked While Subjects Were Taking Vitamin C, Placebo, and Bicarbonate of Soda.

	Mean Cigarettes on	
Drug	*First Drug Day*	*Second Drug Day*
Vitamin C	38.43	42.14
Placebo	39.36	34.21
Bicarbonate	37.21	35.71

Source: From "Studies of the Interaction of Psychological and Pharmacological Determinants of Smoking. 2, Effects of Urinary pH on Cigarette Smoking," by S. Schachter, L. T. Kozlowski, and B. Silverstein, *Journal of Experimental Psychology*, 1977, 106, 13–19. Copyright 1977 by the American Psychological Association. Reprinted by permission.

be achieved, hence reducing the need for excessive smoking. A second group received vitamin C, thus increasing acidic levels and increasing the loss of nicotine from the body. Greater levels of smoking were expected for this group. Finally a third group, which received an inert pill, was included as a placebo control. The results shown in Table 7–1 were consistent with the view that smokers seem to monitor or at least react to differences in their internal pH levels by smoking in amounts necessary to regulate and maintain their customary levels of nicotine as indexed by the alkaline levels. Although no differences were found on the first day, the Vitamin C group, which had the lowest alkaline level, smoked the most.

Under normal circumstances, of course, other factors besides pills probably act to influence the pH levels. Schachter et al. decided to test the influence of other methods of altering pH levels on amount of smoking. For example, the stress levels people experience seem to be related to smoking, as many smokers report a greater need to smoke when stress rises.

Schachter, Silverstein, Kozlowski, Herman, and Liebling (1977) conducted an experiment in which subjects were told the purpose of the study was to determine the effects of noise on tactile sensitivity. However, all subjects were told they would serve in the control group so they would not actually experience noise. Two levels of stress, high and low, were created for different groups by varying the level of shock intensity which was used to measure the tactile pain tolerance of the subjects. During a break in the test, subjects were offered water and cigarettes. The real purpose of this hospitality, of course, was to provide the researchers with a disguised means of comparing the effects of high and low stress on smoking. It was assumed and found that higher stress would cause a drop in alkalinity, thereby prompting greater smoking in order to restore alkaline levels through the increase of nicotine.

Another type of experiment by Schachter, Silverstein, and Perlick (1977) provided subjects with either sodium bicarbonate pills (to increase alkaline levels) or a placebo. Subjects were then exposed to the stress situation described above and the amount of cigarette smoking was recorded. As shown in Table 7–2, smoking due to high stress increased for the control group since the stress produced a decline in alkalinity. In contrast, in the sodium-bicarbonate group, the ability of high stress to reduce alkalinity was offset by this substance so there was less physical need for smoking and high stress did not lead to this behavior. This interaction of stress level with alkaline level supports the theory that smoking serves to maintain a comfortable level of alkalinity. It should be emphasized that the model does not depend on mere assumptions about the alkaline levels in different conditions. Schachter and his associates obtained urine samples before and after subjects took

TABLE 7–2. Mean of Cigarette Smoking.

Condition	No. Smoked During Stress		No. Smoked During Entire Experiment	
	Cigarettes	*Puffs*	*Cigarettes*	*Puffs*
Placebo				
High stress	2.33	23.67	2.75	28.92
Low stress	1.58	11.33	2.00	14.00
Bicarbonate				
High stress	1.92	13.92	2.08	14.67
Low stress	1.79	18.04	1.88	19.13

Note. For all conditions, $n = 12$.
Source: "Studies of the interaction of psychosocial and pharmacological determinant of smoking. 5. Psychological and pharmacological explanations of smoking under stress," by S. Schacter, B. Silverstein, and D. Perlick, *Journal of Experimental Psychology*, 1977, **106**, 31–40. Copyright 1977 by the American Psychological Association. Reprinted by permission.

the pills. Table 7–3 shows the pH indices (higher numbers refer to greater alkalinity) which are equal prior to the stress but increase after stress for the sodium bicarbonate groups. In contrast, high stress reduced the pH for the placebo group whereas low stress had a negligible effect.

Any psychological theory or model is strengthened when predictions derived from its assumptions can account for a greater variety of findings. On the other hand, if experiments designed to test the predictions are not upheld, some doubt is cast on the theory. As more negative outcomes occur, it may be necessary to abandon or drastically revise the formulation.

An example of this situation in the case of Schachter's model can be seen in its ability to handle differences in smoking upon arising in the morning as opposed to later in the day. During the night's sleep, the lack of opportunity to smoke results in a very low nicotine level when the smoker arises. The smoker has a high need to smoke to restore the low alkaline levels to normal.

Schachter, Silverstein, and Perlick (1977) proposed that the effects of stress on smoking should vary, depending on the time of day. Specifically, because smokers are already so deficient in alkalinity upon arising, stress would not lead to more smoking than nonstress conditions. Since alkaline levels would already be low, stress could not significantly lower it. Smoking, then, should be at a high level regardless of the level of external stress. Furthermore, ingestion of sodium bicarbonate should not reduce smoking because the morning alkaline levels are so depleted.

The study described earlier (in which stress did increase smoking)

TABLE 7-3. Effects of the Manipulation on Urinary pH.

	Mean pH			No. Subjects Whose pH		
Condition	*Pre Stress*	*Post Stress*	*Post–Pre*	*De-creased*	*Stayed Same*	*In-creased*
Placebo						
High Stress	6.00	5.83	–.17	8	3	1
Low Stress	5.99	6.13	+.14	4	1	7
Bicarbonate						
High Stress	6.08	7.44	+1.36	0	0	12
Low Stress	6.20	7.01	+.81	2	1	9

Note. For all conditions, $n = 12$.
Source: "Studies of the interaction of psychological and pharmacological determinants of smoking. 5. Psychological and pharmacological explanations of smoking under stress," by S. Schacter, B. Silverstein, and D. Perlick, *Journal of Experimental Psychology*, 1977, **106**, 31–40. Copyright by the American Psychological Association. Reprinted by permission.

was conducted in the afternoon, a time when stress can depress alkaline levels and increase smoking. In short, an interaction is predicted between the factor of degree of stress and the time of day in which smoking will be greater under stressful conditions, provided the test is not performed early in the morning. Smoking will also be high even if sodium bicarbonate is taken in the morning. The results of an experiment confirmed these predictions, as shown in Table 7–4. In contrast to the results of the afternoon experiment (refer back to Table 7–2), no differences in smoking due to stress level for either the placebo or bicarbonate groups exist. Since the model can not only predict the effects of stress on smoking, but also uses the same assumed process (the relationship between nicotine and alkaline levels) to derive predictions about the effects of stress at different times of the day (which were upheld in another experiment), we have more confidence in the theory.

TESTING RIVAL THEORIES

Martin Seligman (1975), in his highly influential book *Helplessness,* suggested that when organisms are subjected to situational consequences or outcomes that are beyond their control, they become inept or unable to take action to produce desired outcomes. In the laboratory, learned helplessness will befall animals receiving inescapable shock, whereas in real life learned helplessness results from dictates and decisions handed down from authorities. Learned helplessness will also

TABLE 7–4. Mean Cigarette Smoking for Morning Subjects.

	No. Smoked During Stress		No. Smoked During Entire Experiment	
Condition	*Cigarettes*	*Puffs*	*Cigarettes*	*Puffs*
Placebo				
High stress	2.63	21.38	3.25	25.50
Low stress	2.63	23.50	2.88	26.25
Bicarbonate				
High stress	1.88	20.88	2.25	24.00
Low stress	2.38	21.25	2.63	23.63

Note. For all conditions, $n = 8$.
Source: "Studies of the interaction of psychological and pharmacological determinants of smoking. 5. Psychological and pharmacological explanation of smoking under stress," by S. Schacter, B. Silverstein, and D. Perlick, *Journal of Experimental Psychology*, 1977, **106**, 31–40.

eventually be associated with affective states similar to depression, and the organism will despair and give up. The critical ingredient appears to be the lack of control imposed on organisms which leads them to believe that there is nothing they can do to affect what happens to them.

A number of experiments have been generated to test and extend the theory proposed by Seligman. Many of them involve testing the limits of generalizability of the theory to see how pervasive the phenomenon is. This set of studies essentially serves to find facts and "fill the holes" in the knowledge network. Another set of related studies has derived methods of minimizing the development of learned helplessness. Thus "immunization," in which organisms received competence training, show less adverse reaction to imposed control than a group that did not (Seligman & Maier, 1967). Other studies focus on the test of therapeutic techniques derived from the theory that learned helplessness is an antecedent of depression.

One set of issues of great importance has been that of generalizability. For example, if a person is subjected to lack of control at home, why does learned helplessness not pervade other parts of that person's life such as work or school experiences? Other examples of the lack of withdrawal, apathy, and depression to imposed control have been dealt with extensively by Brehm's (1966) reactance theory which argues that persons become angry and hostile in such circumstances and make vigorous attempts to regain control and freedom. This reactance is greater to the extent that the person expected to have freedom in the first place, and in proportion to the strength of the imposed threat. Motivation to engage in the threatened activity will increase, as does the attractiveness of any "forbidden fruit."

It might appear that learned helplessness theory and reactance theory are making opposite and conflicting predictions about the reactions to lack of control or freedom. However, Wortman and Brehm (1975) argued that the conditions under which each phenomenon occurs may be different, so these theories do not actually conflict. In the integrative theory of Wortman and Brehm, which was proposed to reconcile the apparent conflict of the two theories, reactance should occur only if the person *expects* to have *control* over some valued or important behavior. Now, if repeated experience still thwarts the individual from achieving control, the expectancy of control should eventually dwindle to nothing. Thus, exposure to lack of control may initially lead to reactance since there was expectancy of control; however, reactance becomes transformed into learned helplessness over time as repeated lack of control creates a new expectation that the person has no control.

The factor of *importance* of the situation to the individual must also be considered. Wortman and Brehm proposed that reactance should occur only in proportion to the importance of the behavior to the individual, since one should not experience reactance for trivial situations.

In summary, whether or not a given situation involving lack of control causes reactance or learned helplessness will depend on factors such as the degree to which the individual has been exposed to it, the importance of the activity, and the individual's initial expectancy regarding control. If expectancy of control is sufficiently high initially, lack of control leads to reactance but it eventually turns into learned helplessness and apathy if lack of control continues long enough. Important outcomes one cannot control also generate reactance when lack of control is first encountered; if lack of control persists and the expectation of no control increases, learned helplessness will develop even for highly important outcomes. Figure 7–2 diagrams the interrelationship of these factors; expectancy of control, importance to the individual, and amount of past exposure to helplessness. The model holds that whether or not the outcome is helplessness or reactance depends on the particular combination of these three variables that are involved in a given situation.

Wortman and Brehm's analysis of previous research provides some support for this conceptual integration of two models which seem, at first glance, to disagree. If their integration is valid, it is a useful synthesis of two influential theories. Although it may seem plausible, it is still necessary to test the model directly by deriving predictions which can be tested in subsequent experiments. Thus, Roth and Kubal's (1976) experiment that tested the effects of importance of outcome and amount of helplessness experience is directly relevant for evaluating predictions derived above. In Roth and Kubal's study, students served in two allegedly unrelated studies on concept learning which were held in separate rooms and involved separate experimenters.

In the "first experiment," the subjects tried to choose the member of a series of pairs of stimulus figures that represented an unknown, under-

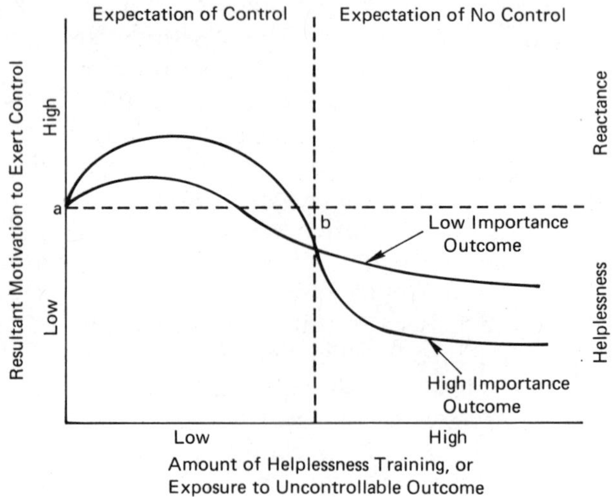

FIGURE 7-2. The integrative model. (From: Wortman, C. B., and Brehm, J. W. Responses to uncontrollable outcomes: An integration of reactance theory and the learned helplessness model. In L. Berkowitz (Ed.), Advances in Experimental Social Psychology. (Vol. 8). New York: Academic Press, 1975. Reprinted by permission.)

lying concept. One group was led to believe the task was related to ability to succeed in college (high importance) while the other group was told the task was a concept-learning problem (low importance). The second independent variable concerned the type of informative feedback received. At each importance level, three subgroups were used, contingent feedback on one problem (accurate information about the correctness of their choices), noncontingent feedback on the problem or random reinforcement so that it was impossible to solve the problem (low helplessness training), or noncontingent reinforcement on *three* problems, the last two of which were alleged to be easier than the first (high helplessness training).

Then subjects were sent to the supposedly unrelated "second experiment," which was really used to obtain a measure of the effects of the differential treatments given to the six different groups in the "first experiment." In this phase of the study, all subjects received identical treatment on a series of concept-learning tasks and their results were also compared with that of an additional control group which did not participate in the "first experiment." A subject who wanted to "give up" on a problem could signal the experimenter to move on to the next problem.

The results obtained by Roth and Kubal were consistent with the Wortman and Brehm integrative model of the two theories. If the subjects were in the high-importance condition, a small amount of helplessness experience was associated with more problems being solved as well as greater persistence on old problems. With higher amounts of helplessness experience when the task was of high importance, performance was poorer with fewer solved problems and persistence was lower with more requests for new problems. When task importance was low, the amount of helplessness experience was a less important factor.

Although the third factor in the model, expectancy of control, was not manipulated in the Roth and Kubal study, it is reasonable to assume that it was high since the subjects were college students. The model predicts that when expectancy of control exists, initial failure should produce reactance with an increased motivation initially followed by eventual decline in motivation and performance quality with continued exposure to helplessness experience for important tasks. The results generally confirm these predictions of the model.

PARADIGMS OF RESEARCH

Sets of experiments are related when they use a common set of procedures, tasks, or a similar conceptual approach to a problem. If experiments employ the same or highly similar tasks, apparatus, or procedures, their results can be compared more easily. In addition, studies based on the same theoretical conception may tend to use a common method. Once a paradigm or set of procedures and methods is accepted by a number of different researchers, subsequent investigators tend to consult this body of experiments as a guide for the design and conduct of new experiments. For example, researchers have developed large bodies of research on achievement motivation based on the tests and theoretical concepts of Atkinson (1957) and McClelland (1958) for identifying individuals of different levels of achievement motivation. Milgram's (1963) basic apparatus and procedure for studying obedience to authority has been used in similar situations where the experimenter wants to induce subjects to engage in aggression toward another unseen person without infliction of actual harm.

A Case History: The Risky Shift

While there are some obvious advantages when a standard paradigm becomes established, what are some of the dangers? Cartwright (1971, 1973) has thoroughly examined the numerous studies of the "risky-shift" effect and provided a thought-provoking analysis of the history of the psychosocial determinants of research on this topic, which may be applicable to many other areas in varying degrees.

The risky shift, as it was dubbed, referred to the finding by Stoner

(1961) that small groups of individuals recommended group decisions riskier than the average of their individual views prior to participating in a group discussion about risk-taking situations. This finding stimulated interest because it contrasted prevailing conceptions in social psychology which maintained that group influence should lead individuals to conform and be conservative rather than risky. In addition, the potential practical importance of research on this issue may have contributed to the surge of new experiments published over the next decade.

As initial experiments corroborated Stoner's basic finding, subsequent experiments explored other factors that might influence the extent of the effect. Rival explanations arose to account for the shift, which was not in question. One theory held that the group situation permitted diffusion of responsibility so that groups choose greater risk levels than individuals. Another theory held that group discussion served to activate the cultural values that hold risk taking in high esteem, while another theory suggested that the more influential members of groups were the riskier individuals who were able to persuade the more cautious members. Experiments were designed to obtain evidence in favor of one's own theory and to refute those of rivals. Eventually, however, experiments showed that the risky shift was not universal. In fact, some evidence even suggested that group discussion following individual evaluation of risk problems could even engender a cautious shift. By the early 1970s, the peak in research on the risky shift occurred and the effect so many researchers were trying to explain no longer seemed as real.

In his careful analysis, Cartwright (1973) suggested that the case history of research on the risky shift is similar to the course of scientific progress in other fields. As the philosopher of science, Thomas Kuhn (1962) has argued, a given paradigm or set of methods becomes accepted and established over time. It dominates research in that area and stimulates additional study, some of which eventually provides evidence that discloses its own inadequacies. Cartwright maintained that the attempts to explain the risky shift were misdirected since the effect is not as pervasive as originally supposed. The bandwagon effect many researchers participated in was facilitated by the acceptance of the set of risk-taking problems devised by Stoner and his procedure for measuring risk-taking levels. The characteristics of this paradigm, which became synonymous with the risky-shift concept, happened to favor riskier outcomes. However, this limitation went unsuspected and undetected for a long time because of the widespread acceptance of the Stoner technique as the basic paradigm for all research in this area.

Let us briefly describe the Choice Dilemmas Questionnaire (CDQ) used by Stoner. It consisted of twelve hypothetical risk dilemmas covering a wide variety of fictitious male characters who had to make choices. In one example, a man was faced with the choice of going to either a highly-prestigious university, which entailed the risk that he might not graduate, or to a less well known institution with a higher chance of success. Another problem involved a man with a serious illness who was contemplating an operation that involved some survival risks. Should he take the risk or reject the operation and endure his illness? Other problems dealt with a marriage decision, a chess decision, and a football play-calling decision by a quarterback.

After reading each problem, the individual was to decide what was the lowest acceptable odds of success the subject would recommend before the decision maker should embark on the riskier alternative in each of the twelve problems. Then groups of two to seven subjects met together and discussed each problem before making a group recommendation for each of the twelve problems.

Stoner's procedure for measuring the risk-taking level of each individual was to sum the scores over all twelve problems and then determine the mean score to use as the best index. The wide variations in the types of problems were ignored because Stoner assumed that the mean, based on all twelve problems, would provide a fair representation of the individual's general level of risk taking. For the groups, all of the means of the group members were then averaged together following their group discission. A comparison of the mean of the initial individual scores was then made with the subsequent mean group scores; lower group scores indicating greater risk levels were interpreted to demonstrate the risky-shift effect.

This procedure was simple enough but it obscured the fact discovered later that some of the problems tended to yield cautious shifts and some of them consistently showed no shift in either direction. It would then follow that if Stoner had included mostly problems from these two categories, he would have instead found evidence for a conservative influence of the group discussion or a cautious shift. This finding would have been highly congruent with conformity theory and thus would hardly have raised any interest or stimulated much research. Paradox is a great stimulant of research!

Cartwright noted that another major shortcoming of this body of research was the lack of analysis of the actual content of the group discussions. An examination of this material would have shed much light on the nature of the process by which group discussion influenced decision. Without such evidence, one cannot be sure that the criteria used by subjects dealt with risk factors at all. Researchers focused on differences between treatments while virtually ignoring the intervening processes that led to the choice responses of the subjects.

What lesson, if any, can be learned from this situation? Was the entire series of experiments a waste of time and effort? Cartwright felt that such a verdict would be unjustified since the body of evidence still represents a substantial set of "hard facts." The problem stems more from the faulty theoretical interpretation of the original finding, which also served to guide (misguide) numerous subsequent experiments. Instead of rejecting this evidence, Cartwright argued that a search for a new conceptualization of the processes involved in this paradigm would be worthwhile and, if successful, could accommodate the set of findings generated originally under the label of "risky shift."

This case history illustrates the dangers that can occur when a large amount of research effort is directed and organized along a single paradigm or line of investigation. On balance, however, Cartwright concluded that the long-range gains outweigh the liabilities since systematic and organized sets of experiments on a given topic facilitate comparability of findings and stimulate additional research. He recommended that attempts be made to find ways of offsetting the negative consequences associated with paradigms that become so well-established that they prevent alternative approaches, methods, and conceptualizations of a problem from being developed.

CRITICAL REVIEWS OF RESEARCH LITERATURE

Integrative summaries of the research literature on specific topic areas are of invaluable assistance in organizing the findings of existing published material. Such critical review articles provide understanding of the relationship among individual articles that can be overlooked when reading isolated individual reports of research. This integration can be helpful in pointing the way for needed additional research since the nature of gaps in our knowledge may be more readily evident. Comparisons of different experiments can also disclose important methodological questions about the accuracy and appropriateness of different procedures, operational definitions, assessment measures, and research designs which have been used in past research. Review articles can also focus on the significance of findings to theoretical issues and controversies over interpretations of data.

Journals such as the *Psychological Bulletin* and the *American Psychologist* often contain integrative reviews of the research in a given area. Examination of a few examples of these reviews may help you develop the critical approach that is useful in evaluating, comparing, and organizing sets of experiments dealing with a specific topic of investigation. There is no fixed or standard format or content for such summary articles but most of them will contain many, although not all, of the following types of materials:

Descriptive summary of existing studies and their findings
Review of major theories about causes, processes

Discussion of conceptual issues
Comparison of alternative procedures or paradigms used to define a concept
Comparisons of alternative dependent variables used to assess outcomes
Review of major independent variables which have been tested
Discussion of methodological problems and issues
Discussion of other limitations of the research such as generalizability, reliability, validity

We will now examine several examples of critical reviews of research in a variety of content areas. In addition to providing some concrete examples to illustrate the nature of review articles which may help you eventually prepare your own critical reviews, it is hoped that you will also see how such reviews can help identify other yet unanswered questions which can be investigated by means of future experiments. To further your learning, suggestions will be provided for designing your own experiments on the same topics covered by the reviews.

Example 1: Are There Sex Differences in Achievement Self-Confidence?

Sex differences have been a topic of growing interest in recent years. One area of concern has been that of self-confidence in achievement situations. It has generally been held that women have less self-confidence than men, possibly due to a generalized outlook based on differences in socialization (Maccoby and Jacklin, 1974). However, a review of the research by Lenney (1977) has identified several types of factors that seem to alter the extent to which sex differences in achievement self-confidence exist. Such evidence has led to the conclusion that lower self-confidence in women is not a generalized belief among women but one that depends on the type of situation involved.

For example, some experiments have shown that the type of task is critical; while some tasks have traditionally been regarded as more appropriate for one sex, the opposite has been true for other tasks. Accordingly, while females might show less self-confidence on a male-appropriate task, they should have greater self-confidence than males when presented with a female-appropriate task. In terms of the language of experimentation, there is an interaction between the independent variable of type of task and that of sex which points out the limitations to the generalization that women have less self-confidence in achievement situations.

Lenney also noted that other factors such as the presence and clarity of feedback about one's task performance are also important to consider. When there is either ambiguous feedback or a lack of it, women had less self-confidence as compared with men, but there were no such differences if clear feedback was available. A third factor which interacted with sex of the person was the extent to which there was an emphasis on social comparison such as when competition is stressed. When competition was involved, women had less self-confidence than men but when it was minimal, as when subjects worked alone, there were no sex differences.

Each of these factors, type of task, performance feedback availability, and presence of social comparison can be viewed as additional independent variables that experiments have found to modify the extent to which sex differences in achievement self-confidence occur. Undoubtedly, future research may disclose still other factors. It would be useful for you to attempt to think of other factors which could be investigated in experiments that you might be able to undertake yourself, using simple materials and procedures such as those used by House (1974) to show how competition on an anagram task lowered the confidence of females.

It would also be worthwhile for you to speculate about the processes that give rise to the pattern of sex differences found in the research literature. Are they innate or learned? What type of experiment or observations would help you answer this type of question? At what age do such differences first show up? If developmental comparisons show that they are absent prior to a given age, it would imply that they are not innate. In order to uncover some of the specific factors which create or cause the sex differences, it may be useful to conduct experiments with young children. A different question might be whether or not specific procedures and experiences could be used to increase the lowered self-confidence of women in those situations where it does exist. Experiments could be designed to test the effectiveness of such treatments. The research process is a self-sustaining one which is never completed since the answers provided by one experimental finding give rise to still further questions for future investigation.

Example 2: Are Women More Responsive to the Young?

A different topic but one which still concerns sex differences is the question of whether or not women are more responsive to young children and infants than men are. The common belief is that women, whether due to some mysterious maternal "instinct" or simply due to social roles, have greater responsiveness to the young. Such an observation, however, does not involve a true experiment since there is no manipulation of an independent variable. Instead, what we have here is a descriptive or correlational study of a nonexperimental nature showing that the individual difference dimension of sex is associated with differences in responsiveness to the young.

However, once we discover differences by the use of careful observation it is usually possible to formulate questions which do lend themselves to investigation with the experimental method. For example, if we wanted to develop methods of increasing responsiveness to the young we could use experiments to evaluate our procedures. What are the effects on the young of any such increased responsiveness? Again, experiments could be employed to determine any positive or negative effects of increased attentiveness.

Berman (1980) reviewed the research literature in this area and noted some methodological issues. What is the best or most valid technique for measuring "responsiveness"? She found that the main methods used were self-report, physiological responses, and behavior in some interaction with a child or infant. To what extent are these measures comparable and are they measuring the same thing? These questions are especially important since the types of conclusions obtained in different studies tended to depend somewhat on the particular type of response measure used to define responsiveness. Berman discovered that while self-report indices suggested that females were more responsive, there was less support of sex differences when only physiological indices such as arousal or behavioral responses such as talking or playing with the child were employed.

In addition, another important finding reported by Berman was that not only were different methods used to measure responsiveness but that the type of stimulus presented to the subjects tended to vary with the type of measurement method. Thus, when a self-report procedure was involved, pictures or videotapes of the young were commonly used as stimulus material whereas a live child was obviously required if the measure involved direct behavioral measures of the subject during an interaction with a child. This confounding between the measurement method and the type of stimulus raises the question of how much each variable affects the obtained results. It would be necessary to design a controlled experiment in which both of the factors were varied while the other was held constant in order to answer this important methodological question.

One might also wonder if the sex of the young child is another major factor that influences the responsiveness of adults. Age of the child might be examined to see if adult attentiveness diminishes with increased age of children. Perhaps the personality of the young must also be considered since some children are easier while others are more difficult to rear.

It should be relatively easy for you to design and conduct an experiment on this topic if someone in your class or a faculty member has a young child or infant that can be used as a "stimulus person". One could observe male and female college students who are instructed to interact or play with the child for a short period while you make unobtrusive observations. An experiment such as the one reported by Feldman and Nash (1978) that used this type of situation could be used as a model from which to depart in planning and designing your own experiment on this topic. If no children are available, you could use other young animals such as kittens.

Example 3: Why Are Groups Less Likely Than Individuals to Help Someone in Distress?

A large number of experiments have been conducted since the early 1970's to determine some of the factors which make members of a group of strangers less likely to provide assistance to a person in need of help than might be expected by an individual who is alone. In part, this research was stimulated by the publicity over the brutal murder of a young woman, Kitty Genovese, on a New York street. What was unusual about this case was the apparent fact that at least 38 nearby residents heard the victim's cries for help but no one summoned the police, let alone tried to intervene to rescue her.

Latané and Darley (1970), in one of a series of investigations, tried to produce experimental or laboratory analogues of this inhibiting effect of the presence of others on the willingness of members of an audience to help victims. Using a group discussion situation in which two-to-six individual subjects worked in several isolated cubicles while communicating with each other over an intercom, Darley and Latané (1968) had a confederate, acting as a subject, fake an epileptic seizure to see how long it would take for one of the other subjects to summon assistance. In comparison to the condition in which the subjects worked in pairs (one being the confederate) so that the real subject was the only witness to overhear the seizure, slower response in seeking aid occurred when there were several witnesses. This seemingly paradoxical phenomenon of group inhibition occurs in the laboratory just as it happens in the outside world.

Since then over 50 experiments have been published on this topic which have explored the influence of a variety of emergency and nonemergency situations where the subject is presented with the opportunity to help. Sometimes the victim is in some danger such as an apparent heart attack on a subway car but in other studies the victim only needs help in picking up some dropped pencils or books. Sometimes the requests are explicit such as for donations while in other studies the need for help is obvious such as when a motorist has a disabled vehicle but there is no direct request for aid. Despite this wide variation in precipitating situations, Latané and Nida (1981) concluded from their review of the literature that the group inhibition effect shows a wide generalizability across situations.

A number of other independent variables have been used in research on this topic including:

Ambiguity of the situation
Laboratory vs. naturalistic settings
Characteristics of bystanders such as age, sex
Characteristics of other bystanders in the audience
Characteristics of the victim, especially sex
Degree of communication among bystanders

Latané and Nida described the influence of these factors in their review. Despite the additional effects of these factors on helping behavior, the basic phenomenon of group inhibition was found to be upheld in the majority of situations, creating greater confidence that the effect is a strong one.

An understanding of the underlying psychological processes can be useful in making predictions about the effects of various factors on the group inhibition phenomenon. Such a theory would also be valuable in trying to discover how, if at all, it is possible to counteract or reduce the group inhibitory effect. Latané and Nida suggested that three factors must be present to create group inhibition: *audience inhibition* whereby the presence of others makes each member of the audience fearful of acting lest one makes a mistake, *social influence* or the reliance of each member on the audience for cues as to the proper action to take, and *diffusion of responsibility* which is a process by which each member can excuse his or her own lack of altruistic behavior by placing equal blame on other audience members for their noninvolvement. Perhaps methods that offset all three of these factors can be developed to see if the group inhibition effect can be minimized.

Some of the research on helping behavior has involved somewhat elaborate situations such as a staged beer theft from a liquor store or feigned injuries on subway cars that are impractical and ill-advised for you to use as models for designing your own experiments. A simpler situation is one devised by Latané and Dabbs (1975) who had a confederate drop pencils and coins in elevators to determine whether the number of occupants affected the likelihood of receiving aid. The group inhibition effect was obtained in each of three different metropolitan areas where the study was conducted.

What other factors can you think of that might affect the level of helping? Would the effect be greater in an elevator that is stationary when the objects are dropped than if it has already started moving up or down? If you can not locate a convenient elevator to use for your laboratory, you could try other public areas such as the library or the cafeteria.

Example 4: What Are the Psychological Effects of Immoral Actions?

Does the person who lies, cheats, or intentionally harms another person experience negative emotional and psychological consequences later? How does subsequent behavior related to the moral transgression change, if at all? It is commonly assumed that guilt, remorse, and other unpleasant states are the price we pay for immoral behavior. If we were to compare those individuals who committed some transgression with those who did not, we might find some differences in their reactions but it would be difficult to be certain whether such differences were caused by the different choices of behavior or if the kinds of individuals who engage in different actions may not already be different in their tendencies.

This type of interpretative problem is not present in laboratory experiments in which subjects are randomly assigned to treatments where they are either induced to violate some strongly held value such as honesty or are not required to transgress. On the other hand, these experiments are often artificial and of short duration so that one may question whether the results are generalizable to moral transgressions outside the laboratory. It is also likely that the tendency to give socially desirable responses may also be a disadvantage of this laboratory approach.

With these limitations in mind, let us examine the evidence reviewed by Klass (1978) dealing with laboratory situations requiring violation of some important social value by the subjects. One widely used situation calls for the apparent harm of another subject since the task requires that electric shock be administered by the subject. Another paradigm involves pressure for the subject to write an essay or make a persuasive speech containing arguments on some controversial topic which are contrary to the one held by the subject in return for some type of material incentive.

It is not surprising that the amount of guilt suffered after a transgression in these types of tasks is one dimension of great interest to researchers. Other dependent variables or reactions, however, have also been examined in many studies. The effect of moral transgressions on self-esteem, bad feelings about the action per se, decreased liking of the victim, compliance with later requests for help (even if the aid does not eliminate the earlier offense), victim compensation, and self-punishment have all been measured in this research. Klass reported that while immoral actions of the variety examined in this research did not have negative effects on self-esteem in general or feelings about the transgression situation, there was negative feeling about the behavior itself, greater belief in the truth of any lies told, and more compliance with requests for aid from others. Evidence on other consequences such as concern for the victim or feelings of responsibility for the action is ambiguous.

No single theory can account for the pattern of overall findings. Some type of guilt-reduction theory as well as cognitive dissonance theory is popular especially since these theories are concerned with diverse reactions such as reparation, expiation, and rationalization. Unfortunately guilt is often invoked as an explanation in this area of research without any independent measurement of the process. Equity theory suggests that transgressors create an imbalance between themselves and their victims that calls for some effort by the offender to restore balance. Victim compensation, self-punishment, denial of responsibility, minimization of the amount of harm, and derogation of the victim are among the diverse reactions which might be considered as methods of restoring equity. Negative state relief theory focuses on the search for positive rewards by the transgressor after the offense as a means to offset aversive feelings.

Despite this abundance of explanatory views, Klass concluded we are still far from accounting for the known consequences of transgression. Part of the problem seems to be the inability of theories to make clear predictions as to which specific reactions are more likely to occur following transgression. Thus, what factors determine whether the response to a violation will be a form of self-punishment as opposed to denial or derogation of the victim?

Factors such as the personality of the transgressor and the type of relationship between the transgressor and the victim may be important to consider. It would be worthwhile for you to devise some hypotheses about the role of these factors in determining the extent to which transgressors will comply with requests for assistance received from other parties after the violation occurs. Situations such as those devised by Freedman, Wallington, and Bless (1967) might be easily adapted for your experiment. In one procedure subjects learned from a confederate about the experimental task prior to testing. Shortly thereafter the experimenter asked subjects if they had any foreknowledge about the experiment and virtually all of them lied and claimed lack of information. In comparison with a control group which did not receive prior information, subjects who lied were more willing to comply with a request at the end of their test session to help another experimenter by serving in an additional experiment. Similar effects of guilt induced by the experimenter were obtained with subjects who "accidentally" knocked over a large ordered pile of the researcher's materials that the experimenter had placed near the subject's location in advance.

Example 5: What Are the Effects of Therapy?

One large category of research of an applied nature deals with the general issue of the assessment of the effectiveness of some specific therapy or method of treatment for the elimination or reduction of some unwanted behavior or psychological state ranging from clinical disorders and behavioral problems to the provision of instruction and tutoring. Regardless of the specific problem under treatment, a common feature to most of these studies is the lack of random assignment of subjects to the different treatment conditions, if there should be more than one treatment available. More often than not, there may not even be a zero or no treatment control group but even when it is included there may not be random assignment of subjects to conditions.

Instead, there is a self-selection procedure in which certain types of individuals may seek or be assigned more often to treatment of one type while other types of individuals receive other types of treatment. Convenience, attitudes, economic resources, or social factors may be responsible for these inequalities that create insurmountable obstacles to any adequate evaluation of the effectiveness of the independent variable or type of treatment. In all fairness, however, it must also be recognized that individuals with serious problems in need of treatment do not come to a therapist for the purposes of scientific investigation. In short, they do not expect to be placed in a "control group", however valuable such a group may be for the scientifically-oriented investigator. The client only wants to be in the therapy treatment or experimental condition. This is a valid concern but one that we will not elaborate on further at this point other than to indicate that researchers have developed control procedures that satisfy both methodological and ethical problems fairly well. When such controls are absent or assignment to different treatments is not random it is not possible to draw conclusive inferences about the true influence of some specific therapeutic treatment.

It is not likely that you will be able to design and conduct an experiment dealing with the evaluation of a therapy for a major psychological problem. Our present discussion is intended more as a lesson in some of the difficulties in performing good experiments in this type of applied psychology. An analysis of the pitfalls here may prove instructive in helping you appreciate the value of experimental design and control.

Research on a wide variety of topics where therapy has been developed has been systematically reviewed including studies of hypertension (Seer, 1979), children's fears (Graziano, DeGiovanni, and Garcia, 1979), homosexuality (Adams & Sturgis, 1977), and smoking (Leventhal & Cleary, 1980), to cite a few examples. Many of the shortcomings and problems in performing sound studies in one area are similar to those associated with other areas. Although we will limit our present discussion to Curran's (1977) review of research on treatment of heterosexual dating anxiety, keep in mind the fact that the issues involved with this body of research apply to many other areas of investigation.

Many studies have examined the utility of a social skills training program to relieve the social anxiety that many adolescents have in heterosexual dating encounters. This approach assumes that the lack of adequate social skills is the primary cause of the problem. As Curran noted, other views such as the conditioned anxiety hypothesis holds that socially anxious persons may have actually experienced aversive consequences in the presence of cues associated with heterosexual encounters and it is these past conditioned reactions rather than lack of skills that creates dating anxiety. Another view suggests that faulty cognitive appraisal of heterosexual interaction such as imagined problems is responsible for anxiety. Perhaps these views overlap or work together but to the extent that the lack of social skills plays a major role there should be some benefits from a program providing social skills training.

Curran summarized the findings of this research that has involved the use of techniques such as modeling, self-observation, and behavioral rehearsal. Overall, the evidence suggests that this approach has merit but Curran also pointed out a number of weaknesses due to uncontrolled factors. Future research is needed to remedy some of these problems.

First, the validity of the response measures or dependent variables has not been established. Investigators seem to make the untested assumption that any measure that seems plausible ranging from self-report to nonverbal responses such as smiling or mutual gazing in a dating type context, ratings by dates, physiological measures, and behavioral ratings by experimenters is acceptable. It is not clear either how equivalent different measures are so that studies that use one method may or may not be comparable to those using different measures. Inconvenient measures that actually deal with the behavior in need of change, i.e., increases in long-term dating frequency are rarely used.

There may be no clear consensus as to the criteria for defining successful treatment, with a tendency to accept subjective indices such as self-report in many areas. As is true of many clinical procedures that are developed in highly controlled but artificial settings, there is no demonstration that any improvements will generalize to natural settings. The work on dating skill training similarly needs to be verified in real life situations. Furthermore, a test of the success of any treatment also calls for followups at intervals of some length after the completion of a program to provide some indication of the durability of any improvements. Research in these problems is often difficult to implement for practical reasons but it is important that some efforts be made in this direction.

Another problem with therapy research in general that also pertains to social anxiety research is the tendency to use rather complex "independent variables" or treatments. While a control group may receive no treatment or perhaps a simple attention or placebo control, the experimental group may often receive a treatment package consisting of several components such as modeling, self-observation behavioral rehearsals, and so forth.

If benefits are found in favor of the experimental or therapy group, do we attribute the gains equally to each of the treatment components or is it possible that some elements are more influential than others? It may be that some components are ineffective, thus wasting time and money. Even worse, there is a chance that some components counteract the benefits provided by other components, with the net effect of reduced benefit, no difference, or even harm. Without better controlled research procedures we cannot identify the relative influence made by each ingredient in the total treatment package. After evidence is obtained showing that a program is beneficial, it is useful to conduct additional more refined experiments that try to narrow down more precisely the role of each part of the program.

A final issue cited by Curran is the need to search for interactions between treatments and types of individuals. There may not be a universal set of skills that are useful for everyone. Although the total group of subjects may be alike insofar as they all suffer from dating anxiety, there may be important subgroups worth distinguishing in terms of age, sex, background, personality, and so forth. Programs which work effectively for one type of person may not succeed with another type, and vice versa.

In discussing this last example of a critical review of a research topic, we have concentrated on methodological issues that are not unique to a specific content area but apply widely. Without sound method, the findings of experiments will be at best, inconclusive, and possibly misleading. As is the case with all of the examples provided, the critical review organizes the available research, evaluates it, and suggests directions for the course of needed future investigation.

SUMMARY

When researchers compare the results of different experiments dealing with the same problem, they may discover experimental discrepancies and conflicts. These apparent contradictions may lead researchers to develop and revise theories that can accommodate or reconcile different sets of information. Additional experiments may be implied or even dictated by the pattern of findings among independent experiments. Later experiments may provide evidence that calls into question the validity of previous experiments, or at least questions their generalizability. In short, experiments lead to more experiments because no single experiment can answer all questions. One experiment may also generate new questions to be explored.

Interrelationships exist between different experiments as well as between theoretical formulations and experiments. It is necessary and possible for researchers to plan new experiments to test hypotheses about the effects of certain variables suggested by previous theories and experiments. The outcomes of these later experiments support or contrast existing evidence and explanations; thus a continuous process of revision and gathering additional evidence characterizes the research enterprise.

History of research on the risky shift illustrates the psychology of investigation dealing with the motivational and cognitive factors that might affect the way researchers approach their work. Some of the problems that occurred in research on the risky shift illustrate the complex social psychological nature of research as it actually unfolds. This complexity can be totally overlooked if one looks only at the final outcome of a set of experiments.

Critical reviews of the research literature are available for many topic areas. These articles summarize existing experiments and point out methodological, theoretical, and conceptual problems. Gaps in our knowledge may become readily evident from the examination of these integrative summaries. Several examples covering different content topics were described to illustrate the nature of these review articles, with suggestions provided for possible experiments that students could readily attempt as learning activities.

REFERENCES

Adams, H. E., and Sturgis, E. T. Status of behavioral reorientation techniques in the modification of homosexuality: A review. *Psychological Bulletin*, 1977, *84*, 1171-1188.

Adams, H. E., and Sturgis, E. T. Status of behavioral techniques in the modification of homosexuality: A review. *Psychological Bulletin*, 1977, *84*, 1171-1188.

Atkinson, J. W. Motivational determinants of risk-taking behavior. *Psychological Review*, 1957, *64*, 359-372.

Berman, P. W. Are women more responsive than men to the young? A review of developmental and situational variables. *Psychological Bulletin*, 1980, *88*, 668-695.

Brehm, J. W. *A theory of psychological reactance*. New York: Academic Press, 1966.

Cartwright, D. Risk taking by individuals and groups: An assessment of research employing choice dilemmas. *Journal of Personality and Social Psychology*, 1971, *20*, 361-378.

Cartwright, D. Determinants of scientific progress: The case of research on the risky shift. *American Psychologist*, 1973, *28*, 222-231.

Curran, J. P. Skills training as an approach to the treatment of heterosexual-social anxiety. *Psychological Bulletin*, 1977, *84*, 140-157.

Darley, J. M., and Latané, B. Bystander intervention in emergencies: Diffusion of responsibility. *Journal of Personality and Social Psychology*, 1968, *8*, 377-383.

Feldman, S. S., and Nash, S. C. Interest in babies during young adulthood. *Child Development*, 1978, *49*, 617-622.

Freedman, J. L., Wallington, S. A., and Bless, E. Compliance without pressure: The effect of guilt. *Journal of Personality and Social Psychology*, 1967, *7*, 117-124.

Glass, D. C., and Singer, J. L. *Urban stress: Experiments on noise and social stressors*. New York: Academic Press, 1972.

Graziano, A. M., DeGiovanni, I. S., and Garcia, K. A. Behavioral treatment of children's fears: A review. *Psychological Bulletin*, 1979, *86*, 804-830.

House, W. C. Actual and perceived differences in male and female expectancies and minimal goal levels as a function of competition. *Journal of Personality*, 1974, *42*, 493-509.

Klass, E. T. Psychological effects of immoral actions: The experimental evidence. *Psychological Bulletin*, 1978, *85*, 756-771.

Kuhn, T. S. *The structure of scientific revolutions*. Chicago: University of Chicago Press, 1962.

Latané, B., and Dabbs, J. M. Sex, group size, and helping in three cities. *Sociometry*, 1975, *38*, 180-194.

Latané, B., and Darley, J. M. *The unresponsive bystander: why doesn't he help?* New York: Appleton-Century-Crofts, 1970.

Latané, B., and Nida, S. Ten years of research on group size and helping. *Psychological Bulletin*, 1981, *89*, 308-324.

Lenney, E. Women's self-confidence in achievement settings. *Psychological Bulletin*, 1977, *84*, 1-13.

Leventhal, H., and Cleary, P. D. The smoking problem: A review of the research and theory in behavioral risk modification. *Psychological Bulletin*, 1980, *88*, 370-405.

Maccoby, E. E., and Jacklin, C. N. *The psychology of sex differences*. Stanford, Calif.: Stanford University Press, 1974.

McClelland, D. C. Methods of measuring human motivation. In J. W. Atkinson (Ed.), *Motives in fantasy, action, and society*. New York: Van Nostrand, 1958.

Matthews, K. A., Scheier, M. F., Brunson, B. I., and Carducci, B. Attention, unpredictability, and reports of physical symptoms: Eliminating the benefits of predictability. *Journal of Personality and Social Psychology*, 1980, *38*, 525-537.

Milgram, S. Behavioral study of obedience. *Journal of Abnormal and Social Psychology*, 1963, *67*, 371-378.

Seer, P. Psychological control of essential hypertension. Review of the literature and methodological critique. *Psychological Bulletin*, 1979, *86*, 1015-1043.

Roth, S., and Kubal, L. Effects of noncontingent reinforcement on tasks of differing importance: Facilitation and learned helplessness. *Journal of Personality and Social Psychology*, 1976, *32*, 680-691.

Schachter, S., Kozlowski, L. T., and Silverstein, B. Studies of the interaction of psychological and pharmacological determinants of smoking. 2. Effects of urinary pH on cigarette smoking. *Journal of Experimental Psychology*, 1977, *106*, 13-19.

Schachter, S., Silverstein, B., Kozlowski, L. T., Herman, C. P., and Liebling, B. Studies of the interaction of psychological and pharmacological determinants of smoking. 4. Effects of stress on cigarette smoking and pH. *Journal of Experimental Psychology*: General, 1977, *106*, 24-30.

Seligman, M. E. P. *Helplessness: On depression, development, and death*. San Francisco: Freeman, 1975.

Seligman, M. E. P., and Maier, S. F. Failure to escape traumatic shock. *Journal of Experimental Psychology*, 1967, *74*, 1-9.

Stoner, J. A. F. A comparison of individual and group decisions involving risk. Unpublished Master's thesis. School of Industrial Management, Massachusetts Institute of Technology, 1961.

Tolman, E. C. *Principles of purposive behavior*. In S. Koch (Ed.), *Psychology, the study of a science*. (Vol. 1). New York: McGraw-Hill, 1959.

Underwood, B. J. Individual differences as a crucible for theory. *American Psychologist*, 1975, *30*, 128-134.

Weidner, G., and Matthews, K. A. Reported physical symptoms elicited by unpredictable events and the Type A coronary-prone behavior pattern. *Journal of Personality and Social Psychology*, 1978, *36*, 1213-1220.

Wortman, C. B., and Brehm, J. W. Responses to uncontrollable outcomes: An integration of reactance theory and the learned helplessness model. In L. Berkowitz (Ed.), *Advances in Experimental Social Psychology*. (Vol. 8). New York: Academic Press, 1975.

LEARNING ACTIVITIES

1. Researcher A finds that men are more aggressive than women, whereas Researcher B obtains exactly the opposite results. What are some possible reasons for these discrepant findings and how could you conduct subsequent experiments to test your analysis?
2. Suppose, upon closer comparison, we found that Researcher A always paired subjects of the same sex together so that the aggressor was of the same sex as the victim. In contrast, Researcher B decided to use opposite sexed pairings so that males had a chance to aggress against females only and vice versa. Can you think of reasons why this difference in procedure may have led to the apparent

conflict in results? Could any experiment or set of experiments be designed to test your analysis?

3. Different experiments dealing with the same topic and examining the influence of the same variables may use different operational definitions or measurement procedures. Could such differences account for the discrepancies in results among different experiments? Give a hypothetical example to illustrate your conclusion.
4. Even if we were to repeat the same experiment with the same investigator and identical procedures, but with different subjects who were selected at random from the same population, it is possible to obtain widely divergent results. Explain why. (Hint: Review Chapter 4's discussion of statistical significance.)
5. Browse through several issues of a journal such as *Psychological Bulletin* for articles reviewing a body of experiments on a given topic. Try to identify the interrelationship among the various experiments described in the article to see how the kinds of variables examined in more recent experiments may have been influenced by the nature of the results of the earlier research in that area.

CHAPTER 8

Doing Your Own Experiments

Chapter at a Glance

Learning how to do experiments cannot be fully grasped by reading books about the logic and the mechanical aspects of the procedures involved. Ultimately, the student must become actively involved starting with identifying a problem for research, searching for and examining relevant past studies, forming a testable hypothesis, and designing an appropriate experiment. Then comes actually executing the experiment, compiling and analyzing the data, and evaluating and interpeting the results. Finally, one must prepare a written presentation of the research in a style similar to that of research journals. Only by this process of planning, performing, and reporting an experiment can the student completely understand some of the abstract principles and specific techniques about experimentation presented in textbook discussions.

In the following sections, we will assist and guide you in this process. Keep in mind that the process depicted here is a fictional profile based on a composite summarization, and not a rigid standard. In actuality, variations of procedure exist, and all are valid research strategies.

SOURCES OF RESEARCH IDEAS: NATURAL OBSERVATION

In order to conduct an experiment, we obviously must be interested in learning more about a specific subject area or topic. Inspiration for such ideas does not come totally out of the blue. When our curiosity is aroused—for example, when we make unexpected or discrepant observations of some phenomenon—we begin to formulate explanations or theories to account for the total set of findings. As researchers interested in empirical or concrete evidence, we devise new, controlled observations to test our hypotheses and predictions. Although many students can understand the principles and logic of designing and performing experiments in the abstract, they often find it difficult to develop interesting ideas for original experiments.

Most of our ideas ultimately originate from natural observation of behavior or phenomena as they occur under normal, everyday conditions. A careful eye for detail and accuracy in noticing and describing real-life events is essential for capturing the full picture of the patterns of factors related to the behavior of interest. Suppose, for example, we were interested in charitable donations. Why we were interested—just for curiosity's sake or for some practical purpose such as how to increase donations—is irrelevant. Our naturalistic observations might disclose a number of relationships between donations and a number of factors, such as the season of the year, the format or content of the request, and the personality of the individual, to cite a few. From any of these observed patterns, we propose explanations. To avoid circular explanations-for example, giving is due to a "donating instinct"—we try to test our theory under conditions that introduce and vary factors that should lead to specific predictable outcomes if our theory is tenable, or different outcomes if our theory is unwarranted.

A Case Example: ". . . Even a Penny Will Help"

The inspiration for ideas to test with experiments may come unexpectedly, but as Louis Pasteur noted long ago, creativity is not a matter of luck because, "chance favors the prepared mind." If one is curious and observant, one will raise questions those who are less "prepared" will not even consider. The account of a social psychologist, Robert Cialdini (1980), regarding the origins of some interesting research questions about the types of effective charitable appeals he and Schroeder addressed (1976) illustrates how good questions are developed.

One day a door-to-door solicitor came to Cialdini's door seeking a donation to a charity to which he had already donated. As he prepared to turn the solicitor away empty-handed, the fund raiser commented, "even a penny will help." This tactic caught Cialdini off guard, and he ended up donating all over again. Later, he puzzled over the unusual effectiveness this type of approach had on him and he wondered if it affected other persons equally, and if so, why it was so influential.

Cialdini postulated that this form of plea served to "legitimate a trivial contribution"; in plain terms, it made it o.k. to give just a little money. Moreover, if he didn't give at all, he might have formed a negative self-image of either being too poor or too stingy to give even one cent! Being an experimenter, Cialdini decided, with the collaboration of Schroeder, to test his hypothesis with research.

In cooperation with their local American Cancer Society, the researchers instructed assistants collecting funds for this cause to state half their appeals to donors in a more or less standard format, "Would you be willing to help with a donation?" and to add the phrase "even a penny will help" to the remainder of their appeals. As shown in Table 8–1, twice as many people gave in the "even a penny will help" condition as in the standard or control condition. The *average* size ($1.54 vs. $1.44) of the donations, however, did not differ as a function of these two types of appeal.

Does this evidence prove Cialdini and Schroeder's explanation correct or are rival explanations compatible with these findings? These researchers recognized that another theory—called the norm of social responsibility (Berkowitz & Daniels, 1963)—may also be involved. This idea refers to the notion that people generally recognize the social norm that help should be given to those in need. Maybe a higher percentage of persons donated when they heard the extra plea because it led them to believe the American Cancer Society was in more desperate need.

TABLE 8–1. Percentage of Subjects Donating, Total Amount Contributed and Need Scores in Experiment 2 of Cialdini and Schroeder (1976).

	Type of Request			
	Control	*Even-a-Dollar*	*Even-a-Penny*	*Social Legitimation*
Percent Donating	32.2	46.7	58.1	64.5
Total Donated ($)	20.74	19.35	31.30	28.61
Need Scores	3.30	2.67	3.42	2.83

Source: "Increasing contributions by legitimizing paltry contributions: When even a penny helps," by R. B. Cialdini and D. A. Schroeder, *Journal of Personality and Social Psychology*, 1976, *34*, 599–604. Copyright 1976 by the American Psychological Association. Reprinted by permission.

In order to rule out this alternate possibility, another condition in the experiment (social legitimation) called for the solicitor to say, "We've already received some contributions ranging from a penny on up." The researchers hoped that this appeal would still provide social legitimation–potential donors could identify with other donors who gave small donations–but it would not imply that the organization was in dire need. The highest percentage of donors occurred for this treatment, which suggests that the "even a penny will help" plea is successful probably because it entailed legitimation–that is, it's o.k. to give a small amount–rather than created a feeling of a greater need for funds. Finally, a more direct check that the perceived need was equal for the control and "even a penny" conditions came from ratings subjects made on this dimension, as seen in Table 8–1.

Could other forms of pleas be as effective as the "even a penny will help" request? In a fourth condition, Cialdini and Schroeder had the solicitor add the phrase, "even a dollar will help" instead of using the minimal amount of a penny. Since this larger amount may be asking "too much" from some donors, they may not feel as much pressure to give and will not suffer as much threat to self-esteem in failing to match the $1.00 recommendation as they would if they could not match or exceed the 1¢ reference. The researchers predicted that the rate of donation for this condition would fall between that of the standard request control group and the "even-a-penny" group. The results upheld this prediction.

In this example, then, we can see that personal experience and observation is one source of ideas for experiments to test. A second point illustrated by this example is that by including several variations of appeals, Cialdini and Schroeder were able to obtain evidence that better supports their explanation because some of the alternative accounts are not supported. If yet other explanations are proposed, it will be necessary to design and conduct further experiments to obtain data that will help us choose among the competing explanations.

IDEAS STIMULATED BY OTHER RESEARCH

A second major source of ideas for research comes from already-published research as we pointed out at the end of Chapter 7. By reading the analyses and interpretations of results obtained by other investigators, we may become stimulated to think more about some topic. We may disagree with their interpretations; we may wonder what effect other variables might have; we may hold different theories or make different predictions; or we may believe that other techniques and measures are more suitable. In actual practice, investigators often use a combination of both natural observation and examination of published experiments to develop their ideas for subsequent studies. A few topics exist for which no past research of relevance is available. Even if no past research deals directly with a given topic, past research that deals with an analogous situation may exist. For example, suppose researchers discover a new incurable illness. With no past research on this specific illness, we might look for parallels from similar known illnesses in order to derive testable hypotheses about possibly effective treatments.

Similarly, in the case of charity appeals, one may not find much past research involving controlled experiments dealing with actual charitable organizations. However, numerous laboratory experiments have been conducted dealing with various forms of helping behavior such as giving directions, doing favors, aiding accident victims, and so forth. Although these specific situations do not involve monetary donations, some of the factors affecting these forms of helping and some of the theories about the process may offer testable hypotheses about the nature of charitable assistance and donations. Accordingly, the prospective researcher of charitable donations would search past research literature not only for this topic but also for research on other forms of helping behavior. We will discuss some of the resources and techniques for conducting such searches of past research in more detail shortly.

Returning to the question of how to find researchable questions, let us pursue the specific topic of charitable donations further. The characteristics of the format of the appeal was the factor emphasized by Cialdini and Schroeder (1976) in our example. We might ask ourselves what other aspects of the appeal itself might be important? Again, some ideas can be obtained by carefully analyzing the kinds of appeals actual charities have employed. For example, the appeal may contain implications about the donor ("You are a *good* person if you

TABLE 8–2. Selected Examples of Potential Variables Which Might Influence Level of Donations.

Setting:
- Home of Potential Donor
  - face-to-face
  - telephone
  - mail
  - radio, television
- Public place
- Place of Employment

Temporal:
- Time of day
- Day of Week
- Time of Month
- Month of Year

Donor Characteristics:
- Age
- Sex
- Ethnicity
- Socioeconomic Level
- Political Affiliation
- Religious Affiliation
- Intelligence
- Personality
- Mood

Type of Charitable Cause:
- Birth defects
- Accident victims
- Disease victims
- Disaster victims
- Political-social causes
- Religious causes

Beneficiary Characteristics:
- Age
- Sex
- Ethnicity
- Similarity with Donor

Solicitor Characteristics:
- Age
- Sex
- Ethnicity
- Attire
- Physical Attractiveness
- Friendliness
- Aggressiveness
- Persistence
- Number

donate), emphasize the beneficiary ("these people are needy and deserving"), arouse guilt and shame ("how can we let them suffer by not helping"), and so forth. Which of these types of appeals is more effective in eliciting donations? A controlled experiment might provide some worthwhile answers.

Other possible variables worth studying might include those listed in Table 8–2. You might try using these examples for "practice" to see what kinds of effects you would predict for some of these factors. What is your logic for such predictions?

IDEAS STIMULATED BY THEORIES

In analyzing a specific behavior, it is often useful to incorporate observations about other types of behavior. For example, numerous experiments have been conducted on modelling effects (e.g., Bandura and Walters, 1963; Mischel, 1966) which deal with the social learning and imitation achieved by observing the behaviors of other persons or models. In children, for example, modelling has been found to affect a wide variety of behaviors ranging from aggression to resisting temptation to acquiring internal standards or criteria for self-evaluation of one's level of performance.

If models can affect the behavior of observers in a variety of situations, perhaps similar effects exist in the specific case of charitable donations or more generally with respect to helping and altruistic behavior. We might make some natural observations or reflect upon past observations and personal experiences, and recall that people often make donations in group settings. Could this be a case of modelling so that when other donors set a "good example," observers also want to donate?

This type of evidence, however, is uncontrolled since many other unknown factors may be involved. The later donors may not be paying attention to the model's behaviors but may be acting independently based on personal motives. Or, if observers do not donate, they may have noticed the model's example, but could not afford to donate or had already donated "at the office." We would want to set up a controlled experiment, two randomly assigned groups of subjects, and expose only one group to models who donated. We might even add a third group with models who declined to donate when explicitly requested in full view of observers. Such a condition allows us to see if models can also have inhibitory or adverse effects on the donation tendencies of observers. Combined with the other two conditions, this experimental design contains a zero-control condition (the no-model group) which, as discussed in Chapter 3, allows us to determine if higher donations from the donating-model condition is mainly due to the positive influence of donors, the negative influence of nondonating models, or to a combination of both models. We would compare the donation levels of the two types of model conditions relative to the no-model condition.

TRANSLATING IDEAS INTO ACTUAL EXPERIMENTS

Suppose we decide to test the general observation that seeing a good example will increase positive behavior while observing a bad example will decrease it. How do we translate this somewhat abstract or general idea into specific concrete terms? What is the operational definition of "good example," "positive behavior," and so forth? What specific procedures enable observers to witness various modelled examples? In what setting or environment will the experiment be conducted? How many observers will be present at a given time? How will we measure "positive behavior" in objective and quantitative terms?

These and other practical questions must be answered when we decide to conduct an experiment. We need explicit and specific definitions and procedures that can be implemented, rather than vague or general propositions and hypotheses. Decisions about independent and dependent variables, as discussed in Chapter 2, must be faced in every experiment. The researcher must decide how many independent variables to use, as well as the number of levels of each. Similarly, the researcher decides how many dependent variables to measure as well as the specific ones to study.

A choice about the type of experimental design—between-subjects, within-subjects, factorial design, matched groups, and so on—is also involved. In the present example of comparing the influence of different types of models on donations, a within-subjects design may be inappropriate. Thus, it is not meaningful to test some subjects under a donating-model condition first, followed by a no-model condition, given the potential carryover effects as discussed in Chapter 5. If we decide to use a between-subjects design, what are the pros and cons of a matched-groups procedure for assigning subjects to treatment conditions?

An Example: The Effects of Type of Model on Donations

Let us assume that we make these decisions eventually and perform an experiment such as the charitable donations example, as diagrammed in Table 8–3. Suppose that the general pattern of the results shows higher percentages of the subjects donated when the models gave, followed next by the no-model condition, with the lowest percentage coming from the group with models who declined to donate when requested.

Rival Explanations

Does this evidence satisfy us that modelling is the process responsible for the outcome? Does an alternative explanation also fit these results? If so, the results are not conclusive and one must devise further experiments whose outcomes may help us choose among rival accounts.

TABLE 8–3. Outline of Hypothetical Experimental Design and Results of the Experiment Relating Type of Model and Donations.

Type of Model	Per cent of Observers Who Donate
Donates	Highest
No Model	Intermediate
Does not Donate	Lowest

In the present example, a critic of the modelling explanation might hold that conformity or yielding to group pressure is an alternative explanation for the findings. Since the requests for donations were made in a group setting, the donations of models and earlier donors may have exerted strong group pressure for conformity from those group members who had not donated yet. In the condition where models declined to donate, the group pressure was also present but in the opposite direction so that would-be donors may have felt inhibited.

Thus, we have a situation where two different processes may have been operative. Are the results due to modelling or to conformity or perhaps even to a combination of both factors? Our hypothetical experiment does not allow us to reach any clearcut decision.

Designing Further Experiments to Test Rival Hypotheses

At this point it is necessary to design an experiment that will enable us to determine whether modelling or conformity—or both—were operative. We have to think more critically about the nature of the two rival processes to aid us in choosing a situation or adding new independent variables that may yield more differentiable outcomes. We might argue, for example, that while both processes require the presence of others for the observer to identify or witness the appropriate or desired type of modelled behavior, the actual donation *by the observers* need not be made in the presence of others. Charitable donations are often given anonymously or as privately-made contributions. In contrast, conformity to group pressure by the observers may be strongest or limited to situations where public behavior is involved. After all, if no one knows the nature of a person's behavior, the pressure for conformity may be successfully avoided.

In the light of this reasoning, we might introduce this public-private factor as a second independent variable in a new experiment in the same type of situation used in our example above. However, instead of having everyone being asked for public donations, as shown in Tables 8–4A, 4B and 4C, we allow half of the subjects in each of the three model conditions the opportunity to respond with private or anonymous donations. If modelling is the primary influence, the donations should be roughly the same for public and private conditions, as shown in Table 8–4A. On the other hand, if conformity is the primary cause, private donations should be smaller; furthermore, we may find no difference in the superiority of the public condition due to the type of model condition if conformity pressure is the only influence, as depicted in Table 8–4B.

Conceivably, *both* factors could work together or combine in their influence on donations so that donating models combined with public conditions yield the highest tendency for donations, as suggested in

TABLE 8–4. Percentage of Subjects in Each Condition Who Donated.

	Modelling Condition A		
	Model Donates	*No Model*	*Model Does Not Donate*
Group Pressure			
High (Public)	15	5	1
Low (Private)	15	5	1
	Modelling Condition B		
	Model Donates	*No Model*	*Model Does Not Donate*
Group Pressure			
High (Public)	15	15	15
Low (Private)	5	5	5
	Modelling Condition C		
	Model Donates	*No Model*	*Model Does Not Donate*
Group Pressure			
High (Public)	20	10	1
Low (Private)	10	7	4

Table 8–4C. The absence of any model along with private conditions for giving combines to produce a relatively low level of donation, 7 per cent. When at least one of the factors assumed to promote giving, either a donating model or public condition for giving, an intermediate level of 10 per cent make donations.

Table 8–4C also illustrates the possible influence of the reluctant model who fails to give. The adverse effect of this model on donations is likely to be more potent under public conditions than private circumstances where the observer may more easily ignore the modelled behavior. The results depicted in Table 8–4C represent an interaction among the two independent variables, the type of model, and the type of conditions for making the donation.

Let us review the reasoning process thus far. We began with a hypothesis based on naturalistic observation about the possible influence of modelling on charitable donations. A controlled experiment was designed to test our predictions. However, the results supported not only the modelling hypothesis but could have also been due to the influence of the social pressures of being asked to donate in the presence of others. It was suggested that additional experiments must be designed which can hopefully provide results to support one explanation while refuting rival accounts.

A factorial design added the independent variable of private vs. public conditions for making donations to our first independent variable, type of model. We reasoned that if modelling was the only or major factor that affected donations, the private vs. public condition variable should show similar results for each of the three modelling conditions. In contrast, if only the factor of the type of conditions for donating was crucial, the type of model should not affect results. Finally, it was suggested that an interactive relationship might be involved, so that the magnitude of the model effect would be greater under public than for private conditions. The model would still affect donations, as predicted by the modelling hypothesis, but its influence would vary depending on whether public or private conditions were involved.

By performing the proposed factorial experiment and comparing the obtained results with the hypothetical ones outlined above, we would draw conclusions as to which explanation was more consistent with the actual results. In practice the results are usually not as clearcut as those given in our hypothetical example, so the actual decisions about interpretations are also less definitive and conclusive. The example, then, provides a guide for understanding the basic aspects of the research process rather than a universal standard for all research.

LITERATURE SEARCHES

Regardless of the specific problem we wish to research, we want to know what research others have done so that we can benefit from their findings and learn about some of the difficulties they may have encountered. Furthermore, by searching the published literature on a topic, we can avoid needless duplication of efforts.

How do we most efficiently and thoroughly find out about previous research? We obviously do not want to search randomly through the vast "haystack" of information contained in the scores of psychological journals. Fortunately, several reference publications exist which compile indices of past experiments according to subject matter and by author for numerous journals for each month. If we know either the subject matter or the author, we should be able to search these indices for any given years to locate the title, reference citation giving the name of the journal of publication as well as the volume number and page numbers, and a brief 100–200 word abstract of the research. The abstract summarizes the distinctive features of the study such as the issues, methods, independent and dependent variables, major findings, and implications so that we can usually discern whether or not that article is relevant to our purposes. If it is, we can consult the full report of the original article for additional details.

The American Psychological Association publishes the journal, *Psychological Abstracts*, which provides such abstracts for all articles published each month in nearly 1,000 different psychological journals.

One of the biggest problems, especially for someone unfamiliar with psychological terms and jargon, is discovering the proper entry words for locating the relevant research. Colloquial terms like "hitting" might be indexed under *aggression* or even *agonistic behavior*, "doing a favor" might be catalogued under *altruism*, while "patience" is encoded as *frustration tolerance*. Esoteric terms such as *massed practice*, retroactive inhibition, *or locus of control* may be unfamiliar to the novice. Other terms may have different meanings for psychologists and laypersons, such as *intrinsic motivation*, *fear of success*, or *arousal*. Consequentially, it may often prove frustrating to try to locate relevant research without knowing the proper labels that pertain to specific concepts, a situation similar to going to the hardware store to buy a thingamajig or what-you-ma-call-it!

One valuable resource for locating possible entry terms is the *Thesaurus* of *Psychological Terms Index*, which is published by the American Psychological Association and should be in your college or university library. A revised edition is due in 1982. A scan of this reference book may help you find terms you want, but you must always try them out to see if they work or you will be dependent on the assistance of persons with more background in psychology or must wait until your own familiarity with the terms used by psychologists increases.

Once you decide on the appropriate labels to search for, you can start with recent issues of *Psychological Abstracts* and look them up in the subject index of each monthly issue or in the semi-annual cumulative indices which cover the issues of either the first or second half of each year. Some temporal lag between the actual publication date and the time when a given article is included in the *Psychological Abstracts* exists, but the gap is now usually only a few months.

Unless you are interested only in a specific year's research or in some previous interval, such as 1940–1950, it is best to start with the most recent issues and work backward in time as far back as you find it necessary to go. You will most often focus on the subject indices unless you have some special interest in the work of a particular investigator highly prolific in an area of research. As you compile your list of past research, check the references cited in each article.

A more recently developed reference resource is the *Social Science Citation Index*, which is actually not one, but three interrelated indices. The *Permuterm Subject Index* involves a thesaurus of possible terms under which references may be indexed. This list of terms is derived by taking all important words from the titles of articles and then generating all pairwise permutations or combinations of these keywords. A detailed example based on a single article is shown in Table 8–5. As may be noted, each significant term in the title is listed alphabetically as a "primary term" with each of the other title terms listed as "co-terms" in alphabetical order. Thus, each term gets its turn to be listed as primary while the others are its co-terms. Some of the permutations from some titles may be meaningless or confusing, but at least all of the useful terms should be represented somewhere in the index.

Suppose you are researching children's learning. The Permuterm index shows an entry "children" and one of its co-term listings is "learning." This entry sounds like what you are looking for, and under the term you will find a list of author names taken directly from the original articles whose titles include the words, "children" and "learning" as shown in the top half of Table 8–6. Now your task is to refer to the *Source Index* and look up each author in your list. The bottom half of Table 8–6 gives an example showing that this index will provide you with the title of the article, the name of the journal that published it, and the data of publication, volume number, and starting page of the article, as well as a list of references to other articles cited by the author. You must then find the original article in the journal in which it was published to see if it fits your interests.

The third index, the *Citation Index*, focuses on providing lists of *other* articles that refer to or cite a specific article in their list of references. Thus, if Smith published a paper in 1975, we can check any subsequent year's citation index to see which later articles cited the Smith article. Why would we want this information? Assuming that important articles are cited more often than less important or influential articles, we can see that this index may conveniently give us a rough estimate of the significance or impact of a specific study. On the other hand, infrequently cited papers are not necessarily of poor quality or unimportant. For example, some research may be "ahead of its time," and be unrecognized by other researchers at that time in history. Nor should we automatically assume that every article frequently cited by others is a "good" article. To the contrary, a controversial study or a poor one used as an example of previous erroneous thinking will also receive a high number of citations. Generally, however, frequently cited articles are influential.

Perhaps most importantly, the Citation Index helps us update information on a topic of interest to us. If our experiment is related to Smith's 1975 article, we would like to consult all subsequent articles that cited Smith because it is highly likely that most of these articles deal with the same research question or topic. The best way to determine the relevance of these articles to your goals is to read the original articles themselves.

TABLE 8–5. The Concept of the Permuterm® Subject Index. The name "Permuterm" is a contraction of the phrase "permuted terms." Here "permute" is used in its correct mathematical sense. In the Permuterm Subject In Index, Permuterm indexing involves the permutation of all significant words within each sentence of the title and subtitle of an article to form all possible pairs of terms. Thus in the article by T. S. Hyde, *Journal of Experimental Psychology* 97:111, 1973, entitled "Differential Effects of Effort and Type of Orienting Task on Recall and Organization of Highly Associated Words," the Permuterm technique results in the following index entries:

Primary Term	Co-Term
Associated	See Stop Lists
Differential	Associated
	Effects
	Effort
	Highly
	Organization
	Orienting
	Recall
	Task
	Type
	Words
Effects	See Stop Lists
Effort	See Stop Lists
Highly	Associated
	Differential
	Effects
	Effort
	Organization
	Orienting
	Recall
	Task
	Type
	Words
Organization	Associated
	Differential
	Effects
	Effort
	Highly
	Orienting
	Recall
	Task
	Type
	Words
Orienting	Associated
	Differential
	Effects
	Effort
	Highly
	Organization
	Recall
	Task
	Type
	Words
Recall	Associated
	Differential
	Effects
	Effort
	Highly
	Organization
	Orienting
	Task
	Type
	Words
Task	Associated
	Differential
	Effects
	Effort
	Highly
	Organization
	Orienting
	Recall
	Type
	Words
Type	See Stop Lists
Words	Associated
	Differential
	Effects
	Effort
	Highly
	Organization
	Orienting
	Recall
	Task
	Type

No entries are created for the words "OF", "AND", "ON". These illustrate "full stop" words and are not indexed. The words "EFFECTS", "EFFORT" and "TYPE" illustrate "semi-stop" terms. Semi-stop words are suppressed as Primary Terms but do appear as Co-Terms. Hyphenated words or phrases are treated as one term. A list of full, semi-, and paired word stops appears in this issue of the *Social Sciences Citation Index*.

Reprinted by permission of the Institute for Scientific Information.

After you practice using these reference materials, you will find them much easier to work with and understand. Most reference librarians can also assist you in first using these materials. Since the print is generally small, you might want to use a magnifying glass.

Retrieving information is a slow, tedious, and often frustrating process, so come to the library prepared for a long session. However, if you

TABLE 8–6. An Example of Listings in the Permuterm Subject Index and Source Index.

Search Technique:
Select **Children/Learning** as the pair of terms with which to begin the search (**Boys/Learning**, **Girls/Learning**, and **Adolescent/Learning** are other possibilities). This entry is located in the **Permuterm® Subject Index** section of the **Social Sciences Citation Index** .

Children (cont)		
Leadership		HARDY RC
Learn	►	PRISUTA RH+
Learned		BERNSTEI.IL
Learning	►	AUGUST GJ
		BRYAN TH
		CARLSON JS
	►	CARTELLI LM
	►	DANIELSO LC
	►	EBERLE G
		FINCHAM F
		FULLER PW
		HALLAHAN DP
		LUKEMAN D+
	►	MACARTNE.F +
		MAGEE PA
		MEGEE PA
	►	MCLOUGHL.JA
		MOLNAR ET
		BK# 20366
		SHAYWITZ SE
		SHEARE JB
		SHURE MB+
		VANCE H+
	►	YSSELDYK.JE
		ZINGALE SA

This entry indicates that during the period indexed, 21 authors have used the words **Children** and **Learning** in the titles of their works.

At this point the searcher notes the names of the authors located and turns to the **Source Index** section of *SSCI* to get full descriptions of the articles. The searcher finds full bibliographic information on book number 20366 in the **List of Books Covered**.

TABLE 8-6. (continued)

Search Results:
Looking up the name of each author in the **Source Index** leads to entries such as the following:

August GJ
Rychlak JF–Role of Intelligence and Task.
Difficulty in Affective Learning Styles of Children with High and Low Self-Concepts
J Educ Psyc *70(3) 406-13* *78* *10R*
Penn State Univ. Dept Psychol., Sharon, PA 16146, USA

Abramson Y	69 J Exptl Research Per	4	65
August GJ	75 J Educ Psychol	67	801
	77	69	253
Cermak LS	72 J Exp Child Psychol	13	210
Divesta FJ	66 J Verb Learn Verb Be	5	249
	69 J Expt Psychology	80	498
Johnson RC	61 Can J Psychol	15	199
Kajl RV	74 Exp Child Psychol	18	426
Marceil JC	75 Hesis Purdue U		
Osgood CE	57 Measurement Meaning		

can afford it, some computer retrieval systems can do all of the dirty work for you. For example, the American Psychological Association will provide an information search through a service called PASAR (Psychological Abstract Search Automatic Retrieval). If you can provide a brief description of the topic area by giving key or main terms dealing with the phenomenon of interest and the kinds of independent variables important to you, a search will be made for a fee through a data base which includes all of the items listed in the *Psychological Abstracts* since 1967. A complete listing of references will be sent to you, but you should realize that aside from the cost (varies with size of topic), the lists may be incomplete or inadequate for your needs if you have used a poor choice of key words for the search. Unless you can afford the expense, try conducting your own slow and painful searches so that you can learn more about the organization of the reference resources.

HOW TO READ A RESEARCH REPORT

A journal article is a technical account of a research project and involves a writing style and objective different from many other materials. Complex concepts, detailed descriptions, and technical procedures are conveyed in objective but often somewhat dry prose. You cannot approach the reading of a journal report with the same techniques that you would use to read a newspaper or a novel.

While no single, best method of reading a journal article exists, partly because the reasons why one reads a journal article vary, some general suggestions may be useful. First, do not try to read and comprehend an article fully from the first reading. During this first reading, you need not always read the article in the exact sequence in which it was written. On successive readings, you may find it worthwhile to focus on different parts of the article and even omit re-reading parts that are either irrelevant to your needs or are already well understood by you.

In general, a good approach involves carefully studying the brief abstract which precedes most journal articles or the article's summary. Abstracts are more prevalent in journals published by the American Psychological Association for the past 15 years or so; prior to that, summaries usually concluded articles. In either case, these capsule descriptions save time and give you an overview which may help structure your attention when you read the more detailed body of the full report. By giving you a brief description of the scope of the problem studied in the research, the general methods and design of the experiment, and the overall findings and conclusion, the abstract or summary enables you to skip irrelevant articles you might mistakenly have judged relevant by their titles. Even abstracts may be misleading, however, and you may decide after reading the entire article that it is not useful for your own research. Most of the time, however, the abstract will prove helpful.

The first major section, the *Introduction*, offers you an account of the major purposes of the research, a description of the background issues and past research leading up to the present research, an explanation and logical justification for the experiment reported in the article, along with hypotheses and predictions in many, but not all, reports. If at this point in your reading you are still interested, you might continue to the second major section called *Method*, especially if you plan to do your own experiment in this area. On the other hand, if you are primarily reading the study to learn what the author learned, you might want to skip ahead to the *Discussion* section which presents an analysis and evaluation of the findings of the research.

The *Method* section is highly detailed, descriptive information about the number and type of subjects, the design of the experiment, the step-by-step procedures, the nature of the stimulus materials, description of apparatus, definition of major terms, and other information especially vital for a reader who wishes to do a similar study or merely wants to make a thorough evaluation of the appropriateness of the procedures of the study. Sometimes, readers will skim this section initially but later return to it, searching for possible flaws in the design or factors that might invalidate the experiment. Another approach might actually be to read the *Method* section *before* reading the *Introduction*. The *Method* section is concrete and specific whereas the *Introduction* is usually more abstract and sometimes too general for the reader to fully grasp what the experiment actually involves.

The *Results* section, which follows the *Method* section, is the empirical bread-and-butter of the experiment, the basic evidence or facts we wish to examine in relationship to the hypotheses of the experiment. Statistical evaluations of the significance of the results are also reported as well as the actual means, correlations, or percentages, and so on, that summarize the performance of groups receiving different treatments. In complex experiments with numerous independent variables or several dependent variables, the presentation of results can be difficult to follow. One can get bogged down in a sea of data; thus it is sometimes useful to skip ahead to the *Discussion* section which follows the *Results* and presents an interpretation of the major findings. A well-written report involves a carefully orchestrated argument, not at all unlike the train of thought employed by a skilled debater or salesperson. Unfortunately, data can not "speak for themselves" and their importance may be overlooked unless the author takes pains to call the readers' attention to the implications of various aspects of the findings. Explicit statements about the relationship of the results to the hypotheses of the experiment are needed so that the reader learns how the author interprets the findings. Of course, not everyone will necessarily agree with the author's interpretation of the results, but at least the initiative for such persuasion rests with the author. After the reader hears the case made by the author, it is the reader's prerogative to cross-examine the author, in a sense, by going back over the report and assessing the validity of different aspects of the study such as predictions, design, operational definitions, analysis of results, and so forth.

Most often numerous experiments pertain to a specific topic. As we read a given article, we may begin to compare it with other experiments. Sometimes the strain on memory can be rather great so that one ends up reading a given part, say the *Method* section, of several different articles concurrently to facilitate comparison. It is helpful to skim each article in its entirety and then go back and reread parts of each of them again to answer questions that may come to mind based on such interarticle comparisons. As similarities and differences among the various articles are detected, you may start to form your own integration of the total set of evidence. Always remember that the earlier publications did not have the benefit of the knowledge obtained in later articles; consequently their reasoning and interpretations may have made sense at the time they were written, but are no longer as valid as a synthesis formulated by someone like yourself who has the later as well as the earlier findings to examine as a total set.

While you may be able to fit most of the findings from the set of studies into a logical explanation, invariably some data just won't "fit." This situation may reflect the fact that your theory is wrong or, on the other hand, that some flaws may exist in the design and execution of these experiments. As you reread the article for what may seem like the tenth or fifteenth time, you may be trying to check on procedural details or aspects of the results you did not consider important during some of your earlier readings. In short, you must reexamine articles to evaluate your own thinking about the total pattern of results from a set of different experiments on the same phenomenon. Do not think that after you have read an article once you will have been able to extract all of the information you need from it.

You can expedite your task in the long run if you learn to take notes about each article as you read it, preferably on large index cards. Be sure to include the journal citation and the journal name, volume number, and inclusive pages as well as the names of the authors and the title of the article for future use when you need to locate and reread the article.

One outcome of this critical rereading is the development of your own hypotheses and explanations about the processes that may be involved. By comparing different articles, you begin to suspect that certain factors not examined in past articles may be important determinants of the behavior. You may discover that you want to redesign some of the studies and repeat them under varying circumstances to see how the outcomes might be altered. In short, active comparison of a body of studies can be a powerful source of ideas for additional research.

As you examine the set of research articles on a given topic, you are a judge who weighs evidence and evaluates the persuasiveness of the arguments provided by the authors. When different studies conflict, you must be careful to be objective and use the same degree of rigor and the same types of standards to evaluate them. There is a dangerous tendency, even among trained researchers, to be less critical of evidence one happens to concur with while being more skeptical about findings that are at odds with one's expectations and assumptions.

ACTUAL CONDUCT OF YOUR OWN EXPERIMENT

Sooner or later you will finally get the go-ahead signal and feel that you have adequately surveyed past research and prepared a worthwhile proposal for an original experiment. You have a hypothesis, space to test the subjects, adequate materials and equipment, and you are ready and anxious to get rolling!

At this stage, it is useful to run a few practice subjects through the steps of your study to iron out rough spots in your research procedures. You are apt to be a bit nervous and until you have practiced, you may botch up the testing of the first few subjects. Try going through the entire procedure from reading the instructions, administering the procedures, recording data, and so forth. Interview your practice subjects for their reactions and suggestions for improving the operation.

Experienced researchers have numerous anecdotes of unexpected surprises that confront them during the conduct of research, ranging from equipment failure to uncooperative subjects to accidental testing of the wrong persons due to honest mistakes. Be ready for almost anything and try to stay calm since most problems get resolved satisfactorily.

The old axiom about "if something can go wrong, it will go wrong," is certainly true for research. Try to anticipate problems and you may prevent them. For example, when you recruit subjects you may find that a fair number fail to showup on time and/or at the right place. You may find it worthwhile to give them a written reminder, such as mailing them a postcard or phoning them just prior to the scheduled date.

After you complete the running of several subjects in each treatment condition, you may feel a strong urge to check on the preliminary results. As we will note in Chapter 13, this feedback can be dangerous in that it may bias our experiment if it leads the investigator to alter his or her behavior unevenly over the different treatment conditions. Perhaps this problem is absent or reduced if the investigator has data collectors as assistants and does not get directly involved in the testing of subjects. On the other hand, it could be argued that in some experiments where the investigator is not really sure what to expect, it may be fruitful to examine early returns and treat the experiment as a pilot or exploratory study. If the original predictions seem to be totally wrong, the experiment may be abandoned or revised, which saves countless hours of fruitless work. If the early data returns seem to support predictions, the research is allowed to continue. One danger of this selectivity is that the vast majority of completed experiments are those that successfully confirm predictions, an outcome that may lead us and others to mistakenly assume we have a very high batting average with our ability to predict outcomes. We somehow quietly and conveniently overlook all of the aborted studies that were dropped near the outset due to unpromising early data.

If the term "pilot study" is to avoid becoming a euphemism for biased research, perhaps the investigator should make a decision *at the outset* that a specified small number of subjects will be tested, and after their results are examined, this data will be discarded regardless of whether it is positive, neutral, or negative. In this manner, these studies will truly be pilot or exploratory rather than potential sources of biased research.

The vast majority of experiments do not involve potential physical or mental stress or harm to the research participants. It is often difficult, however, for the investigator to be the most impartial judge. Ethical considerations, discussed extensively in a later chapter, must be faced by every responsible researcher. The ultimate responsibility of ethics rests with the individual researcher, regardless of the opinions of other consultants. Ethical matters are complex and often the answers are not clearcut. It is useful to discuss your experiment from an ethical standpoint not only with your peers and instructors, but also with the subjects themselves either after the experiment or with practice subjects.

After the test session is completed for an individual subject, you may find it useful to interview the subject about her or his perceptions of the experimental task. This feedback can be educational for you, and can sometimes lead to important revisions and improvements. Verbal reporting, however, is fallible and you may have to exercise care in assessing the accuracy of some of the information you receive.

The postexperimental interview also provides some educational feedback for the subjects. You can tell them about the general purpose and predictions of the study. If deception was employed, you may provide corrective information at this time and ask them to pledge not to discuss the procedures with other persons who might be future participants.

WRITING YOUR OWN REPORTS

After you design, perform, and interpret your own experiment, your task becomes one of communicating to other interested parties the nature of your research problem, methods, and findings. During your search of published articles related to your own experiment, you undoubtedly will have learned a lot about the format and style of articles in psychological journals. We will provide a brief overview of the basic ingredients of a typical report of a psychological experiment, but note that each individual article you read may vary somewhat from this model due to special aspects unique to different research.

Abstract. This section appears at the beginning of published articles, but it is not necessarily the first part to be written. As we already noted in discussing how to read articles, the goal of the abstract is brevity, clarity, but also completeness. Details are avoided, but the reader wants to learn about the purpose, hypothesis, general method or design, independent and dependent variables, major findings and conclusions.

Introduction. A presentation of the background issues and previous findings that have led up to the present research reported in the paper is the goal of this section. Development of the reasoning behind the hypotheses and predictions is provided so that the reader can evaluate the validity of your thinking. As you write this section which is not labelled, by the way, ask yourself if your presentation of past work is sufficient in detail and completeness to make the reader aware of the significance or contribution of your own experiment. You do not need to cite every study that you can locate on a given topic; often it is adequate to cite representative examples. Specification of the general outline of your experiment, identification of the independent and dependent variables, and description of the tasks and materials, if any, are sometimes included in this section.

Method. This section includes a number of subheadings in which you report the important procedural details so that the reader could repeat your study, if desired, with reasonable faithfulness by following your report.

Identify the number and source of subjects. Report recruitment techniques and methods for assignment of subjects to treatment conditions. In some cases, other characteristics may be worth reporting, such as the age, ethnicity, or education level, depending somewhat on the type of research problem. If the experiment deals with auditory discrimination, it is relevant to report whether the subjects were of normal or impaired hearing, but this information may be irrelevant for some experiment on taste judgments.

A description of any equipment, test materials, or apparatus, especially if it is unique or especially devised for your study rather than a standard piece of commercially-available equipment, should be given. You should also describe the characteristics of any stimulus materials, such as word lists, pictures, auditory signals, anagrams, psychological tests and scales, and so on, presented to subjects in the study.

If verbal instructions are used, it is sometimes sufficient to describe their general nature, but often it is desirable to provide a verbatim transcript, especially if the independent variable involves some variation in the wording of instructions for different treatments. The reader may wish to evaluate your instructions for possible ambiguity or miswording of critical aspects of the instructions.

Design. Although the design of many experiments is fairly simple—such as a two-group, experimental vs. control group design—some experiments involve more complex designs that should be more fully described.

Procedure. This section provides the reader with a description of the different phases or steps in the sequence of events subjects might encounter in the different treatment conditions. Usually this description follows a chronological order, which helps the reader envision the perspective of a subject in the experiment. The duration of each phase as well as the time between different phases is important to report so that the reader knows how long the total experiment runs for a given subject.

A description of the setting is often useful. For some types of experiments, it may be critical to know details, such as size of the test room, physical location of the room, contents of the room, or even the presence or absence of windows. The writer must use reasonable judgment in deciding what information is relevant, depending on the nature of the topic under investigation.

Results. After the experiment is completed, what empirical facts were obtained? The reader wants to examine the evidence but needs your guidance in this section. Do not present the "raw" data or results of individual subjects except in special cases. The use of summary indices such as means, standard deviations, percentages, and total frequencies for different treatment conditions is generally preferred.

This information is usually displayed in tables or graphs (referred to as "figures" in journal articles), especially if the information is difficult to follow because of complex relationships or large quantities. Common errors include the tendency of students to provide both a table and a figure for presentation of exactly the same data. Use one form, but not both, although you might try both formats out initially so that you can choose the clearest one. Be sure to provide clear and complete labels and titles for your tables and for both the horizontal and vertical dimensions of your figures as well as the curves showing results for different treatments.

Student reports often fail to provide any descriptive accounts of the information in their visual displays. While readers may be able to extract the information on their own, it is desirable for the writer to call attention to key features of the pattern of results, in case some readers fail to notice them. The authors needs to point out which aspects of the data are important and not assume that the reader knows.

The results of statistical tests of significance used to evaluate treatment effects should also be provided in this section. Provide the names of the statistical tests used, but do not include actual formulas or computations.

Discussion. The line between the *Results* and *Discussion* sections is often narrow, and some journals combine them. Strictly speaking, the *Results* section is descriptive reporting of the facts while the *Discussion* section is an interpretation of such facts in relation to the predictions of the study. The reader learns how the researcher draws conclusions about the soundness or weakness of the evidence from the experiment in support of the original hypothesis.

Secondly, this section allows the greatest opportunity for speculation, second-guessing, and synthesis. If results were not positive or confirmatory, the author may offer plausible guesses as to what went wrong and how these problems might be remedied. The author may also show the significance of the findings for this topic of study as well as for any other areas where they may be applicable. Some degree of speculation or analysis of the underlying processes or mechanisms responsible for the results may also be appropriate.

References. Finally, *References* consist of a listing of relevant past articles cited in a study. Names of authors, titles of articles, and full citation of the location of the article are listed in alphabetical order.

Writing laboratory reports is not an easy assignment for most students. You can not expect to do it successfully in one last-minute draft, but you should expect to write several preliminary versions since you will find it necessary to revise as you go along. It may help to make an outline first to provide some structure to the overall report. It is also helpful to start early, well before your report is due, so that you can allow adequate time for revisions. If you can find another student, especially one who is familar with principles of psychological research but who does not know anything about your specific experiment, you will benefit if you can get this student's reactions and questions to a draft of your report. When we are familiar with a topic, we tend to write about it in a manner that may be perfectly clear to us, but may be incomplete and confusing to those unfamiliar with it. This type of egocentric thought is often evident in *Introduction* sections of reports where the logic and rationale for conducting the experiment is weakly developed for the reader. Similarly, in the *Method* section, the author fails to provide critical procedural information assumed to be obvious because the author performed the experiment. From the reader's perspective, however, the procedures are either illogical or, worse yet, may be misinterpreted because the reader fills in the missing gaps with different assumptions about the actual procedures.

Again, when reading journal articles for background information, you should also direct some attention to the format and style of technical writing. You may better understand some of the general comments offered above by examining specific journal articles. As you read articles published in journals of the American Psychological Association, you should take note of details about form such as the citation of references in the text of articles as well as the proper form for listing them at the end of the article. For a complete description of these details you must consult the *Publication Manual* of the American Psychological Association which your library or bookstore probably has. We have not focused on these matters of form, preferring to emphasize issues related to the content and substance of your reports. The format of reports differs somewhat in psychological journals published by different organizations; in fact, even the guidelines of the American Psychological Association itself change from time to time. Thus, the term "subjects" was formerly represented in the abbreviated form "*S*s" but must now be fully spelled out. A similar change took place for the titles of journals in reference lists so that abbreviations are no longer acceptable. Obviously, these conventions are arbitrary procedures and subject to change in the future, so we have provided no details on this topic here. Consult the Publication Manual or recent issues of American Psychological Association journals as well as your instructor for details of acceptable format for your reports.

Finally, a word about titles of research reports. Although the title appears at the top of the first page along with the name of author(s) and their professional affiliations, it is sometimes the last item of a report the author prepares. Titles, of necessity, must be brief due to space limitations, thus it is a real challenge for authors to come up with a clear, yet complete and informative, title. As you can realize, poor titles can make resources such as the Social Science Citation Indices into inaccurate retrieval systems. The majority of titles take the form of "The effects of X on Y" or a variant format, "Y as a function of X", where X is the independent variable and Y is the dependent variable.

When several independent as well as more than one dependent variable are involved, it is almost impossible to provide a comprehensive title. In recent years, many titles have grown in length partly to accommodate the penchant of authors to be poetic or witty by including metaphors or proverbs as part of their titles, for example, the "Pygmalion effect," "basking in reflected glory," "a lady in distress," or "does the trigger pull the finger?" Sometimes these literary touches are helpful as well as fun, but first be sure that your title, whether it is dull or cute, is an accurate and informative cue for the reader.

SUMMARY

A variety of sources for ideas for original experiments exist. Careful observation of naturalistic or uncontrolled events and behavior in the real world may provide you with hypotheses about the factors influencing certain behaviors. The example of charitable donations illustrated the way in which questions about a specific phenomenon can be raised that could be subjected to experimental evaluation.

The reading and evaluation of reports on completed experiments is another valuable source of stimulation for further research. One can identify discrepancies in the research literature as well as areas that have not been fully explored as one becomes acquainted with existing research.

As we try to formulate explanations about phenomena we want to understand, we sometimes find that findings and theories dealing with other behavior may hold parallels and similarities with the behavior we are investigating. Predictions can be derived from theories which can be tested with new experiments.

Regardless of the source of the ideas, they must eventually be translated into concrete terms and procedures before we can actually conduct experimental tests of our predictions. Decisions and choices must be made about the kinds and numbers of variables to include, the type of experimental design, and so forth.

The results of an experiment, even when they support our hypotheses, may sometimes also be consistent with rival explanations. Then we try to design further experiments and add other independent variables we hope will enable us to obtain results that more clearly support one of the alternative explanations.

In order to spare ourselves from wasted duplication of past research and to learn from the mistakes as well as the experience of others, we must engage in thorough searches of previous, related research. Descriptions of the major bibliographic indices of published psychological research were provided along with suggestions for efficient utilization of these resources.

Journal articles are highly technical and often difficult to read, especially for novices. Advice was given about some useful strategies for reading this type of material.

A number of the practical aspects of the actual conduct of your own experiments was described. The use of preliminary or practice subjects was recommended as a procedure for debugging the experiment as well as desensitizing the student experimenter to the anxiety and tension that may be involved when actually running an experiment for the first time. Unexpected problems invariably arise when conducting research, and one has to learn to stay calm, do the best one can, and eventually learn to anticipate problems so that they can be minimized.

Your final task as an experimenter is to communicate to others the nature of your research problem, your design and method, the results of the experiment, and your interpretation of the implications of the findings. The laboratory report is a written account of your experiment, which is modelled after the style and format of published journal articles. The major sections of such reports were described and suggestions were offered about some of the important aspects of report writing.

REFERENCES

American Psychological Association, *Publication manual of the American Psychological Association* (2nd ed.). Washington, D.C.: Author, 1974.

Bandura, A., and Walters, R. H. *Social learning and personality development.* New York: Holt, Rinehart, and Winston, 1963.

Berkowitz, L., and Daniels, L. Responsibility and dependency. *Journal of Abnormal and Social Psychology*, 1963, *65*, 429-436.

Cialdini, R. B. Full-cycle social psychology. In L. Bickman (Ed.) *Applied social psychology annual.* (Vol. 1) Beverly Hills: Sage, 1980.

Cialdini, R. B., and Schroeder, D. A. Increasing contributions by legitimizing paltry contributions: When even a penny helps. *Journal of Personality and Social Psychology*, 1976, *34*, 599-604.

Mischel, W. Theory and research on the antecedents of self-imposed delay of reward. In B. A Maher (Ed.), *Progress in experimental personality research.* (Vol. 3). New York: Academic Press, 1966.

LEARNING ACTIVITIES

1. Using the example about possible variables that could be examined in experiments on charitable donations, prepare a similar list for experimentation on one of the following: how to sell used cars, how to enlist votes for a political candidate, or how to get drivers to conserve gasoline.
2. Examine several recent issues of the journal, *Psychological Bulletin*, in your library and locate several review articles that summarize and evaluate the present state of research knowledge on some specific topic such as conformity, short-term memory, or migraine headaches. Study the organization of the articles to see how the authors group the various studies on that topic. Try to apply a similar structure to guide you in discovering ideas for research on topics of interest to you.

   (*Using the reference section of your library, determine the answers to activities 3-9 below.*)
3. How many articles were published in 1978 on sex education, metamemory, or the hippocampus?
4. Has the amount of research in the area of sports psychology changed over the past five years?
5. How many articles did Tom Trabasso publish in 1974 and 1975?
6. How often was the article, "Chronic fear produced by unpredictable electric shock" by M. E. P. Seligman published in the *Journal of Comparative and Physiological Psychology*, 1968, *66*, 402-411, cited by other authors in 1973? In 1979; What importance do you attach to this difference, if any?

7. How often was any of the work of Richard L. Solomon cited by others in 1980, and which single article was often most cited?
8. A study dealing with internal and external locus of control was published by Julian B. Rotter in 1966. Can you determine the title, journal, and complete citation?
9. Were there any articles on experimenter bias published in 1975?

PART II

THE EXPERIMENTER'S DILEMMA

CHAPTER 9

What Is the Experimenter's Dilemma?

Chapter at a Glance

In the first part of this book, we have seen that the experiment is the method highly regarded by psychological researchers as a means of providing analytical precision in determining causal relationships. Nonetheless, some serious shortcomings and limitations associated with the experimental method raise concerns about its central role in psychological research. Part 2 of this book primarily examines these issues concerning the usefulness of the experimental method. Most, but not all, of these issues pertain to research involving human participants.

Unlike the naturalistic observations described earlier in which we observe behavior as it ordinarily occurs in everyday life, the experimental situation is quite different. It is an artificial and contrived situation in which experimenters try to compare at least two groups assumed equivalent on the average in all respects except on the treatment or independent variable.

You should recall from Part 1 of this book that if differences in some aspects of the behavior of the two groups develop, one can reasonably assume that the different types of treatment received in the experiment contributed substantially to these differences. The alternative explanation that the two groups may have already been different cannot be seriously entertained since efforts were made at the outset to ensure that the groups were equivalent prior to their different experimental treatment.

Despite these advantages of the experimental method, it also involves a number of problems, particularly when it is used to study many important aspects of human behavior, which although not readily apparent, seriously jeopardize, detract from, or reduce the usefulness of this method. We are now ready to begin a thorough discussion of these problems which pose as obstacles and create what we will call "The Experimenter's Dilemma." This dilemma, or actually set of dilemmas, faced by the researcher seeking knowledge about human behavior, consists of a number of difficult choices that must be made during the process of experimentation. At this point, it might be useful to briefly preview some of these problem areas.

THE REACTIVE NATURE OF EXPERIMENTATION

Subjects are generally aware that they are being experimented upon and, being human, may modify their "normal" behavior to conform to the "role of subject." Some may try to please experimenters by trying to do what they think is wanted; others may behave in ways they think will make themselves "look good"; finally, some will try to confound and frustrate experimenters, either to just be "ornery" or to prevent themselves from feeling manipulated. They may detect cues in the situation that act as "demand characteristics" to influence their behavior so as to match their perception of what behavior is appropriate. One could try to solve these problems by observing subjects in natural rather than laboratory settings so that they would be less aware that they were under observation. However, the more natural the situation, the less is control attainable.

THE GENERALIZABILITY OF EXPERIMENTAL FINDINGS

The human subjects in most experiments are not a random sample of the population. The validity or generalizability of results can be affected by the selection method if it favors the inclusion of certain types of subjects to the exclusion of others. The most readily available human subjects, the introductory psychology student, is not most representative of the larger population whose behavior is being studied. Thus, selection on the basis of convenience conflicts with the goal of developing laws of behavior that are valid for humans as a species. Convenience is a major factor in the widespread preference for college sophomores and albino rats as subjects in experiments, but how representative are they of humans as a species or mammals as a zoological class, respectively?

EXPERIMENTER EXPECTANCY BIAS

Experimenters generally have a considerable emotional and intellectual investment in their research such that certain experimental outcomes may be more desirable than others. A large body of evidence indicates that the expectancies, hypotheses, or biases of experimenters may be communicated in some yet unknown fashion to their subjects. Although such communication is unintentional and neither experimenters nor subjects may even be aware of it, this source of bias seriously reduces the validity of the experimental findings. One possible solution to this problem would be to replace experimenters with a "neutral" tape recording made by someone who did not know the hypothesized outcome of the experiment. But while such a change might solve one problem, it could create others, such as reducing the motivation of the subjects.

ETHICAL DILEMMAS

In order to investigate some phenomena, psychologists have found it difficult, if not impossible, to conduct studies with subjects who know about the purposes and procedures in advance. Deception about one aspect of the study or another has been a common procedure in many experiments. In other studies, subjects may be exposed to physically and psychologically stressful or harmful stimuli. Even when no deception occurs in the latter type of studies, many subjects may feel pressure to participate in order to please professors or fulfill course requirements.

Since the experimenter holds more power in the experimental situation, the ethical decisions of using procedures that safeguard rights of the subject, such as privacy, confidentiality, safety, and self-esteem, rest with investigators. In many instances, the choices are not easy since to proceed in the most methodologically desirable manner may be ethically questionable whereas adherence to strict ethical codes and principles may jeopardize a study's methodological soundness.

SOCIAL RESPONSIBILITY

Some experimenters hold science to be value-free and objective, although some psychologists personally and ethically feel bound to work on social issues or topics whose results may benefit humanity. Even those psychologists who avoid such direct involvement with the potential societal applications of research findings will find that their work may be cited by other persons and groups to promote their own interests and causes.

It has been suggested that even the choice of problems for investigation involves value judgments, or at least has implications for social policy and applications. The choice facing the researcher may not be one of getting involved or staying disengaged, but rather of which issue or problem area to be associated with.

THE LIMITS OF THE EXPERIMENTAL METHOD AND APPROACH

Doubts and concern have grown that the approach based on the use of the experimental method cannot provide useful answers to important questions about human behavior, especially social psychological aspects. Researchers are now criticizing the conceptual limits of the experimental approach's emphasis on the search for general laws, inability to deal with complex, interacting, multiple causes of behavior, and neglecting social systems in favor of studying isolated individuals.

The experimental psychologist is thus in a dilemma, a situation requiring choices between equally undesirable alternatives. Every alternative that diminishes the problems raised by experimental procedures also diminishes the advantages provided by those procedures. As we shall see, psychologists have responded to this dilemma in a variety of ways, ranging from refining further the traditional experimental method to suggesting that we should abandon these procedures and adopt a more "human" approach to psychology. This section of the book aims to stimulate a thoroughgoing discussion of these problems and to suggest some courses of action that may extricate us from the experimenter's dilemma.

IDEAL VERSUS ACTUAL EXPERIMENTS

Friedman (1967) challenged the myth of the "standardized experiment," which is sometimes depicted as an ideal by textbook explanations about the nature of experiments. In these accounts, one gets the impression that there are universally-accepted standards which researchers adhere to in conducting experiments. However, based on filmed experimental sessions of a task devised by Rosenthal and Fode (1961), which will be described in detail in Chapter 10, Friedman has obtained objectively analyzable records of what most researchers have long suspected; namely that there is substantial uncontrolled variability in how researchers conduct experiments.

Even the social interaction between subjects and experimenters during the test session varies considerably, and we can reasonably suspect that the nature of this interaction could affect the results of some experiments. More seriously, perhaps, is the lack of standard procedures within the experiment proper, starting with the giving of instructions, to the administration of stimuli, recording of responses, and dismissal of subjects. During this period, the amount of social interaction and conversational small talk also varies. Some experimenters are formal and professional, others are more casual and nonchalant about uniformity of procedures for all subjects. The pace and style of stimulus presentation vary with different experimenters, as do the accuracy and conscientiousness for recording the subject's responses. Most experimental reports describe to some extent the subject's characteristics and his or her behavior in the experiment, but rarely, if ever, does one find a description of the experimenter's traits and behavior reported, unless, of course, these factors are being studied systematically as independent variables. Even the verbal interchange at the conclusion of a session varies. Although such differences could not possibly affect the subjects' behavior in the just completed session, it well might influence their attitudes and performances in future experiments.

Friedman emphasized the social nature of psychological research.

Unlike the phenomena of the physical sciences–which psychology has emulated as a model–the interaction between subjects and experimenters in an experiment is quite different and involves unique problems. Whereas chemicals do not respond differently as a function of the personality of experimenters, human, and also animal subjects to some degree, respond differently in some situations to different types of experimenters. In addition to the differential effect of different experimenters, the fact that human subjects know they are being studied can, in itself, alter behavior.

Accepting the fact that wide differences exist among experimenters in how subjects are handled, just how serious is this lack of standardization? How do we know that such procedural variations actually influence the results or conclusions of an experiment? If positive evidence is available, just how widespread is the problem? Even if it can be shown that procedural variations can alter the findings in one type of task or situation, there is no guarantee that it will also modify those in a different type of experiment.

Furthermore, could lack of standardization even be a virtue? Thus, if the same results occurred with different data collectors in one experiment, or in several different experiments, despite wide procedural differences, we could be more confident about the generalizability of our findings. On the other hand, if results cannot be replicated under altered conditions either in the same laboratory or in different ones, we know there are some limits to the generality of our findings, and can study them in additional experiments. If standardization were the first rule, we might never discover the other variables affecting the behavior under study. On the other hand, if test conditions vary in different experiments, we can worry about standardization only when results can no longer be reproducible under differing conditions. However, if the results can be repeated under varying conditions, then we have gained generalizability. We would still not know exactly how much the variations among experimenters affect the behavior of subjects; all we would know is that despite any possible experimenter variable effect, the influence of other variables are even greater and still occur. This issue is another aspect of the experimenter's dilemma.

The Experimenter's Perspective

Also problematic is the fact that experimenters and subjects perceive an experiment differently since their goals differ. For the experimenters, the experimental method obtains answers to questions under study. They want to understand, control, and predict behavior. Use of the experiment allows experimenters to draw conclusions about causal relationships.

As a result, the experimenter's attitude toward subjects can be quite impersonal since the subject is a guinea pig, a number, or a piece of data. As Lyons (1964) observed,

> The experimenter keeps looking for the perfect servant—who will carry out the master's wishes with understanding and intelligence yet not go beyond them; who will accede without obsequiousness and cooperate without being servile; who will be independent and unrestricted yet neither negativistic nor resistive; and who will never cut through the entire master-servant relation, and thereby destroy it by seeking to put himself in the master's place, for example, by trying to know as much about the experiment as does the experimenter himself [p. 105].

Thus, in the experimental situation, experimenters do not trust subjects, and instead try to keep them as naive and ignorant as possible about the purposes of the experiment.

The Subject's Perspective

In contrast, subjects are not primarily interested in the problem under attack by experimenters, although they may be somewhat curious about it. They are generally cooperative so that they can learn something about themselves and others. To a lesser extent, or as a fringe benefit, they are "aiding science." Sometimes, however, they are pressured into volunteering by requirements for their psychology course, by their instructor, or by their friends. Other times, they are lured into the experiment either by being paid, by curiosity, or by challenge. The exact motives for participating probably depend on whether subjects volunteered or were "drafted" into service. In any case, once they get into the experiment, they are not passive organisms but very active ones who attempt to decipher the secret purpose or true meaning of the experiment. Such an attitude is quite natural but can create difficulties for experimenters as when different subjects have different hypotheses about the study's purpose. In studies where deception is necessary, the validity of findings is at stake if subjects can see through to the real purpose. Lyons (1964) realized that experimenters must deal with the very persons they want to study, so they can never reveal the true purpose to their subjects prior to the study.

Subjects vary in their attitudes toward experiments, but most of them are either in fear, awe, or respect of experimenters, who after all are psychologists, and everyone, thanks to the popular magazines, movies, and so on, knows what psychologists can do! "Being-experimented-on" feelings lead many subjects to be docile, subservient, and obedient to virtually any request imposed upon them while under the power of experimenters. Compliance, however, is often accompanied by hostility toward experimenters and attempts to outwit them (Jourard, 1968).

Some evidence concerning the nature of the "implicit contract" held by subjects in experiments comes from a survey in Epstein, Suedfeld, and Silverstein (1973). As suspected by many analysts, subjects come to experiments expecting that they should be cooperative, honest, and punctual. However, only a few feel they should maintain secrecy about experimental purposes and procedures. In turn, subjects expect experimenters to be respectful, maintain confidentiality of information, and to display professional competence. Subjects often mentioned invasion of privacy, exposure to pain, and to a small degree, the experiences of deception as justifications for withdrawing from experiments. In actual practice, however, few subjects walk out during the middle of experiments, possibly because they feel pressure to stick it out. Since the survey dealt only with subjects' reasoning about hypothetical experiments, it did not reveal how frequently subjects actually do withdraw from studies.

A second study using female subjects examined their rated expectations, desirability, and appropriateness of a number of negative consequences that might take place during an experiment, which are listed in the three columns of Table 9–1. The majority expected professional behavior from experimenters in the form of respect, competence, and confidential treatment of their data. They did not, however, expect disclosure of the experimental purpose, but rather seem to assume deception is highly likely and appropriate, even though they did not rate same desirable. Other undesirable negative events subjects still perceived as appropriate for experiments included receiving electric shock, being asked personal questions, and being paid late for their participation.

Schulman and Berman (1975) also examined the expectations held by subjects about the manner in which experimenters and subjects would play their roles in the experimental context. Equal numbers of male and female subjects identified the 10 most likely aspects of the behavior they expected from experimenters by completing a fill-in questionnaire.

Three independent dimensions were inferred from their responses: professionalism such as logical, serious, and scientific attitudes; interpersonal warmth or coldness; and attentiveness or degree of involvement and eagerness. Subjects expected that experimenters would be scientific and organized, interacting with them in an objective but involved manner.

Schulman and Berman similarly analyzed subjects' appraisals of how they thought they should behave. One group of attitudes, such as interested, cooperative, and honest, was termed "faithfulness," whereas another set of terms, including nervous, tense, and defensive, was labelled "apprehensiveness." Finally, a dimension of "skepticism" was

TABLE 9–1. Mean Ratings of Expectations, Desirability, and Appropriateness by Subjects about Various Aspects of Experiments.

Statement	Rating	Rating	Rating
1. Instructions will not be clear	9.28	9.0	8.2
2. Subject will not be told purpose of experiment	3.65	6.5	4.8
3. Experimenter will not be respectful	9.93	9.8	9.3
4. Subject will be asked personal questions	5.73	7.5	5.3
5. Subject expects possibility of electric shock	7.90	9.0	5.1
6. Embarrassing information about the subject will be seen by other subjects participating at the same time	9.80	10.2	8.4
7. Persons not directly connected with the research will have access to the subject's data	9.70	9.0	8.6
8. Experimenter will be late	8.58	9.0	8.8
9. Subject will be deceived	6.08	7.6	4.7
10. Experimenter will be incompetent	9.65	9.8	9.4
11. Experiment will require more than one hour	8.10	8.0	4.7
12. Subject will be paid one week after experiment	7.40	4.6	4.1
13. Bell will ring during experiment	6.65		
14. Experiment will not be enjoyable	7.65		

Note. 1 = expect; 11 = do not expect.
1 = desirable; 11 = not desirable.
1 = appropriate; 11 = not appropriate.

Source: Adapted from Y. M. Epstein, P. Suedfeld, and S. J. Silverstein. "The Experimental contract: Subject's expectations of and reactions to some behaviors of experimenters," *American Psychologist*, 1973, **28**, 212–221. Copyright 1968 by the American Psychological Association. Reprinted by permission.

indicated, as reflected by the choice of terms like cautious, suspicious, and reserved.

It appears then, that subjects do not approach their experimental participation with a specific attitude, but rather with a composite of several orientations. A more detailed discussion of these factors and their consequences for outcomes of experiments will be presented in Chapter 11 which deals with several conceptions of the roles subjects adopt while performing as subjects.

From the preceding analysis of the experimental situation as shown from the perspective of both involved parties—the experimenter and the subject—we can see that some important differences exist. What implications does this conception of the experiment as a social psychological interaction—as opposed to the model of the experiment based on the methods of physical sciences—have for psychological research? What kinds of solutions and remedies have psychologists developed to deal with the problems associated with gaining valid knowledge from experiments? The goal of the present section of this book is to discuss these issues in light of the social nature of the experimenter–subject relationship inherent in psychological experiments with human subjects.

Chapter 10 examines the problem of *reactivity*, the fact that subjects who know they are tested may react to this realization and behave atypically. The concept of the demand characteristics of an experiment will be introduced as a possible source of artifact or error in the kinds of conclusions that may be drawn from experiments. Chapter 11 will discuss in greater detail some of the different attitudes and roles that affect the subject's motivations and reactions to being in an experiment.

The sources of human subjects and the factors in their selection that may lead to biased results—such as how they are recruited, differences between characteristics of volunteers and nonvolunteers, and amount of experience as subjects—will be the major concerns of Chapter 12.

Chapters 13 and 14 focus on the unintentional influence of the experimenters themselves on experimental outcomes. First, evidence will be presented in Chapter 13 about the effect experimenters' expectancies or hypotheses have on outcomes of studies, followed by an appraisal in Chapter 14 of the possibility that the physical and psychosocial attributes of experimenters can influence results.

In Chapter 15 the ethical issues involved in the use of human subjects in psychological experiments that have received much attention in the past decade will be identified. Views, as well as empirical studies, related to topics such as informed consent, harm, deception, and debriefing will be discussed. Chapter 16 presents some discussion of alternative methods to deal with the problems of experimentation. The nature of naturalistic research and its pros and cons in comparison to traditional experiments where subjects know they are being observed will be discussed as a solution for reactivity. Then we examine role-playing methods as an alternative to the ethical problem of using deception in experiments.

Chapter 17 examines the broader ethical concerns of the social impact of psychological experiments and the responsibility of investigators to society. To what extent can or should psychology as a scientific discipline exist as an objective, value-free enterprise? Should experimenters be concerned about how the findings of studies are used or misused? Finally, Chapter 18 considers future prospects in light of contemporary unrest and skepticism about the utility and validity of the experimental method and approach itself. What is the future role of the experiment in the quest for further understanding of the complexities of human psychology?

SUMMARY

Despite the methodological advantages of the experiment for achieving conclusions about the determinants of behavior, the use of experimentation with human subjects can be jeopardized by a number of sources of faulty inferences. Taken collectively, these problems are referred to in this part of the book as "The Experimenter's Dilemma." Included among these problems are the reactive nature of experiments, which alters the behavior of human subjects from what it may be in natural or nonexperimental situations because they realize they are being observed; over-reliance on college students as a source of participants, which reduces the generalizability of results to other types of persons; and biases of both experimenters and subjects due to their expectations. In addition, the experimenter faces issues of an ethical nature such as how to obtain informed consent of subjects, the protection of the well-being of subjects, and the legitimacy of deception. In some types of investigations, the personal values of the experimenter may affect the choice of the problem or the method of study, which destroys total objectivity. The ultimate dilemma involves the question of whether other methods may be preferable to the experiment in studying some aspects of human behavior.

The two parties involved in any experiment—the subject and the experimenter—do not perceive the situation in the same light. Whereas the experimenter is primarily interested in testing some theoretical issue or confirming an hypothesis, the subject may be more concerned about his or her personal adequacy of performance. Furthermore, in agreeing to serve as subjects, they have implicitly contracted to cooperate, expose themselves to mild discomfort in some situations, and possibly be deceived. In return, they expect experiments to be trustworthy, objective, and professional, among other things.

REFERENCES

Epstein, Y. M., Suedfeld, P., and Silverstein, S. J. The experimental contract: Subject's expectations of and reactions to some behaviors of experimenters. *American Psychologist*, 1973, *18*, 212-221.

Friedman, N. *The social nature of psychological research.* New York: Basic Books, 1967.

Jourard, S. *Disclosing man to himself.* New York: Van Nostrand Reinhold, 1968.

Lyons, J. On the psychology of the psychological experiment. In C. Scheerer (Ed.), *Cognition-theory, research, promise.* New York: Harper & Row, 1964.

Rosenthal, R., and Fode, K. L. The effect of experimenter bias on the performance of the albino rat. *Behavioral Science,* 1963, *8*, 183-189.

Schulman, A. D., and Berman, H. J. Role expectations about subject and experimenters in psychological research. *Journal of Personality and Social Psychology,* 1975, *32*, 368-380.

CHAPTER 10

Does "Being Experimented On" Alter Behavior?

Chapter at a Glance

THE REACTIVE NATURE OF EXPERIMENTS

Unlike the situation in most natural sciences, the study of human psychology can be drastically affected by the fact that participants in experiments clearly know that their behavior is being observed and analyzed. This reactive process, is, of course, not limited to experimental contexts. As we all know from personal experience, whenever we have felt ourselves under scrutiny by others in everyday life, we often act differently or at least feel highly conspicuous. This obvious reaction, however, is often surprisingly ignored or minimized by many researchers, although there is growing awareness and concern that this process may restrict the usefulness of laboratory findings.

Some subjects act in more socially desirable ways when they realize they are being observed, while others may act defensively or even defiantly. Some subjects become more outgoing while others become more restrained and subdued. Being in an experiment is rather like being on stage or on television. Some people stare at the audience or camera while others wave and smile, and still others become self-conscious and nervous.

These reactive effects may reduce the generalizability or external validity of experimental results if the behavior displayed during the experiment becomes distorted from what it would ordinarily be like. This danger of methodological imperfection or artifact due to reactivity is by no means a new threat or one unique to psychological research.

Shapiro (1960) has documented the history of the use of placebo conditions in medical and drug research. It was recognized long ago that the power of suggestion often led to dramatic effects. The ingestion of placebos, or pills consisting of innocuous ingredients, has sometimes produced changes equal to those caused by actual medicines. The doctor's patient is like the experimental subject in being influenced merely because one is being observed.

Sommer (1968) examined a similar effect, known as the *Hawthorne effect* after the Hawthorne industrial studies (Roethlisberger and Dickson, 1939). Regardless of environmental changes, worker production seemed to always improve, much to the surprise of the investigators who were trying to identify optimal working conditions. In actuality workers were responding to the observation process itself and behaving in ways atypical of work under natural conditions. Sommer pointed out that the term Hawthorne effect has negative connotations, for when present it suggests that the experimental results may be artifacts. However, Sommer argued that it is a pervasive feature of most field research because persons are usually aware when they are being studied.

Awareness of the psychological effects of experimentation upon subjects is crucially important. To the extent that behavior is altered by subjects' awareness of participation in an experiment, the experimenter has limited generalizability of findings to the real world. We will consider this problem more fully later, but it should continually be kept in mind.

The experimental situation involves a special type of interpersonal interaction between an experimenter and one or more subjects. The experimenter holds more power and control over the situation, knowing the purpose and procedures of the study. The subjects are the "guinea pigs" who are more or less trusting and willing participants in often ambiguous circumstances. Even when the subjects are explicitly informed that they are not being "psychoanalyzed" or individually evaluated, they may be apprehensive about how well they will do or look in the study. Although researchers may honestly tell subjects that comparisons of average or overall performance of groups undergoing different treatments is their only interest, typical participants are usually so personally involved and interested that they still tend to worry.

In short, in the psychological experiment, humans are not passive subjects who respond reflexively or mechanically to stimuli. They have thoughts and feelings about their performance, the purpose of the study, the nature of the responses expected of them by the experimenter, and the amount of satisfaction or dissatisfaction experienced.

This situation, however, is at odds with the concept of the "naive" subject held by many experimenters in the past. This view portrayed the subject as a docile input-output machine which did not try to discern the purpose of the study or worry about the quality of performance. It should be added that naive subjects were not always desired; in fact during the early introspectionistic days of experimental psychology before 1900 when sensory psychology and psychophysics were primary topics of concern, researchers distinctly preferred highly trained and experienced *observers*, as they were then called. However, with the rise of behaviorism in the early 1900s, psychologists rejected mental experiences, verbal report, and subjectivity. The eventual rise in the use of deception as a general technique also precluded use of any subjects except those who were as naive and uninformed as possible about the nature of psychology.

Experimental situations involving the use of deception are especially prone to difficulties stemming from the reactive nature of experiments. For example, consider studies in the area of stress, harm, and danger which require that subjects be convinced of the authenticity of the threat. Of course, in laboratory studies, experimenters are limited in what they can do, and no real physical harm can come to subjects. Experimenters must cleverly contrive situations that deceive subjects into thinking some harm is possible. But just how credible are such deceptions?

When subjects participate in an experiment, they assume (sometimes erroneously) that investigators are bound by certain ethical codes, and they are regarded as responsible and trustworthy professionals. The possibility that genuine harm can occur to subjects as part of the experiment appears quite remote.

With this attitude on the part of most subjects, what problems of interpretation can this create for experiments that attempt to induce fear and stress in subjects via deceptions? Would not such an attitude attenuate the effectiveness of any deceptions aimed at creating stress? In fact, many subjects who are familiar with psychological research know that much deception is practiced. When they are in an experiment that apparently involves danger, their assumption that experimenters are trustworthy increases their tendency to be suspicious of the alleged procedures within the experiment. Nowadays subjects are not naive enough to believe experimenters' cover stories about an experiment, but they do assume that experimenters are restricted when it comes to potentially harmful situations.

Darley and Latané (1968) studied some factors that influenced helping behavior in emergency situations. They recruited subjects to come to the laboratory for a group discussion of personal problems. Each subject was told that since some individuals are embarrassed by such discussions, they would be tested in a private cubicle equipped with intercoms connecting the rooms where other subjects were housed; after the session started one subject suddenly went through an epileptic fit which was heard over the intercom. The experimental question was how long it would take before the subject would report this emergency to the experimenter who was in another room.

Of course, the emergency was faked by a confederate whose seizure was tape recorded. How well were the subjects deceived by this manipulation? Darley and Latané do not report attempting to determine the credibility of the deception. While it is plausible that most subjects would have been totally surprised by the occurrence of the apparent emergency, it is possible that some subjects just did not believe it was "real" because they knew they were in an experiment.

Similar questions could be raised about the credibility of situations and procedures in many experiments. As long as subjects are aware that they are in an experiment, we cannot ignore the possibility that they are prepared to regard virtually any event—however unlikely—to be part of the experiment; and feel that since it is an experiment, it is safe. Of course, many studies with deception do not entail stress, but it may still be important to successfully involve the subjects in these experiments.

Psychologists have been prone to ignore the question of whether or not deception actually works. Stricker's (1967) survey of 390 published articles showed that only 24 per cent of the 88 studies using deception bothered to measure or report the efficacy of their deceptions. Furthermore, in studies that assessed subjects' perceptions of the experiment, Stricker maintained that the criteria for judging awareness were not always sound.

NATURE AND SOURCES OF DEMAND CHARACTERISTICS

Naive subjects may be docile and cooperative, but abundant evidence suggests that they are not so naive after all. Even when no real purpose underlies the tasks assigned to subjects, they will search for and, if necessary, impute meaning and purpose nonetheless. Some striking demonstrations of this process were reported by Martin Orne (1962) in a classic and influential paper. Some pilot studies were done to find a dull and meaningless task to use in an experiment dealing with hypnotic control. One such task involved long addition of rows of random digits, requiring over 200 computations per page. An impressive stack of about 2000 sheets was given to each subject who was instructed to work until the experimenter returned. Compliance was so high that usually the experimenter "gave up" before the subjects did, which was usually several *hours* later. A modification of the task called for the subjects to tear up each completed page into at least 32 pieces before continuing with a new sheet of additions. This change was made to make the task appear even more absurd, and subjects continued to persist for long periods. Apparently they were able to supply some meaning to the situation which was not intended. Requests to perform the same behaviors outside the guise of an experiment would probably be ignored or ridiculed. Being a subject in an experiment is like being under a powerful spell!

Based on these failures to find boring and monotonous tasks subjects would not persevere with for long periods, Orne concluded that subjects in a psychological experiment are highly motivated to be cooperative. Furthermore, this helpfulness will occur despite some degree of boredom and discomfort. Finally, Orne suggested that subjects search for cues to the meaning and purpose of the study, try to figure out the hypotheses or identify the nature of the appropriate responses, and try to confirm the experimental hypothesis by being "good" subjects. This latter point will be discussed in more detail in the next chapter.

Note that this process engaged in by subjects is not assumed to be willful or conscious. Orne postulated the concept of *demand characteristics*, a term that covers many different aspects of the experimental situation, to refer to cues noticed and used by subjects in arriving at their interpretations of the purpose of the experiment and the nature of the experimenter's hypothesis.

As shown in Table 10–1, a number of factors, taken singly or together, can serve as cues to create or activate demand characteristics in an experimental context to influence subjects. The physical environs, per se, such as the laboratory room located in a psychology building on a college campus, may awe or impress subjects. The awareness that the experiment is a scientific investigation conducted by a professional psychologist in appropriate and serious circumstances optimizes cooperation. If expensive or exotic equipment and apparatus is involved, they may also add to the subjects' interest and motivation. The physical features such as age, sex, and attire of the experimenter as well as his or her personality and style of interpersonal interaction are other important factors affecting subjects' attitudes toward the study.

As the experiment gets underway, the instructions to the subjects strongly affect them in unintended as well as intended ways. Subtle wording differences may convey different nuances as to what they should do or what they will construe to be the purpose of the study. Slight procedural variations may produce entirely different types and amounts of motivation. Expectancies about the performances subjects should exhibit may be unintentionally conveyed to them by subtle cues such as intonations in reading instructions, nonverbal reactions such as smiles or frowns at the performance of subjects, and so forth.

TABLE 10–1. Sources of Demand Characteristics.

Physical Setting
- Laboratory room
- Apparatus, Equipment

Experimenter
- Age, Sex, Attire
- Hypotheses
- Attitudes
  - Toward experimental procedures
  - Toward subject during interactions
- Unintentional cues

Instructions (which vary across different conditions)
- Wording, Clarity, Length, Jargon

Actual Procedures, Tasks, Feedback, Reactions (which vary across different conditions)

Subject Factors
- Individual differences, e.g., personality, intelligence, motivation
- Prior experimental experiences, number and type, especially with deception studies
- Rumors, gossip, and campus scuttlebutt about experiments

The actual procedures subjects undergo during the experiment also provide cues. Some tasks, such as personality inventories, may arouse apprehension. Implausible "cover stories" used to disguise true purposes of studies involving deception may still activate suspicious reactions. Even if subjects can not identify the true hypothesis, they may nonetheless formulate their own hypotheses and act on the basis of these conceptions, as humorously suggested in Figure 10–1.

The problem is greater when one realizes that for a given experimental setting with identical procedures, wide individual differences among subjects as to the demand characteristics that affect them may exist. Different amounts, as well as types, of past experiences with experiments may affect the demand cues perceived by individual subjects. Prior acquaintance with deception may sensitize them to be suspicious even when no deception is involved. Personality, age, sex, and other individual difference dimensions may also play a major role.

WHEN DO DEMAND CHARACTERISTICS REPRESENT PROBLEMS?

The fact that demand characteristics exist is not the problem; these cues subjects use to extract meaning from experiments are inevitable, given that subjects know they are being observed. Demand characteristics become a problem for experimenters when they threaten internal validity of experiments so that erroneous conclusions are made about the effects of the independent variables or factors of interest to the researcher. Thus, if the behavioral change we observe in subjects receiving drug X is really not due to the pharmacological substances but rather to the subjects' expectations that the drug will produce a specific type of reaction, due to some demand cues in the situation, we can not conclude there is a genuine drug effect.

The type of task is an important determinant of the likelihood that such problems will occur. If the task primarily involves ability, skill, or capacity to perform, there is little ambiguity as to what represents "good" performance. With these *task-ability situations* (Riecken, 1962), all subjects who are motivated to cooperate as well as "look good" know what responses to make. On the other hand, with tasks Riecken (1962) called *self-quality problems,* there can be considerable ambiguity as to what behavior is desirable or appropriate. Such situations, often negative and stressful, are like personality assessments in which one's behavior implies something about one's personal qualities and character. The demand characteristics in the situation will suggest to the subject what kinds of behavior the experimenter will judge positive and negative. The researchers must know how the subject per-

In certain of the psychology courses the system of democratic blackmail is practised whereby you are forced to volunteer as experimental subjects or you lose 5% of your term mark.

However students, being the sophisticated devils they are these days, tend to spot the purpose of the experiment which can really foul-up the results sometimes. Hence the experimenters are forced to use elaborate red-herring, disguise techniques in order to further the ends of their 'science'.

In one experiment I was in, I figured it was concerned with group-cooperation. A team of five others and myself, with two buckets between us, had to transfer the water from the field house swimming pool to a series of polyethylene bags which were suspended from the ceiling of the old dining hall.

As we were panting up and down the hill, some guy in a white coat timed us with a stop watch and made sure we didn't spill any water. When all the water was safely in the old dining hall we had to complete a questionnaire to say how much we had enjoyed the experiment

I discovered afterwards that the water-carrying bit has just been a subterfuge and that the questionnaire we completed was actually a test for latent homosexuality.

In the last experiment I had to take part in I found myself alone in a cubicle affair — just four bare walls. I figured the experiment was either about the general effects of sensory deprivation or possibly the isolation factor in stamina-destruction. Anyways, I stuck it out in there as long as I could but I finally collapsed after the fifth day. It turned out that the actual experiment was next door but I had wandered into an empty broom-closet.

FIGURE 10–1.

ceived this type of situation in order to understand what kind of behavior will occur.

We must be careful that the concept of demand characteristics not be used as a convenient after-the-fact explanation to account for results that disagree with predictions or to discredit the validity of interpretations other investigators may make of their own data. For example, if the hypothesized results do not occur, it is easy to speculate that the subjects misinterpreted the instructions or that they thought the study dealt with conformity, when it did not.

If these speculations are to be useful, experimenters need some independent and objective measure to show the nature of these perceptions. Methods of assessing the nature and the extent of the demand characteristics affecting subject interpretations of the experiment are needed to substantiate or refute the validity of these *post hoc* analyses.

Examples of Demand Characteristics as Alternative Explanations

Sensory deprivation studies (e.g., Bexton, Heron, and Scott, 1954) are among the most dramatic of psychological situations, involving a type of solitary-confinement experience. Usually only paid volunteers are used in these studies which involve the isolation of a subject to small chambers that minimize or eliminate all visual, auditory, and other sensory inputs from the environment for about a day or more. These procedures have been found to produce severe, although short-lived, impairments in cognitive, perceptual, and motor abilities.

However, Jackson and Pollard (1962) suggested that some of the experimental results could have stemmed from the power of suggestion. Consistent with this view is an experiment conducted by Orne and Scheibe (1964) to determine how much of the sensory deprivation effect was attributable to demand characteristics of the experimental task. After all, the subjects did know that they would be isolated for long periods of time and may have had some preconceptions as to what should happen to them psychologically. Is it possible that some, if not all, of the effects ascribed to the sensory deprivation are generated by the demand characteristics of the situation?

Both an experimental and a control group was subjected to four hours of isolation in a room with a window. Paper and pencil was available on a table. These conditions are not nearly as extreme as those usually employed in most sensory-deprivation studies. Before being isolated, the experimental group received an extensive physical examination, signed a release form, and was reassured that if at any time in the experiment they could not "take it any more," they could press a "panic button" in order to be rescued. In addition, they were "assured" that there was no danger in the presence of an emergency medical tray full of drugs and syringes. In contrast, control-group subjects did not undergo this phase of the study but were simply informed before they were isolated that they were control subjects for a sensory-deprivation study.

Despite the fact that the isolation treatment per se was identical for experimental and control groups, there were marked differences afterward on a battery of perceptual, cognitive, and motor-skills tests which showed impairment in the experimental group. Orne and Scheibe attributed this poorer performance to the demand characteristics of the situation, the medical exam, the concept of the panic button, and so forth, which led experimental group subjects to expect bizarre effects. Orne and Scheibe concluded that similar processes could have operated in previous studies that obtained sensory-deprivation effects. This is not to say that sensory deprivation has no effects of its own, but that demand characteristics may produce effects similar to them.

Perhaps no phenomena are more fascinating in terms of the intriguing potential for dramatic behavioral changes than those involving hypnosis. Theatrical demonstrations of the power of this process are familiar to everyone and no doubt this experience greatly increases individuals' belief in its potential to transform persons under its spell. Orne (1959) examined the possibility that demand characteristics may play an important role in mediating the effects typically obtained with hypnosis. If subjects know how they are supposed to be affected by hypnosis, perhaps some, if not all, of their behavior when hypnotized is due to role playing rather than genuine hypnotic trances.

To test this interpretation, Orne (1959) instructed one group of subjects to behave *as if* they were under hypnosis to provide a test of the ability of a different experimenter whose task was to distinguish between them and a group of hypnotized subjects. Simulating subjects were told that this other experimenter would not (as was true) know which subjects did not undergo hypnosis so their task was to see if they could fool this other experimenter. The results showing that the other experimenter was unable to distinguish above chance the actual and simulated hypnosis subjects is consistent with the argument that demand characteristics of the situation, rather than hypnosis per se, could produce the behavior shown by the subjects actually receiving hypnosis. In other words, subjects act the way they think hypnotized subjects should behave so that even if the hypnotic induction procedure itself had no effect, one would still observe some behavioral changes. This conclusion does not imply that hypnosis never has true effects, but raises the possibility that some "hypnotic" effects may be due to demand characteristics rather than to any special properties of the hypnotic procedures.

Under hypnosis people are apparently under the control of the hypnotist to such a degree that they may commit illegal, immoral, or unethical deeds. The following study provides one such example.

Rowland (1939) had two deeply hypnotized subjects pick up a large rattlesnake. Even though one subject actually attempted to do so, he was prevented from endangering himself by invisible glass. Subjects performed other dangerous behavior—such as throwing acid at other persons—when instructed to do so under hypnosis. These anti-social behaviors under hypnosis have been replicated by Young (1952).

But Orne and Evans (1965) questioned the validity of these dramatic demonstrations. They replicated Young's experiment successfully. However, they also added a control group of nonhypnotized subjects. Even these subjects displayed the antisocial behavior, suggesting to Orne and Evans that such behaviors were not really judged as dangerous by the subjects when performed in the context of an experiment. Interviews with subjects afterward revealed that although some of them had felt uncertain about some of the tasks, "they were quite convinced that they would not be harmed because the context was an experimental one, presumably being conducted by responsible experimenters" [Orne & Evans, 1965, p. 199]. In short, knowledge that they were being experimented on allowed subjects to engage in what otherwise would be considered very dangerous activity.

A similar objection has been made by Orne and Holland (1968) to the widely-cited study of obedience by Milgram (1963). Pairs of subjects (one an accomplice of the experimenter) served in a study alleged to deal with the effects of punishment on learning. The real subjects always ended up by "chance" as the teacher and the stooge served as the learner. The task of the subject was to administer increasingly painful shocks to the learner each time he made a mistake. The stooge's behavior was rigged so that he made more and more errors, requiring the subject to give increasingly stronger intensities of shock. Although the learner was in another room, the subject could hear the moans, grunts, and screams of the apparently tormented learner. Milgram wanted to demonstrate the blind obedience of subjects to authority even when ordered to cause severe pain for a fellow human.

Orne and Holland (1968) questioned the plausibility of this situation. They noted, "Despite the movie image of the mad scientist, most subjects accept the fact that scientists—even behavioral scientists—are reasonable people" [p. 287]. If this were the case, the obedience would simply stem from the demand characteristics of the situation.

In a similar vein, Mixon's (1971) criticism of Milgram's study questioned whether it is valid to conclude that subjects perceive the consequences of their actions to match what is commonly attributed to them. Perhaps they did not believe they were harming others—despite the realistic feedback—because they did not expect the experimenter, presumably an ethical and responsible person, to allow such consequences. Mixon used a role-playing procedure to replicate the study in which he asked subjects to imagine they were in the original Milgram situation. His results confirmed Milgram's that a very high percentage of subjects would obey authority. However, with another group of subjects who clearly understood that they would probably *harm* the other subject who was supposedly in the other room (the other subject being described as having a heart condition), obedience levels were drastically lower.

MEASURING DEMAND CHARACTERISTICS

The usefulness of arguments that specific findings from an experiment may be artifacts due to demand characteristics depends on our ability to provide convincing evidence concerning the nature of these factors. Otherwise, we are left with speculative arguments about what might have occurred without any method of deciding which analysis is valid. How can we determine the nature of demand characteristics in a given experiment?

Postexperimental Inquiry

The most typical procedure has been some form of postexperimental inquiry. Prior to *debriefing*, where the experimenter discloses the actual purpose of the study, subjects are asked about their perceptions, suspicions, and thoughts about the experimental procedures and purposes. This interview is more commonly used with deception experiments since one wants to eliminate data from any subjects who saw through the deception. However, even where no deception is used, it is often worthwhile to determine the subjects' perspective on the experiment, especially since it may provide some surprises that could alter the interpretation of the findings.

This method does have serious problems. Orne used the term *pact of ignorance* to refer to the unwillingness of any aware subjects to let on that they know for fear that they would be criticized by the experimenter and the reluctance of experimenters to probe too intensively for fear that they might learn that many subjects were aware. Awareness, however, is a complicated process, varying in subtle degrees and with respect to different facets of the procedures. Brief interviews may be insensitive to detecting some of these subtleties especially since subjects usually do not know the exact meaning of some of the interview questions. On the other hand, too intensive an inquiry may sensitize the subjects to notice things they might not have considered. This problem is particularly serious when subjects are unaware of some aspect of the procedures or their performance during the actual experiment, but come to realize it retrospectively during the postexperimental inquiry and confusingly claim the awareness occurred earlier. In short, the postexperimental inquiry has its own demand characteristics which may bias its results.

A good example of these problems can be seen in the debate between Page (1969) and Staats (1969) concerning the possible role of demand characteristics in the classical conditioning of attitudes (Staats & Staats, 1957). In this paradigm, subjects are told that the purpose of the study is to learn two word lists simultaneously, one presented visually and the other aurally. The visual list contained six nonsense syllables, one followed on each trial by a positive adjective and one by a negative adjective. The other four nonsense syllables were associated with neutral words and served to disguise the nature of the pairings with the two syllables of primary interest.

This paradigm was designed to see if the affective associations between the nonsense syllables and adjectives might influence the ratings of the nonsense syllables on a dimension of pleasantness–unpleasantness. It was assumed that the syllable paired with positive words would acquire pleasant meaning via the process of classical conditioning and that the syllable associated with negative words would be judged unpleasant due to the same process.

A brief single-item, postexperimental inquiry suggested to Staats and Staats (1957) that almost none of the subjects were aware of the actual pairings. The results of the evaluations of the words did support their prediction and they concluded that classical conditioning was involved. The criticism by Page (1969) focused on the possibility that the Staats' assessment of awareness was inadequate and that actually many subjects had been aware of the pairings, realized what the investigators were trying to prove, and rated the two critical nonsense syllables to match the kinds of words they knew had been paired with them. Such a process would not constitute classical conditioning, which assumes lack of awareness by the subjects.

Page devised the postexperimental questionnaire shown in Table 10–2 for use in his replication study. Substantially better "conditioning" was obtained from the third of the subjects who were judged from the questionnaire as being aware of the pairings and aware of what the experimenters' were expecting to happen. The remaining subjects who were unaware showed little indication of conditioning. Page concluded that demand characteristics can account for the effect obtained by Staats and Staats without recourse to an explanation involving classical conditioning.

In reply, Staats (1969) raised the possibility that Page's intensive method of assessing awareness may have had far greater demand characteristics than the Staats' paradigm itself. The pointedness of the ques-

TABLE 10-2. A Detailed "Funnel-type" Postexperimental Inquiry Used to Assess Awareness in a Classical Conditioning of Attitudes Study.

1. What was the purpose of this experiment and what were you supposed to do?
2. During the experiment did you ever have the idea that its purpose might be something other than what I was telling you? What?
3. Thinking back to the experiment, did you notice at the time any relationship between certain syllables on the screen and the words that were spoken? What?
4. If you noticed any relationship between the lists, is this something you were actually aware of during the experiment or is it something you thought of while filling out these questions?
5. Do you remember approximately when it was that you noticed this? (1) right away, (2) first 1/3 of learning, (3) second 1/3, (4) last 1/3, (5) while taking the first learning test, (6) while taking the second learning test.
6. What did you think was the purpose of the rating scales at the time you were filling them out, if anything?
7. How did you go about deciding what rating to give the various nonsense syllables?
8. Did you think that the experimenter might have expected that you would rate certain of the nonsense syllables in any certain way? Explain.
9. Was your answer to Question 8 something you were actually aware of before or during the marking of the rating scales, or something that you thought of afterwards?
10. What syllable was always or usually paired with travel words?
    a. How certain are you of this or are you guessing?
    Guessing——:——:——:——:——:——:——Certain
    b. Is this something you were aware of during the experiment or something you thought of since? Please explain if necessary.
11. What syllable was always or usually paired with words of pleasant meaning?
    a. How certain are you of this or are you guessing?
    Guessing——:——:——:——:——:——:——Certain
    b. Is this something you were aware of during the experiment or something you thought of since? Please explain if necessary.
12. What syllable was always or usually paired with words of unpleasant meaning?
    a. How certain are you of this or are you guessing?
    Guessing——:——:——:——:——:——:——Certain
    b. Is this something you were aware of during the experiment or something you thought of since? Please explain if necessary.
13. Were you ever aware during the experiment that yof [wuh for the other group] was always paired with words of pleasant meaning or connotation and that wuh [yof] was always paired with words of unpleasant meaning? And, if so, were you aware of any effect this might have had on you as you marked the rating scales? Explain.
14. Assuming that you knew the pleasant and unpleasant words and what was expected on the marking of the rating scales, rate your attitude while marking the rating scales.
    Resist the influence——:——:——:——:——:——:——Mark the right answers.

TABLE 10-2. (continued)

15. Please make any other comments that you feel might help us understand your reaction to this experiment.
16. Have you had any previous courses in psychology such as in high school?
17. Do you know the meaning of the term conditioning? If so, did you think about it during this experiment?

Source: "Social psychology of a classical conditioning of attitudes experiment," by M. M. Page, *Journal of Personality and Social Psychology*, 1969, **11**, 177–86. Copyright 1969 by the American Psychological Association. Reprinted by permission.

tions virtually cry out for the subjects to notice or imagine that they notice something. The questionnaire seems to assume that subjects have something to hide from experimenters.

Other evidence concerning the effect of type of assessment of awareness in the Staats and Staats paradigm comes from Weber and Riddell (1975) who replicated the classical conditioning study using the single-item global postexperimental inquiry for one group and Page's longer questionnaire for another group. The single-item approach was inadequate since it failed to detect many of the aware subjects. Since exclusion of aware subjects eliminates the classical conditioning effect, it is obvious that the type of assessment of awareness is critical. One similarity of results for the two methods was the fact that although one method detected more aware subjects, there was no difference in amount of "conditioning" shown by the aware subjects identified by the two different questionnaires.

In defense of the use of the more intensive "funnel type" questionnaire which procedes from general items to more specific ones, Page (1973) argued that there was less danger in having an overly sensitive method, which mistakenly classifies some unaware subjects as aware since these subjects' data would usually be deleted. This conservative approach would not lead to false confirmation of the hypothesis as would be the case with an insensitive method that erroneously classified aware subjects as unaware.

Preinquiry or Nonexperiment

A second procedure (Orne, 1959; Riecken, 1962) for identifying the demand characteristics of a particular experimental task is the preinquiry or nonexperiment which is a "dry-lab" type of procedure.

This method is akin to roleplaying procedures, which will be discussed as an alternative to deception paradigms in Chapter 16. It also calls for subjects to imagine they are receiving the actual procedures. They may be shown the equipment and room where the actual study will be conducted and given the instructions as well as any questionnaires or forms actual subjects might receive prior to the experiment. The only difference between the preinquiry and the actual experiment should be the absence of the actual treatment for the former condition.

One example of the use of this procedure is the study by Stare, Brown, and Orne (1959) which showed that preinquiry subjects were able to identify how real subjects would react to a sensory-deprivation study. Once again, this finding does not prove that actual subjects reacted only to demand characteristics, but suggests the possibility that such a process could potentially have occurred.

Control of Demand Characteristics As Independent Variables

The study cited earlier by Orne and Scheibe (1964) on sensory deprivation illustrates how hypotheses about demand characteristics derived from the preinquiry can be tested. Instead of speculating about the nature of demand characteristics, the experimenter may create different conditions for different groups that involve different demand cues. In the Orne and Scheibe study, one group received strong cues that something might go wrong. Medical tests were given, release forms were required, and emergency medical equipment was conspicuously present to foster the suggestion that the experimental procedures could create problems for subjects. These disturbing props were absent for another group of subjects who otherwise received the same "sensory deprivation" experience.

In this study, which was aimed at proving that demand characteristics may contribute to the psychological impairments typically found in sensory-deprivation studies, the experimenter knows that the demand cues are different because they represent the independent variable manipulated by the experimenter rather than after-the-fact speculations.

Simulator Method

The final method suggested by Orne (1970) for use as a quasi-control, to use his term, is the simulator procedure, which does not rely on verbal report as does the postexperimental inquiry. Simulator subjects are treated the same as the actual treatment subjects except for the critical factor, as in the study described earlier on the demand characteristics of hypnosis (Orne, 1959). In that study, blind experimenters who did not know which treatment subjects actually received attempted to guess which subjects had actually been hypnotized and which were merely simulating. Simulators knew the task of the judges and knew that they were making blind ratings.

If the behavior of simulators differs from that of actually treated subjects, we may conclude that the treatment of interest has some effect since it cannot be faked or created only by demand characteristics. However, if both groups are identical, no proof exists that all of the treated group's behavior is due to demand cues. We have not learned much about the actual processes underlying the phenomenon.

The simulator method, like the preinquiry, identifies what processes could potentially occur simply due to the demand characteristics of the situation since the independent or treatment variable is withheld from these quasi-control conditions. Such demonstrations do not prove, however, that such factors do operate in the same way for subjects who do receive the real treatments. This disparity is especially likely in cases where the simulators undergo an intellectual or hypothetical experience rather than an actual run through all of the procedures, save the treatment factor. Since the hypothetical experience is often more concentrated in time, it may make some factors of the situation more salient or obvious to the simulators than it would to actual subjects who undergo the procedures directly rather than in an imaginary version.

For example, Kahle and Page (1976) instructed subjects to pretend to either be satiated or food deprived just prior to receiving a learning task in which they were shown pairs of nonsense syllables and words, some being food and others being nonfood words. They wanted to show that simulators who were aware of the hypothesis could match the results obtained by Staats, Minke, Martin, and Higa (1972) using this paradigm which suggested that food-deprived subjects liked the nonsense syllables paired with food words better than those paired with nonfood words. Although Kahle and Page succeeded, it should be noted that Staats et al.'s subjects were actually food deprived or satiated rather than instructed to pretend. Staats et al.'s subjects were probably less aware of their bodily states about food than were Kahle and Page's subjects about their mental states concerning food. Thus, the simulator method here may be overstating the degree to which demand cues were operating in the actual treatment conditions of the Staats study.

Conclusions

It is not necessary or practical to measure demand characteristics for every experiment, but where it might be suspected that such cues may be alternative explanations for the findings in a given study, some attempt to measure them would be useful. Studies involving the use of deception are one of the most likely types of situations where this problem might arise. One wants to be sure that the deception was effective, that is, that the manipulation was credible. One wants to rule out the possible criticism that demand cues rather than the treatment factor of interest may have been the cause of any behavioral differences.

This type of reassurance is sometimes desirable even if no deception was employed. A situation is potentially problematic when it may be likely that the experimenter's assumption about how the task appears differs from the way subjects perceive and interpret the task. Measuring the demand cues enables one to check and hopefully rule out this source of artifact.

As we shall see in the next chapter, even if all subjects in a given situation perceived the same demands, they will not all necessarily react the same way. While some may act in compliance with these cues, others may act in ways to contradict these demands. Furthermore, the same type of reaction will not necessarily be prompted by the same motives since subjects may differ in their conception of their proper role as a subject.

SUMMARY

The human subject is not a passive recipient of stimuli and generator of responses in an experiment, but rather is an active problem-solving agent seeking to identify the purpose of the study and the most appropriate form of behavior. Subjects form their own impressions and perceptions about experiments, termed demand characteristics, on the basis of a variety of cues ranging from the physical surroundings, the instructions, the equipment, the appearance of the experimenter, and the subject's own level of performance during the experiment.

All experiments involve demand characteristics but they represent a problem only when they lead to behaviors that are mistakenly attributed to the independent variable by the experimenter. Thus, if a memory experiment is perceived to be a measure of intelligence by subjects, little difficulty should arise since subjects would probably try to perform well and remember as much as they could. On the other hand, if some aspects of the situation suggested or implied that the test performance reflected some negative quality such as lack of imagination, this demand characteristic would induce subjects to perform poorly.

It is crucial that some independent assessment of the demand cues involved in a given experiment be made. Otherwise it would be too easy for critics of a given study to argue that the results were due to demand characteristics rather than to the independent variable under study.

Several methods have been used to measure demand characteristics: the simulator method, in which a control group that does not receive the independent variable is asked to act as if they had to fool judges who are blind as to whether or not they received the treatment variable; the preinquiry method, which calls for subjects to "dry-lab" the experimental procedures by reacting to a verbal description rather than undergoing the actual procedures; and postexperimental inquiry, in which subjects are interrogated about their perceptions after the experiment is concluded.

The likelihood that demand characteristics exist that may invalidate the findings of an experiment varies with the type of problem or task. In ambiguous situations or those involving deception, it is more likely that some, if not all, subjects may hold perceptions about the purpose of the study or the expected type of behavior that differ from the experimenter's. When tasks are seen to involve the assessment of the individual's personal qualities, such as personality traits, it is also more likely that demand characteristics held by subjects may conflict with those intended by the experimenter.

REFERENCES

Bexton, W. H., Heron, W., and Scott, T. H. Effects of decreased variation in the sensory environment. *Canadian Journal of Psychology*, 1954, *8*, 70-76.

Darley, J., and Latane, B. *The unresponsive bystander*. New York: Appleton-Century, 1968.

Jackson, C. W., Jr., and Pollard, J. C. Sensory deprivation and suggestion. *Behavioral Science*, 1962, 7, 332-342.

Kahle, L. R., and Page, M. M. The deprivation-saturation effect in attitude conditioning without deprivation but with demand characteristics. *Personality and Social Psychological Bulletin*, 1976, *2*, 470-473.

Milgram, S. Behavioral study of obedience. *Journal of Abnormal and Social Psychology*, 1963, *67*, 371-378.

Mixon, D. Behavior analysis treating subjects as actions rather than organisms. *Journal for the Theory of Social Behavior*, 1971, *1*, 19-31.

Orne, M. T. The nature of hypnosis: Artifact and essence. *Journal of Abnormal and Social Psychology*, 1959, *58*, 277-299.

Orne, M. T. On the social psychology of the psychological experiment: With particular reference to demand characteristics and their implications. *American Psychologist*, 1962, *17*, 776-783.

Orne, M. T. Hypnosis, motivation, and the ecological validity of the psychological experiment. In W. J. Arnold and M. M. Page (Eds.), *Nebraska Symposium on Motivation* (Vol. 18). Lincoln: University of Nebraska Press, 1970.

Orne, M. T., and Evans, F. J. Social control in the psychological experiment: Antisocial behavior and hypnosis. *Journal of Personality and Social Psychology*, 1965, *1*, 189-200.

Orne, M. T., and Holland, C. H. On the ecological validity of laboratory deceptions. *International Journal of Psychiatry*, 1968, *6*, 282-293.

Orne, M. T., and Scheibe, K. E. The contribution of nondeprivation factors in the production of sensory deprivation effects: The psychology of the "panic button." *Journal of Abnormal and Social Psychology*, 1964, *68*, 3-12.

Page, M. M. Social psychology of a classical conditioning of attitudes experiment. *Journal of Personality and Social Psychology*, 1969, *11*, 177-186.

Page, M. M. On detecting demand awareness by postexperimental questionnaire. *Journal of Social Psychology*, 1973, *91*, 305-323.

Riecken, H. W. A program for research on experiments in social psychology. In N. F. Washburne (Ed.), *Decisions, values and groups*, Vol. 2. New York: Pergamon Press, 1962.

Roethlisberger, F. J., and Dickson, W. J. *Management and the worker*. Cambridge, Massachusetts: Harvard University Press, 1939.

Rowland, L. W. Will hypnotized persons try to harm themselves or others? *Journal of Abnormal and Social Psychology*, 1939, *114-117.*

Shapiro, A. K. A contribution to a history of the placebo effect. *Behavioral Science*, 1960, *5*, 109-135.

Sommer, R. Hawthorne dogma. *Psychological Bulletin*, 1968, *70*, 592-595.

Staats, A. W. Experimental demand characteristics and the classical conditioning of attitudes. *Journal of Personality and Social Psychology*, 1969, *11*, 187-192.

Staats, A. W., Minke, K. A., Martin, C. H., and Higa, W. R. Deprivation-saturation and strength of attitude conditioning: A test of attitude-reinforcer-discriminative theory. *Journal of Personality and Social Psychology*, 1972, *24*, 178-185.

Staats, C. K., and Staats, A. W. Meaning established by classical conditioning. *Journal of Experimental Psychology*, 1957, *54*, 74-80.

Stare, F., Brown, J., and Orne, M. T. *Demand characteristics in sensory deprivation studies*. Unpublished seminar paper, Massachusetts Mental Health Center and Harvard University, 1959.

Stricker, L. J. The true deceiver. *Psychological Bulletin*, 1967, *68*, 13-20.

Weber, S. J., and Riddell, J. C. An examination of postexperimental questionnaires used to assess awareness. *Representational Research in Social Psychology*, 1975, *6*, 1-6.

Young, P. C. Antisocial uses of hypnosis. In L. M. LeCron (Ed.), *Experimental hypnosis*. New York: Macmillan, 1952.

CHAPTER 11

What Different Roles Do Subjects Play in Experiments?

Chapter at a Glance

When people serve as subjects in a psychological experiment, their behavior may be affected by their preconceptions about the nature of psychological research and the role subjects play. Even a naive subject who has never been in an experiment knows something, even if it is erroneous, about psychology. These perceptions are general attitudes about research and, unlike demand characteristics, are not tied to specific research situations. Instead they reflect the subject's beliefs about experiments in general. These attitudes and beliefs subjects bring with them may distort or alter their behavior while under the scrutiny of the researcher, but psychologists do not agree on the precise nature of subjects' conceptions of their own roles. Several of the most influential formulations will be briefly listed below before a fuller discussion is provided.

MAJOR CONCEPTIONS OF THE ROLE OF SUBJECTS

1. Riecken (1962): Subjects want to "put the best foot forward" and appear in the best possible light by concealing or trying to suppress the qualities they think will be undesirable while emphasizing and drawing attention to behaviors they think will be flattering.
2. Orne (1962): Subjects are cooperative and eager to be "good subjects" so that they can aid science. They not only try to figure out the experimenter's hypothesis but they are motivated to perform in ways they think are suitable for attaining this goal based on the demand characteristics of the situation.
3. Rosenberg (1965): Subjects are anxious about the impressions they make since they assume they are being evaluated in an experiment. This apprehension leads to behavior they think places them in the best possible light.
4. Fillenbaum (1966): Subjects are "faithful" and follow instructions precisely; they refrain from attempting to second-guess or outsmart the experimenter.
5. Masling (1966): Sometimes, subjects will adopt a "screw you" attitude and resist the attempts of the experimenter to study them. They may even be uncooperative to the point of deliberately trying to undermine the experiment by behaving in unusual ways.
6. Argyris (1968): Subjects may be negativistic, resentful, and hostile, or even fail to come to their appointments because of the rigorous situational control inherent in the social relationship between the experimenter and subjects in experiments.
7. Sigall, Aronson, and Van Hoose (1970): Subjects are primarily concerned with protecting their own images, not the goals or predictions of the experimenter. In situations where these goals of

the experimenter and subjects are incompatible, subjects will behave in ways that maintain their own interests by trying to "look good."

8. Newberry (1973): Subjects have a "no hassle" outlook and are prone to be apathetic and uninvolved rather than "good" or negativistic.

Thus we see that psychologists have formed a number of views about the kinds of attitudes subjects hold about their proper role in the research setting. It should be clear, however, that several formulations do overlap. It may well be the case that there are different types of subjects, good and bad as well as indifferent with respect to their involvement in their role as subjects.

EVIDENCE FOR SELECTED MAJOR ROLES

Before proceding to a discussion of some of the conceptual problems and methodological implications of the various active roles played by subjects, we must take a fuller look at some of the evidence for the major subject roles.

Orne's "Good Subject"

This formulation is closely tied to Orne's work on demand characteristics, discussed in detail in the preceding chapter. The view of the subject as one who cooperates with the experimenter by attempting to identify *and* confirm the hypothesis also requires the subject to be keenly alert and sensitized to any demand cues in the situation. However, other roles, such as apprehension, would also lead to such attentiveness. The conception of the good subject probably owes its origins more to Orne's (1962) failure to find conditions that were sufficiently boring or tiring to make subjects quit or give up than to any experimental proof that this attitude is more valid than rival roles. It was a common-sense idea that seemed logical—after all, the subjects did volunteer.

One procedure that provides an empirical test of the good-subject role is illustrated in a study by Goldstein, Rosnow, Goodstadt, and Suls (1972), who enhanced the demand cues for half of the subjects by explicitly instructing them regarding the exact treatment they would receive. The task involved verbal conditioning using a paradigm in which subjects had to make up a series of sentences using verbs supplied by the experimenter in combination with a personal pronoun such as he or she, and so on. After sentences starting with one preselected pronoun, the experimenter would say the word "good" as a reinforcer to try to increase the frequency of sentences starting with that pronoun. Some researchers interpret this increase to be similar to conditioning whereas other investigators maintain that it involves cognitive processes at a higher level since the degree of such increase is usually greater the more aware the subjects are of the contingency between the correct response category and the reinforcement.

In any case, Goldstein et al. (1972) predicted that the opportunity for "good subject" behavior would be greater for subjects who knew what procedures would occur. In addition, they had two types of subjects, volunteers and nonvolunteers, to test the idea that volunteers would also be more prone to play the "good subject" role. As expected, higher levels of conditioning occurred for those subjects assumed to be more likely to adopt this role.

Rosenberg's "Apprehensive Subject"

Rosenberg's (1965) view of the subjects' attitude emphasized evaluation apprehension. They realize that their performance may reflect something about themselves to the experimenter although they may not be sure exactly what it is. He suggested that this process can produce difficulties for interpreting results if the degree of apprehension is not equal in all experimental conditions. Those conditions in which greater evaluation apprehension is aroused will more likely cause subjects to interpret the situation as a threat and lead them to more efforts to win positive evaluations from the experimenter than those subjects in other conditions. As a consequence, differences in behavior among different conditions may not be entirely due to variations in experimental variables but could be due, at least partially, to these unequal degrees of apprehension.

One example where there may be differential amounts of evaluation apprehension is research on cognitive dissonance. This theory predicts that a person who must argue publicly in favor of a view that is contrary to their true conviction will be more likely to undergo real attitude change when small rather than large justification is provided. This counterintuitive prediction is based on the notion that high dissonance exists if you do something you do not believe in and yet receive little justification for doing so. Such dissonance is further assumed to be a negative state that leads the person to seek ways of reducing it, such as by changing one's views in the direction of making the previously unacceptable behavior seem more attractive.

Although evidence has been provided (e.g., Festinger & Carlsmith, 1959) in support of the prediction, Rosenberg (1965) provided an alternative explanation, suggesting that high justification (low dissonance) is a condition more likely to arouse suspicion among subjects that they are being evaluated. Thus if you were offered a big sum of money to try and convince the next subject that the boring task you had just performed was very interesting, you might wonder if your integrity was being tested. This perception might make you more resistant to attitude change whereas the low justification (high dissonance) condition would be less likely to make you feel you were being bribed. You would be less suspicious and apt to show more attitude change.

Thus, the same data can be explained either in terms of different amounts of cognitive dissonance or evaluation apprehension. To try to get evidence supporting his view, Rosenberg (1965) replicated the study using two different experimenters, one for the induction of dissonance and a different one for the measurement of attitudes on the assumption there would be less apprehension if the two phases of the study appeared to be unrelated to each other.

When evaluation apprehension was reduced with this technique, Rosenberg found no support that the high justification subjects showed little attitude change. Instead the greatest attitude change occurred when justification was high (low dissonance).

Other research by Rosenberg (1969) on evaluation apprehension searched for other factors that might affect the arousal of this process. Since evaluation apprehension can distort the validity of the experimental results, it is useful to determine how it operates so that it can be minimized or equated for all treatment conditions.

Rosenberg's replication of the Festinger and Carlsmith (1959) study did vary conditions so that a test could be made of the presumed influence of different levels of evaluation apprehension, rather than merely remain a conjecture about the possible operation of this factor. It illustrates how the experimental method can be used to test hypotheses about its own nature.

Fillenbaum's "Faithful Subject"

The faithful subject is cooperative, but not to the extent of Orne's good subject. Faithful subjects do not try to figure out the purpose of the study but "faithfully" play the objective part of impartial participant. Fillenbaum (1966) arrived at this conception after discovering that prior experience with deception and debriefing did not apparently increase the suspiciousness of many subjects when they participated in another deception study which followed immediately. The faithful concept implies that although these subjects should have been suspicious, they did not let this tendency influence their performance in the later experiment. In this later experiment, subjects were instructed to cancel out certain words in a prose passage.

Then the study's "true" purpose was revealed when subjects were given an unannounced incidental learning task to see how much of the content of the passage they could recall. Fillenbaum assumed that they should have learned very little of the passage content during the word-cancelling task unless they had been suspicious that the experimenter was deceiving them. Compared to a control group that had not been given a prior deception experience, and thus should not have been unduly suspicious, Fillenbaum's deceived subjects generally showed no better performance than the control group on the incidental learning of the prose passage received in the second experiment. These findings led Fillenbaum to argue that these subjects must have assumed a "faithful" role.

It is difficult to imagine what subjects think they are being "faithful" to, if indeed they are doing so. The demonstration of this effect has been limited to incidental learning situations and needs to be shown in a variety of contexts if it is to prove valuable.

Masling's "Negativistic Subject"

Undoubtedly some subjects go to an experiment in either a hostile mood, perhaps because they feel coerced into coming, or who develop negative attitudes during the course of the study due to such factors as poor performance or lack of harmony with the experimenter. However, evidence on the pervasiveness of this type of attitude is not condusive enough to suggest that it is extensive. More importantly, unless there are different degrees to which this tendency is activated in the various conditions of an experiment, no confounding occurs between this factor and the independent variables of the study. In studies where unpleasant experiences such as stress, shock, frustration, or even boredom are involved, it is possible that precisely this type of differential arousal may occur such that the groups receiving the unpleasant experiences are more hostile toward the experiment than those encountering neutral events. Unfortunately, little systematic research has been done on this problem.

Even the argument that some subjects, distributed evenly across conditions of the study, are negativistic is based more on intuition and impression than on careful systematic studies. Epstein, Suedfeld, and Silverstein (1973) reported one demonstration that shows one possible factor leading to negativism. For half of the subjects, the experimenter arrived 20 minutes late, either with or without a reasonable excuse. A control group waited 20 minutes with the experimenter present before taking the digit-symbol task, while a second control group was tested immediately upon arrival. In all conditions, testing was done by an assistant who was blind as to the treatment since another person arranged schedules and made excuses when experimenters were late. A later evaluation of the study showed that subjects who had had unexcused late assistants were more negative toward their experimenter; unfortunately, no data on actual task performance was reported.

Sigall, Aronson, and Van Hoose's "Looking Good Subject"

Motives often do not exist in isolation but may compete with opposing motives. The attitude dominant one moment may suddenly shift within the same experiment, such as when apprehension becomes so strong that uncooperativeness develops as a form of defence to prevent identification of the subject's "true personality."

One view that illustrates the interaction of motives is that of Sigall, Aronson, and Van Hoose (1970), who argued that the motives of the subject may sometimes clash with behaviors expected by the experimenter. Like Riecken (1962), they suggested that the subject is primarily concerned with looking good, which may increase cooperativeness, thus confirming the experimenter's hypothesis. However, suppose the situation required behavior that would make the subject appear foolish or act in an unflattering manner. Under these conditions, Sigall et al. predicted that the subject would no longer cooperate to fulfill the experimenter's hypotheses but would instead behave so as to give the best possible self-presentation.

Sigall et al. tested this analysis by creating a task that pitted the motive of pleasing the experimenter against the motive of looking good. The study allegedly involved a test of the effect of reduced room lighting on the copying of a long list of telephone numbers. One group was told that they should do poorly while another was led to believe they would do well. A third group was provided with no expectancy.

The results showed that both of the expectancy groups showed improvements when contrasted with the no-expectancy group. Thus, even when they thought they should do worse,subjects did not perform at a level to confirm this prediction, but instead achieved higher performance which placed them in a more positive light.

This interpretation especially applies to the performance of a fourth group that was led to expect to do poorly and also told that people who performed well were probably "obsessive-compulsive." Under these circimstances, performance did *decrease*. However, as Sigall et al. argued, this decrease is more likely due to the motive to avoid "looking bad" or obsessive-compulsive rather to any wish to make the experimenter look good by fulfilling the hypothesis.

Some reservations about the interpretation of the Sigall et al. study have been raised by Adair and Schachter (1972). They argued that demand characteristics in the instructions for the decreased performance expectancy group may have prompted subjects to try harder. Specifically in this condition, Sigall et al. told subjects that their performance would decrease relative to a preliminary practice trial because the room illumination was reduced during the test session.

In the replication study by Adair and Schachter, the reduced room illumination was emphasized for one group while it was minimized for another group. Both groups showed gains in performance relative to the practice trial but larger gains occurred when the reduced illumination was emphasized, suggesting that subjects did try harder when challenged by the more difficult circumstances.

Another failure to repeat the findings of Sigall et al. was reported by McGinley, Kaplan, and Kinsey (1975) who learned from postexperimental interviews that many subjects assumed that they should improve regardless of what they may have been told by the experimenter. After all, they had all received a so-called practice trial so it was reasonable to infer that performance should be better on the "real" test. According to McGinley et al., the practice trial acted as a cue that led subjects to try to improve; their actual improvement stems from this perception rather than a motive to "look good."

Although the interpretations of the Sigall et al. study vary, their approach, which suggests the simultaneous existence of several roles that sometimes may work together and at other times work in opposition, probably is a more accurate description of the complexity of the subject's motivations than one that assumes a single or unitary role. A blend of curiosity, apprehension, interest, desire to aid science, cooperativeness, and self-interest exists side-by-side and leads the subject to be more patient and tolerant of the experimenter and the treatments administered to them. Some reasonable amount of discomfort, pain, and deception will be accepted although if they, or any other procedures, are perceived as frivolous, hostile, or unnecessary the attitudes of the subject may rapidly become those of resentment, apathy, and negativism.

Other evidence from a different area, attitude change, agrees with the type of analysis made by Sigall et al. Silverman and Shulman (1970) also predicted that whenever subjects are in conflict between complying with the demand characteristics of the task and promoting their own image favorably, they will act to enhance themselves, to the detriment of the experimenter's hypothesis.

Their analysis was based on attitude-change studies that involve situations where subjects are generally aware that the purpose is to assess their attitudes and how they might be altered under various conditions. How should subjects react in such situations? If they allow themselves to be persuaded, might they not appear to be weakminded and malleable; if they resist the propaganda messages, might they not appear to be independent and individualistic? On the other hand, if they are persuaded, might this not reflect cooperativeness and openmindedness whereas if they steadfastly resist, might they not be regarded as rigid and dogmatic? Clearly, subjects face considerable conflict in attitude-change studies in deciding whether or not to comply with demand characteristics.

Silverman and Shulman (1970) made several predictions. In accord with Sigall et al., they predicted compliance or attitude change when there was a relative lack of evaluation apprehension. However, if the latter factor was present, subjects were predicted to act to maintain favorable self-presentation, even if this behavior did not match demand characteristics. In fact, it was predicted that if demand cues were too strong, subjects might intentionally become negativistic or act in exactly the opposite direction, possibly to avoid giving the bad impression of being easily manipulable.

CONCEPTUAL PROBLEMS

In an important analysis, Weber and Cook (1972) raised a number of issues concerning the usefulness of arguments on the nature of the subject's role. Although a number of plausible conceptions have been proposed, no independent evidence has generally supported them or ruled out the validity of alternative roles. Often, the nature of the role assumed by subjects is postulated after the experiment is over and one has observed their behavior.

One exception to this criticism was a study by Earn and Kroger (1976), who manipulated subjects' conceptions of their roles by providing half of them with a prepared script urging them to be active, alert, cooperative and giving the other half the prepared role of passive, relaxed, objective, and faithful followers of instructions.

Using the task developed by Sigall et al. (1970), subgroups were led to expect performance increases or decreases, or given no expectancies. The results showed active-role subjects showed greater changes in the directions expected by the experimenter, as compared with the performance of the passive-role subjects. This study supports the view that the role assumed by subjects is an important determinant of behavior; moreoever, since Earn and Kroger controlled the type of role subjects played, their conclusion is strengthened because it avoids the circularity of *ex post facto* explanations.

Weber and Cook (1972) concluded that it is difficult to rule out the operation of evaluation apprehension in experiments and that it probably can account for behaviors attributed by Orne to the "good subject" role and by Fillenbaum to the "faithful subject" role. They argued that the primary subject role is that of apprehension which may sometimes lead to good or faithful role behavior.

They rejected Orne's assumption that subjects try to figure out the hypothesis and then perform accordingly on the grounds that it is often impossible for subjects to correctly identify hypotheses, as when subjects serve in only one of a number of different treatment conditions. Without knowing the nature of these other treatments, a subject can not logically infer the purpose of the overall study.

In one sense, Weber and Cook are correct. However, subjects may still generate their own impressions and hypotheses, even if not identical to the experimenter's, that will affect their behavior. Moreover, it is not necessary for subjects in one treatment condition to know or figure out the overall design of the study to guess the kind of behavior the experimenter may be looking for. Milgram's (1963) subjects, for example, may have had no idea that they were in a study of obedience to authority. They may even have accepted the cover story that the painful shocks they were required to administer to the "other subject" really were for the purpose of providing feedback on the learning task assigned to the victim. Yet they may have also realized from the demand characteristics of the situation that the experimenter expected them to comply with his commands to increase shock intensity levels over the course of the session and certainly not to refuse to cooperate.

In addition to the usefulness of acknowledging the existence of individual differences in roles assumed by subjects and the conception that several simultaneous motives may operate within a given subject, we should also consider the possibility that the role adopted by a subject may *change* over the course of an experiment. As diagrammed in Figure 11-1, most subjects come to experiments with some degree of evaluation apprehension created merely by the thought of being tested. Upon reaching the laboratory and meeting the experimenter, this

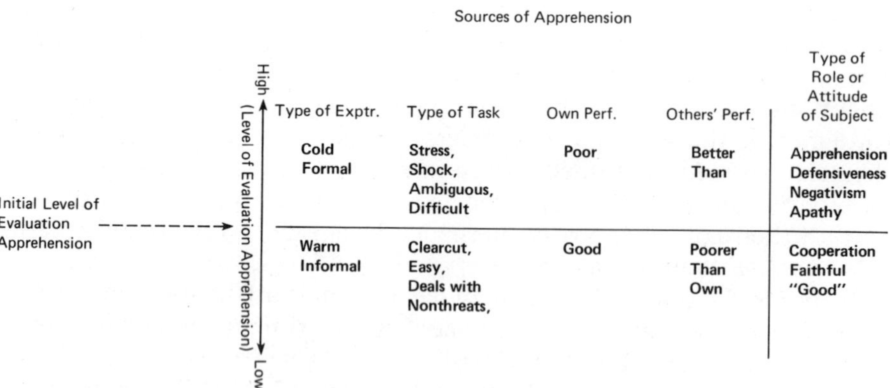

FIGURE 11-1. Diagram showing how initial levels of evaluation apprehension when subjects arrive at the experiment can be shifted up or down during the course of the study by several factors.

initial level of apprehension may be altered in either direction or remain unchanged, depending on these initial experiences. Formal conditions may intimidate most subjects, adding to their anxiety, whereas informal circumstances may reassure them and relax tension.

As the session gets underway, the quality of the subjects' performance as well as that of others in some kinds of studies, may modify apprehension levels again. Subtle reactions, such as nonverbal responses by the experimenter, can also affect the subjects' attitudes. In comparison to the initial level of apprehension, an overall reduction in anxiety may promote cooperation and faithful behavior from subjects, whereas an increase in apprehension may encourage defensiveness. In extreme cases such as where the experimenter or assistants and confederates deliberately insult or criticize the subject, the increased apprehension may turn into negativistic or apathetic attitudes.

A factor that might lead the same subject to assume different roles is the extent to which the subject has encountered deception or negative experiences in prior studies. Cook, Bean, Calder, Frey, Krovetz, and Reisman (1970) examined the effect of different amounts of experience with deceptions and subsequent debriefings in which the true purpose was revealed. Subjects served in five consecutive experiments dealing with different problems in the area of social psychology of attitudes, but they were supposed to be seen as totally unrelated studies. Actually, Cook et al. were interested in attitudes toward each study for different subgroups of subjects who, due to varying sequences in which they experienced the different studies, had been exposed to deception in varying amounts. One unique feature of this study is the large number of studies each subject underwent and also the fact that they were distributed over such a long time period–five weeks. This aspect of the procedure makes it less likely that subjects will think of the different studies as being tied together as might be the case when subjects receive two back-to-back experiments in the same session even if the experimenters are different and the investigator tries to make them believe the two studies are unrelated (e.g., Fillenbaum, 1966).

The results led Cook et al. to conclude that prior experience with deception did *not* affect the roles assumed by subjects. Although they may have become more suspicious, they did not act differently. This finding might be seen as consistent with Fillenbaum's faithful subject role, but not supportive of Masling's negativistic subject role.

Cook et al. conducted a second study under conditions that might optimize the arousal of suspicion of deception to provide a better test of how such awareness affects roles. Subjects received two consecutive but apparently unconnected studies in the same session conducted by two different experimenters. In the first study, all subjects were deceived but only half of them were debriefed. The second study also involved deception; for one subgroup the instructions used a term, "cognitive organization," several times to try to make subjects associate it with the first study, which also emphasized that same term.

Despite these increased cues for suspicion of deception, it does not appear to have altered the subject roles. In fact, Cook et al. suggested this example may have, as noted by Orne (1962), such obvious demand cues that the subject bends over backward to be honest. Greater amounts of suspicion seem to have occurred for subjects in the condition deceived on the first task, but given no cues that the two tasks were related. Suspicion was also high for subjects in another condition who were *not* deceived but only read a passage about the use of deception in experiments as part of their first task and also received cues implying that their second task was related to the first. This complex set of results led Cook et al. to conclude that there may not be a single reaction to prior experience with deception. This analysis may account for the disparity reported by other investigators of this issue who have found anything from faithful behavior (Fillenbaum, 1966) to apprehension (Silverman, Shulman & Wiesenthal, 1970) to resistance or negativism (Brock & Becker, 1966; Edelman, 1970; Christensen, 1977). These findings, discussed further in Chapter 12, need not be incompatible with each other but may merely reflect the complexity of reactions of subjects to suspicions of deception.

METHODOLOGICAL IMPLICATIONS

Thus far we have examined the variety of subject roles that might be assumed as well as some of the evidence supporting each conception. Now we must discuss the important question of how such roles can bias the outcomes and conclusions of experiments.

Weber and Cook (1972) distinguish three types of artifacts stemming from the roles played by subjects: false positive, false negative, and false serendipitous. When subjects play the "good subject" role, they may tend to provide false positive results and confirm the hypothesis in their eagerness to please the experimenter. Conversely, false negative findings occur if subjects are negativistic and refuse to cooperate. Finally, false serendipitous results can also be generated by negativistic subjects, especially if the experimenter does not realize this attitude is present. They may produce a pattern of results that, although it fails to support the original hypothesis, may be compatible with some *other* formulation the experimenter may serendipitously "discover" after he or she gets over the initial disappointment from examining the data.

We have already pointed out that Weber and Cook (1972) concluded that the underlying subject role in most situations is evaluation apprehension. How can this role create artifacts? If, according to Weber and

Cook, one treatment condition activates more apprehension than others, the results may reflect differences in this factor rather than treatment differences imposed or intended by the experimenter. Whenever unusual procedures are employed, as in the case of many social-psychological studies, Weber and Cook argued that it is likely that some conditions will involve more apprehension and suspicion than others. Control treatment groups typically receive rather dull activities in comparison.

These differences in evaluation apprehension can sometimes be responsible for false positive findings, such as when the treatment producing the highest apprehension is also the one predicted to produce the most extreme scores. False serendipitous results can be expected if variations in apprehension across treatments occur that are inconsistent with the original theory but yet are consonant with an alternative formulation the investigator creates after the initial theory is disconfirmed. Finally, one might obtain false negative results or a failure to confirm the predictions because the differences in apprehension produce too much variation among subjects in their behavior so that any effect of the independent variable is masked.

In addition to these preceding threats to *internal validity,* subject roles also jeopardize *external validity* or generalizability of laboratory experiments. In the real world, subjects or people are not or do not think they are being evaluated for research purposes much of the time, so their behavior is not influenced by this reactive process. This critical difference between the experimental and real-world contexts suggests a major reason why results from experiments often fail to apply to real behavior. The "good" or "faithful" subject roles generate behavior that is more cooperative and compliant than that ordinarily found in the real-world counterparts of an experiment. The evaluation-apprehensive role will often produce higher motivation and better performance in the experimental context.

A dilemma exists when we seek ways of reducing the influence of subject roles, such as evaluation apprehension. To the extent that we succeed, we may also reduce the realism and seriousness of the situation. Apprehension may be an unavoidable but also desirable, in some ways, aspect of experiments.

An important experiment by Carlston and Cohen (1980) avoided some of the limitations of most analyses about subject roles by using explicit instructions for different groups of subjects designed to reflect four of the major conceptions of the role assumed by subjects in experiments. To the extent that subjects obeyed the instructions, we can assume safely that the four different groups were approaching the experimental task differently.

In addition, Carlston and Cohen designed a task that should lead to different types of behavior for each of the four subject roles. Prior studies usually do not have tasks that enable one to infer which specific role was assumed by the subject, since several roles may have led to the same responses. Or, subjects with the same roles may have produced variations in response on the same behavioral tasks. Carlston and Cohen planned their experiment to compare all four subject roles under conditions where the dependent variables would differ for each role so that better inferences could be made about the relationship between each subject role and behavior.

There were these four roles, described by excerpts from the actual experiment:

> *Good subject:* We would like you to play the role of a good, cooperative subject . . . you are anxious to help out the experimenter by providing valuable scientific data.
>
> *Faithful subject:* We would like you to play the role of the faithful, compliant subject . . . your responsibility is to follow all instructions as closely as possible, without speculating on what is going on.
>
> *Negativistic subject.* We would like you to play the role of a hostile, antagonistic subject. You didn't want to come here in the first place . . . try to mess up the experiment by providing useless data.
>
> *Apprehensive subject.* We would like you to play the role of a subject who is out to impress people with his intelligence. You are concerned about being evaluated in an experiment . . . prove that you measure up.

A fifth condition was used as a control group which was provided with an instructional set to be curious:

> *Curious subject.* We would like you to play the role of the curious subject. You feel that psychologists are usually deceptive, so you try hard to figure out what the experiment is really about . . . act in accordance with your theory rather than with what the experimenter said.

A final control group was included and was given no role-play instructions at all.

Each subject was seated before a computer monitor and told to pick one nonsense syllable out of each series of three nonsense syllables which would be displayed in a row for use on a later memory task. They were told that prior research has shown that the two hemispheres of the brain differ in dominance, and that right-handed persons have a dominant left hemisphere and vice versa for left-handed persons. They were told that the purpose of the present study was to see if this dominance affected visual perceptions. The hypothesis was stated that right-handed persons should choose the nonsense syllable located on the right side of the display and vice verse for left-handed persons.

Since the subjects all knew what the experimenter was predicting, it was assumed by Carlston and Cohen that good subjects would try to confirm the hypothesis and pick the nonsense syllable location that corresponded with their handedness. In contrast, negativistic role subjects should try to make the experimenter look wrong by picking the location opposite to their handedness.

The rows of nonsense syllables were shown either at the top, middle, or bottom of the screen, depending on the subject's choice. It was after explained that the top row would contain easiest items, with harder items being in the middle row, and that the most difficult items would occur in the bottom row. The number of points awarded would be proportional to the row difficulty selected by the subject.

It was assumed that the typical subject would generally choose the more difficult items so they could impress the experimenter by earning more points and appearing more intelligent, especially if the subjects were apprehensive.

Faithful subjects, however, might obey instructions that actually gave them *lower* scores. Carlston and Cohen tested this assumption by interrupting all of the subjects just as the item selection was to begin by giving them a note asking them to choose the top (easier) rows most of the time. It was predicted that only the faithful role subjects would be likely to follow this otherwise unexplained instruction.

In summary, the instructions contained a series of procedures designed to lead subjects following different roles to make different types of responses, either in terms of the left–right spatial location of the selected nonsense syllable or in terms of the chosen row location that reflected difficulty level.

The overall results are summarized in Table 11–1. After the experiment, a series of questions was used to determine if the different instructions had succeeded in creating different motives for the various subject roles. The self-reported motivation was highest for the good role while it was lowest for the negativistic role.

Other questions were aimed at determining how much subjects remembered about the purpose of the experiment, especially about the stated or ostensive hypothesis. As Table 11–1 shows, lowest knowledge occurred for the apprehensive and negativistic subject roles.

An examination of the row choices indicated that the request to concentrate on the easier top rows, which gave fewest points, was followed best by the faithful and good subjects while negativistic subjects were neutral. Apprehensive subjects who were concerned about looking good disobeyed and chose the bottom rows the most often, in order to impress the experimenter.

Table 11–1 shows that conformity to the ostensive hypothesis by choosing the particular word within a row that matched their dominant hand was highest for the good and faithful subjects. Negativistic subjects tended to provide response choices that refuted the hypothesis whereas the other three roles led to neutral evidence.

Finally, a recognition test containing the selected words as well as

TABLE 11–1. Experimentally Identified Attributes of Various Subject Roles.

Variable	Subject Role					
	Good	*Faithful*	*Apprehensive*	*Negativistic*	*Curious*	*Control*
Self-reported motivation to provide good data	Very high	Moderate	Moderate	None[a]	Moderate	Moderate
Recall of ostensive experimental hypothesis	Correct	Correct	None	None	Correct	Correct
Compliance with a non-self-enhancing instruction	High obedience	High obedience	Moderate *dis*obedience	None	Moderate obedience	High obedience
Conformity to the ostensive experimental hypothesis	Positive	Positive	None	Negative	None	None
Relative performance on recall task[b]	Good	Good	Good	Poor	Poor	Good

[a]"None" indicates a neutral rather than negative score on each variable.
[b]As indicated by the number of nonappearing words erroneously identified.
Source: "A closer examination of subject roles," by D. E. Carlston and J. L. Cohen. *Journal of Personality and Social Psychology*, 1980, **38**, 857–70.

some new distractor items showed that the curious and negativistic subjects incorrectly chose more of the new items although they were equal to the other groups in picking out the correct items.

CONCLUSIONS

Taken as a whole, the results of the Carlston and Cohen experiment show that different roles can not only be created by instructions but that these roles can lead to different types of behavior, at least in a situation involving cognitive skills. However, as Carlston and Cohen pointed out, most experiments do not spell out in advance such explicit roles for subjects to assume, offer such obvious cues about the purpose or hypotheses of the study, or have dependent measures that unequivocably reveal the nature of the underlying motivations of the subjects. Moreover, in order for biases due to subject roles to alter the outcome of a given experiment, it is first necessary for a large majority of the subjects to assume the same role.

In the Carlston and Cohen study, a measure of the type of behavior of typical subjects who are not given an explicit role to play can be inferred by examination of the control group. Their behavior seems to fall in a neutral area, both with respect to an active-passive and a positive-negative dimension when compared with the behavior of the subjects playing explicit roles provided by the instructions. As a result, Carlston and Cohen concluded that biases due to subject roles are probably rare and are not a serious problem for most research.

Although the conclusion drawn by Carlston and Cohen seems warranted and reassuring, it must be noted that their results may depend to some degree on the type of experimental task involved. Their memory task, while ego-involving, is perhaps not as threatening as many other tasks. While one strength of this experiment was the controlled observation of the different roles by creating them through instructions, one might wonder if such blatant instructions aroused suspicion or even poor role playing for the apprehensive, negativistic, or even the curious role subjects who were told to be especially suspicious and negativistic.

SUMMARY

The human subject in a psychological experiment who knows that he or she is being observed may assume a variety of different attitudes or roles. These roles may be diverse, ranging from cooperation to apprehension to negativism.

Perhaps the most pervasive attitude of subjects is that of apprehension due to the awareness that their performance will be evaluated and may reflect adversely upon them. It is also possible that subjects may simultaneously be anxious to cooperate with and assist the experimenter by being a "good subject." In most cases, these two different roles may have the same effect on behavior and make it difficult to isolate the influence of each role. On the other hand, if the type of behavior required to meet the experimenter's hypothesis makes the subject appear in a less favorable light, there is evidence that the subject will be more concerned about performing in a manner to "look good" rather than to fulfill the experimenter's hypothesis.

Many of the speculations about the role subjects play in experiments are conjectural, and alternative views can not be discounted in a given experiment. In addition, the roles or attitudes of subjects may shift during the course of an experiment rather than remain constant.

The roles subjects adopt may represent sources of threats to internal validity, as when the roles are different for different treatment conditions. Thus, if more apprehension is aroused in the experimental than in the control condition, the results of the study may stem from this difference rather than to the independent variable of interest. False positive findings can occur if subjects cooperate to such an extent that they yield to the demand cues in order to please the experimenter. False negative results may occur if subjects assume a negativistic role and obscure any real effects of the independent variable.

REFERENCES

Adair, J., and Schachter, B. S. To cooperate or to look good? The subject's and experimenter's perceptions of each other's intentions. *Journal of Experimental and Social Psychology,* 1972, *8*, 74-85.

Argyris, C. Some unintended effects of rigorous research. *Psychological Bulletin,* 1966, *19*, 185-197.

Brock, T. C., and Becker, L. A. "Debriefing" and susceptibility to subsequent experimental manipulations. *Journal of Experimental and Social Psychology,* 1966, *2*, 314-323.

Carlston, D. E., and Cohen, J. L. A closer examination of subject roles. *Journal of Personality and Social Psychology,* 1980, *38*, 857-870.

Christensen, L. The negative subject: Myth, reality, or a prior experience effect. *Journal of Personality and Social Psychology,* 1977, *35*, 392-400.

Cook, T. D., Bean, J. R., Calder, B. J., Frey, R., Krovetz, M. L., and Reisman, S. R. Demand characteristics and three conceptions of the frequently deceived subject. *Journal of Personality and Social Psychology,* 1970, *14*, 185-194.

Earn, B. M., and Kroger, R. O. The subject in psychological experiments: Effects of explicitly induced subject roles on laboratory experiment. *Personality and Social Psychological Bulletin,* 1976, *2*, 466-469.

Edelman, R. I. Some variables affecting suspicion of deception. *Journal of Personality and Social Psychology,* 1970, *15*, 333-337.

Epstein, Y. M., Suedfeld, P., and Silverstein, S. J. The experimental contract: Subject's expectations of and reactions to some behaviors of experimenters. *American Psychologist,* 1973, *28*, 212-221.

Festinger, L., and Carlsmith, J. Cognitive consequences of forced compliance. *Journal of Abnormal and Social Psychology,* 1959, *56,* 203-210.

Fillenbaum, S. Prior deception and subsequent experimental performance: The "faithful" subject. *Journal of Personality and Social Psychology*, 1966, *4*, 532-537.

Goldstein, J. H., Rosnow, R. L., Goodstadt, B. E., and Suls, J. M. The "good subject" in verbal operant conditioning research. *Journal of Experimental Research in Personality,* 1972, *6*, 29-33.

Masling, J. Role-related behavior of the subject and psychologist and its effects upon psychological data, *Nebraska Symposium on Motivation* (Vol. 14). Lincoln: University of Nebraska Press, 1966.

McGinely, H., Kaplan, M., and Kinsey, T. Subject effects and demand characteristics. *Psychological Reports,* 1975, *36*, 267-278.

Milgram, S. Behavioral study of obedience. *Journal of Abnormal and Social Psychology,* 1963, *67*, 371-378.

Newberry, B. J. Truth telling in subjects with information about experiments: Who is being deceived? *Journal of Personality and Social Psychology,* 1973, *25*, 369-374.

Orne, M. T. On the social psychology of the psychological experiment: With particular reference to demand characteristics and their implications. *American Psychologist,* 1962, *17*, 776-783.

Riecken, H. W. A program for research on experiments in social psychology. In N. F. Washburne (Ed.), *Decisions, values and groups,* Vol. 2. New York: Pergamon Press, 1962.

Rosenberg, M. J. When dissonance fails: On eliminating evaluation apprehension from attitude measurement. *Journal of Personality and Social Psychology,* 1965, *1*, 18-42.

Rosenberg, M. J. The conditions and consequences of evaluation apprehension. In R. Rosenthal & R. L. Rosnow (Eds.), *Artifact in behavioral research.* New York: Academic Press, 1969.

Sigall, H., Aronson, E., and Van Hoose, T. The cooperative subject: Myth or reality. *Journal of Experimental and Social Psychology,* 1970, *6*, 1-10.

Silverman, I., and Shulman, A. D. A conceptual model of artifact in attitude change studies. *Sociometry,* 1970, *33*, 97-107.

Silverman, I., Shulman, A., and Weisenthal, D. L. Effects of deceiving and debriefing psychological subjects on performance in later experiments. *Journal of Personality and Social Psychology,* 1970 *14*, 203-212.

Weber, S. J., and Cook, T. D. Subject effects in laboratory research: An examination of subject roles, demand characteristics, and valid inferences. *Psychological Bulletin,* 1972, *77*, 273-295.

CHAPTER 12

Who Serves as Subjects in Psychological Experiments?

Chapter at a Glance

Several analyses have confirmed the commonly held stereotype of the typical subject in human psychological research as college sophomores enrolled in introductory and other psychology courses. Smart (1966) examined the 1962–1964 *Journal of Abnormal and Social Psychology* and *Journal of Experimental Psychology* and discovered that 73 and 86 per cent, respectively, of the experimental articles reported there used college psychology students as subjects. Furthermore, a disproportionate number of these subjects were male. A later survey (Schultz, 1969) of journal articles showed high agreement.

Menges (1973) conducted a survey of about 1000 articles from several journals in 1971 and obtained evidence suggesting a somewhat lower, but still high, reliance on college students. About half of the articles in the *Journal of Personality and Social Psychology* and the *Journal of Experimental Psychology* were based on college students fulfilling psychology course required participation. Many of the subjects used for research published in other journals, although from a college population, were obtained by personal solicitation. Thus, 75 per cent of articles reported in *Journal of Abnormal Psychology* and the *Journal of Counseling* used this approach. About one-third of the articles in these latter journals bypassed direct recruitment of subjects since they involved data analysis of information, such as test scores, which were routinely given to students in conjunction with some other primary purpose, such as personal guidance and counselling.

A different approach was used by the author (Jung, 1969) to obtain estimates of the extent to which college psychology students were used for research purposes by psychologists associated with colleges and universities. A survey of 60 major graduate psychology programs was conducted since it was assumed that these leading Departments of Psychology conduct the most research and also that their practices would influence those used by other institutions. The results showed that over 90 per cent of the human subjects used in academia were college students, with about 80 per cent coming from introductory psychology courses.

This highly selective source of subjects was not always the favored type of research participant. As noted in Chapter 10, early psychologists who were interested primarily in sensory processes preferred highly experienced rather than unsophistocated or naive subjects, using themselves, colleagues, and graduate students rather than college sophomores. Changes in topics of interest toward personality and social psychology as well as the emphasis on group differences rather than individual cases encouraged the move toward use of college psychology students who were not only naive but also in plentiful supply. Since many studies with more complex designs required several hundred subjects, it would have been virtually impossible to do research without this convenient and ample source. Despite these obvious advantages, use of this source introduces serious problems.

One does not need statistical information to be convinced that college students are not typical of the general population. They differ in intelligence, age, and social-class background to name a few obvious factors. Furthermore, they do not hold the same patterns of attitudes, values, and interests that noncollege populations typically have (Bereiter & Freedman, 1962; Sternberg, 1955). In addition, there may be differences among students as a function of size, location, or prestige of their colleges.

Within the college population, one would expect differences to exist among students majoring in different fields. Introductory psychology courses probably consist more of psychology majors than of students enrolled in other introductory courses.

Results of studies performed with college students—mostly introductory psychology students—are frequently applied to other populations differing substantially in a variety of dimensions. For some types of phenomena, these generalizations may hold, but for many other processes, we may expect different findings for college and noncollege populations. It appears urgent that psychologists make greater efforts to utilize subjects other than introductory psychology students. Although they are less convenient to use than college students, there are other sources of large captive audiences such as hospital patients, prison inmates, and military personnel which might be used as subjects more frequently under appropriate circumstances.

But such changes will not come easily because they are costly both in terms of time and money. Probably as long as psychologists can justify or rationalize the required participation of psychology students as subjects, little headway will be made toward studying other types of people. One incentive for changing present sources of subjects might be the demonstration in numerous studies of empirical differences in results between college and noncollege subjects.

This pessimism is reinforced by an anecdote reported by Argyris (1968). He reported that some students had speculated about the possibility of creating a source of subjects similar to the Manpower Supply of Business Help. Through such a union, students who served as subjects might get paid, be better treated by experimenters, and receive more thorough feedback about the study than they could by serving as subjects for course requirements. Argyris described the reactions of some psychologists to this idea as "... similar to the reactions of businessmen who have just been told for the first time that their employees were considering the creation of a union" (p. 189). There was also nervous laughter and scorn. It appears that human experimental psychology may continue to be the psychology of the college sophomore for many years to come!

However, as just noted, one obvious problem is that not all college sophomores or psychology students are alike. It may often be misleading to make generalizations about college research participants and there is a real need for comparison of subgroups on dimensions such as sex, ethnicity, age, and other demographic variables. In the past, description of such features of subjects was often omitted in research reports; thus, Carlson and Carlson (1961) surveyed a number of published articles and found that few reports identified even the sex of their subjects. Schwabacher (1972) found that about half of the studies published in 1970–1971 in one journal included both sexes. In these studies, one could have compared results as a function of sex, but such comparisons were rare as investigators were either uninterested in this variable or assumed it made no difference.

Reardon and Prescott (1977) examined the same journal several years later and noted that a shift had occurred in the sex composition of subject, with a four-fold increase in all-female subject studies and an over fifty per cent drop in all-male subject studies. In many of the studies, especially those with all female subjects, there was a tendency to overgeneralize findings to both sexes. It should be pointed out that this surveyed journal deals only with topics in social and personality psychology and may not reflect the distribution of sex with research in other subfields.

The important issue for our purposes is the infrequent examination of results as a function of subject variables such as sex. A given investigator may choose to use only one sex for a theoretical reason or due to lack of availability of subjects of the other sex, but whatever the reason, this aspect of the composition of the sample should be reported and mention of the limits of generalization of the results should be made clear.

THE HUMAN SUBJECT POOL

In all likelihood a "human subject pool" exists in every Department of Psychology that has an active program of research using humans. This supply of research participants consists of students enrolled in introductory psychology for the most part who must fulfill some type of course requirement or option by serving as subjects in research conducted by faculty and advanced students. Although commonly described as "volunteers," the term "draftee" or "quasi-volunteer" is more accurate in describing these subjects. This primary source of subjects may be augmented by true volunteers, sometimes paid but occasionally gratis participants who are under no pressure to serve. However, only about 7 per cent of all human subjects—psychology or nonpsychology students—were found to fall into this category (Jung, 1969).

Scheduling Methods

In most psychology departments (67 per cent), the scheduling of appointments and the choice of experiments is left largely to the initiative and convenience of the participants. They sign up or arrange appointments for the experiments of their choice, a procedure that may permit some forms of bias in sampling, which will be discussed shortly.

An alternate method that avoids these types of biases is used by only a few Departments, accounting for only 11 per cent of the subjects used, according to the survey conducted by the author (Jung, 1969). This system involves more administrative work since it requires maintaining a file of all of the students and their times of availability as well as various amounts of background information such as age, sex, phone number, and address and possibly items such as grade point average and scores on a few standardized tests.

Researchers may either draw a random sample or select subjects with certain qualifications that fit the nature of the research problem. Subjects who are selected by the investigator receive notification and if appointment times are agreeable, they are scheduled for testing.

Bias Due to Subject-Initiated Selection of Experiment

As noted previously, most subject pools allow a "cafeteria" system in which subjects choose their own experiments. Is it possible that this method introduces a bias in research? Martin and Marcuse (1958) found that studies described as dealing with personality or with sex attitudes were more popular than those labelled learning experiments. A similar study by Silverman and Margulis (1973) compared characteristics of those who sign up for studies on "Personality Assessment" vs. "Color Preferences." Even though the available appointment times were identical, different kinds of persons chose different studies. The personality study attracted students who were more intellectual, curious, socially interested, and religiously skeptical than those signing up for the color preference study.

Siess (1973) asked subjects to volunteer for 14 different hypothetical experiments which were identified by a descriptive title and a brief descriptive paragraph. They were also asked to take a personality inventory which included measures of the kinds of skills called for on the 14 different experiments.

Sex differences in preferences were found which matched expectations based on traditional sex roles, with females preferring social-service involvement such as preschool teaching aide more than males while males were more likely than females to choose risky activities such as aeronautical simulation. For each sex, there was also a correlation between scores on the personality test and experiment preferences, showing that subjects preferred tasks that matched their own skills and abilities.

While the preceding evidence shows that self-selection of experiments for participation can create biased sampling, it is not clear that this source of bias is frequent. In the author's survey (Jung, 1969), 67 per cent of the Departments of Psychology did allow all subjects to select their own experiments. A followup survey (Jung, 1977) showed an increase up to 81 per cent using this procedure. But it should not be concluded that all of these Departments provide descriptive information or titles about experiments as in the experiments by Siess (1973) and Silverman and Margulis (1973). It is the author's impression that many universities use nondescriptive numbers or code words to identify their experiments so that subject-initiated sign-ups do not allow bias through knowledge about the content or purpose of experiments, except through the grapevine when students leak out information to other students as to which experiments are fun, tedious, or brief, and so forth.

The only empirical study on this issue, however, does cause some concern. Johnson (1973) surveyed 39 Canadian university psychology departments and found that 29 of them did provide content descriptions when recruiting subjects. This unwise procedure may have been considered necessary since only about 25 per cent of the graduate departments involved in this survey had a required participation of students enrolled in classes. Perhaps when participation is optional or genuinely voluntary, it is difficult to obtain subjects without providing more information in advance about the content.

Although there is no study of American universities on the frequency with which subjects are provided with this preexperimental information, the fact that most American universities (Jung, 1969) impose course-required participation would suggest that little or no content descriptions of experiments are provided to prospective subjects.

Bias as a Function of Early vs. Late Term Sign-ups

The common procedure of allowing subjects to choose their own appointment times may create biased sampling through a different process since some subjects will tend to sign-up early in the term while others wait until later. This temporal difference might reflect differences in motivation or interest in participation, anxiety about completing course requirements, or some other personality differences.

Evans and Donnerstein (1974) recruited students for a study of "opinions and beliefs" and compared those who participated early as opposed to late in the term. Early-term subjects of both sexes were more internally controlled, as measured by Rotter's (1966) Internal-External Locus of Control scale, suggesting that they had greater belief in the role of their own effort and initiative rather than luck or chance as causes of events that happen to them. They also were more academically oriented than late-term subjects. Higher achievement motivation was found for early-term subjects but only among males. Perhaps other differences which were not assessed may also exist between early- and late-term participants. The results obtained by Evans and Donnerstein could make comparisons between studies conducted at different times of the term confusing if the kinds of subjects obtained at those different times perform divergently. With some tasks, this factor may be unimportant, as appears to be the case in verbal learning where Underwood, Schwenn, and Keppel (1964) found no effect of time of participation. It would be wise, perhaps, whenever a study requires most of the term to complete, for the data of early and late subjects to be compared to make sure that they are equivalent.

Bias Due to Amount of Experimental Experience

Departments of Psychology vary in the number of required participations of students (Jung, 1969), ranging from one to as many as 10 per term. It is not clear how Departments decided upon the exact number to require, but one suspects that to a large extent the total research activity of each Department was the major factor. In other words, the estimated number of subjects needed was divided by the number of students available to determine how many sessions to require of each student. If other factors such as the educational value to each student gained by participation were important, one would expect less variation among institutions.

Evidence exists that subjects who have served in a larger number of studies differ in their attitudes and behavior in some types of studies as compared with subjects with little or no prior experience. It is possible that as one serves in successive studies, one learns how to be a subject. General anxiety may decrease, although specific anxieties such as suspicion about deceptions may increase with experience. Comparisons of subjects who, at the same time of the term, have fulfilled more of their required sessions or volunteered for more studies may have more positive attitudes and greater motivation to serve than those with less participation.

Holmes (1967) found more experienced subjects to be more cooperative in a verbal-conditioning paradigm. The type of experience, positive or negative, must also be considered. Holmes and Applebaum (1970) found that the likelihood of subsequent participation was greater for those who had encountered prior positive experimental experiences.

In Holmes's (1967) study of verbal conditioning, more experienced subjects reported during a postexperimental interview that they were consciously trying to cooperate, although an unexpectedly lower percentage attempted to try to figure out the purposes of studies. Since these subjects were also more likely to become aware during the experiment and show better performance, it is difficult to identify whether their higher motivation existed prior to the experiment or was generated during the experiment by their positive experiences of success.

Another questionnaire given to additional subjects after either one or six prior experimental participations showed that more experienced subjects had more positive attitudes toward experiments and perceived them to be more valuable and scientific. These findings were confirmed with another group of subjects who were compared twice, once after being in a few experiments and then again after they had been in additional experiments.

Experience and Suspicion of Deception. Another important consequence of prior experience in experiments may be the increased suspicion of deception. Since deception is such a widespread procedure, this effect is hardly surprising. Deception is used regarding the true purpose of studies, the nature of subject's actual performance, the performance of other subjects, or the apparatus and equipment. In a few studies, deception occurs about the consequences of serving in the study such as the promise of money (Festinger & Carlsmith, 1959) or photographic slides of nude *Playboy* models which were used as stimuli (Valins, 1966) but subjects never received the promised rewards.

Given these types of practices, subjects are realistic in expecting deception especially if they have encountered it firsthand in prior studies, according to Stricker, Messick, and Jackson (1969). And, even without such direct experience, it is likely that their suspicions that it will happen to them will increase over the academic term as they learn more about psychology from their courses and conversations with their classmates who had been in deception studies.

Awareness and suspicion of deception, however, should be distinguished from accurate identification of the truth as well as from the type of reaction to such discovery. To be suspicious may only mean that everything is not accepted as valid but this suspicion is not equal to knowledge of the actual state of affairs. The nature of subject reactions to their encounters with deception will also vary across individuals, further complicating conclusions. Thus, Rubin and Moore (1971) noted that more authoritarian subjects were more likely to have an increased suspicion of additional deception.

A number of studies have been conducted to determine the possibility that prior experience with deception followed by debriefing enhances suspicion in subsequent experiments. For example, we already saw how Fillenbaum's (1966) findings bear on this issue in connection with the discussion of his concept of the "faithful subject" role in Chapter 11. His studies of incidental learning suggested no effect of deception in a first study on performance in an immediately subsequent experiment.

Brock and Becker (1966) employed a much more dramatic situation than Fillenbaum's deception. After serving on three mental tasks in Experiment 1, subjects were debriefed and told that they had been deceived as to the true purpose. Then another experimenter asked them to serve in a different experiment. In Experiment II, a motor learning task was required in which the subject had to press buttons to light and then unlight some bulbs on a panel in front of him. During the course of the task, due to a rigged setup, one button press "caused" either low (a "pop") or high damage (a "bang" and clouds of smoke) to the apparatus. The purpose of this treatment was not to study motor learning, as the subject was told, but to see if the subject felt guilty for apparently damaging the equipment. It was predicted that subjects who apparently created high damage would be more willing to sign a petition requesting the university to increase tuition to improve the university than those causing low damage.

The fact that some subjects had been debriefed about deception in Experiment 1 had different effects on compliance, depending on the similarity of Experiments 1 and 2. Debriefed subjects did not differ in petition-signing from those without debriefing when the two experiments appeared to be unrelated. However, when the two tasks were perceived as part of the same study, those subjects who were completely debriefed showed much less compliance.

Silverman, Shulman, and Weisenthal (1970) deceived and debriefed one group of subjects on subtests from an intelligence test while another group was given a memory task without deception. Then, in a second study, common personality tests were used for both groups. Differences were obtained, with the previously deceived subjects tending to give favorable self-presentation and lowered compliance with demand characteristics. It was suggested that prior deception sensitizes subjects to look for ulterior purposes of experiments and increases evaluation apprehension.

Christensen (1977) used a verbal conditioning task to see if two different methods of creating suspicion of deception would reduce conditioning performance. One condition involved a prior deception and debriefing before subjects received the verbal conditioning task. A second condition involved no first task but subjects were merely told of the possibility that deception might be employed on the verbal conditioning task.

The results showed that only the direct experience with deception was effective in reducing the conditioning to the level of the control group that received no reinforcements. Christensen did not interpret the lack of conditioning as negativistic behavior but rather as an attempt to avoid the appearance of being manipulable.

A second study by Christensen added an important control group absent from other studies assessing effects of prior deception. Subjects in this control condition received a prior experiment with a *non*manipulative experience before being tested on verbal conditioning. This group did show verbal conditioning, implying that the prior experience must be with deception if it is to alter performance on the second task.

The picture is complicated by the results of Cook et al. (1970) discussed in the previous chapter in connection with the effects of prior experience of deception on the roles or attitudes assumed by subjects. This study may not be comparable to the ones cited in this chapter since Cook et al. used five sessions distributed over as many weeks. They found that while *suspicions* of subjects may have increased with more exposure to deception, their *performance* on the tasks used in that study did *not* differ from control conditions.

Evidence is contradictory that subjects who are themselves still naive about deception become aware and suspicious of deception due to tip-offs and gossip from other students who have already served in deception studies. Wuebben (1967) discovered that 64 per cent of his subjects who received deception and debriefing later divulged their secrets to other subjects, whereas Aronson (1966) reported that he could find little indication that this type of disclosure occurred.

This difference could stem from a number of factors. For one matter, the investigators may have differed in the degree of rapport with their subjects–disharmony may had led to more leaking of the fact that the study involved deception since a hostile subject could "get even" this way. It is also conceivable that the degree to which experimenters could extract "the truth" from subjects who learned of the deception from previous subjects varies with the skill or degree of interrogation. Evidence is available that tipped-off subjects are very reluctant to admit that fact, according to Golding and Lichenstein (1970), Levy (1967), and Newberry (1973). In all of these studies, investigators did not have to rely on verbal reports of subjects to identify whether or not they had been alerted by tipoffs because a confederate was used to provide tips on how to do well or hints that something was "fishy" about the procedures of the study.

In the Golding and Lichenstein (1970) study, even though some subjects were fully tipped off that the experimenter would give them fake heart-rate feedback as they viewed slides of nude models, the effects of this feedback did not differ from that found for the control group. Tipoffs where problem-solving tips are involved, as in Newberry's study, helped the performance of subjects who received them.

Bias Due to Self-Initiated Withdrawal

In some types of studies, especially those that involve several different sessions, some of the original subjects are lost and do not serve in later stages of the study. This attrition may stem from a variety of sources including loss of interest, moving out of the community, absentmindedness, death, and so on. As long as the attrition or dropout rate is small, say less than about 25 per cent, *and* randomly distributed over all the treatment conditions, there is little cause for concern. It does create some added costs and inconvenience, but at least no systematic error or bias is created which would lead to faulty inferences.

On the other hand, when differential dropout rates occur across the various treatment conditions, serious problems arise and conclusions are seriously weakened. What factors cause differential attrition? If some conditions are excessively stressful or aversive, more subjects will be lost from these conditions than in the control group, leaving perhaps the stronger, braver, or more foolish to stick it out in the former conditions whereas a wider range of subjects compose the control group. Other factors such as differences in boringness or interestingness of tasks for different conditions will produce biases due to more subject selection occurring in some than in other conditions.

As in various forms of psychotherapy (Baekeland & Lundwall, 1975), the less motivated and/or more serious cases showing the least progress may drop out at a higher rate in some treatment conditions, so that it is difficult to evaluate the relative effectiveness of the treatments. Thus, alcoholics who are required to abstain totally may drop out more frequently than those who are treated using a criterion of moderate drinking.

Update on Human Subject Recruitment Practices

Despite increased awareness of the problems created by extreme reliance on introductory psychology students obtained from required participation in some type of human subject pool, it does not appear that much change has occurred in the sources of human subjects for research by university psychologists. The author (Jung, 1977) conducted a followup survey to the 1969 study of sources of human subjects. It was expected that some changes would have occurred over that interval during which these issues were heavily chronicled in professional journals.

Returns were obtained from 45 of the 52 psychology departments that cooperated in the original study, although not all of the respondents provided comparable data for some of the items. The results showed a slight reduction in the dependence on introductory psychology students from 79 to 73 per cent of the total human subjects used. There was a corresponding increase, on the other hand, in the percentage of noncollege subjects used from about 10 to 16 per cent, with the balance coming from other college students remaining fairly constant.

One of the most interesting findings deals not with the source of subjects but rather with the method of recruitment. Course-required participation dropped from 45 percent of the total to only 14 per cent of the college students used as subjects as shown in Table 12–1. Part of this shift, however, is more apparent than real since many more departments (57 per cent compared to a previous 25 per cent) allow students an option such as writing a paper instead of required service as a subject.

Although the absolute percentage of paid subjects is small, Table 12–1 shows that this category doubled over the time period between the two surveys. True volunteers who serve without pay, course credit, or other forms of pressure remained at about the same small level, about 4–5 per cent.

Scheduling procedures still fell in two main categories, one where subjects arrange appointments to fit their schedules and preferences and one in which subjects are contacted by the experimenter so that self-selection bias cannot occur readily. The former method which, as noted

TABLE 12–1. Estimated Percentages of College Subjects in Experiments Obtained by Various Methods in Major American University Psychology Departments, 1967 vs. 1976. (From Jung, 1977)

Methods Used for Obtaining College Students (1967 vs. 1976)		
Per cent of College Subjects	*1967 (n = 52)*	*1976 (n = 36)*
Required Bases		
Course Requirement	45.3	13.7
Course Option	25.4	57.2
Optional Extra Grade Credit	22.1	20.0
Entirely Voluntary Bases		
Gratis	4.1	5.0
Paid Money	2.6	6.3
	99.5%	102.2%

earlier, allows several forms of bias has increased in use from 67 to 81 per cent of the departments surveyed. Finally, there does not appear to be much difference in the mean number of participations required which was 4.0, compared to the current 4.6 sessions.

VOLUNTEER VS. NONVOLUNTEER DIFFERENCES

Important differences may exist between persons who serve as subjects on an entirely voluntary basis and those who are more or less coerced or required to participate. Such differences between volunteers and nonvolunteers, in turn, may or may not lead to corresponding differences in behavior. As already noted in surveys of sources of subjects, true volunteers are rare since most university-sponsored research used draftees–subjects who are pressured into "volunteering." The true volunteer subject is primarily a mythical creature or, at best, an endangered species. Many published experiments describe their subjects as "volunteers" whereas in fact they are not, except in the sense that they may have selected one experiment over another. In other research situations such as polls or surveys, however, the distinction between volunteers and nonvolunteers is more valid. Participation here is often optional and respondents frequently differ from nonrespondents. In addition, polls and surveys usually involve wider sampling of the general population than is the case with laboratory experiments.

Most studies attempting to identify differences between volunteers and nonvolunteers have employed intact groups such as whole classes tested in classroom settings. This procedure is different from that usually employed in obtaining subjects for most experiments where an appeal is made for volunteers. A comparison is then made between volunteers and nonvolunteers using results of personality tests given before the appeal. Usually no attempt is made to compare them on actual performance of some subsequent task since by definition, the nonvolunteers do not wish to participate in the experiment.

For example, Lasagna and von Felsinger (1954) compared volunteers and nonvolunteers for a drug experiment. The main concern was a comparison of differences in the personal histories between the two groups, which indicated more severe maladjustment among the volunteers. However, there was no attempt to compare their actual performance on the fictitious drug experiment.

Nonetheless, in order to compare the characteristics of volunteers and nonvolunteers, it is sometimes still necessary to require the nonvolunteers fill-out questionnaires and personality tests. One must wonder whether some of the observations of personality differences obtained in such studies stem from the annoyance or hostility nonvolunteers may feel when pressured to fill out these tests just after they have refused to be in an experiment.

Robert Rosenthal and his colleagues (Rosenthal & Rosnow, 1975) have used a two-stage procedure in which an initial appeal is made for volunteers for one type of study. The response to this request enables one to separate volunteers from nonvolunteers. Later all subjects, regardless of whether or not they volunteered for the first study, are tested on an apparently unrelated and different type of task.

Aside from the ethical problems of requiring everyone to take the second test, there is also a question concerning the validity of the classification of the volunteers and nonvolunteers. This procedure implies that volunteering is a trait-like feature which is stable across situations so that a person who volunteers for one type of study is also more likely to consent to be in other types of studies than the nonvolunteer. This is a questionable assumption since persons who would volunteer for a study of, for example, political attitudes might refuse to participate in a survey on sexual behavior and vice versa.

This issue concerning the relative role of traits and situations as determinants of behavior has recently been a central concern of theorists (Bowers, 1973; Endler, 1973; Mischel, 1968, 1973) as it has been many years ago as well (e.g., Hartshorne & May, 1928). The interactionist view (Bowers, 1973) holds that neither traits nor situations alone can explain behavior since they both interact. Applying this formulation to the act of volunteering for a psychology experiment, this behavior would not be attributed entirely to either an internal disposition or trait of volunteers or to external situational factors such as the type of experiment, but to the joint influence of both factors.

This issue is relevant because the use of one specific request to volunteer as the basis for classifying subjects as volunteers or nonvolunteers is overly simplistic, implying that "once a volunteer, always a volunteer," so to speak. Kruglanski (1975) has also criticized this method of defining volunteers, pointing out that just because a person volunteers for one type of experiment does not guarantee that the person is any more or less likely to volunteer for other types of studies. Moreover, all volunteers for a given study are not alike in their motives. In rebuttal, Rosnow and Rosenthal (1974) maintained that it is practical and valid to lump together persons engaged in the same form of behavior, even though the underlying motives and reasons may be different. Thus, suicides are alike in their actions although a wide variety of factors lead to this behavior. Still, in dealing with suicide behavior, it is useful to combine all such cases. Perhaps both sides of this argument have merit since there are some advantages to grouping persons together on the basis of similar behavior, but it is also true that finer distinctions in our taxonomies can permit a fuller understanding of the complexities of the phenomena we wish to explain.

Another factor complicating any comparisons of volunteers and nonvolunteers is what Rosenthal and Rosnow (1969) termed *pseudo-volunteers.* These subjects are the no-shows who sign up or agree to serve, but fail to show up, thus frustrating data collectors who wait in vain. It is possible that some persons volunteer to requests half-heartedly, perhaps because they do not wish to appear uncooperative. Later, when the scheduled experiment is due, these persons would not feel as much pressure to participate so they simply do not show up. This analysis is plausible in view of Gustav's (1962) study of attitudes of students toward required participation in experiments. The results suggested more irritation and apathy on the part of students than most psychologists think exists.

Based on a comparison of personality differences among volunteers who are shows and no-shows by Leipold and James (1962) and by Levitt, Lubin, and Brady (1962), it seemed conclusive to Rosenthal and Rosnow that these pseudo-volunteers may be more like non-volunteers. Classifying them with the volunteers, as is usually done, may serve to mask the true extent of differences between volunteers and nonvolunteers.

On the other hand, it does not appear reasonable to consider all no-shows as pseudo-volunteers, because a variety of reasons—ranging from forgetfulness to accidents—can prevent subjects from fulfilling their intention to participate.

Findings of Comparisons of Volunteers vs. Nonvolunteers

With these issues in mind, let us examine some of the empirical findings regarding possible volunteer-nonvolunteer differences in characteristics and how they might affect performance on behavioral tasks. Summaries made by Bell (1962) and Rosenthal and Rosnow (1969) of earlier studies suggested that volunteers were generally more intelligent (especially males), more often first-borns, higher in need for social approval, higher in need of achievement, more unconventional, and for some types of studies, less conventional.

A subsequent large-scale study (Rosenthal & Rosnow, 1975) that combined a review of past studies with data from new investigations pointed out some of the limitations of previous generalizations about volunteer-nonvolunteer differences. The type of task for which subjects volunteered or declined turns out to be an important qualifier of many of the earlier conclusions. Volunteers tended to be first-borns, but only for certain studies such as sensory deprivation. Volunteers tended to be higher in sociability, but not if the task did not involve social interaction.

Situational factors were also found to influence volunteering. Provision of monetary incentives increased volunteer rate whereas aversive tasks lowered it, as one might expect. Characteristics of the recruiter, perceived urgency of the need for volunteers, level of personal interest in psychology, and perceived normativeness of volunteering by others were also found to affect volunteering.

The complexity of the factors underlying volunteering makes it difficult to draw conclusions about volunteer-nonvolunteer differences that are applicable to dissimilar situations from that used to identify volunteers. Clearly, a trait-like feature of volunteering that applies across situations is not a valid conception.

For a given situation or task, however, it is still important to consider whether findings obtained with the volunteers *for that task* are probably valid for the nonvolunteers *for that task*. For some tasks, volunteer data probably is an overestimate of the responses of the remaining nonvolunteers. For example, Kaats and Davis (1971) found volunteers for a sexual attitudes survey to be more sexually permissive and experienced than the nonvolunteers. For other tasks or situations, just the opposite tendency should occur toward underestimates if volunteer data is used. In the example of authoritarianism (Rosenthal & Rosnow, 1975, p. 50), volunteers score lower on this dimension than do nonvolunteers. In both of these types of situations, one cannot use results from volunteers as estimates of the responses of the nonvolunteers without risking serious error.

An overview of the main differences found between volunteers and nonvolunteers with respect to background and personality dimensions after a thorough survey of published studies was made by Rosenthal and Rosnow (1975), as shown in Table 12-2. In view of the many complicating factors, they divided the findings into four groups, depending on the degree of certainty they felt was warranted.

Volunteer-Nonvolunteer Behavioral Differences

Now that we have examined evidence about volunteer-nonvolunteer differences in background characteristics and personality dimensions, we will look at evidence on behavioral differences in experiments. As we noted in Chapter 11, Orne has argued that the performance of subjects in experiments is usually affected by the demand characteristics of the situation. Furthermore, Orne's view held that subjects are motivated to be "good subjects" and try to figure out what kind of behavior the experimenter expects from them.

Using this conception, Rosenthal and Rosnow (1975) suggested that it is more likely that volunteer subjects will match this description of subjects whereas nonvolunteers may be more akin to Rosenberg's (1965) evaluation of apprehensive subjects who are more concerned about their own self-image. To test these assumptions, Rosenthal and Rosnow and their associates conducted several experiments.

TABLE 12–2. Volunteer Characteristics Grouped by Degree of Confidence of Conclusion.

I. Maximum Confidence	III. Some Confidence
1. Educated	12. From smaller town
2. Higher social class	13. Interested in religion
3. Intelligent	14. Altruistic
4. Approval-motivated	15. Self-disclosing
5. Sociable	16. Maladjusted
	17. Young
II. Considerable Confidence	**IV. Minimum Confidence**
6. Arousal-seeking	18. Achievement-motivated
7. Unconventional	19. Married
8. Female	20. Firstborn
9. Nonauthoritarian	21. Anxious
10. Jewish > Protestant or Protestant > Catholic	22. Extraverted
11. Nonconforming	

Source: The Volunteer Subject, by R. Rosenthal and R. Rosnow, New York: Wiley, 1975. Copyright by John Wiley and Sons. Reprinted by permission.

In one study by Rosnow and Suls (1970), attitudes on an issue were assessed with a pretest prior to presenting subjects with a persuasive communication aimed at changing their attitudes. Inasmuch as previous work (Lana, 1969) has shown that such pretests act to sensitize subjects as to what the purpose of the study is about and can thus bias results, it was predicted and found that volunteers confronted with such strong demand cues, and being motivated to be "good subjects," showed more attitude change in the direction intended by the communication. In contrast, nonvolunteers who were assumed to be apprehensive showed less change because the pretest sensitization may have alarmed them to feel that if they yielded in their attitudes, it would be a sign that they were easily influenced or manipulated.

Based on these types of studies showing better performance of volunteers in the direction of strong demand characteristics, Rosenthal and Rosnow (1975) proposed a multi-stage model of the process, shown in Table 12–3, by which artifacts might be created when volunteers are used as subjects. First, subjects must be aware or receptive to the demand cues in the experimental situation. In addition, the subjects must be motivated to cooperate with these demands rather than ignore them or act contrary to them. Finally, and obviously, the required responses must be within the performance capacity of the subjects.

It is further assumed that volunteers are more motivated than are nonvolunteers to comply with demand characteristics and confirm the hypothesis, provided they are salient, as when the experiment is con-

TABLE 12-3. Mutually Exclusive and Exhaustive Subject States for Each of Three Mediating Variables.

Mediator	State	Description
Receptivity	Adequate	Subject effectively receives demand characteristics.
	Inadequate	Subject fails to receive, or inadequately receives, demand characteristics.
Motivation	Acquiescent	Subject is in an acquiescent mood pursuant to demand characteristics.
	Nonacquiescent	Subject is not motivated to respond overtly to demand characteristics.
	Counteracquiescent	Subject is in a counteracquiescent mood pursuant to demand characteristics.
Capability	Capable	Subject is capable of manifesting his demand motivation behaviorally.
	Incapable	Subject is incapable of manifesting his demand motivation behaviorally.

Source: The Volunteer Subject, By R. Rosenthal and R. Rosnow, New York: Wiley, 1975.

ducted in a professional atmosphere, subjects are experienced, or the instructions are explicit. On the other hand, these same conditions may affect nonvolunteers differently, leading to resentment or even sabotage in the form of uncooperative behavior which may disconfirm the hypothesis.

Significance of Volunteer-Nonvolunteer Differences

As already noted, the use of the term "volunteer" varies somewhat and often does not involve truly voluntary participation. Yet, the procedure by which Rosenthal and Rosnow (1975) separated volunteers and nonvolunteers focused on consent under minimal pressure so that characteristics of this type of volunteer may not hold for the "coerced volunteer" typical of students who are required to serve as subjects to fulfill course assignments or options.

Nonetheless, despite the rarity of true volunteers (Jung, 1969) in past college subject research, these comparisons are worthwhile for studies using higher percentages of noncollege subjects, such as surveys and questionnaires conducted off campuses. Studies such as the famous Kinsey Reports (Kinsey, Pomeroy, & Martin, 1948; Kinsey, Pomeroy, Martin, & Gebhard, 1953) of human sexual behavior were often critized on the basis that volunteers for these studies were not representative.

Moreover, there may be greater reliance on noncollege sources of subjects in the future, especially as psychologists begin to question the shortcomings of exclusive use of college students. Legal actions and ethical considerations such as the ruling in 1977 (Smith, 1977) that it was illegal to *require* students enrolled in psychology courses at the State University of New York at Albany to serve in experiments. If this type of ruling is upheld and spreads to other universities, more use of noncollege subject sources where participants may more frequently involve volunteers will occur. If such a shift occurs, one benefit will be the extension of our findings to a more diverse population, but at the same time any volunteer-nonvolunteer differences become a new source of threats to generalizability.

FUTURE SOURCES OF HUMAN SUBJECTS

One of the big challenges to researchers will be finding effective ways of persuading and encouraging members of the general public who, unlike psychology students, feel no obligation to participate. Volunteers may not be willing to take the time and effort to serve unless they perceive they will stand to gain some benefits, such as personal insights and satisfactions. They may insist on knowing more about the nature and purpose of a study before agreeing to participate, conditions that may bias their behavior in some cases.

One type of incentive that may avoid this problem but introduce others is material or monetary rewards for service. A small percentage of subjects who have to serve in long or arduous tasks or who need special skills have generally received pay in the past. Future research may also require the use of pay to attract sufficient numbers of noncollege subjects if it becomes no longer possible to require student service.

One obvious question becomes, how will behavior be altered, if at all, in experiments if subjects are paid? If we can assume that pay will often attract volunteers who otherwise would not participate, we can expect this factor to modify some of our findings. In addition, how will the introduction of extrinsic rewards such as money affect the behavior of persons who otherwise would serve without pay for reasons such as curiosity or altruism? Deci (1971) suggested that this procedure would undermine or reduce intrinsic motives to perform tasks subjects were interested in.

If pay does affect or change the behavior of both volunteers and nonvolunteers, compared to how they would perform without pay, some serious problems are created for researchers who try to compare results of studies on the same topic obtained from paid and gratis volunteers.

An example of this problem comes from a study by Oakes (1972) who recruited noncollege subjects with the use of newspaper advertisements for a study of social interaction. The results from this source of subjects did not match those previously found with paid college students. Of course, a number of factors besides the pay differed between the subjects in the two studies, such as age and other background factors, but the comparison serves to illustrate the issue.

Oakes (1972) raised the important point that neither finding is more correct than the other since we have no basis for accepting one population as more valid than the other. All we can safely note is that the results from the two sources are not in agreement.

The use of financial incentives to attract subjects may also create a class of "professional subjects," persons who participate frequently in experiments. Not only would they become less comparable to naive subjects who are serving in only one study due to increased sophistication about psychological research procedures, but if they are primarily enlisting for the pay, their motives will differ from persons who serve mainly for curiosity or fun. They may be apathetic, treating the activity as only a job to endure. Or perhaps some paid subjects will be overly cooperative to keep in the good graces of experimenters—after all, they will want to impress experimenters by being good employees so they will be rehired and used in future studies.

Other methods of obtaining subjects from noncollege sources will depend to some extent on the resourcefulness and ingenuity of investigators. Rubin (1975), for example, has recruited volunteers from airport waiting lounges for his studies of liking and self-disclosure. Other sources of potentially cooperative and large sources of volunteer subjects include hospitals, rest homes, and recreational facilities.

Other large potential sources of subjects, such as schools and prisons, entail special problems. Children and prison inmates may not be entirely without pressure to volunteer. This problem will be cited later in the chapter dealing with ethical problems in research.

Some investigators avoid the issue of recruitment by relying on unobtrusive observations of behavior in natural settings in which "subjects" do not ever realize they are participants in an experiment. Since subjects do not get a chance to refuse participation, there can be no distinction between volunteers and nonvolunteers. However, some ethical concern has been raised about this approach under some circumstances, an issue again to be deferred until a later chapter.

An imaginative proposal by Perloff and Perloff (1977) warrants mention. In the early days of psychology, it was not unusual for enterprising pioneer psychologists such as James McKeen Cattell to set up apparatus in booths at expositions and fairs to test interested passersby. Since people attending these fairs were generally interested in learning more about themselves and the world, many of them were ready volunteers for the kinds of measurements and tests administered by psychologists. Following this model, Perloff and Perloff suggested that such a strategy be employed again as a means to obtain large samples of cooperative, if not eager, persons from a wider range of backgrounds than the current supply of subjects.

There is some merit to this resourceful proposal and there is certainly no harm in trying this strategy. The types of studies that would be possible, however, would not be the same as those favored by university experimenters, which are often of more theoretical interest to the investigator than of practical value for the participant. Since the person attending the fair who would be interested most in participating also wants to gain personal insight, the kinds of feasible studies would probably involve descriptive studies or the establishment of norms for a variety of skills, attitudes, and beliefs. These comments do not mean to imply that these goals are uninteresting or not valuable but only to point out some possible differences in the kinds of research that might be done in a setting with members of the general public as compared with the college subject population.

In the long run, it will turn out that pressures forcing experimenters to seek subjects other than the college psychology student will be a positive factor in the development of a psychology that will be valid for a wider range of individuals. Perhaps some day we will look back in dismay at how reluctant we were to relinquish our almost total reliance on such an atypical source of subjects.

SUMMARY

The primary source of human subjects for experimental research has traditionally been the introductory psychology student population, which is a large and readily available supply. Surveys of actual published articles in selected journals as well as surveys of current policies and practices employed in major university psychology departments both support this conclusion.

Most universities maintain a human "subject pool" by requiring introductory and other psychology students to serve in several experiments as part of their course requirements. In recent years, increased use of an optional assignment have occurred although the primary source of human subjects is still the introductory psychology student.

Aside from the problems of generalizability due to the unrepresentativeness of college psychology students in relation to the general population, the use of these subject pools permits other sources of bias. Thus, when students arrange their own appointments in scheduling sessions, it is possible for different types of experiments to attract different subpopulations of subjects. Students who sign up early in the academic term may differ from those who delay until the end of the term.

Although few human subjects are, strictly speaking, true volunteers, some differences have been found between those subjects who choose to serve in some types of experiments and those who do not. The nature of such differences may not be the same for all types of experiments, but thus far it has been found that volunteers tend to be more intelligent, first-born, in greater need of social approval, and more unconventional. Volunteers may be more motivated to serve in experiments and thus be more attentive to demand cues and more likely to cooperate by being "good subjects."

Future sources of subjects may change with less dependence on college students. Without the incentive of course requirements for such service, greater reliance on monetary rewards or personal fulfillment to subjects may be required. It may become more difficult to obtain large supplies of subjects like those of the past.

REFERENCES

Argyris, C. Some unintended effects of rigorous research. *Psychological Bulletin,* 1968, *70*, 185-197.

Aronson, E. Avoidance of inter-subject communication. *Psychological Reports,* 1966, *19*, 238.

Baekeland, F., and Lundwall, L. Dropping out of treatment: A critical view. *Psychological Bulletin,* 1975, *82*, 738-783.

Bell, C. R. Personality characteristics of volunteers for psychological studies. *British Journal of Social Clinical Psychology,* 1962, *1*, 81-95.

Bereiter, C., and Freedman, M. B. Fields of study and the people in them. In N. Sanford (Ed.), *The American college.* New York: John Wiley, 1962.

Bowers, K. Situationism in psychology: An analysis and a critique. *Psychological Review,* 1973, *80*, 307-336.

Brock, T. C., and Becker, L. A. "Debriefing" and susceptibility to subsequent experimental manipulations. *Journal of Experimental and Social Psychology,* 1966, *2*, 314-323.

Carlson, E. R., and Carlson, R. Male and female subjects in personality research. *Journal of Abnormal Social Psychology,* 1961, *61*, 482-483.

Christensen, L. The negative subject: Myth, reality, or a prior experimental exposure effect. *Journal of Personality and Social Psychology,* 1977, *35*, 392-400.

Cook, T. D., Bean, J. R. Colder, B. J., Frey, R., Krovetz, M. L., and Reisman, S. R. Demand characteristics and three conceptions of the frequently deceived subject. *Journal of Personality and Social Psychology,* 1970, *14*, 185-194.

Cox, D. E., and Sipprelle, C. N. Coercion in participation as a research subject. *American Psychologist,* 1971, *26*, 726-728.

Davis, J. R., and Fernald. Laboratory experience versus subject pool. *American Psychologist,* 1975, *30*, 523-524.

Deci, E. L. Effects of externally mediated rewards on intrinsic motivation. *Journal of Personality and Social Psychology,* 1971, *18*, 105-115.

Endler, N. S. The person versus the situation–A pseudo issue? *Journal of Personality,* 1973, *41*, 287-303.

Evans, R., and Donnerstein, E. Some implications for psychological research of early versus late term participation by college students. *Journal of Research in Personality,* 1974, *8*, 102-109.

Festinger, L., and Carlsmith, J. Cognitive consequences of forced compliance. *Journal of Abnormal and Social Psychology,* 1959, *56*, 203-210.

Fillenbaum, S. Prior deception and subsequent experimental performance: The "faithful" subject. *Journal of Personality and Social Psychology,* 1966, *4*, 532-537.

Golding, S. L., and Lichtenstein, E. Confession of awareness and prior knowledge of deception as a function of interview set and approval motivation. *Journal of Personality and Social Psychology*, 1970, *14*, 213-223.

Gustav, A. Students' attitudes toward compulsory participation in experiments. *Journal of Psychology*, 1962, *53*, 119-125.

Hartshorne, H., and May, M. A. *Studies in deceit.* New York: Macmillan, 1928.

Holmes, D. S. Amount of experience in experiments as a determinant of performance in later experiments. *Journal of Personality and Social Psychology,* 1967, *2*, 289-294.

Holmes, D. S., and Applebaum, A. S. Nature of prior experimental experience as a determinant of performance in a subsequent experiment. *Journal of Personality and Social Psychology,* 1970, *14*, 195-202.

Johnson, R. W. The obtaining of experimental subjects. *Canadian Psychologist,* 1973, *14*, 208-211.

Jung, J. Current practices and problems in the use of college students for psychological research. *Canadian Psychologist,* 1969, *10*, 280-290.

Jung, J. New trends in the sources of and policies for use of humans as psychological research subjects: 1967 vs. 1976. California State University, Long Beach. Unpublished paper.

Kaats, G. R., and Davis, K. E. Effects of volunteer bias in studies of sexual behavior and attitudes. *Journal of Sex Research,* 1971, *7*, 26-34.

Kinsey, A. C., Pomeroy, W. B., and Martin, C. E. *Sexual behavior in the human male.* Philadelphia: Saunders, 1948.

Kinsey, A. C., Pomeroy, W. B., Martin, C. E. and Gebhard, P. H. *Sexual behavior in the human female.* Philadelphia: Saunders, 1953.

Kruglanski, A. W. The human subject in the psychology experiment: Fact and artifact. In L. Berkowitz (Ed.), *Advances in experimental social psychology,* 1975, *8*, 101-149.

Lana, R. Pretest sensitization. In R. Rosenthal and R. L. Rosnow (Eds.), *Artifact in behavioral research.* New York: Academic Press, 1969.

Lasagna, L., and Felsinger, J. M. von. The volunteer subject in research. *Science,* 1954, *120*, 359-361.

Leipold, W. W., and James, R. L. Characteristics of shows and no-shows in a psychological experiment. *Psychological Reports,* 1962, *11*, 171-174.

Levitt, E. E., Lubin, B., and Brady, J. P. The effect of the pseudo-volunteer on studies of volunteers for psychology experiments. *Journal of Applied Psychology,* 1962, *46*, 72-75.

Levy, L. Awareness, learning, and the beneficient subject as expert witness. *Journal of Personality and Social Psychology,* 1967, *6*, 363-370.

Martin, R. M., and Marcuse, F. L. Characteristics of volunteers and nonvolunteers in psychological experimentation. *Journal of Consulting Psychology,* 1958, *22*, 475-479.

Menges, R. L. Openness and honesty versus coercion and deception in psychological research. *American Psychologist,* 1973, *28*, 1030-1034.

Miller, A. A survey of introductory psychology subject pool practices among leading universities. *Teaching of Psychology,* 1981, in press.

Mischel, W. *Personality and assessment* New York: Wiley, 1968.

Mischel, W. Toward a cognitive social learning conceptualization of personality. *Psychological Review,* 1973, *80*, 252-253.

Newberry, B. H. Truth-telling in subjects with information about experiments: Who is being deceived? *Journal of Personality and Social Psychology,* 1973, *25*, 369-374.

Oakes, W. External validity and the use of real people as subjects. *American Psychologist*, 1972, *27*, 959-962.

Perloff, R., and Perloff, L. S. The fair—an apportunity for depicting psychology and for conducting behavioral research. *American Psychologist,* 1977, *32*, 220-229.

Reardon, P., and Prescott, S. Sex as reported in a recent sample of psychological research. *Psychology of Women Quarterly*, Winter 1977, *2* (2), 157-166.

Rosenberg, M. J. When dissonance fails: On eliminating evaluation apprehension from attitude measurement. *Journal of Personality and Social Psychology*, 1965, *1*, 18-42.

Rosenthal, R., and Rosnow, R. L. The volunteer subject. In R. Rosenthal and R. L. Rosnow (Eds.), *Artifact in behavioral research.* New York: Academic Press, 1969.

Rosenthal, R., and Rosnow, R. L. *The volunteer subject*. New York: Wiley, 1975.

Rosenzweig, S. The experimental situation as a psychological problem. *Psychological Review*, 1933, *40*, 337-354.

Rosnow, R. L., and Rosenthal, R. Taming of the volunteer problem: On coping with artifacts by benign neglect. *Journal of Personality and Social Psychology,* 1974, *30*, 188-190.

Rosnow, R. L., and Suls, J. M. Reactive effects of pretesting in attitude research. *Journal of Personality and Social Psychology,* 1970, *15*, 338-343.

Rubin, Z. Disclosing oneself to a stranger: Reciprocity and its limits. *Journal of Experimental and Social Psychology,* 1975, *11*, 233-260.

Rubin, Z., and Moore, J. C., Jr. Assessment of subjects' suspicions. *Journal of Personality and Social Psychology*, 1971, *17*, 163-170.

Schultz, D. P. The human subject in psychological research. *Psychological Bulletin,* 1969, *72*, 214-228.

Schwabacher, S. Male vs. female representation in psychological research: An examination of the *Journal of Personality and Social Psychology,* 1970, 1971. *Journal Supplement Abstract Service,* 1972, *2*, 20-21.

Siess, T. F. Personality correlates of volunteers' experiment preferences. *Canadian Journal of Behavioral Sciences,* 1973, *5*, 253-263.

Silverman, I., and Margulis, S. Experiment title as a source of sampling bias in commonly used "subject pool" procedures. *Canadian Psychologist,* 1973, *14*, 197-201.

Silverman, I., Shulman, A. D., and Weisenthal, D. L. Effects of deceiving and debriefing psychological subjects on performance in later experiments. *Journal of Personality and Social Psychology,* 1970, *14*, 203-212.

Smart, R. G. Subject selection bias in psychological research. *Canadian Psychologist,* 1966, *7a*, 115-121.

Sternberg, C. Personality trait patterns of college students majoring in different fields. *Psychological Monographs,* 1955, *69*, No. 18 (Whole No. 403).

Stricker, L. J. The true deceiver. *Psychological Bulletin,* 1967, *68*, 13-20.

Stricker, L. J., Messick, S., and Jackson, D. W. Evaluating deception in psychological research. *Psychological Bulletin,* 1969, *71*, 343-351.

Underwood, B. J., Schwenn, E., and Keppel, G. Verbal learning as related to point of time in the school term. *Journal of Verbal Learning and Verbal Behavior,* 1964, *3*, 222-225.

Valins, S. Cognitive effects of heart-rate feedback. *Journal of Personality and Social Psychology,* 1966, *4*, 400-408.

Winett, R. A., Fuchs, W. L., and Moffat, S. A. Personal and impersonal methods of recruitment for social research. *Journal of Community Psychology,* 1974, *2*, 376-379.

Wuebben, P. L. Honesty of subjects and birth order. *Journal of Personality and Social Psychology,* 1967, *5*, 350-352.

Are Experimental Outcomes Biased by Experimenter Expectations?

CHAPTER 13

Chapter at a Glance

In most sciences, little danger exists that experimenters can inadvertently bias the outcomes of their research given that they hold expectations about the nature of the results. In psychology, on the other hand, where the experimenter and the subject are involved in a social interaction during the course of many experiments, there has been some evidence and concern that experimenters might somehow unintentionally influence the outcomes of experiments. During the 1960s, there was a large body of research stimulated largely by the work of Robert Rosenthal (Rosenthal 1966, 1976) which seemed to provide clear evidence of such bias due either to expectancies of experimenters or to differential behavior of experimenters indirectly associated with expectancies. However, as we shall see shortly, in the last decade there has been a marked diminution of empirical work on this issue due in part to the failure of efforts to determine the underlying mechanism for such effects.

This interesting case study of the "psychology of research" illustrates how the kinds of topics that are investigated may shift over time. Despite this decline in actual research on this phenomenon and some controversy over the validity of some of the evidence for it, the influence of Rosenthal's work is important since it has made more experimenters aware of and careful about the possibility of such biases. This sensitization of researchers may have contributed to a reduction in the extent to which such biases continue to exist. In the present chapter, we will first describe the background and the primary evidence in support of experimenter-expectancy effects, followed by a discussion of the search for the processes by which they occur. After presenting criticisms of this research and its limitations, we will consider the implications for research that experimenter-expectancy effects contain and examine possible solutions for minimizing any such effects.

In many respects, it is not so surprising that a phenomenon such as experimenter-expectancy effects might occur. Indeed, one might well wonder instead why it took psychologists so long before they began to think about it. After all, experiments are usually undertaken by experimenters to test their carefully formulated hypotheses and predictions. In other words, experimenters do not usually conduct experiments without also having some expectancies or preconceptions as to what the outcomes will be. An experiment is designed to obtain an answer from nature for the questions posed by experimenters. This aspect of science is quite proper but may lead to difficulty in the area of psychological research. A major dilemma exists for psychology if the experimenter's hypotheses not only guide the type of research undertaken but also bias the behavior under study, especially if the bias is in favor of the predictions.

Most published research consists of so-called positive results, findings that more or less support the predictions proposed by experimenters. (This fact should not be interpreted to mean that experimenters are so clever that most of their predictions are supported in most of their experiments. For one thing, journal editors usually do not publish negative results. In view of this policy, and for other reasons as well, experimenters who obtain negative results may not even bother to submit such findings to journals for consideration). Still, what are we to make of the volumes of journals mostly full of positive results? Are we able to safely conclude that at least for these studies experimenters were sufficiently wise and knowledgeable to make valid predictions? Certainly we would like to be able to think so, for these "facts" are generally accepted as "truth."

However, one unpleasant possible alternative basis for such successful predictions is that sometimes the expectancies or hypotheses of experimenters have managed to bias the results in favor of these hypotheses. Such bias, it should be clear, is assumed to be unintentional. We are not concerned with forms of cheating or misrepresentation. Most experimenters are honest and scrupulously attempt to avoid bias. However, despite such noble intentions, is it possible that in some types of situations experimenters somehow unintentionally transmit their expectancies to subjects?

If we make the additional assumption that most subjects are cooperative and wish to be "good subjects," as noted by Orne earlier, or even if they only appear to be cooperative (Sigall et al., 1970), we can see that any subtle cues produced by the experimenter during the experimental session might influence a subject's performance in the direction desired or expected by experimenters. The typical subject is highly motivated and eager to serve as a subject, either to learn something of personal value or to figure out the hidden purpose of the study. As they perform, some of their responses will be those expected by the experimenter. Although experimenters attempt to be objective and doubtless believe that they are, they may get a bit excited or smile a lot whenever predicted behavior is obtained, and frown whenever behavior inconsistent with predictions occurs. Such unintentional cues could serve to reinforce subjects, to continue making responses expected by experimenters.

A fascinating example of an actual case of such unintentional bias is the story of Clever Hans, the remarkable horse who apparently could solve mathematical problems. He answered problems by tapping with his hoof. Careful scrutiny of this incredible behavior, however, led Pfungst (1911) to conclude that Hans was reacting to unintentional cues provided by observers. As Hans approached the correct answer, the questioner would expectantly look up to see if Hans would stop tapping. Of course, this unintentional cue functioned as a signal for Clever Hans to stop tapping. Astonished observers, however, attributed mathematical skills to him.

Thus far, we have speculated on the quite plausible possibility that the results of psychology experiments may be affected by unintentional cues produced by experimenters which guide behavior of subjects in ways that fulfill experimenters' hypotheses. We have also assumed that subjects can, in varying degrees, discern such cues. Finally, if the subjects are also cooperative to the demand characteristics of the situation, we will obtain what Rosenthal (1966; 1976) termed variously as experimenter bias or the experimenter-expectancy effect.

Despite such speculation, it was not until Rosenthal began his systematic program of experiments designed specifically to demonstrate experimenter bias and identify its mechanism that these problems were generally acknowledged. Rather than conjecture that such bias existed, Rosenthal and his associates developed a standard methodology for the systematic study of such effects.

THE ROSENTHAL PARADIGM

The basic paradigm or experimental situation adopted by Rosenthal was an "experiment within an experiment" (Rosenthal, 1966). Experimental assistants or student experimenters were assigned to test subjects on a so-called test of empathy, in which they had to look at a series of 20 photographs of individuals for five seconds each and rate them as to the extent to which the persons in the photographs seem to have been experiencing success or failure. A scale ranging from +10 (extreme success) to -10 (extreme failure) was employed for the ratings.

Actually, the set of photographs had a mean rating of zero, indicating neutrality, according to a prior standardization test administered to other students. Therefore, from what we have just stated, our expectation in this study would be that the mean rating of the set of photos by subjects should also be zero. However, Rosenthal usually attempted to differentially bias his real subjects—namely the student experimenters—by instructing half of them to expect a mean rating of -5. Student experimenters were told that such expectancies were based on well-established findings of past studies they were to replicate. In some studies the expectancies are based on alleged personality tests that had been given to subjects.

Student experimenters were told to read the instructions provided by Rosenthal to subjects but not to say anything other than "Hello" and "Good-bye." The importance of secrecy was stressed to the student experimenters since one goal of the study was to be able to replicate "well-established" findings, just as students in physics are expected to do.

To summarize, two different groups of student experimenters were led to expect opposite types of ratings from their subjects. Since the subjects were assigned at random to experimenters and since the pictures had been standardized earlier as being neutral with respect to success or failure, no difference in the mean ratings of the two groups of subjects should exist, *if* there is no experimenter bias. However, to the extent that the expectations of experimenters' influenced the results of their subjects, one group of experimenters should obtain ratings above zero while the other group should get ratings below zero. Such an experiment was done by Rosenthal and Fode (1963) and the results supported the prediction that experimenter bias occurs.

Since that initial experiment, this person-perception task has been used extensively by Rosenthal and others. At one time (Rosenthal, 1969), it was used in over half of the experiments on this topic. By 1978, however, it was used in only about 25 per cent of such studies, according to Rosenthal and Rubin's (1978) tabulation of over 300 studies. The use of the person perception task actually increased slightly since 1969, but an even greater tenfold gain in bias studies using what Rosenthal and Rubin labelled, "everyday situations" also occurred. Nonetheless it still is the most frequently used single method in this research.

Table 13–1 shows the number of studies before and after 1969 on experimenter-expectancy effects reported by Rosenthal and Rubin

TABLE 13–1. Comparison of Significance Levels of Studies Before and After 1969 in Eight Research Areas.

Research Area	Number of Studies		Proportion Reaching $p < .05$	
	To 1969	Since 1969	To 1969	Since 1969
Reaction Time	3	6	.33	.17
Inkblot Tests	4	5	.75	.20
Animal Learning	9	6	.89	.50
Laboratory Interviews	6	23	.33	.39
Psychophysical Judgments	9	14	.33	.50
Learning and Ability	9	25	.22	.32
Person Perception	57	62	.25	.29
Everyday Situations	11	101	.36	.41
Median	9	18	.33	.36
Total	108[a]	242[b]	.35	.37

[a]Three of these 108 entries represent research conducted in a single study but for more than one research area.

[b]Two of these 242 entries represent research conducted in a single study but for more than one research area.

Source: "Interpersonal expectancy effects: The first 354 studies, by R. Rosenthal and H. Rubin. *The Behavioral and Brain Sciences*, 1978, 3, 377–86. Copyright 1978 by Cambridge University Press. Reprinted by permission.

(1978) using different types of situations as well as the proportion of each type showing significant effects.

Why have there been over 300 studies in this area? Not all of them deal with bias in experimental situations, per se, but many deal with interpersonal expectancy biases affecting behavior in nonexperimental situations as well as interviews or classroom interactions. Only a few of these studies were primarily concerned with demonstrating the occurrence of experimenter bias; most of them were performed to identify variables that modify the degree of experimenter bias. Such variables include personality traits of experimenters and subjects such as anxiety or need for approval, sex of experimenters and subjects, and characteristics of the physical setting of the laboratory, to name a few. In addition, using both subjective reports of subjects and objective records such as filmed and tape-recorded sessions, analyses have been made of the characteristics of the manner in which experimenters run their subjects. Factors such as degree of professional-like conduct of the session, extent of interpersonal rapport between the experimenter and subject, amount of kinesic communication by the experimenter (such as signals from the head and leg regions), and amount of paralinguistic communication by experimenter (such as tone of voice) are the main aspects of the experimenter's behavior that are examined.

Other types of studies of experimenter bias using human subjects are much fewer in number. They have employed a variety of tasks ranging from projective tests such as the Rorschach Inkblot Test to psychophysical judgments, reaction time, and structured laboratory interviews. Although the overall results of these 85 studies cited by Rosenthal (1969) represent mixed support for the experimenter-bias effect, half of them have produced results that could have occurred by chance less than 10 times out of 100. This level of statistical significance is not as infrequent as that (5 times out of 100) usually demanded by psychologists before they will accept evidence as supportive of an experimental hypothesis. However, the large number of findings *taken as a whole* cannot be disregarded even if most of the studies examined individually do not meet the conventional statistical criterion, which after all is an arbitrary rather than a magical criterion.

In addition, nine studies using animal subjects have been done. Most of them tested the performance of rats allegedly selectively bred for maze-brightness versus maze-dullness. The overall evidence showed strong experimenter-bias effects on both maze and Skinner-box performance.

A large sample of experimenters and subjects has been used to demonstrate the experimenter-expectancy effect. Rosenthal (1966, Chapter 17) indicated that as of 1966, over 350 different experimenters, mostly male students majoring in a variety of areas, have been used. Most of them had been volunteers, although sometimes they were students enrolled in a class, but most of the experimenters were paid for their services.

Over 2,000 human subjects, with about 60 per cent of them female students from a variety of majors taking introductory psychology courses, served in these studies. Most subjects did not receive any pay but were volunteers or were enlisted by their instructors to participate.

UNDERLYING MECHANISM FOR EXPERIMENTER BIAS

As we shall see shortly, not all psychologists have accepted the evidence presented by Rosenthal and his associates as support for the occurrence of experimenter-expectancy effects and have proposed alternative explanations. For the present, however, let us assume that experimenter bias does occur in Rosenthal's studies and turn next to a consideration of the obvious question: Just how is experimenter bias transmitted to the subject?

Is Operant Conditioning Involved?

Rosenthal (1963b) examined evidence for an operant conditioning type of explanation for some of the experimenter-bias findings. According to this view, the experimenter subtly reinforces subjects whenever they happen to make a correct response—that is, a response consistent with expectation. Such reinforcement was assumed to be verbal in nature, such as those used in studies of verbal conditioning (Krasner, 1958; Spielberger, 1965). These verbal responses of the experimenters were not assumed to be as explicit as "That's right," but were thought to be more subtle such as "Mmh hmm," "OK," or "Good." If the experimenter made one of these utterances each time a subject made a correct response, it would be possible for the experimenter to bias results.

In view of the high levels of apprehension many subjects have when they serve in experiments, this process seems plausible. As noted earlier, some views of the subjects suggest that they search for cues or demand characteristics in an experiment to guide their responses. The verbal conditioning process by which the subject may be affected by reinforcement from the experimenter should be especially favored by high apprehension. In fact, Minor (1970) found that experimenter-expectancy bias in Rosenthal's person perception paradigm occurred only when subjects were made more apprehensive by implying that poor performance meant some form of psychological maladjustment.

Although verbal conditioning processes can mediate expectancy effects, it does not appear to be a necessary factor. Rosenthal (1969) noted that bias can still occur even under circumstances where verbal conditioning is not possible, such as in a study by Adair and Epstein (1968) in which tape-recorded instructions made by experimenters with opposite expectancies were used instead of live experimenters. Nonetheless, experimenters found differences in performance that corresponded with the expectancies of the experimenters who taped the instructions a given subject received.

In addition, if verbal conditioning were a major factor, experimenter bias should not occur with the very first photo in the series since verbal conditioning requires a number of trials. Yet, Rosenthal reports such instant bias. Furthermore, rather than increased bias as the trials continue—as one might expect if verbal conditioning were involved—the bias actually diminishes over the series of 20 photos.

It should also be noted that verbal conditioning could not be responsible for the experimenter bias demonstrated in animal studies. Apparently the mechanism involved here, according to Rosenthal and Fode (1963), is differential handling and treatment of allegedly maze-bright and maze-dull rats. The former received gentler and greater amounts of handling than the latter, according to the reports of the experimenters themselves after the experiment.

Nonverbal Communication as a Mechanism

Rosenthal (1969) suggested that since the very first response of subjects can sometimes be affected by experimenter expectancies, it would appear that some of the mediating processes occur *prior* to the experimental session such as when the experimenter greets, seats, and instructs subjects. Some types of cues, such as vocal intonation or body postures and gestures, may be operative. The evidence for the idea that nonverbal communication is the basis for expectancy effect is indirect. The aforementioned study by Adair and Epstein (1968) suggests that bias can occur even though the same instructions are presented on tape, but by experimenters with opposite expectations.

Despite this suggestive evidence, Rosenthal (1969, p. 254) lamented: "For all the hundreds of hours of careful observation, and for all the valuable things learned about experimenter–subject interaction, no well-specified system of unintentional cueing has been uncovered." So how does the bias occur? Rosenthal (1969, p. 254) speculated that even though subjects are affected by experimenter expectancies, "Perhaps they do not know, but perhaps within the context of the given experiment, they can come to know."

The process Rosenthal was suggesting is a learning process quite different from the verbal conditioning explanation. In verbal conditioning, the experimenter does the "teaching" or reinforcing by giving a reinforcer each time the subject makes the correct response. Under this alternative conception, the subject does the "teaching," not the experimenter who may even be unaware that such training is even happening. Rosenthal speculated that when the subject first hits upon the correct response, probably due to chance, it becomes more likely for the experimenter to repeat any unintentional cues he or she just happened to be emitting immediately prior to a subject's earlier correct response. With subsequent subjects, an experimenter is apt to be more proficient at this process. What we have in the experimenter-subject dyad is a type of interpersonal learning situation with the emphasis placed on the subject as the shaper of the experimenter's behavior.

In his more recent formulations (Hall, Rosenthal, Archer, DiMatteo, & Rogers, 1978), Rosenthal has expanded the scope of his studies to interpersonal dyads of a variety of types including teacher–student, therapist–patient, counselor–client, and employee–employer rather than looking only at experimenter–subject dyads. Furthermore, instead of viewing these situations as one-way avenues of communication, the focus has shifted toward treating them as two-way or reciprocal interactions. The basic problem of the influence of interpersonal expectancy effects applies to all of these situations, but instead of asking how does the expectancy of A affect B or vice versa, the question is rather how do expectancies of both A and B toward each other affect their behaviors.

Hall et al. have been looking at the role of nonverbal communication as the underlying process by which interpersonal expectancies affect behavior in situations such as those listed above. They developed a film test called the Profile of Nonverbal Sensitivity (PONS) containing 220 brief segments in which a young woman portrays various emotional scenes such as expressing gratitude, talking to a lost child, talking about the death of a friend, or expressing jealous anger. Subjects do not receive total information but are limited sometimes to facial cues, body cues, or auditory cues masked to hide content but preserve pitch and loudness, and so on.

Although the PONS does not deal specifically with experimenter–subject interactions, it could be used to identify subjects who might be more prone to the influence of nonverbal cues emanating from biased experimenters. Persons who score well on this test should be capable of greater influence by the experimenter than those who prove less sensitive to nonverbal cues. Similarly, if communication in the experimental dyad is bidirectional, we might expect those experimenters who score well on the PONS to be more capable of picking up nonverbal cues from their subjects and being influenced by them. These assumptions have yet to be thoroughly tested, but future research may provide some answers to these speculations about the process by which interpersonal expectancies in the laboratory as well as in everyday situations exert their influence.

Artifacts and Experimenter-Bias Effects

Barber (1976) raised a number of doubts about the extent to which demonstrations of experimenter-expectancy effects are valid. He emphasized the important distinction between the *principal investigator* of an experiment and the person who actually collects the data, who may only be an assistant. Whereas the investigator may sometimes be the same person who interacts directly with subjects in large studies or those supported by research grant funds, the investigator who designs and plans experiments often hires student assistants to collect the data.

Perhaps, maintained Barber, more attention needs to be paid to the possibility of *investigator*, as opposed to experimenter or data-collector, bias in studies purporting to show experimenter-expectancy effects when the design and conduct of studies is done by different persons. Even if the experimental assistants did not bias the results during the experimental sessions, it is possible that the expectations of investigators may create bias in the manner in which they design the study, select and train their assistants, choose their subjects, analyze their data, and interpret the findings.

In addition to these sources of bias, Barber also cited several other mechanisms by which experimental assistants can obtain what look like expectancy effects but do not actually involve any genuine influence of experimenter bias on the actual behavior of the subjects. One factor is the failure to follow protocol precisely, the procedures planned by the investigator are not closely or uniformly adhered to. However, in order for this shortcoming to create experimenter bias, the experimenters would have to be sloppy or inconsistent in their procedures for some treatment conditions, but not for all of them. If they were friendlier, for example, toward subjects who were expected to do well but neutral or negative toward those expected to perform poorly, this differential treatment might favor expectancy confirmation.

Barber also suggested the possibility of either intentional "fudging" of data or unintentional recording of errors by the experimenter in the direction of expected outcomes as alternative accounts of studies claimed as evidence of unintentional experimenter-expectancy effects. These factors are not generally considered as likely so they are seldom evaluated, according to Barber, but unless they are ruled out we can not be sure that experimenter-expectancy effects are genuine.

"Fudging" or the deliberate falsification of data is a serious charge which is difficult to prove, especially after a study is published. But it would be naive not to think that it does happen throughout science (e.g., New York *Times,* April 18, 1974; *Time,* Aug. 26, 1974; Gillie, London *Sunday Times,* Oct. 24, 1976) on the part of investigators. Similar fudging by experimental assistants may stem from subtle pressures and hints from investigators who, after all, are paying them. Even though investigators may not explicitly tell assistants to fudge, some assistants may fear they will be regarded as incompetent if their data fail to support hypotheses, or even worse, are in the opposite direction from that expected.

Fortunately, some evidence pertaining to this question is available. Rosenthal (1966, p. 12) described a study done by his collegues which suggests that misrecordings as well as computational errors during data analysis are infrequent and trivial in magnitude. Furthermore, some filmed and tape-recorded studies showed less than 1 per cent discrepancy between experimenter records and independent scoring of other judges (Rosenthal, 1969, p. 247). This is not to say that no errors occur, but that they are mainly "honest errors" which tend to be random in direction and cancel out rather than favor one direction, as would be the case if experimenter bias was affecting the errors.

Silverman (1968) tape recorded sessions involving word associations given to experimental assistants who had been given expectations of either short or long response latencies. Since the assistant had to manually time these latencies, it was possible for their biases to influence the accuracy of their recorded times in comparison with the response times measured from the tape recordings. Although the results were inconclusive due to incomplete data, there was some evidence that misrecording can occur and contribute to expectancy effects.

The magnitude of such errors, however, does not appear to be appreciable. Using the same type of word association task, Johnson and Adair (1970) compared male and female assistants holding expectations of short latencies for some subjects but long latencies for others. Again, inconclusive results were obtained but there did appear to be some misrecording error which was smaller than the influence of the direction of expectancy on the actual responses. More recording error was found with females, possibly due to the fact that the investigator was male, according to Johnson and Adair's speculation.

The final alternative source Barber proposed as a basis for expectancy effects is the influence of the *attributes* rather than the biases of experimenters. Physical and psychological differences among experimenters may influence the reactions of subjects; this problem will be considered in more detail in the next chapter.

In summary, Barber held that a number of investigator as well as experimenter factors other than their expectancies may exist and create the effect attributed by Rosenthal to unintentional influence of experimenter expectancies. If Barber is correct, the expectancy effect would be an artifact and there would be no need to try to identify any underlying process for biases due to experimenter expectancies per se.

METHODOLOGICAL CONSIDERATIONS

The exact extent to which experimenter bias occurs in experiments concerned about the nature of the experimental method itself and the process by which it operates are unresolved issues. Nonetheless, Rosenthal and Rubin (1978) maintained that the overall findings of 345 studies can be statistically shown to support the view that differences do occur between experimenters holding different expectancies. If such differences are due to experimenter bias, it should be apparent that procedures need to be devised that can prevent or reduce such processes that would undermine the validity of conclusions drawn from experiments affected by such bias.

Blind Experimenters

One obvious solution would be for the researcher who is the principal investigator on a project to employ assistants or data collectors who themselves were not informed of the investigator's hypotheses or expectations about the nature of the subjects' responses. It should be pointed out that most published research is based on data collected by such research assistants, and not by the principal investigator(s). It is not as clearly known how frequently these assistants actually know of the investigator's hypotheses, but the suggestion under consideration is that they not be informed about the expected outcomes. It would still be possible, however, for assistants to act just like subjects do and attempt to formulate their own hypotheses about the purpose and expected outcomes of the experiment. There is no guarantee that there will be no experimenter bias merely if the data collectors are not officially informed of the investigator's hypotheses.

In one study, Rosenthal, Persinger, Vikan-Kline, and Mulry (1963), assessed the possibility that the principal investigator's hypotheses could still influence the results of research assistants who were not informed of the investigator's hypotheses. Student experimenters were given different expectancies about their subjects' performance on the person-perception task. Then, these student experimenters were given research "grants" to hire their own research assistants to run additional subjects. The student experimenters were instructed that their assistants should obtain similar results; however, they were not allowed to actually instruct their assistants as to what results to expect. Thus, the student experimenters were biased to expect their assistants to obtain results similar to their own; yet the assistants were not explicitly biased by the student experimenters. Nonetheless, the results indicated that the research assistants obtained results that corresponded with the expectancies of the persons who trained them.

There is some ambiguity about the procedure of this experiment. Just how did Rosenthal et al. (1963) convey to student experimenters the expectation that their assistants would obtain results similar to their own? All they say is that experimenters were "subtly led, by their printed instructions, to expect their assistants to obtain data of the same sort they had themselves obtained from their earlier run subjects" [p. 314].

An assistant may be blind about different aspects of an experiment; the expected or hypothesized behavioral responses of subjects, the conceptual hypothesis, the total design of the study, and various background aspects of the subjects. Even when the assistant is blind concerning one of these dimensions, it may still be possible for the assistant to figure out expected outcomes and to produce biased results unintentionally. Systematic studies on the effects of witholding information about different aspects of the experiment from the assistant are still needed.

Automated Procedures

One would think that the use of automated methods of providing instructions, administering stimuli, and recording responses would eliminate or greatly reduce any influence of expectancies of assistants on outcomes of studies. Of course, there is already substantial use of automation of some aspects of experiments such as those mentioned above. Even when these experiments are done, however, there is a human assistant who greets subjects and often is present in the room with them during many parts of the otherwise automated session.

Automation may also have its own problems, especially since it may arouse greater apprehension or create indifference or resentment. The author can recall his personal reaction the first time he received an automated "junk phone call." As much as I disliked phone solicitations when a "live" voice was involved, I found it even more insulting to have a tape-recorded message trying to sell me some product. Similarly, although there are problems of bias when a "live" person conducts an experiment, different and perhaps worse problems occur if the entire procedure is automated. People feel "silly" talking to the experimenter's machines, just as many of them feel awkward leaving messages with telephone-answering devices.

One study by Johnson and Adair (1972) that compared the effectiveness of automated instructions and stimulus presentation as a means to reduce recording errors in the direction of experimenter expectancies suggested that automation is not the perfect answer. Although male assistants showed less biased recording errors if automation was used, *more* misrecording bias was found with female assistants under these conditions in comparison with nonautomated conditions. Exactly why this puzzling result with the female assistants occurred was not clear.

Expectancy Controls

Instead of preventing expectancies on the part of the experimenter, Rosenthal (1966) suggested that all experimenters be given explicit expectancies by the investigator, with half of the experimenters for each treatment condition receiving opposite expectations. This strategy is not to eliminate experimenter bias, as when a no-expectancy control group is used, but to assess it by allowing it to operate in opposite directions in the very same experiment (see Table 13–2).

Consider the example of a simple drug study in which a stimulant X is administered to the experimental group while a pharmacologically-inert placebo is given to the control group. To control for expectancy bias on the part of the experimenter, Rosenthal would add two more groups to the design such that opposite expectancies would be held by experimenters for half of the subjects in both the experimental and control conditions. Thus, a third group that received the stimulant would have experimenters expecting *lowered* alertness. Similarly, a fourth group would receive the placebo but this time their experimenters would be led to expect *increased* alertness from them.

Few published studies exist that have employed such expectancy controls, but the potential value of such methods to prevent erroneous conclusions about the effects of variables can be seen in a study that did use expectancy controls. Cooper, Eisenberg, Robert, and Dohrenwend (1967) had subjects memorize symbols and their definitions; half were told there was a 50–50 chance they would be tested on this material while the other half were only instructed to examine the material. Presumably, greater effort should be expended in the former group, reasoned Cooper et al. so that they should be more likely to expect a sub-

TABLE 13–2. Example of Use of Expectancy Control Design.

Expectancy	Treatment	
Gp. E > C	Experimental	Control
Gp. C > E	Experimental*	Control*

*These are the expectancy controls treated exactly the same as the corresponding experimental and control groups but are tested by experimenters who are given the opposite expectancies.

sequent test. If actual measures of subject expectations for a test would be made, it is possible that the hypothesis could be confirmed merely because of experimenter expectations that the group with more effort would have greater perceptions of a possible test.

To test this possibility, Cooper et al. used expectancy controls, with half of the subjects at each of the two effort levels being examined by experimenters told that high-effort subjects would be more likely to expect a test and the other half tested by experimenters led to believe that low-effort subjects would be more prone to expect a test.

The results showed that experimenter expectancies were confirmed; that is, whichever level of effort, high or low, the experimenters had been told would be more likely to expect a test were the ones who gave higher ratings of test likelihood. Had there been no expectancy controls used in this study, the role of experimenter bias would have gone undetected and the obtained differences in subject expectancies of tests would have been mistakenly attributed to the independent variable, amount of effort.

Other Methods

Rosenthal (1966) suggested a number of other ways of coping with the problem of experimenter bias. If we only use one or two different experimenters in an experiment, as is the case with most experiments (McGuigan, 1963), any biases that these experimenters have may influence the results in a systematic direction. However, if we randomly sample experimenters just as we do in selecting subjects, thus using several different experimenters within a single experiment, biases of different experimenters might possibly cancel each other out. There is still opportunity for biases of individual experimenters to operate, but overall it is assumed that the effect of experimenter bias will be cancelled out, more or less.

The use of a larger number of experimenters per experiment may also serve to control bias by reducing it, not merely cancelling it out. Rosenthal (1966, Chapter 19) noted that for a given number of subjects in an experiment, there would be fewer subjects tested by each experimenter as we increase the number of experimenters. The advantages of this situation would be to reduce the opportunity for experimenters to learn how to bias, lessen the chances that experimenters would figure out which subjects are members of which experimental treatment, and minimize the effects of trends in early returns from biasing the expectancies experimenters would have for subsequent subjects. All of these benefits would reduce experimenter bias; in addition, we would acquire a bonus in gaining greater generalizability of results.

It is interesting to note that Rosenthal's recommendation of having less experienced experimenters contrasts with present procedures based on the assumption that more objectivity would be obtained with highly-experienced experimenters.

Another approach to reducing experimenter bias suggested by Rosenthal is the careful observation of the experimenter's behavior during the experimental sessions either by subjective or objective means. The knowledge or belief that they are being watched may reduce the operation of bias on the part of experimenters, but they may also become anxious or resentful as well.

CRITICAL EVALUATION

The strongest critics of Rosenthal's work purporting to show experimenter bias have been Barber and his associates. On the one hand, Barber and Silver (1968) have charged that the statistical analyses of the results in many of the studies claiming experimenter bias have been weak or inappropriate. The details of this criticism are complicated, as was Rosenthal's (1968) refutation of these attacks. For example, it was charged that sometimes only selected portions of the total data were used to evaluate hypotheses or that hypotheses were sometimes changed after the results were analyzed. Many of the issues under dispute are not easily resolved since as Rosenthal (1968, p. 372) noted, "The conclusions one wants to draw from an array of data are a matter of taste and judgment." Furthermore, as shown by Rosenthal (1969, p. 350), there is considerable disagreement among statisticians as to the proper use of statistics.

In addition, they (Barber, 1976; Barber & Silver, 1968) attacked Rosenthal's work on methodological rather than statistical grounds, suggesting that intentional bias has not been entirely ruled out in many experimenter-bias studies. Even the actual fudging or doctoring of data cannot be ruled out in some cases. Obviously if these methods are the processes by which experimenter bias is manifested, the phenomenon is not particularly interesting. All we would have would be an additional situation where dishonesty or cheating was operative. What makes Rosenthal's work intriguing is the possibility that it demonstrates bias via some form of unintentional influence. Barber (1976) suggested that before we can worry about the mechanism of unintentional forms of influence, we must be convinced that no intentional types of bias are being employed by the experimenter on the results.

In response to Rosenthal's (1968) countercharge that no proof was given by Barber and Silver of cheating or intentional biasing, they responded that, ". . . the burden of proof is upon those who wish to claim that, in these studies, the student experimenters unintentionally and subtly biased their subjects' responses; the burden of proof is not upon reviewers who point out that alternative explanations have not been rigorously excluded" [Barber & Silver, 1968b, p. 61].

In terms of their evaluation, Barber and Silver (1968b) concluded that experimenter bias occurred in only 12 of the 31 studies available at that time. Further analysis led them (1968b, pp. 58–61) to conclude that in only two studies could one exclude the possibility that factors such as intentional biasing or fudging of the data operated. The notion formulated by Rosenthal that unintentional paralinguistic or kinesic cues serve to bias results seems acceptable to Barber and Silver in only these two studies.

Another criticism by Barber and Silver (1968a, p. 26) is that there has been a confusion between expectancy and desirability by Rosenthal. In instructing his student experimenters, Rosenthal not only provided expectancies about their subjects' behavior, but he also urged upon them the desirability that they be able to replicate previous well-established findings upon which the alleged expectancies were based. This distinction appears to be well worthwhile. It led Barber and Silver to raise the interesting questions of whether expectancies would be fulfilled if the students' experimenters did not regard them as desirable or whether results could be biased when experimenters desired certain results but had no basis for expecting them.

Certain unique problems exist in formal studies of experimenter bias such as Rosenthal's. The investigator must use student experimenters to demonstrate experimenter bias; yet these experimenters are simultaneously functioning in the role of subjects for the investigator. In this respect, they are no different from any other subjects; it just so happens that their task is not to memorize nonsense syllables or fill out questionnaires, but rather to test their own subjects. One must wonder to what degree student experimenters are like other subjects in trying to figure out the true purpose of their participation. To what extent are student experimenters suspicious or aware of the deception imposed upon them by Rosenthal when he tells them what results to expect from their subjects?

And what about the demand characteristics of the situation? Rosenthal's experimenters were probably as eager—if not more so—as other subjects to be "good subjects." Some of them were students in Rosenthal's class and they were told how important it was to replicate the expected results. Furthermore, in many studies they were paid $2 an hour if they succeeded, but only $1 otherwise.

Therefore, the situation involved strong pressure on student experimenters to "deliver the goods." Otherwise, they have failed to replicate well-established findings that would cast doubt on their ability as experimenters. In addition, they would get only $1, rather than $2 an hour. Rosenthal (1966, Chapter 13), however, did show that if excessive rewards are offered one actually gets less bias. Excessive rewards of $5 led to less bias than $2 rewards. Rosenthal suggested that the $5 reward may have appeared to be a bribe, so experimenters bent over backward to avoid bias so it would not appear that they could be bribed.

In real experiments, as contrasted with the metaexperiments or "experiments about experiments" of Rosenthal, it is doubtful that most research assistants and data collectors would be under as much pressure to come up with the expected results. Often they are not even informed of the investigator's hypotheses. They receive the same rate of pay, regardless of whether or not the data confirms the hypothesis. Even if the principal investigator—who obviously knows the hypothesis—ran the subjects, there would not be as much pressure as that encountered by the student experimenters because the investigator would not be a subject at the same time.

The investigators who study experimenter bias represent an interesting paradox since, in principle, they could be biasing their own results! For example, it is conceivable that Rosenthal himself, in attempting to confirm his belief that experimenter bias exists, may have unintentionally biased the results of his studies himself (Lester, 1969). Yet, ironically such bias would constitute evidence itself that studies can be influenced by experimenter bias. One implication of this speculation is that studies of experimenter bias by an investigator who did not believe in experimenter bias might fail to replicate Rosenthal's findings because of his or her opposite bias. Interestingly enough, the major critic of Rosenthal's work, T. X. Barber, along with five colleagues (Barber, Calverley, Forgione, McPeake, Chaves, & Brown, 1969), have done five studies that have all failed to replicate Rosenthal's results. This predicament leaves us in quite a dilemma for it suggests that we may obtain as many different results as we have investigators with different hypotheses and expectancies!

Where does this discussion leave us? What conclusions can we draw? The possibility that some process like experimenter bias can exist is important to evaluate, for to the degree that it operates, our whole approach to psychology based on experimentation is undermined. We owe a large debt to Rosenthal and his colleagues for their thorough and painstaking analysis of the phenomenon and for his imaginative suggestions for improving experimental methodology.

However, the possibility that experimenter bias is a pervasive and significant factor throughout psychological research does not appear to be as strong as one might get the impression from reading Rosenthal's work. A similar view was proposed by Masling (1966) who noted that, "One possible danger of the current enthusiasm for investigating the Rosenthal effect is that it may lead to the conclusion that all psychology, under all conditions, is subject to this phenomenon" [p. 92].

Furthermore, he observed that where it does occur, it may not be a strong factor affecting the conclusions made in the study. Such reservations have also been voiced by Aronson and Carlsmith (1968).

Even if we were persuaded that experimenter bias affects results in the types of situations such as those studied by Rosenthal where the effects of the independent variables are weak relative to the yet unidentified but presumed differential behavior of experimenters, there is little reason to argue that such biases can have similar effects in other experiments where more powerful independent variables might be involved or if the nature of the task does not involve much experimenter–subject interaction.

The possibility that experimenter-expectancy effects can be demonstrated in a metaexperiment or study designed specifically to evaluate the processes inherent to experiments should not lead one to conclude that the same effects occur to the same extent in "real" experiments. The author (Jung, 1978) has pointed out the possibility that metaexperiments may be atypical and designed to favor demonstration of expectancy effects. Furthermore, increased awareness on the part of researchers to the problem of bias may paradoxically produce a "self-defeating prophecy" whereby there is a decrease in such an effect. Once publicized, social-science findings, according to Gergen (1973) and Mills (1961) may alter the behavior of those who learn of these results so that they no longer are valid. Following this argument, successful demonstrations of expectancy effects in metaexperiments could eventually lead to less experimenter bias in experiments in general.

Is it worth the considerable time, effort, and concern to take as many precautions to guard against experimenter bias as recommended by Rosenthal? Or is it reasonable to take the risk that experimenter bias may occur undetected due to the lack of elaborate controls against expectancy bias? Most experiments do not employ measures to check if bias occurs so that it would appear that most investigators assume the problem is unlikely or that an objective "attitude" and "good intentions" may be sufficient safeguards.

Ideally, it would be preferrable to include procedures that measure any possible bias, but in terms of practical considerations the costs seem too great so that most investigators do not bother to assess this prospect. Until some evidence that bias is likely to occur in a given area of research, investigators in that area are unlikely to take preventive measures. Perhaps this pragmatic approach represents a compromise answer to this dilemma.

In addition to preventive measures that might be used during a study, it is also possible that publication policies of journals could be altered in ways that might reduce the tremendous pressure to find significant results. An investigator invests substantial time, energy, and effort in any major piece of research. Often the professional advancement of the investigator depends on the successful publication of research findings, findings very unlikely to be accepted by major journals if they do not "turn out right" in the sense of showing differences that confirm the experimenter's hypotheses.

One obvious reason why nonsignificant results are not accepted is because they are inconclusive; it is logically unsound to argue that one has evidence in a study that proves the null hypothesis of no difference between the treatment and control groups. However, if one price we pay for this strategy for judging the merit of research is the increased influence of biased results due to experimenter expectancies, we might wish to change this policy.

In 1976, the journal *Representative Research in Social Psychology*, which is published by graduate students at the University of North Carolina, took this bold step in announcing an editorial policy that bases its acceptances of articles entirely on the merit of research proposals that give a description of the rationale for the problem to be studied, its method and design, and the appropriateness and completeness of plans for data analysis. Articles accepted on the basis of submission of this information will be published regardless of whether or not the data eventually collected is statistically significant. It will be interesting to see how this policy fares since this innovation may reduce the influence of the artifact of experimenter expectancies.

SUMMARY

Although experimenters try to be objective, their expectancies and hypotheses may unintentionally influence the outcomes of studies so that they confirm their predictions. The work of Rosenthal and his associates, using a variety of tasks and many different data collectors, has provided direct evidence that the results obtained by experimental assistants who were provided with different expectancies tend to fulfill those biases.

The precise mechanism by which experimenter-expectancy effects are produced is not known, although it is likely that nonverbal cues may be emitted during experiments by both the experimenter and the subject, which in turn may affect their behavior. In contrast, it has been argued that in some demonstrations of experimenter bias, there is the possibility of intentional "fudging" or faking of data or at least some type of data-recording errors.

If the evidence on expectancy effects is upheld, how can measures be taken to reduce or eliminate such sources of error? The use of blind or naive experimental assistants, automated methods of stimulus presentation and data recording, control groups given no or opposed expectancies, and the use of larger numbers of experimenters who would each test fewer subjects are among the procedures that have been tried.

Even if experimenter-expectancy effects exist, it is possible that studies aimed at demonstrating the effect may overstate the magnitude of the effect. Investigators who believe the effects are large may design and conduct studies on this phenomenon in ways that may favor the finding of such bias. The generalizability of experiments on experimenter bias to other studies investigating other processes may be limited. In addition, the Rosenthal-type studies may serve to sensitize researchers to be wary of expectancy biases so that greater precautions are used, thereby reducing the overall incidence of these effects.

REFERENCES

Adair, J. G., and Epstein, J. Verbal cues in the mediation of experimenter bias. *Psychological Reports*, 1968, *22*, 1045-1053.

Aronson, E., and Carlsmith, J. M. Experimentation in social psychology. In G. Lindzey and E. Aronson (Eds.), *Handbook of Social Psychology* (Sec. Ed.). Reading, Mass.: Addison-Wesley, 1968.

Barber, T. X. *Pitfalls in human research*. New York: Pergamon, 1976.

Barber, T. X., Calverley, D. S., Forgione, A., McPeake, J. D., Chaves, J. F., and Brown, B. Five attempts to replicate the experimenter bias effect. *Journal of Consulting and Clinical Psychology*, 1969, *33*, 1-6.

Barber, T. X., and Silver, M. J. Fact, fiction, and the experimenter bias effect. *Psychological Bulletin Monographs*, 1968, *70*, 1-29 (a).

Barber, T. X., and Silver, M. J. Pitfalls in data analysis and interpretation: A reply to Rosenthal. *Psychological Bulletin Monographs*, 1968, *70*, 48-62 (b).

Cooper, J., Eisenberg, L., Robert, J., and Dohrenwend, B. S. The effects of experimenter expectancy and preparatory effort on belief in the probable occurrence of future events. *Journal of Social Psychology*, 1967, *71*, 221-226.

Gergen, K. J. Social psychology as history. *Journal of Personality and Social Psychology*, 1973, *26*, 309-320.

Gillie, O. Crucial data was faked by eminent psychologist. London *Sunday Times*, Oct. 24, 1976, pp. 1-2.

Hall, J. A., Rosenthal, R., Archer, D., DiMatteo, M. R., and Rogers, P. L. The profile of nonverbal sensitivity. In P. C. McReynolds (Ed.), *Advances in psychological assessment*. (Vol. 4). San Francisco: Jossey-Bass, 1978.

Johnson R. W., and Adair, J. G. The effects of systematic recording error vs. experimenter bias on latency of word association. *Journal of Experimental Research in Personality*, 1970, *4*, 270-275.

Johnson, R. W., and Adair, J. G. Experimenter expectancy vs. systematic recording error under automated and nonautomated stimulus presentation. *Journal of Experimental Research in Personality*, 1972, *6*, 88-94.

Jung, J. Self-negating functions of self-fulfilling prophecies. *The Behavioral and Brain Sciences*, 1978, *3*, 397-398.

Krasner, L. Studies of the conditioning of verbal behavior. *Psychological Bulletin*, 1958, *55*, 148-170.
Lester, D. The subject as a source of bias in psychological research. *Journal of Genetic Psychology*, 1969, *81*, 237-248.
McGuigan, F. J. The experimenter: A neglected stimulus object. *Psychological Bulletin*, 1963, *60*, 421-428.
Masling, J. Role-related behavior of the subject and psychologist and its effects upon psychological data. *Nebraska Symposium on Motivation*: University of Nebraska Press, 1966, *14*, 67-103.
Mills, C. W. *The sociological imagination*. New York: Oxford University Press, 1961.
Minor, M. W. Experimenter-expectancy effect as a function of evaluation apprehension. *Journal of Personality and Social Psychology*, 1970, *15*, 326-332.
N.Y. *Times* Charge of false research data stirs cancer scientists at Sloan-Kettering. April 18, 1974.
Rosenthal, R. Experimenter attributes as determinants of subjects' responses. *Journal of Projective Techniques and Personality Assessment*, 1963, *27*, 324-331.
Rosenthal, R. *Experimenter effects in behavioral research*. New York: Appleton-Century-Crofts, 1966. Irvington, Sec. Edition, 1976.
Rosenthal, R. Experimenter expectancy and the reassuring nature of the null hypothesis decision procedure. *Psychological Bulletin Monograph*, 1968, *70*, 30-47.
Rosenthal, R., and Fode, K. Psychology of the scientist. V. Three experiments in experimenter bias. *Psychological Reports*, 1963, *12*, 491-511.
Rosenthal, R., Persinger, G. W., Vikan-Kline, L., and Mulry, R. C. The role of the research assistant in the mediation of experimenter bias. *Journal of Personality*, 1963, *31*, 313-335.
Rosenthal, R., and Rubin, H. Interpersonal expectancy effects: The first 354 studies. *The Behavioral and Brain Sciences*, 1978, *3*, 377-386.
Sigall, H., Aronson, E., and Van Hoose, T. The cooperative subject: myth or reality. *Journal of Experimental Social Psychology*, 1970, *6*, 1-10.
Silverman, I. The effects of experimenter outcome expectancy on latency of word association. *Journal of Clinical Psychology*, 1968, *24*, 60-63.
Spielberger, C. D. Theoretical and epistomological issues in verbal conditioning. In S. Rosenberg (Ed.), *Directions in psycholinguistics*. New York: Macmillan, 1965.
Time, Psychic scandal. Aug. 26, 1974.

CHAPTER 14

Are Experimental Outcomes Affected by Experimenter Attributes?

Chapter at a Glance

SOME MAJOR ATTRIBUTES OF EXPERIMENTERS AFFECTING OUTCOMES

Not only may the expectancies of experimenters bias the results of experiments, but their physical and psychosocial attributes such as sex, age, race, status, friendliness, and anxiety—to cite a few—may also affect results. For many years the experimenter has been ignored as a possible factor affecting results (McGuigan, 1963), even though Rosenzweig (1933) warned about this problem as long ago as 1933. McGuigan surveyed several randomly-selected issues of the *Journal of Experimental Psychology* to determine how many different experimenters or data collectors had been used in each study. As he noted "In no article was any mention made of techniques of controlling the experimenter variable and in only one of the articles was the number of data collectors actually specified" [pp. 421–422]. He was able to draw some inferences, however, about the number of "possible" data collectors in the 37 articles he surveyed. It was clear that in 10 articles, only one data collector was used, and by inference he concluded that in most of the other 27, more than one data collector was used. Yet, none of these studies provided analyses of results as a function of different types of experimenters to show that this factor itself was not an independent variable affecting results. Thus, male experimenters may obtain different kinds of results than female experimenters, or hostile experimenters may get different findings from those obtained by friendly experimenters. If only one data collector is used in a study, we have no way of determining to what extent that one experimenter's results could be replicated by experimenters with markedly different characteristics. Even if a number of data collectors are used, unless we specify how the experimenters differ and also compare the results obtained by different kinds of experimenters, we still are in the dark about the effects of specific experimenter characteristics on the results.

It is obvious that experimenters vary on an infinite number of dimensions. Thus it would be impossible to vary all of them. However, sometimes the nature of the topic under investigation may suggest which specific experimenter attributes might strongly affect the experimental outcomes—such as sex of the experimenter in a study of arousal toward erotica or the race of the experimenter in a study of attitudes toward minority groups. In such situations it may be useful to use several experimenters who differ along the dimension assumed to affect results so that comparisons of data by different experimenters can be made.

A survey (Harris, 1971) of several volumes of some major journals disclosed that as many as 85 per cent of the articles did not bother to report the sex of the experimenter. It is unlikely that any other attributes were reported either. Undoubtedly, some of those studies used more than one data collector, and in some cases there may have been subgroups of experimenters differing on some attribute, such as age or sex, which would have allowed comparisons to be made to see if the data of subjects varied as a function of these experimenter attributes. However, no such analyses were reported since this type of factor is rarely regarded as important in most studies.

Inspection of articles published in three major journals in 1968–1969 by Silverman (1974) revealed results similar to those found by Harris, confirming McGuigan's (1963) lament that the experimenter is a neglected stimulus object. Fortunately, Silverman was able to get a 70 per cent return of a questionnaire he sent to the authors of these studies to retrieve data about the attributes of the experimenters. The following composite portrait of the experimental assistant was obtained: An undergraduate or graduate, male, in his early to mid-twenties, who is paid to assist the principal investigator.

The survey also revealed that only 20 per cent of the studies involved more than one data collector, but it does not appear that whenever several experimenters were used was there any effort to test the effects of some experimenter attribute since one third of these studies with more than one experimenter did not require each experimenter to collect equal amounts of data from all treatment conditions. Only 7 per cent of the articles included any analysis of results obtained by different subgroups of experimenters to assess for bias. Finally, a followup was done by Silverman by examining the first 30 articles in the same journals in 1973. Little change was found, with only two of these studies reporting experimenter attributes. If journal editors were concerned about this matter, they could very readily require this information from all investigators submitting manuscripts.

Page and Yates (1974) assessed attitudes of 250 psychologists from 12 institutions, but only received returns from half of them. Although this sample was biased (with mean age of 35 and five publications), the vast majority indicated a need for the use of more than one data collector in an experiment but also felt that their own research was minimally affected by this issue.

Some evidence supports these suspicions that the attributes of experimenters can affect results of experiments. Unfortunately, some of these studies are equivocal since very limited sampling of experimenters varying on an attribute was done. Thus, while sex of experimenter was varied in the following examples, only one male and one female experimenter was used so that it may not be their difference in sex, per se, that caused differential results.

One of the early experimental studies examining the effects of experimenter traits was a verbal conditioning study done by Binder, McConnell, and Sjoholm (1957). The task of subjects was to emit sentences as they came to mind; meanwhile the experimenter reinforced all sentences containing hostile words by responding, "Good." For one group of subjects, an attractive, soft-spoken young lady, 5′5 1/2″ tall and weighing 90 lbs. was the experimenter, while the experimenter for the other group of subjects was a very masculine, 6′5″ tall, 220-pounder who was 12 years older than the lady experimenter. Binder et al. stated that the lady experimenter could have passed for a high-school sophomore whereas the male experimenter might have been thought to be a faculty member.

Clear differences in conditioning occurred as a function of the type of experimenter. Hostile words were produced more frequently over trials for both groups, but at a faster rate for the lady experimenter. Binder et al. interpreted this result to mean that subjects were less inhibited in using hostile words in the presence of the lady experimenter. Of course it is not clear exactly which attribute distinguishing the two experimenters was the main factor producing the different results, since they differed in sex, age, size, and personality, but it is obvious that results did vary as a function of experimenters.

A comparison of results obtained by a female versus a male experimenter was also made by Deutsch, Canavan, and Rubin (1971) on a task in which pairs of male subjects had to negotiate in order to achieve a goal. Greater competitiveness or lack of cooperation occurred between the males when the experimenter was female, possibly because each was trying to impress her by outperforming the other subject.

The influence of experimenter traits on behavior is not always as straightforward as in the preceding study. Sometimes there may be an interaction between the traits of the experimenters and those of the subjects. Thus, in the previous study, differences might exist between men and women subjects in how they react to male versus female experimenters.

A case in point is a study on sensory deprivation reported by Walters, Shurley, and Parsons (1962). Male and female subjects floated in a tank of water for several hours; thereafter they were interrogated about their experiences during this isolation. Questions were concerned with feelings such as fright, sex, unpleasantness, and so on. Half of the subjects of each sex were interviewed by an experimenter of the same sex and half by one of the opposite sex. The manner in which subjects responded to the question about sexual feelings differed, depending on whether the experimenter and subjects were of the same or of the opposite sex, with higher scores being reported when they were of the same sex.

The extent to which a given attribute of experimenters will affect subjects will undoubtedly depend on the type of task, the potency of the independent variable, the specific dependent variable, and some attributes of the subjects, to cite a few factors. Findings in one situation that a given experimenter attribute does or does not affect a particular response of one category of subjects to a given independent variable may not be generalizable to a totally different task, for example.

Sex of the Experimenter

Perhaps the sex of the experimenter has been the most frequently studied attribute as a factor affecting results. Whether differential results obtained by male and female experimenters are due merely to their physical differences, per se, or to correlated real or perceived differences such as friendliness, competence, and so on, is not clear.

One type of task in which it might appear obvious that the sex of the experimenter would make a difference is where the content might include sexual or erotic material. For example, Masling and Harris (1969) examined the differences in administration of the Rorschach inkblot test under the four combinations of male and female experimenters and subjects. The four stimulus cards allowing for romantic-sexual fantasy were presented more frequently to females than to males by male experimenters. This cross-sex effect did not occur for female experimenters who were more objective in their treatment of male and female subjects. Harris and Masling (1970), again using the Rorschach and varying the sex of subjects and experimenters, found that more responses were elicited from female than from male subjects when the examiner was male. It is not entirely clear why these biases occurred, but such findings do show how one attribute of the experimenter can produce different results, as least on this type of task.

In a review of studies of the effect of sex of the experimenter, Rumenik, Capasso, and Hendrick (1977) concluded that the age of the subjects is an important additional factor. Whereas female experimenters elicit better performance from children, it appears that male experimenters obtain better performance from college-age subjects.

Race of the Experimenter

Sattler (1970) provided an extensive review of the evidence of the effect of black versus white investigators on performance not only in experiments but in other forms of interaction such as intelligence testing and psychotherapy. Many of the findings are similar, but we will restrict the discussion to the influence of experimenter race—black versus white—on experimental outcomes.

One area of interest has been performance on various types of learning tasks such as digit-symbol copying, verbal learning, and perceptual-motor tasks. Sattler concluded that the overall evidence shows black children are affected by the race of the experimenter, performing better with black experimenters especially when the tasks involved cognitive rather than perceptual motor skills. On the other hand, age is also important to consider as Sattler noted that studies by Katz (e.g., Katz, 1967, Katz, Roberts & Robinson, 1965) with college students showed that better performance was obtained with white experimenters in some situations.

The magnitude of these experimenter race effects are larger in situations such as interviews, studies of attitudes, and personality assessments where anxiety may be greater when subjects and experimenters are of different races. This conclusion is based on more studies with only black subjects than with subjects of both races or with whites only; less is known about the effects of experimenter race on white subjects.

The criticism of studies of experimenter-sex effects made earlier that only one experimenter of each sex was used also holds for many studies of experimenter race. Other factors besides race also differ when only two experimenters are compared. One important other factor is the racial attitude of the experimenter, a factor that may be more influential than the skin color per se of the experimenter. In addition, it would seem essential to consider the racial attitudes of the subjects for each race. Finally, the extent to which experimenter-race effects may occur will also vary with tasks, being lower with those that are more objectively administered and scored.

Psychosocial Aspects

It is difficult to separate psychological or psychosocial attributes from the physical characteristics such as sex, race, or age. Persons varying on physical dimensions may in fact differ or merely be perceived by others as being different in their personal traits, beliefs, and attitudes. Whether or not an older experimenter is in fact more formal and cold toward the subject or is merely perceived as such makes no difference in terms of the influence on the subject's behavior, for example.

Rosenthal, Persinger, Vikan-Kline, and Mulry (1963) had male experimenters test subjects on the photo-rating test of person perception used in the experimenter-expectancy studies. The extent to which experimenter bias was obtained varied with two psychological attributes of the experimenters. More bias was shown with more anxious experimenters while less bias was found with experimenters with lower need for social approval.

Sarason and Winkel (1966) observed experimenter-subject interactions in which subjects had to describe themselves. Then both subject and experimenter rated each other. In addition to varying the sex of both subject and experimenter, high versus low hostility subjects and experimenters were also contrasted.

Male experimenters elicited more evaluative self-statements while female experimenters were perceived as friendlier. Perhaps subjects assumed a more serious attitude with male experimenters due to their expectations that males were more serious. Hostile experimenters were less liked, but elicited more personally significant disclosures and fewer ambiguous self-disclosures. These results illustrate how actual or perceived psychological attributes of experimenters can affect the reactions of subjects at least for this type of situation.

UNDERLYING MECHANISMS FOR EXPERIMENTER-ATTRIBUTE BIAS

Regardless of which experimenter attribute we are concerned with, if it alters behavior of subjects, what is the process by which it occurs? Following Rosenthal's (1976) distinction between *active* and *passive* effects of the sex of the experimenter as an example, we can make a similar distinction for any other attribute that affects behavior. An active effect of sex of experimenter would refer to the modification of subject behavior due to actual differential treatment by male and female experimenters. In contrast, a passive effect occurs when the subjects themselves respond differently to male versus female experimenters due to sex difference or because of preconceptions held by subjects about abilities of experimenters of different sexes or how they will be treated by experimenters of different sexes.

Complex processes develop as the course of the experimental session continues. Thus, if the initial reactions of subjects to their experimenters, based on their preconceptions, alters experimenter behavior, this reaction may feed back into the interaction and thus affect subsequent reactions of the subjects. In Masling's (1957, 1959) studies, female confederates acted as either "warm" or "cold" subjects. The manner in which examiners gave and scored their intelligence tests and projective test protocols differed, with better scores "given" to the "warmer subjects."

Evidence for Active Effects

Rosenthal, Persinger, Mulry, Vikan-Kline, and Grothe (1964) filmed sessions of experimenters and subjects interacting with the person-perception task. Male experimenters were friendlier than females, regardless of the sex of the subject. A doctoral dissertation by Katz (1964), cited by Rosenthal (1967), found that male experimenters took more time to present the photos in the person-perception task when testing females; similarly there was a slight tendency for female experimenters to give more time to male subjects.

Sarason and Winkel (1966) had observers watch male and female experimenters interact with either male or female subjects. They noted that female experimenters tended to look at their subjects, smile, and agree with their subjects more often than male experimenters did. Male experimenters exhibited greater tendencies to fidget with objects.

Evidence for Passive Effects

It is difficult to obtain clear-cut evidence for passive effects of experimenters in studies where there is actually live interaction, but studies that have used videotapes of experimental sessions can provide some information. Piacente, Penner, Hawkins, and Cohen (1974) told subjects to judge the ability of trainee experimenters as they watched them perform in a videotaped interaction with another subject. These trainees were actually confederates who were instructed to perform in a competent or incompetent manner. As might be expected, ratings of competent trainees were higher but there were also differences in ratings for male and female trainees. Male experimenters were seen as better, especially among the confederates who appeared to be incompetent.

However, a similar study by Silverman, Shulman, and Wiesenthal (1972) had contrary results. Female experimenters were perceived as more competent and vigorous whereas male experimenters were seen as warmer, judging from videotapes of their interactions with other subjects. Unlike the Piacente et al. procedure, however, experimenters were not aware that they were being filmed nor were they presented to the judges on film as "trainee experimenters."

Evidence for Complex Interactive Effects

A second session was conducted in the Silverman et al. study in which subjects who had judged the videotaped experimental interactions were asked to make self-ratings on a number of descriptive adjectives. For male subjects there was a correlation between their ratings of themselves and the traits they earlier attributed to male experimenters whom they had observed on the tape, but no correlation existed with ratings assigned to female experimenters. Silverman et al. viewed this result as a case of identification modeling, their term to imply that traits of male experimenters had induced similar traits in male subjects.

In contrast, female subjects had self-ratings that correlated *inversely* with traits ascribed to female experimenters, but not with those assigned to male experimenters. This reference modeling, as it was called by Silverman et al., suggests that the females did not imitate female experimenters but used their traits as a frame of reference against which they compared themselves in contrast. Since female experimenters in this study, it will be recalled, had been seen as competent, female subjects tended to perceive themselves as incompetent. Direct modeling by subjects after their experimenters occurs for males; if this process contributes to experimenter-attribute bias, it should be greater for male-male dyads.

A study by Shulman and Berman (1975) also illustrates the complex manner by which subjects may be influenced by experimenter behavior. Subjects were told they were in a study dealing with the relationship between moods and motor performance; half were led to expect a warm, and half a cold, experimenter. Then, each of these groups was divided again, with half receiving an experimenter whose behavior confirmed their expectation and half did not.

Subjects who had experimenters that matched their expectations rated them as more professional and attentive, regardless of whether the experimenters were acting warmly or coldly toward them. However, this factor did not affect either motor performance or the subjects' descriptions of their own mood states.

Shulman and Berman did find, however, differences on independent ratings by judges who watched videotapes of the test sessions that had been edited to delete the sight and sound of either the subject or the experimenter. These ratings indicated that a correlation existed between the behavior of the members of experimenter-subject pairings. Warm experimenters had subjects who also displayed warmth, as measured by more smiles, eye contact, and so forth. Cold experimenters had subjects who also behaved in a cold manner of passivity and withdrawal. Since the subjects had been randomly assigned to the different types of experimenters, it would appear that the attitude of the experimenter induced the similar moods among their subjects.

It appears, then, that experimenters who differed on certain attributes may have affected their subjects' behavior in different ways. The situation is complicated when there are interactions between the experimenter attribute and type of subject who is affected, such as in the case of the sex of experimenter where the effect of this experimenter attribute differs, depending on the sex of the subject.

IMPLICATIONS

Regardless of the exact process by which experimenter attributes affect subject behavior, it should be apparent that we cannot afford to ignore the possibility that results may differ as a function of variations among experimenters along certain attributes such as sex, race, or age, and various personality dimensions.

Since it is rare for more than one data collector to be used in a study or to compare results obtained by different subgroups of assistants where several are used, it is possible that the findings may be affected by experimenter attributes without our knowledge. McGuigan (1963) has suggested that this contaminating factor may account sometimes for the inability of one investigator to replicate the findings of another, an event that occurs not infrequently in psychology. Our journals are full of controversies stemming from failures of others to replicate previously published findings.

It is not argued that differences in experimenter traits are the main or only difference between two studies yielding conflicting results. The subject populations and test conditions also vary frequently from study to study. In addition, other aspects of the two studies are frequently slightly different. And, when the two investigators happen to be of different theoretical persuasion—as is often the case when a second investigator sets out to replicate the work of another—the differences in outcome could be due to differences in experimenter expectancy rather than differences in experimenter traits. The present evidence suggests that we must now add the nature and characteristics of experimenters to our list of possible variables in all experiments.

POSSIBLE SOLUTIONS

The suggestion has often been made (Friedman, 1967; McGuigan, 1963, Rosenzweig, 1933; Rosenthal, 1966, Rumenik et al., 1977) that investigators use more than one data collector in an experiment. Ideally, experimenters could be randomly selected, but in practice this would prove difficult to implement. However, a minimal improvement would be to use at least two different assistants in each study. If the results obtained were essentially equivalent, one could feel a bit more comfortable although still other attributes that did not vary between the two assistants used might affect results. On the other hand, if the results collected by the two assistants disagreed, we would know that some difference in their attributes might be affecting the results and we would have to be more cautious in our conclusions. We might then repeat the study and add even more data collectors who varied systematically along some attribute we think might reasonably affect the behavior under examination to see if this factor was influencing the results.

Experimenter as an Independent Variable

The only way to discover if a given experimenter attribute affects behavior or has no influence is, of course, to use it as an independent variable in the design of the study. We should not automatically presume experimenter attributes are inconsequential; on the other hand, we cannot realistically vary every conceivable experimenter attribute in our study just to rule out the possibility that if affects results. Some reasonable judgment has to be exercised in deciding which attributes to examine, depending on the type of phenomenon being investigated.

When we do find an effect of experimenter attributes, there may be two quite different types of situations, according to McGuigan (1963). The effect may exist but it may not be a differential one for various conditions of the experiment. Thus, one type of experimenter may obtain better or different performance from both the experimental and control groups, but the mean differences could still be comparable to those produced by a different type of experimenter. Although the actual numerical values of performance scores would differ for the two types of experimenters, combined data from all subjects would show about the same overall differences between the experimental and control groups. This is a situation where experimenter attributes would affect the *results,* but not the *conclusions* drawn about the effects of the independent variable in the study. Rosenthal (1966, p. 110) made essentially the same important distinction.

For example, suppose we are studying learning as a function of the time of day. In addition, we vary the type of experimenters—say, cold versus warm—because we suspect this factor affects learning. It may happen that although one type of experimenter may obtain more learning from subjects, there is no differential effect of the time-of-day variable. That is, regardless of the type of experimenter, learning is better in the morning than in the afternoon, perhaps due to fatigue being greater at the later hour. As long as there is no interaction between the experimenter variable and the independent variables in the study, the conclusions drawn about it will not be affected by the influence of experimenter traits.

However, in some types of research, such as surveys, where the goal is to measure the actual opinions or attitudes and not how some other variables affect them, the influence of experimenter traits can be a serious problem. For example, in a survey about racial attitudes, the race of the interviewer can influence the nature of the results so that our conclusion about the nature of racial attitudes of the interviewees will vary, depending on the race of experimenter (Sattler, 1970).

In contrast, in the other type of situation described by McGuigan, an experimenter effect may occur whereby one type of experimenter obtains differences between the experimental and control conditions but another type of experimenter does not. There is an interaction between type of experimenter and the other variable. In this situation, there is an effect of the experimenter on *both* results and conclusions.

The exact effect of the experimenter on the results and conclusions of an experiment obviously cannot be identified if there is only one experimenter or there is no breakdown of the data for different types of experimenters when multiple experimenters are employed. For these reasons, McGuigan and others have recommended that the experimenter be studied as an independent variable in its own right, which like other variables may influence behavior. The old conception of the experimenter as a background factor in the experiment who is "invisible" and is an element of the situation whose presence is neutral must be abandoned.

However, there may be limitations to the solution proposed by McGuigan. Lyons (1964, pp. 94–95) did not feel that this remedy is adequate for assessing the effects that experimenters have on subjects. In fact, it simply makes the situation more complex. The investigator who is systematically studying the influence of different types of experimenters on their subjects is still in the same bind as is any other experimenter studying his or her own subjects. After all, there may be differences in the experimental designs selected by different investigators to study this problem, which might bias the outcome in their favor. Thus, it is possible that some investigators would find that experimenter traits make a difference and other investigators might not, depending on their own views. As Lyons (1964) stated, "All that has been accomplished is to make each experimenter into an experimentally manipulable object who is in no essential way different from the subjects already familiar to us" [p. 95].

Use of Automation?

Lyons suggested that the only viable solution is to eliminate the experimenter with some form of automated administration of the experiment. Even then, presumably there will be some form of human contact encountered by subjects who participate in experiments, either the person greeting them at the experiment before turning them over to the computer, the person recruiting volunteers, or the psychology professor for their course. Might not characteristics of these humans associated indirectly with participation of subjects in an experiment have some effect? Of course, it should be much smaller than any influence of an experimenter. Therefore, in this respect, automation would be a big advance in eliminating this type of bias. However, automation is expensive and perhaps not too readily attainable.

Not all psychologists, however, would agree that automation is the solution. Aronson and Carlsmith (1968) maintained that a live experimenter is "not simply a bias-producing machine; he is frequently a necessary ingredient in the experimental process" [p. 52].

In particular, they point out the advantages of a live experimenter over taped or printed instructions for subjects who fail to understand what they are to do in the experiment. Aronson and Carlsmith held that the live experimenter can and should use judgment in determining which subjects are confused and take extra effort to provide clarifying instructions. They recognize that many psychologists, the author included, would question the feasibility of allowing the experimenter to modify instructions for different subjects due to the possibility of biased treatment of subjects. However, Aronson and Carlsmith did not see this outcome as a serious threat, since they felt this bias can be avoided. But while they did discuss means of eliminating experimenter bias during the experiment, they did not actually mention methods for controlling experimenter bias during the instructional period preceding the experiment.

Are there any other arguments in favor of using live experimenters? One could argue that the presence of a live experimenter may permit the detection of phenomena that were not anticipated when the experiment was first planned. By observing the subjects, the experimenter might be able to suggest ways of improving the actual procedures within the experiment. However, while these are good arguments, such gains due to the use of a live experimenter must always be weighed against the cost of contamination of results by factors related to the experimenter, such as those described in this and the preceding chapters. If we are aware of these problems and exercise care to minimize or prevent forms of bias-associated attributes of the experimenter, then the use of live experimenters is preferable.

SUMMARY

For some types of studies, physical and psychosocial attributes of the experimenter such as age, sex, race, and personality traits may affect the nature of the subjects' responses. Since the majority of published studies use only one or a few experimenters to collect the data, it is possible that any biases due to experimenter attributes will go undetected. Surveys of published studies also show that many studies do not include any descriptions of the characteristics of the experimental assistants.

Studies have been conducted in which some attribute of the experimenter has been used as an independent variable in order to provide evidence on the influence of this attribute on the results. Findings have supported the concern that for some types of tasks there will be different results, depending on the characteristics of the experimenter.

The process by which this type of bias occurs may be either active or passive. In the former case, it appears that experimenters who differ along some attribute actually treat their subjects differently whereas in the latter type the expectations of the subjects toward different types of experimenters may be the primary basis for differential behavior by the subjects. Similarity of features between subjects and experimenter may produce more rapport, and hence different outcomes than those obtained from subjects who do not share these attributes with their experimenter.

Proposed solutions to this type of bias are similar to those used to reduce experimenter-expectancy effects, namely the use of several data collectors who are dissimilar in their attributes or the use of automated procedures where possible. These precautions may not be needed in all types of studies, but should be considered if it appears likely that the attributes of the experimenter might influence the nature of the subjects' behavior.

REFERENCES

Aronson, E., and Carlsmith, J. M. Experimentation in social psychology. In G. Lindzey and E. Aronson (Eds.), *Handbook of social psychology*. Sec. Ed. Reading, Mass.: Addison-Wesley, 1968.

Binder, A., McConnell, D., and Sjoholm, N. A. Verbal conditioning as a function of experimenter characteristics. *Journal of Abnormal and Social Psychology,* 1957, *55*, 309-314.

Deutsch, M., Canavan, D., and Rubin, J. Effects of size of conflict and sex of experimenter upon interpersonal bargaining. *Journal of Experimental Social Psychology,* 1971, 7, 258-267.

Friedman, N. *The social nature of psychological research.* New York: Basic Books, 1967.

Harris, S. Influence of subject and experimenter sex in psychological research. *Journal of Consulting and Clinical Psychology,* 1971, *37*, 291-294.

Harris, S., and Masling, J. Examiner sex, subject sex, and Rorschach productivity. *Journal of Consulting and Clinical Psychology,* 1970, *34*, 60-63.

Katz, I. Some motivational determinants of racial differences in intellectual achievement. *International Journal of Psychology,* 1967, *2*, 1-12.

Katz, I., Roberts, S. O., and Robinson, J. M. Effects of task difficulty, race of administrator, and instructions on digit-symbol performance of Negroes. *Journal of Personality and Social Psychology,* 1965, *2*, 53-59.

Katz, R. Body language: A study in unintentional communication. Unpublished doctoral dissertation, Harvard University, 1964.

Lyons, J. On the social psychology of the psychological experiment. In C. Scheerer (Ed.), *Cognition–Theory, research, promise.* New York: Harper & Row, 1964.

McGuigan, F. J. The experimenter: A neglected stimulus object. *Psychological Bulletin,* 1963, *60,* 421-428.

Masling, J. The effects of warm and cold interaction on the interpretation of a projective protocol. *Journal of Projective Techniques,* 1957, *21*, 377-383.

Masling, J. The effects of warm and cold interaction on the administration and scoring of an intelligence test. *Journal of Consulting Psychology,* 1959, *23*, 336-341.

Masling, J., and Harris, S. Sexual aspects of TAT administration. *Journal of Consulting and Clinical Psychology,* 1969, *33*, 166-169.

Page S., and Yates, E. Attitudes of psychologists toward experimenter controls in research. *Canadian Psychologist,* 1974, *14*, 202–208.

Piacente, B. S., Penner, L. A., Hawkins, H. L., and Cohen, S. L. Evaluation of experimenters as a function of their sex and competence. *Journal of Applied Social Psychology,* 1974, *4*, 321–329.

Rosenthal, R., Covert communication in the psychological experiment. *Psychological Bulletin,* 1967, *67*, 356–367.

Rosenthal, R. *Experimenter effects in behavioral research.* New York: Appleton-Century-Crofts, 1966. Irvington, Sec. Edition, 1976.

Rosenthal, R., Persinger, G. W., Vikan-Kline, L., and Mulry, R. C. The role of the research assistant in the mediation of experimenter bias. *Journal of Personality,* 1963, *31*, 313–335.

Rosenthal, R., Persinger, G. W., Mulry, R. C., Vikan-Kline, L., and Groethe, M. Emphasis on experimental procedure, sex of subjects, and the biasing effects of experimental hypotheses. *Journal of Projective Techniques and Personality Assessment,* 1964, *28*, 465–469.

Rosenzweig, S. The experimental situation as a psychological problem. *Psychlogical Review,* 1933, *40*, 337–354.

Rumenik, D. K., Capasso, D. R., and Hendrick, C. Experimenter sex effects in behavioral research. *Psychological Bulletin,* 1977, *84*, 852–877.

Sarason, I. G., and Winkel, G. H. Individual differences among subjects and experimenters and subjects' self-descriptions. *Journal of Personality and Social Psychology,* 1966, *3*, 448–457.

Sattler, J. Racial "experimenter effects" in experimentation, testing, interviewing, and psychotherapy. *Psychological Bulletin,* 1970, *73*, 137–160.

Shulman, A. D., and Berman, H. J. Role expectations about subjects and experimenters in psychological research. *Journal of Personality and Social Psychology,* 1975, *32*, 368–380.

Silverman, I. The experimenter: A (still) neglected stimulus object. *Canadian Psychologist,* 1974, *15*, 258–270.

Silverman, I., Shulman, A. D., and Wiesenthal, D. L. The experimenter as a source of variance in psychological research: Modeling and sex effects. *Journal of Personality and Social Psychology,* 1972, *21*, 219–227.

Walters, C., Shurley, J. T., and Parsons, O. A. Differences in male and female responses to underwater sensory deprivation: An exploratory study. *Journal of Nervous and Mental Disease,* 1962, *135*, 302–310.

CHAPTER 15

What Are the Experimenter's Ethical Dilemmas?

Chapter at a Glance

All types of formal human social interaction, whether between a teacher and student, a doctor and a patient, an employer and an employee, or a merchant and a customer, involve certain established but sometimes unwritten laws of conduct and expectations about the legitimate ways of interaction. Such ethical principles are often similar in a variety of situations, generally dealing with issues of trust, fairness, honesty, and justice. Many of the issues involved in these interpersonal situations also apply to the relationship between the experimenter and the subject.

Questions exist concerning the proper manner of recruiting participants for research, the types of experiences they encounter during experiments, the amount and type of feedback they obtain about their own performance and its meaning, and the purposes to which findings from a study are used. Issues such as the legitimacy of the use of procedures with possible risks to subjects at both the physical and psychological level during the experiment, the propriety of the use of deception of subjects and misrepresentation of various aspects of the study to them, and the responsibility of experimenters to provide educational and therapeutic debriefing to subjects are examples of the main concerns.

The present chapter examines these issues and discusses the reactions of psychologists, individual and collective, to these problems and to the kinds of solutions that have been developed or proposed.

MAJOR ETHICAL ISSUES

Informed Consent

Before any experiment can be conducted, one obviously must have a supply of subjects, unless unobtrusive or naturalistic experiments are involved in which persons are observed in public and are unaware of the experiment. How do we go about the task of gaining the consent or agreement of participants? The issue is how complete and how accurate must be the background information provided to prospective participants about the purpose of the study and its procedures. If the study is boring, are we justified in making it sound more exciting? If the study is dangerous, are we warranted in hiding this information? If the study requires several hours, can we lie and say it is a relatively brief study? In short, is it ethical to deceive subjects by either falsifying or deleting some details about the experiment that might otherwise lower their willingness to consent to serve?

In many situations where subjects with foreknowledge about the procedures or goals of the study would be unuseable, the experimenter faces a serious dilemma. While complete disclosure may be ethical but provide no subjects, misrepresentation may obtain subjects but in a manner of questionable propriety. Although the subjects may have "consented" and even signed an agreement form, there is no "informed consent" because subjects did not receive adequate and accurate information to enable them to make their decision. *Informed consent* is a concept that is difficult to precisely or objectively define. Just how much information is needed for a decision based on it to be truly "informed"? Does the subject need to know the theoretical purpose of a study, for example? Can there be intermediate degrees of "informed consent" or is it an all-or-none situation?

It is perhaps easier to identify situations in which informed consent is absent than when it is present. If electric shock will be administered but subjects are not told about this event, consent would probably be considered "uninformed" since insufficient information was received for subjects to know what kinds of risks they might reasonably expect. Although informed consent is sometimes vague, it is a step in the right direction since it requires the experimenter to take some initiative and assume some responsibility for the safety and well-being of human subjects.

Informed consent, like some other ethical issues, applies to situations other than psychological research such as business and medicine since they all involve interpersonal dealings. A good example of this problem in the medical field is an unfortunate incident which happened in Los Angeles recently. Several Mexican-American women were sterilized at a local hospital without their understanding what was happening. The doctors defended themselves on the grounds that the women had signed consent forms, but testimony of these women, all Spanish-speaking, reevealed that they had not fully understood what they were asked to sign. Although there was allegedly no intentional deception, it appears that misunderstanding did occur and that the "consents" were not informed.

Informed consent may also be jeopardized by the use of highly attractive incentives to encourage agreement to serve in experiments due to potential conflict between the motivation to decline participation and the need for the offered incentives. Payment for services, provision of extra points toward course grades, and required participation as a condition of a course all involve some types of pressure that might lead persons who might otherwise not consent to agree to participate. An historic settlement was made between the New York State Health Department and the State University of New York at Albany (Smith, 1977) which had violated several state and federal regulations concerned with protection of human subjects. Part of the settlement agreement called for the discontinuation of their policy of required participation in experiments or the use of an option of writing of a term paper by introductory psychology students, a policy we have already seen in Chapter 12 is nearly universal in American colleges. The impact of this decision on practices throughout the country could be quite significant and bears further scrutiny.

By contrast, of course, the incentives and pressures offered by departments of psychology are quite weak compared to those offered to "volunteers" for medical and psychological studies among inmates of other institutions such as correctional facilities and mental hospitals.

The requirement of informed consent as an ethical procedure creates a methodological problem for many types of studies where it must be assumed that subjects are unaware of certain aspects of the study. One solution to this dilemma developed by Bersheid, Baron, Dermer, and Libman (1973) calls for an inexpensive and convenient procedure of determining the rate of consent that might be expected for a given study by using a roleplaying panel that would not actually serve in the study. A sample of subjects from the population to be studied would be chosen for this panel and would be informed about the purpose, procedures, and so on, of the study and asked if they would consent to serve. Bersheid et al. felt that use of peers would be more valid for this judgment than relying on the experimenter or other researchers.

To test the objection that panelists' judgments might be misleading since they would know they were only roleplaying, Bersheid et al. led half of the panelists to believe that they would actually be in such a study and the other half to know that they definitely would not be in any such study.

Six descriptions of actual published experiments were used, four involving stress, such as having to apparently shock other subjects or place one's hand in painfully cold ice water. Two nonstressful situations, such as competitive bargaining or listening to a persuasive message while watching an amusing film, were also used. It was predicted that panelists who faced the possibility of actual participation would report less willingness to be in the stressful studies whereas panelists who were merely roleplaying would show little difference in preference for the two types of studies.

Four different levels of information were provided: rationale or deceptive cover story only; procedural information also given after the cover story; cover story and procedural information plus an expectation that they would behave in either a desirable or undesirable manner, that is, that the typical behavior in such a study by subjects is either normal or deviant in some way.

Finally, three different types of debriefing—positive, neutral, and negative—were given to the roleplaying group only but not to those subjects told to expect possible participation because such information would reduce the credibility of such a prospect.

The results showed no differences between the two groups of panelists, suggesting that the roleplayers took the task as seriously as the group who believed they might have to serve. As might be expected, subjects were less willing to be in stressful studies except when very little information was provided, a situation where they could not realize how much stress was involved. Such consent can hardly be considered "informed." Consent rates for the nonstressful studies did not vary with the amount of information received.

The usefulness of this approach for an investigator planning a study is that one can determine the extent to which the procedures might be objectionable to participants, without destroying the naivete of potential subjects, unless, of course, word about the study spreads around the campus by word of mouth.

Protection from Harm

Once we have resolved the problem of obtaining informed consent, what are the ethical responsibilities of experimenters during the experiment itself? Although subjects may be confronted with some stimulus situations and events that may cause distress, discomfort, and dismay during the experiment, it is certainly safe to assume that no responsible investigator wants to cause any long-lasting or permanent physical or psychological harm to participants. The problem is how to be able to foresee all of the potential dangers involved with a specific set of procedures. If subjects receive electric shock, are injected with certain types of drugs, or required to exert strenuous physical effort, we would realize that there is higher risk of physical harm to some, if not all, subjects. Careful screening of subjects for physical health would be conducted and emergency medical provisions would be available. But this situation still requires us to justify to ourselves, the subjects, and others that it is ethically proper to conduct such studies.

Safeguards are more difficult to institute and the potential problems are harder to detect when dealing with psychological stress. A situation relished as a challenge by one person may induce anxiety and depression in another person, states that may persist long after the session is over. Even if we could identify individuals who may be prone to adverse psychological reactions to certain types of experiences represented in psychological experiments, we still must face the question of the ethics of confronting subjects with these experiences.

From a moral point of view, the fact that subjects may have given "informed consent" does not alleviate our burden of responsibility toward subjects if they suffer harm from serving in our studies. Subjects who, for example, are told that a task will involve threats to their self-esteem may consent, thinking that they can cope with the situation; but when actually confronted, they may react quite badly. In such a case, is the experimenter ethically bound to try to remedy the situation and "restore" the harmed subjects to the condition they were in at the outset of the study, if possible?

Many investigators justify the imposition of treatments with potential harm to subjects on the grounds that the benefits of the study outweigh the risks of harm to the subjects. Aside from the fact that these subjective judgments are made by the investigator who is apt to be biased in favor of conducting the research, there is also the problem that these supposed benefits to science, humanity, and society are being paid for by the subjects who run the risks. Unlike the situation in therapy, as opposed to basic research, where the clients about to undertake treatment that may be risky do so with the promise and hope that they themselves will improve their own condition, the situation in the experiment calls for subjects to risk themselves as guinea pigs who may be exposed to harmful risks—but risks that, if successful, will benefit others.

Undoubtedly some altruistic individuals would be willing to take such risks, but since there are individual differences in the levels of risk people are willing to take and differences in the amount of benefit they must expect in order to make the sacrifice, it would appear mandatory that each subject, rather than the experimenter, make the choice after receiving full information about the risks and benefits.

Deception

In everyday life situations, deception between two persons creates mutual distrust and suspicion, leading eventually to terminated interactions. Although deceptive practices are widespread in real life because it often provides advantages to the deceiver, it is generally regarded as unethical as a principle of human conduct. The same logic has been extended to a criticism of the use of deception by experimenters in their treatment of subjects. But is it possible that there are important differences between real life and experimental situations so that deception might be more permissible in the latter?

In Chapter 9, it was noted that the implicit contract or expectation of subjects was examined by Epstein et al. (1973) who discovered that subjects have come to actually expect deception in experiments. Furthermore, they seem willing to continue despite such deception perhaps because they want to see if they can see through the deceptions. It may be that some subjects are so involved in experiments because they hope to learn something about themselves or some knowledge of personal value that they are willing to accept deception within the context of the experiment.

This acceptance or tolerance of deception, of course, has its roots in their previous knowledge of experiments and their nature. Just because subjects accept deception does not make it ethically "right," but it does suggest that the experimental interaction between experimenter and subject is rather different from everyday interpersonal exchanges where deceptive practices would be highly objectionable.

The stereotype held by prospective subjects that experiments typically involve deception may be overstated, but it is true that in some fields of psychology, deception is a common practice. The exact extent to which deception is used is not known, but useful approximations may be gained from surveys of published studies, although these are based only on the research published in a few specific journals during a specific brief time period.

A survey (Menges, 1973) of this type examined the incidence of deception of several types: purpose of study, information about subject's own behavior, information about behavior of others, and instruments. Studies published in five important journals for 1971 were examined, providing about 1,000 articles in all. In the case of two journals, *Journal of Abnormal Psychology* and *Journal of Personality and Social Psychology*, it was possible to obtain a temporal comparison by contrasting the incidence of deception in those journals with the 1961 volume of the *Journal of Abnormal and Social Psychology*, which was later split into the two former journals.

Table 15–1 shows the percentage of studies in each journal using various deception practices. As many as almost half of the studies in the *Journal of Personality and Social Psychology* contained deception whereas a low of about 3 per cent occurred in the *Journal of Experimental Psychology* which deals mainly with research on perceptual and cognitive processes in nonsocial settings. The overall rate of deception was about 20 per cent, but much higher in social psychological studies. The category in which deception occurs least was that regarding the purpose of studies. The overall rate of use of deception showed little change between 1961 and 1971.

Although many psychologists have expressed concern over the widespread use of deception, it is not entirely clear how much of the objection is on ethical grounds as opposed to methodological considerations. There is the danger that overuse of deception will lead subjects to be overly suspicious of deception, looking for it even in studies where it does not actually exist. In this way, the experimenter is ultimately the victim of the very weapon used to approach the problem. Accurate assessment of the extent of such subject suspicion itself is difficult to obtain since evidence shows that subjects in studies where they clearly know that deception is involved will not reveal this fact to experimenters when asked.

Faced with such a dilemma, psychologists have been adept at rationalizing. Aronson and Carlsmith (1968), for example, attempted to reduce the concern about possible adverse effects of deception by in-

TABLE 15–1. Type of Deception (Inaccurate Information) by Journal.

Journal	All Studies	Deception Studies*	% Using Deception	Type of Deception: *Purpose of Study*		*Subject's Own Behavior*		*Information About Others*		*Instruments*	
				N	%	*N*	%	*N*	%	*N*	%
Journal of Personality and Social Psychology (1971)	248	117	47.2	8	6.8	40	34.2	44	37.6	25	21.4
Journal of Abnormal Psychology (1971)	144	31	21.5	7	22.6	7	22.6	13	41.9	4	12.9
Journal of Abnormal and Social Psychology (1961)	86	14	16.3	0	0	4	28.6	4	28.6	6	42.9
Journal of Educational Psychology (1971)	82	7	8.5	2	28.6	2	28.6	2	28.6	1	14.3
Journal of Counseling Psychology (1971)	80	5	6.3	2	40.0	1	20.0	1	20.0	1	20.0
Journal of Experimental Psychology (1971)	353	11	3.1	1	9.1	3	27.3	0	0	7	63.6
Total	993	185	18.6	20	10.8	57	30.8	64	34.6	44	23.8

[a]Studies using inaccurate information about either independent or dependent variable.
Source: "Openness and honesty vs. coercion and deception in psychological research," by R. J. Menges, *American Psychologist*, 1973, **28**, 1030–1034.

sisting that most subjects realize that they are in an experiment and consequently may either expect deception or at least not be unduly upset by its occurrence within the context of an experiment.

While this situation may hold for some subjects, this argument to placate those such as Kelman (1967) who hold strong ethical reservations about the use of deception is self-defeating. In essence, it holds that deception is not too effective. But if it is not, why do we persist in deluding ourselves by using it so widely, especially in view of its ethical problems?

Another leading social psychologist, William McGuire (1969), acknowledged the moral cost of deception but felt that "it might be necessary to pay this cost . . . rather than to cease our research" (p. 50). Thus, for McGuire, research takes precedence over other goals as he argued, "Those who are doing experiments which involve deception" are less of an ethical problem than "those who are doing too few experiments or none at all" (p. 53).

Much of the criticism of the use of deception has focused on experiments that also held potential risk of physical or mental harm to participants, such as Milgram's obedience experiment where the deception is that the subjects are harming someone else. Use of deception would probably cause less adverse reaction if the content of the deception was innocuous or less serious. Thus, after subjects worked on very difficult puzzles for a short time either with or without a monetary reward, Deci (1971) excused himself allegedly to go score some tests the subjects had completed. Actually he wanted to allow the subjects to be alone so he could surreptiously measure whether or not being paid to work on the puzzles would affect the amount of intrinsic interest in the puzzles, as inferred by the amount of time they would work on them while the experimenter was absent from the room.

Although deception was used in this study, it was a mild hoax few would object to in comparison to deception about some aspect of the subjects' abilities or personalities such as those of studies (e.g., Aronson & Carlsmith, 1962; Aronson & Mettee, 1968) in which fake scores were provided on tests that indicated some subjects had poor or unstable personalities. In contrasting these two examples of the use of deception, it is clear that deception is questioned primarily when the content of the deception can harm the subjects.

Debriefing of Participants

After the experiment is finally concluded and the subjects are about to be dismissed, what is the ethical responsibility of the experimenter to debrief subjects by providing them with information about various aspects of the experiment and their own level of performance? Should anxieties and frustrations created by service in the study be reduced by the researcher, especially if they were instilled primarily by deceptive practices used during the session? Is there also some burden upon the experimenter to make the experience an educational one in which the purpose of the study and the significance of the findings are explained to participants?

Debriefing, as actually practiced, varies widely in its nature and frequency. Menges' (1973) analysis of about 1000 published journal articles in 1971 found only about 10 per cent reported the use of debriefing, although many of the studies not mentioning this procedure may have in fact used it. Even the journal with the most deception studies showed only a 29 per cent level of use of debriefing. Fortunately, by 1971 a higher incidence of debriefing was being reported.

Details of actual procedures used in debriefing vary considerably but are usually quite skimpy; the typical description is contained in a sentence to the effect that "subjects were then thoroughly debriefed." And if stress was involved, another sentence is usually added which says more or less, "As far as could be detected by reports from the subjects, none of them expressed any serious or long lasting negative feelings." Finally, if deception is also employed, a statement indicating that none of the subjects reported suspicions about the deception, or in cases where a few subjects saw through the deception, we learn that these subjects were not included in the data analysis.

In Milgram's (1963) well-known obedience to authority study, a vague comment is provided about debriefing indicating that there was "a reconcilation" with subjects at the end. Darley and Latané (1968) failed to report any information about debriefing in their study of bystander intervention in emergencies. Nor was debriefing used in Brock and Becker's study of guilt-induced compliance with regard to the staged incident in which subjects apparently were responsible for the apparatus "blowing up." Nor was debriefing employed in Valins' (1966) study in which false heart-rate feedback was given to male subjects as they watched slides of nude female models. One could go on in citing specific studies, but the general point should be clear that a number of prominent and influential psychologists do not debrief, or if they do, they are quite vague about their procedures.

Mills (1976) made careful observations of the manner in which his assistants debriefed subjects and concluded that their procedures were invariably too cursory and superficial. If the debriefing is too rapid, there may be insufficient time for the feedback to fully register so that the subject can think about the meaning of the experiment and its personal value.

Mills (1976) suggested that adequate debriefing entails several parts. First, there is a general justification to the subject on the necessity for deception in research without referring specifically to the current experiment in which the subject is serving. It is pointless to ask, "any questions?" since subjects tend to not ask questions for fear they will appear foolish. In turn, it may be more difficult later to convince them about the deception if they have earlier admitted having no questions or suspicions about procedures.

The next phase of debriefing, according to Mills, should offer another chance to the subject to make guesses about the study by suggestively saying in effect, "Actually there is more to the study than what you were told. Do you have any ideas about what this study is about?"

Novice experimenters tend to be overly technical and use too much jargon in their debriefing rather than everyday terms. Mills suggested that experimenters pay careful attention to each subject's reactions and adjust the debriefing procedure for each subject based on such feedback. There should not be an attempt to force the subject to accept or agree with the purpose of the study but an effort to insure that the subject understands why the deception was necessary.

The final aspect of debriefing recommended by Mills is the attempt to alleviate anxiety of the subject about the experience and to persuade the subject to pledge secrecy about the study. The emphasis to the subject is that the study is concerned with group averages rather than measures of individuals in terms of their personality, character, or ability. If subjects realize there will be a need to test more persons who are naive about the deception, they may be more likely to cooperate. Of course, if they are disgruntled or hostile toward the experimenter for some reason, they would be less willing to maintain secrecy although they probably would not let the experimenter know their feelings.

Methodological concerns also get entangled with ethical issues in discussions about debriefing practices. If debriefed subjects may divulge some aspects of the procedures and the true purpose of some types of studies, there is the danger that there will be fewer naive subjects or, even worse, the risk that some informed subjects will serve anyway but remain undetected by the experimenter.

In addition, as was noted in an earlier chapter, the subjects who undergo deception *followed by debriefing* may become overly suspicious to deception in future studies. Since both of these adverse consequences of debriefing jeopardize the methodological rigor of experiments, it may be tempting to withhold debriefing from subjects, at least until the completion of the study. The methodological gain occurs, however, at the risk of introducing ethical losses. A deceived subject who was given fake scores to lower self-esteem might have to suffer weeks or months under this procedure before learning the truth. Educational and motivational factors must also be considered since subjects will learn less and be less motivated to serve in studies if there is a long interval between participation and debriefing.

Despite the introduction of methodological problems, it is necessary for experimenters to debrief subjects if the use of deception is to be ethically acceptable, according to Rosenberg (1969). He observed that, "Candid and thorough debriefing, unmarred by any proclivity towards gloating, can do much for the experimenter's self-image and probably it also serves the enrichment of the subject's experience and knowledge" (p. 339).

The fear held by some psychologists that debriefing only increases the chances that some subjects will tell other future subjects about the true purpose of certain experiments is not seen as such a threat by Rosenberg. He believed that mutual trust between the experimenter and subjects formed by full and candid debriefing, will enhance cooperation. This view was similarly held by Jourard (1968), a critic of experimental psychology.

On the other hand, other psychologists such as Campbell (1969) have qualified their acceptance of debriefing. Campbell, in essence, felt that "no harm, no debriefing," since debriefing eventually leads to contamination of the naive subjects. He even suggested debriefing can be harmful to subjects since knowing that "one had been had" may lower one's self-image. Campbell regarded the nondebriefed subject as one case where ignorance can be bliss.

Brock and Becker (1966) based their views on debriefing in terms of methodological considerations too. They suggested that minimal debriefing be provided for subjects who may be in similar experiments in the future. Such a criterion is for the benefit of the experimenter and is based solely on the need for naive subjects and shows little consideration for their well-being.

There does not appear to be an easy solution to the dilemma of deception for it is closely tied to methodological problems. It seems that there is an inverse relationship between the two aspects of deception. If we choose the most ethical procedures, we end up with methodological impasses, but if we resolve our methodological problems, we can come face to face with unresolved ethical issues.

We need more research aimed at the question of whether or not deception is harmful. If possible, impartial observers rather than the investigators themselves should be employed for this evaluation. Similarly, more investigation of the effectiveness of debriefing is needed. Research has been done in these areas in recent years but much more is still needed to clarify the situation.

Effectiveness of Debriefing. There is no guarantee that the provision of debriefing, however careful and well-intentioned, will automatically erase any negative effects of participation in an experiment. Evidence on this important question of the effectiveness of debriefing is hard to find since followups are rarely conducted after the end of a session unless one has compelling reason to fear that ill effects persisted.

One can logically argue that debriefing might be ineffective because the credibility of experimenters is already weakened since many subjects come to the laboratory expecting to be deceived. If deception occurs throughout different phases of the study, why should it stop when debriefing is given? The argument that debriefing is given *after* the data for a given subject is all collected and therefore the experimenter has no need to deceive further may be valid, but subjects do not always know when an experimental session is "over" and may regard the debriefing as yet another part of the procedures by which they are assessed. In a few experiments, in fact, debriefing after a first part of the study is still followed by an allegedly separate study (e.g., Brock & Becker, 1966; Fillenbaum, 1966). The first debriefing is actually a deception in which different groups are given different feedback to see how this information will affect behavior on the second task.

Debriefing also involves deception aimed at more honorable goals, such as when discussing the performance of subjects who did poorly due to lack of ability. Rather than let the subjects leave feeling deflated and in low spirits, the experimenter may tell a "white lie" and try to convince subjects that their performance was good or even above average.

The single study that has created the most ethical concern has undoubtedly been Milgram's (1963) obedience to authority experiment. In response to Baumrind's (1964) charges that harm may have been suffered by subjects, Milgram (1964) reported evidence that suggested debriefing had been successful in restoring the subjects to their original mental and emotional state after they learned that no one had actually been harmed by them and that their obedient behavior during the experiment was normal under the circumstances.

A follow-up several months later indicated that about 1 per cent had negative feelings about their participation experience, although this conclusion was based on only one question that furthermore did not directly check on how subjects feel about themselves after performing obediently to a request to harm others. Psychiatric interviews conducted a year later, however, suggested that the subjects suffered no long-term effects.

Ring, Wallston, and Corey (1970) provided an independent test of the effectiveness of debriefing in a Milgram-type situation that involved following orders to administer noxious auditory stimuli of increasing intensity to learners who made errors. As Milgram found, most subjects obeyed. Two types of debriefing were used for different subgroups after both had been dehoaxed about the deception. Defiance-justification subjects were led to believe that it was a sign of mental health to refuse to administer the painful stimuli, whereas an obedience-justification group was told that better-adjusted subjects tended to obey the requests. A third group that received no debriefing until later served as a control.

The extent to which subjects reported being upset on an allegedly anonymous post-experimental survey was least for the obedience-justification group, followed by the defiance-justification, and then by the control group. It appears then that even highly stressful experiences can be acceptable to subjects under certain types of debriefing. However, a limitation to this study noted by Holmes (1976b) was the absence of a no-stress control group or the measurement of preexperimental stress levels so that one can not determine if debriefing was totally successful in returning subjects to their original states.

Holmes repeated the Ring et al. experiment, adding both a no-stress control group and taking predeception measures of stress such as self-ratings and pulse rates. Debriefing included attempts to convince subjects that their behavior in following instructions to inflict apparent harm to another person was "normal" in this type of situation but does not generalize to other types of situations. The results showed that debriefing was effective at both the physiological and self-report levels, with the debriefed group showing no difference with the no stress control group, which suggested that the subjects were restored to their preexperimental levels of well-being..

Holmes and Bennett (1974) conducted an experiment to determine how effective debriefing was when subjects were deceived into thinking they would receive shock, a belief that should increase autonomic arousal levels. Immediately after debriefing, in which it was explained that it had been necessary to mislead subjects to expect shock but that they would not receive any shocks, arousal levels were measured and compared to those of a control group that had not been led to expect shock. A second control group also expected shock, which they did not receive, but they were not debriefed until after their arousal was assessed. The results supported those found earlier in a similar study (Holmes, 1973) and suggested that debriefing was effective in reducing the induced arousal. Both the immediate debrief and the control group that never expected shock showed equally low arousal as compared to the delayed-debrief group.

This type of situation in which the deception dealt with some aspects of the procedures used by the experimenter may be quite different from situations where the deception deals with some aspects of the subject's own personality or performance. Hollingsworth (1977) argued that dehoaxing may be effective in the former but not in the latter type of situation where it is more difficult to convince the subject that some environmental or external factor is responsible for their reactions.

Evidence that debriefing may be inadequate to remove beliefs instilled by deception in subjects about their personal qualities can be found in a study by Walster, Bersheid, Abrahams, and Aronson (1967) in which female subjects were told they had good or poor social skills, judging from aptitude tests they been given earlier.

During debriefing the subjects were told that it had been necessary to use fake test scores so that the experimenter could determine how self-esteem affected the liking of similar people. Finally, in order to measure the extent to which the fake test scores had any persistent effect on the self-appraisal of the subjects despite the debriefing, subjects were then told that the experimenter was really interested in assessing some of their personal feelings. They were asked to complete a questionnaire which included items asking how well they thought they had done in the study and how well they would do in future interactions. The results showed that such estimates were higher for subjects who had been given fake good scores, suggesting that debriefing had not been completely effective in restoring subjects to their original condition, so to speak.

Details of the debriefing procedure were vague, however, as Walster et al. only stated that they were "debriefed at length." Perhaps other methods of debriefing could have been effective. The only description given about the reactions of subjects when they were told they had been deceived was also skimpy, "virtually all of them indicated that they were happy to have participated" (Walster et al., 1967, p. 376.).

In a similar study, Ross, Lepper, and Hubbard (1975) examined the persistence of self-perceptions of subjects after debriefing that they had been given fake feedback about their successes and failures on a series of trials on a cognitive task.

The debriefing process in this study involved showing the subjects the actual prearranged reinforcement schedule in hopes that it would strongly convince them that their own efforts had nothing to do with their outcomes on the task. After apologizing for the necessity of deceiving them, the experimenter gave the subjects a questionnaire asking for their estimates of how many they had gotten correct as well as how well they thought they would do if they received a similar test.

The results showed that the higher the fake scores were, the higher were the postdebriefing estimates of both past and future performance. These findings, like those of Walster et al., show the persistence of first impressions about one's own performance despite contrary information. Apparently subjects do not believe experimenters when they tell them fake scores were used, but persist in thinking the scores are valid not only when they are good but also for bad scores.

Finally, Ross et al. employed a more involved debriefing for another group in which the experimenter emphasized the persistent nature of first impressions. Under these circumstances, debriefing was somewhat effective although Ross et al. acknowledged the possible artifact due to the strong demand characteristics of the situation. One other interesting effect found in this study was that another group of subjects who merely observed the performance of the deceived subjects and also overheard the debriefing they received still predicted higher performance from subjects who were given high fake scores! It is not only difficult to undo deception in the subjects who were deceived but it is hard to erase the first impressions of witnesses.

In a different type of situation, however, debriefing has been found to be effective in counteracting the effects of a deception. Tennen and Gillen (1979) used the learned-helplessness paradigm in which subjects first undergo a situation in which they cannot control the outcomes followed by a new task where their responses can influence the types of consequences they receive. The typical finding is that of poor or impaired performance on the second task, as compared to control groups which either do not encounter the first experience or experience that situation under conditions where their own responses do control outcomes.

Tennen and Gillen (1979) gave subjects a series of trials on which a loud noise was presented and told them that they should try to terminate the noise by pressing a button on a small box before them. One group had inescapable noise in that there was nothing they could do to end the noise under the experimenter's control. A second group had escapable noise since the noise ended if they pressed the button four times. A third group received equivalent amounts of noise but was not told anything about trying to end them. Based on prior evidence (e.g. Hiroto & Seligman, 1975), it has been found that the inescapable noise group would acquire a sense of "learned helplessness" and perform poorest on a subsequent unrelated task such as anagram word solution.

In addition to these conditions, a fourth group was tested also with inescapable noise but was then thoroughly debriefed about the deception and told that it had been impossible for anyone to escape the noise. The results showed that debriefing was effective in offsetting the potential adverse effects of the inescapable noise, with performance on the anagram task equalling that of the group that encountered escapable noise.

Debriefing, then, was successful under this type of situation, which is quite different from that of the one used by Ross et al. (1975) that involved fake information about abilities of subjects showing resistance to correction via debriefing.

A useful distinction between two aspects of debriefing was made between *dehoaxing* and *desensitizing* (Holmes, 1976a,b). When subjects are given corrective information about the deceptions foisted upon them by the experimenter, dehoaxing is the term suggested by Holmes. Desensitizing is used to deal with attempts to change any feelings subjects have at the end of the session about their behavior during the study which stemmed from some aspects of the deception so that they are returned to the level at which they entered the experiment. This distinction has not usually been clearly identified in the debriefing research and may account for some of the discrepant findings and views.

Holmes' review of the limited research on effectiveness of either type of debriefing concluded that the overall evidence suggests that dehoaxing as well as desensitization can be accomplished if done properly. Improvements in dehoaxing could occur, according to Holmes, if more efforts were made to demonstrate to the subjects that deception was used, such as showing them how the hoax was perpetrated. Desensitization can involve different procedures, such as telling subjects their behavior or traits were normal or similar to that of other subjects. Another approach is to point out that their laboratory behavior was not representative of their true nature and did not imply that their everyday behavior was similar.

Holmes raised a warning that the issue of the ethics of deception is a separate matter from that of the effectiveness of debriefing in eliminating the effects of deception. He called for more research on the effectiveness of debriefing, research that was unavailable but should have been collected as part of the development of an empirically-based ethics code.

Tesch (1977) also called for more research on the effectiveness of debriefing, such as identification of the variables that affect the success of debriefing. Factors such as the sex and status of the debriefer, whether or not a person different from the experimenter should be the debriefer, whether or not the debriefing would be more effective in a setting other than the experiment, are examples of variables that could be evaluated in controlled experiments.

Although future research may help identify some of the variables affecting the effectiveness of debriefing, it may be essential that individual investigators dealing with sensitive topics and areas of high risk to the psychological and physical well-being of participants verify the success of their debriefing efforts in correcting any misconceptions induced by the experiment. It can not always be correctly assumed that dehoaxing alone will be adequate to desensitize subjects who encountered serious threats to their self-esteem due to deception and stress induced in the study. For example, Bramel (1962, 1963) provided male subjects with false feedback on a psychogalvanic skin conductance measure of emotion as they viewed slides of nude males which implied that they had homosexual tendencies. Later, the subjects were dehoaxed in that they were told that the scores were invented by the experimenter. However, it may be that some subjects still believed the fake scores after the experiment or were otherwise upset by their reactions to the experience. Debriefing in this case was necessary but it may not have been sufficient to undo harmful effects of the deception. Unfortunately, no evidence was reported that provides any light on this question.

Tesch also pointed out the lack of research to assess the educational benefits gained through debriefing by subjects, citing a system reported by Davis and Fernald (1975) as one that may be successful in achieving this goal. Most universities with human-subject pools emphasize the educational value of participation in experiments, but there is a glaring lack of objective evidence as to the extent of learning and the relative effectiveness of this type of learning versus some nonparticipatory experience. One survey (Britton, 1979) found that the educational value of participation was rated by subjects as above average but still far short of the highest possible rating. Observing other students serving as subjects may be as useful or even more beneficial as a learning exercise than actual service as a subject, especially if debriefing procedures are poor. Issues like this deserve further investigation.

Other Issues

Another important condition where researchers must protect the well-being of participants is the requirement of confidentiality. Although many experiments do not deal with situations where the data collected would prove embarrassing or threatening to subjects if their responses were made available to others, there are many situations where such adverse consequences would occur, such as studies in which subjects must report private feelings, discuss personal matters, describe personal traits and attitudes, or provide private information. The promise of confidentiality may encourage more honest and willing cooperation by participants. Even if the information were obtained without this pledge, the researcher must realize that the subjects are assuming that their participation in the study is to assist the experimenter and may be dismayed if their data is released to other parties without their permission.

Since the participant in the kinds of studies we have been discussing so far realize they are being studied and agree to participate, the issue of invasion of privacy is less relevant. Some personal questions may be regarded by some subjects as an invasion of their privacy, but in principle, they do have the right to refuse to respond. However, in the context of a study, the subject may feel conflict and pressure to cooperate and be reluctant to refuse. There may also be the fear that failure to respond is like an admission of weakness. The problem of invasion of privacy is a greater issue in some types of naturalistic experimentation conducted on unsuspecting "participants," a topic discussed in detail in Chapter 16.

THE AMERICAN PSYCHOLOGICAL ASSOCIATION CODE OF ETHICS

Background and Purpose

A profession generally attempts to formulate policies and guidelines for the professional conduct of its members. Psychologists, through its major professional organization association, the American Psychological Association (APA), realized that it is important to develop, maintain, and promote a code of ethics as a set of guidelines for its members. This form of self-regulation is more likely to be effective than a set of controls imposed from external sources, such as governmental regulatory agencies. Self-regulation is preventive insofar as it may circumvent violations of ethics and ideals whereas external controls usually tend to be reactions after incidents of abuse occur which arouse indignation on the part of the public.

In the 1960s, the general activism in our society which led to critical examination of issues ranging from civil rights, sex roles, and the Vietnam war also led to scrutiny of practices in the behavioral sciences (e.g., Panel on Privacy and Behavioral Research, 1967; U.S. Department of Health, Education, and Welfare, 1971). This public and governmental interest may have helped prompt the APA to devote attention to putting its own house in order. An Ad Hoc Committee on Ethical Standards in Psychological Research was formed (Committee on Ethical Standards, 1973). The Committee extensively examined these problems and proposed revisions to the earlier code (American Psychological Association, 1963). The result was the publication of a code emphasizing the ultimate responsibility of the individual investigator and focusing on ten major principles (Ethical Principles in the Conduct of Research with Human Participants, 1973), shown in Table 15–2.

Principles

An inspection of the principles shows that they are general guidelines applicable to a wide variety of research situations. No specification is made regarding the consequences of failure to follow these guidelines, no threats of punishment are described or even implied. Instead, the implicit assumption is that the consciences or superegos of individual investigators will guide them and help them obey the spirit of these rules. As one member of the drafting committee pointed out (Smith, 1973), the emphasis was on sensitization rather than on regulation. Smith went on to say in his editorial in the *American Psychological Association Monitor,* a publication distributed to all association members, that psychologists must seriously attempt to regulate themselves

TABLE 15-2. The American Psychological Association Ethical Principles for the Conduct of Research.

The Ethical Principles
The decision to undertake research should rest upon a considered judgment by the individual psychologist about how best to contribute to psychological science and to human welfare. The responsible psychologist weighs alternative directions in which personal energies and resources might be invested. Having made the decision to conduct research, psychologists must carry out their investigations with respect for the people who participate and with concern for their dignity and welfare. The Principles that follow make explicit the investigator's ethical responsibilities toward participants over the course of research, from the initial decision to pursue a study to the steps necessary to protect the confidentiality of research data. These Principles should be interpreted in terms of the context provided in the complete document offered as a supplement to these Principles.
1. In planning a study the investigator has the personal responsibility to make a careful evaluation of its ethical acceptability, taking into account these Principles for research with human beings. To the extent that this appraisal, weighing scientific and humane values, suggests a deviation from any Principle, the investigator incurs an increasingly serious obligation to seek ethical advice and to observe more stringent safeguards to protect the rights of the human research participant.
2. Responsibility for the establishment and maintenance of acceptable ethical practice in research always remains with the individual investigator. The investigator is also responsible for the ethical treatment of research participants by collaborators, assistants, students, and employees, all of whom, however, incur parallel obligations.
3. Ethical practice requires the investigator to inform the participant of all features of the research that reasonably might be expected to influence willingness to participate and to explain all other aspects of the research about which the participant inquires. Failure to make full disclosure gives added emphasis to the investigator's responsibility to protect the welfare and dignity of the research participant.
4. Openness and honesty are essential characteristics of the relationship between investigator and research participant. When the methodological requirements of a study necessitate concealment or deception, the investigator is required to ensure the participant's understanding of the reasons for this action and to restore the quality of the relationship with the investigator.
5. Ethical research practice requires the investigator to respect the individual's freedom to decline to participate in research or to discontinue participation at any time. The obligation to protect this freedom requires special vigilance when the investigator is in a position of power over the participant. The decision to limit this freedom increases the investigator's responsibility to protect the participant's dignity and welfare.
6. Ethically acceptable research begins with the establishment of a clear and fair agreement between the investigator and the research participant that clarifies the responsibilities of each. The investigator has the obligation to honor all promises and commitments included in that agreement.

TABLE 15-2. (continued)

7. The ethical investigator protects participants from physical and mental discomfort, harm, and danger. If the risk of such consequences exists, the investigator is required to inform the participant of that fact, secure consent before proceeding, and take all possible measures to minimize distress. A research procedure may not be used if it is likely to cause serious and lasting harm to participants.

8. After the data are collected, ethical practice requires the investigator to provide the participant with a full clarification of the nature of the study and to remove any misconceptions that may have arisen. Where scientific or humane values justify delaying or withholding information, the investigator acquires a special responsibility to assure that there are no damaging consequences for the participant.

9. Where research procedures may result in undesirable consequences for the participant, the investigator has the responsibility to detect and remove or correct these consequences, including, where relevant, long-term aftereffects.

10. Information obtained about the research participants during the course of an investigation is confidential. When the possibility exists that others may obtain access to such information, ethical research practice requires that this possibility, together with the plans for protecting confidentiality, be explained to the participants as a part of the procedure for obtaining informed consent.

so as to safeguard the safety, freedom, and dignity of the human participant in our research. He pointed out a number of governmental proposals for legislation to protect human subjects as well as the creation of the National Commission for the Protection of Human Subjects, reflecting perhaps the public and governmental doubts that psychologists would effectively police themselves.

Method

The APA code of ethics was formulated after members had been invited to submit responses in the form of reports of incidents of psychological research where they felt or worried that ethical improprieties may have occurred. Using this case approach as the major source of evidence, the committee tried to identify the basic ethical concerns of researchers and used them to formulate the principles. A useful adjunct may have been to also invite nonpsychologists to examine the case incidents and obtain their reactions for the conceptions of what represents ethical violations may differ for psychologists who conduct experiments and for members of the general public.

The Risk-Benefit Ratio

One of the interesting concepts in the code on research ethics is the risk-benefit ratio which does not involve an absolutist stance on ethical issues, but represents a pragmatic consideration of relative consequences. It tries to straddle the fence by protecting the opportunities of investigators to do research while also trying to protect the well-being of subjects. This juggling act is difficult in some situations, as when the risks to the subjects are high but the benefits to science and society are great. It is clearer and easier to argue that a study with the same risks but with smaller benefits would be more objectionable by this criterion.

One problem with this procedure is that the subjects are not consulted or given a choice as to whether they want to make the "sacrifice" in the first type of study. Even when the investigator does the weighing of risks and benefits, there is no objective method of comparing the two events since no common units of measurement exist. The subjective decision ultimately involved is apt to be biased in favor of going ahead since some experimenters are apt to err in favor of their own interest—doing research. Risk of harm to the subjects can easily be rationalized by ambitious researchers.

As Baumrind (1971) observed in her critical reactions to the first draft of the Ethics Code, the risk/benefit criterion is unworkable and hypocritical since it justifies the neglect of the welfare of subjects in the name of science. She observed, "I can not think of a single actual psychological study in which the potential benefits to society justified the legitimation by a respected investigator of violations of basic human rights" (p. 894).

Other Safeguard Policies

Despite the formulation of the APA Ethics Code, outside agencies such as federal granting sources (Weinberger, 1974, 1975) to which investigators submit research proposals seeking financial support have also been concerned with the implementation of practices aimed at the protection of human subjects. Such proposals to agencies such as the National Science Foundation and the National Institutes of Mental Health require that applications for research funds be screened and approved for ethical soundness at several levels.

Institutions such as universities where the researcher is affiliated must first screen proposals, usually using a departmental level screening followed by a university-level review based on recommendations of interdisciplinary committees of colleagues, called Institutional Review Boards (IRB). Then, when panels of reviewers that make recommendations on the substantive merits of proposals at the national level examine the applications, they must also certify that adequate precautions have been taken to safeguard the rights of human subjects.

Needless to say, all of these precautions are time-consuming, awkward, and sometimes irritating to investigators, especially since most research seems to be free of these problems. The elaborate machinery seems unwieldy, but what are the alternatives for preventing the rare but objectionable studies? The requirement of institutional review of research grant proposals is inefficient. In many ways it is also inadequate because IRB's are interdisciplinary in composition so that many members are not competent to pass judgment on research in other fields. There is also the lack of any mechanism of appeal for an investigator whose proposal is rejected on ethical grounds. Perhaps more attention needs to be directed toward correcting this weakness of peer review of proposed research. In fact, policies are continually being reevaluated as they need to be. Proposals are currently being considered for some reduction of red tape by exempting relatively safe projects from IRB scrutiny (Flotz, 1980) at institutions receiving research funds from the Department of Health and Human Services.

Some ethical standards and guidelines are desirable even though most of the ethical violations may be minor and cause no serious harm. On the other hand, it only takes one controversial study to create a problem to damage the public acceptance and support of research. If unethical studies involving serious stress and harm are not prevented, the adverse reactions to these few studies can jeopardize the opportunities of other researchers to conduct their own studies which may involve less serious or no ethical problems.

Although these bureaucratic hurdles may weed out the potentially dangerous and unethical studies from among those receiving federal grant funds, unsubsidized research may not receive the same degree of scrutiny. What is to prevent researchers from conducting studies that, by the criteria of the APA Ethics Code, are objectionable? As Elms (1975, pg. 974) observed, "most discussion of ethics in psychological research including the Ethics Code does little more than appeal to everyone's good will and presumably shared assumptions of right and wrong." There are no sanctions or penalties that can be imposed upon violators of the code, other than possible expulsion from the membership of the American Psychological Association, if one is cited, but even this contingency is not specifically stated. Indeed, the first principle of the code indicating that the ultimate responsibility for ethical conduct lies in the hands of individual investigators shows how weak the power of the code actually is in dealing with violations.

A good illustration of this problem is the exchange between Schnur (1978) and Schachter (1978) over some of the procedures in the latter's research on the relationship of stress, social activity, cigarette smoking, and urinary acidity levels, which was cited in Chapter 7. Schur questioned the lack of informed consent, adequacy of debriefing, risk of harm, and the subversion of a college seminar to the purpose of conducting research. Rather than answer any of the specific points or clarifying any issues, Schachter chose instead to make light of the matter by citing several mostly sarcastic and *ad hominem* comments obtained from some of his students. Inasmuch as Stanley Schachter is among the most influential and well-known researchers, his response is apt to encourage similar attitudes among other investigators.

Reactions to the APA Ethics Code

While there may be some who feel the code did not go far enough to protect the rights of subjects, there are probably more researchers who feel it is overly restrictive and damaging to the rights of investigators to conduct their research. Certainly, when viewed in contrast to the situation prior to the APA Ethics Code, a more difficult situation faces the experimenter who wants to use human participants. Not only must subjects be located, encouraged to volunteer, and told of their rights, but the experimenter is also faced with screening committees that review ethical aspects of projects at several levels, departmental, institutional, and in cases when federal research funds are sought, federal granting agencies. All of these safeguards appear to involve bureaucratic "red tape" and overkill which frustrate the experimenters, threatening to make them an endangered species.

A different type of objection has been made by Gergen (1973) who argued that more empirical evidence is desirable before the implementation of all of these time-consuming safeguards. Instead of arguing only on speculative terms, for example, that deception is harmful, we should conduct studies to see if the behavior of deceived and nondeceived subjects differs in the assumed direction.

One problem with this approach is that experimenters, who do have a conflict-of-interest in this matter, stand as both judge and jury. It would be in the best research interest of the experimenter to discover no difference between "ethical" and "unethical" practices. As we already know from Chapter 3, experimenter bias can influence outcomes to conform with experimenter expectations.

Another aspect of Gergen's objection to the promulgation of a formal code of ethics is that it would make some forms of research difficult or impossible to perform. If one had to provide informed consent to subjects in a situation where some form of deception was required, for example, it would be pointless to conduct the study.

Such a demonstration that use of the ethical principles would lead to different results in a verbal conditioning task was reported by Resnick and Schwartz (1973). In comparison to the typical procedure in which subjects are not told in advance that the experimenter will reinforce a class of their responses, another group was added that *did* receive this information so that they would be truly informed. It should come as no surprise that verbal conditioning was obtained in the standard procedure, but not for the latter modified "ethical" procedure. Resnick and Schwartz used this *reductio ad absurdum* approach to discredit the validity of findings obtained from studies that adhere to the ethical principles. In situations such as verbal conditioning, informed consent certainly leads to *different* reactions.

While this criticism is valid, it misses the point underlying the concern of ethics—one's values as to what forms of experimenter behavior are right, not expedient or practical. If we found subjects who did not object to receive painful electric shocks in our study, but we believed there was no justifiable grounds for exposing subjects to such risks in our study, it would be unethical to continue the study. We should examine our values first, and use them as a guide toward deciding which practices to employ. If we emphasize doing our research at all costs, then ethical issues will be ignored or conveniently rationalized away.

West and Gunn (1978) have expressed the fear that the ethical code may force researchers away from more rigorous methods toward less powerful techniques. Furthermore, they may simply find topics to study that involve fewer ethical difficulties. They lamented the likelihood of what they called a "bowdlerized approach" to psychology, especially since the code was developed without the benefit of much empirical research to demonstrate the presumed effects of the various aspects of research the code regulates.

The consequences forecast by West and Gunn may be upheld, but it would seem that their argument places a greater priority on the freedom of the investigator than in considering the rights of the participants. The challenge is to find a means of achieving a solution that can fulfill the rights of both researchers and participants without jeopardizing those of one party at the expense of the other.

Diener and Crandall (1978, p. 14) in their analysis of ethical issues in social science and psychological research concluded that, "The personally ethical scientist, with the guidance of a professional code and local ethics committee, is the surest and wisest safeguard against ethical wrongdoing." They recognized correctly that any researcher who wishes to ignore ethical codes can readily violate them almost with impunity. Thus, if the investigator is not already of an ethical persuasion, no number of committees can do much to prevent abuses. Diener and Crandall advocated the use of ethical codes as sensitizers that might help educate researchers to the problems and argued that self-control by researchers is needed if ethical guidelines are to be followed and accepted.

Certainly education and awareness can do much to alert researchers to issues of an ethical nature and reduce abuses, but in some cases it may be necessary for professional organizations to police its own members if they commit ethical abuses by reprimanding or censuring activities which violate professional codes. Although such actions may seem drastic, the seriousness of the problem may necessitate such remedies, if for no other reason, to protect the public image of the profession.

EMPIRICAL STUDIES OF ETHICAL ISSUES

Perspectives of Subject vs. Experimenters

Sullivan and Deiker (1973) designed a survey to obtain empirical ratings from experimenters and subjects concerning risk and benefit evaluations of four well-known and controversial published experiments. Over 300 student and 400 randomly sampled psychologists were asked to rate descriptions of these studies on several ethical dimensions. All of the experiments were preceded by a fake cover story that it dealt with learning of nonsense syllables but they actually dealt with topics such as induced stress, experimentally-induced pain, alteration of self-esteem, and prompted unethical behaviors. Each rater was asked to rate only one of these studies and the students were also asked if they would volunteer for such a study if they had the chance. Both samples of raters were also asked if they thought subjects would volunteer for one of these studies if there had been no deceptive cover story about the purposes (raters knew the true purpose of the study by the time they made this judgment).

Raters were additionally asked their view on the ethical propriety of the deception and whether any other aspect of the study was unethical. Finally, they were asked if the deception was justified, and if any other procedure was deemed unethical, was it justified?

Results showed that the sample of psychologists was more strict or conservative than the sample of students since the majority of experimenters felt the deception was unethical, but this was true for only one study judged by the students. Sullivan and Deiker imply that the proposed code may be overly strict, judged by the fact that subjects seem less concerned than the experimenters. However, it is possible that the psychologists were more attuned to demand characteristics and answered cautiously so as to be appear more concerned than they were, especially since they had been sensitized to the ethical issues.

The important point, however, is whether or not psychologists should let their values be the primary criterion in governing their research in situations where procedures might be harmful to subjects who are either unaware, unconcerned, or unable to comprehend the risks. This attitude is not the same as paternalism, where the psychologists are asked to protect the best interests of the subjects, but argues that the psychologists must face themselves as to what types of research conduct are consistent with their own values.

If psychologists know or fear that a procedure will harm subjects, they cannot ethically conduct the study even though they may be interested in the data that would be obtained. The problem is that faced with this dilemma, many psychologists ignore the ethical aspect and proceed with the conduct of the study. When faced with such a conflict of interest, the psychologist should allow impartial third parties to provide valuable input to aid decision making.

Subject Ratings of Specific Experimental Procedures

Farr and Seaver (1975) were also concerned that the APA ethics code might be too cautious. For example, the code suggests that procedures possibly harmful to subjects should not be used without first obtaining the informed consent of the participants, a practice that would destroy the validity of studies dealing with topics such as conformity where deception is typically used.

Following Gergen's (1973b) call for empirical rather than speculative arguments, Farr and Seaver decided to obtain evidence on perceptions of the extent to which harm is involved in a variety of hypothetical experiments. A list of 71 situations, 30 involving physical discomfort of varying degree (see Table 15-3), 15 with threats to psychological well-being (see Table 15-4), and 36 with possible invasions of privacy (see Table 15-5 for partial listing).

Tables 15-3, 15-4, 15-5 show the mean ratings for each of the three types of situations given by 86 introductory psychology students on a 5-point scale, with higher values indicating greater threat and discomfort. This role-playing procedure enabled Farr and Seaver to assess the relative aversiveness of various experimental procedures, as perceived by subjects who did not actually undergo these experiences. Although their actual reactions to such conditions might be different, inasmuch as Farr and Seaver were interested in factors affecting the informed consent decisions of subjects, these data are useful since real subjects also must make their initial decision to participate based only on perceptions rather than actual contact with the experimental procedures.

Farr and Seaver realized that their study used only a few situations but felt that their data might provide a set of reference points against which other experiments could be evaluated to estimate the potential risks subjects would perceive. They also concluded that invasion of privacy does not appear to be an issue for subjects. It should be pointed out, however, that the same request for personal information or the observation of certain forms of behavior that might not arouse defensiveness or anxiety in the context of an experiment might generate hostility, resentment, and lack of compliance under other circumstances. As we have already noted, the experiment is a special type of situation in which subjects may be unusually cooperative and compliant.

TABLE 15-3. Ratings of Perceived Physical Discomfort for Various Experimental Procedures.

Procedure	$\bar{X}$	SD
Run up and down steps for 1 minute	1.37	.63
Eat no food for 6 hours prior to study	1.83	1.05
Wear earphones over which was heard continuous white noise like that made by a small fan	1.90	.99
Hold a hand in a bucket of ice water for 1 minute	1.92	1.00
Blood sample taken by pricking a finger	1.94	1.08
Solve word puzzles for an hour in a room heated to 85°	2.14	1.02
Lie motionless for 1 hour in a totally dark, soundproofed room	2.15	1.23
Lie motionless for 1 hour in a lighted, soundproofed room	2.23	1.24
A 4-ounce steel weight dropped on the finger from a height of 6 inches	2.54	1.17
Run up and down stairs for 10 minutes	2.55	1.10
Run up and down stairs for 15 minutes	2.73	1.09
Eat no food for 12 hours before the study	2.76	1.26
Blood sample drawn from a vein in the arm	2.79	1.34
Hear repeated short blasts from an air horn located in the same room	2.90	1.18
Receive a single electric shock of painful but not harmful intensity	2.99	.89
Solve word puzzles for 1 hour in a room heated to 110°	3.02	1.10
Wear earphones over which was played continuous white noise like that made by an alarm clock buzzer	3.05	1.28
Lift a 10-pound weight repeatedly for 1 hour in a room heated to 85°	3.14	1.16
A 4-ounce steel weight dropped on the finger from a height of 12 inches	3.29	1.13
Band tightened around the arms as tightly as could be tolerated	3.40	1.10
Hear a continuous 2-minute blast from an air horn located in the same room	3.40	1.29
Receive a series of electric shocks of increasing intensity which the subject stops when they are too painful	3.43	1.00
Solve thought problems in a room that smelled strongly of rotten eggs	3.44	1.17
Do physical work in a room that smelled strongly of rotten eggs	3.48	1.21
Eat no food for 24 hours prior to the study	3.49	1.33
Lift a 10-pound weight repeatedly for 1 hour in a room heated to 110°	3.55	1.20

TABLE 15-3. (continued)

Procedure	$\bar{X}$	SD
A 4-ounce weight dropped on the finger from a height of 24 inches	3.78	1.09
Hold a hand in a bucket of ice water for 1 hour	3.85	1.10
Band tightened around the head to see how much pain could be tolerated	4.07	.99
Receive repeated electric shocks of the maximum tolerable intensity	4.19	.87

Source: "Stress and discomfort in psychological research: Subjects' perceptions experimental procedures," by J. L. Farr and W. B. Seaver. *American Psychologist*, 1975, **30**, 770–73. Copyright 1975 by the American Psychological Association. Reprinted by permission.

The Farr-Seaver, as well as the Sullivan-Deiker, study is useful in providing some limited information about the perceptions of experiments by experimenters and subjects alike. One should be cautious, however, in generalizing from their findings since the perceptions may vary with the type of experiment, the types of subjects, and even the expectations of the experimenters. The approach described earlier by Bersheid et al. is more useful to an investigator concerned with evaluating the ethics of a specific study about to begin since it is possible to collect a sample of reactions to that specific study with a sample of subjects representative of those who will eventually be used in the study if it is undertaken.

Changes in Ethics Policies in Use of Human Subjects

A different approach to assessing the impact of the increased general awareness and concern about ethical issues is the comparison of practices governing the use of human subjects by major departments of psychology before the surge of interest in ethics and sometime afterwards. The author (Jung, 1977), as part of his followup survey in 1976 of a study of the use of human subjects in major psychology departments in 1969, included a few questions that shed some indirect light on the impact of the 1973 APA Ethics Code and related discussions of ethical issues.

The data in Table 15–6 are based on the percentages of surveyed departments of psychology that used various procedures related to several ethical concerns. This index is not as precise as one based on the number of actual subjects tested under various conditions since departments vary widely in the volume of human subjects used, but there is no reason to suspect that ethical practices vary systematically with size of departmental research programs.

TABLE 15-4. Ratings of Perceived Psychological Discomfort for Various Experimental Procedures.

Procedure	$\bar{X}$	SD
Judge the more attractive person in each of 50 pairs of photographs of college students	1.49	.79
Be the elected leader of a group that had to work together to construct an object out of tinker toy parts	1.62	.83
Move a handle to keep a pointer aligned with a fast-moving target	1.66	.88
Judge the weight of several objects, but other subjects consistently estimated much greater weights than you did	1.74	.84
Go through the pages of a booklet and cross out the letter "e" each time it appeared	1.76	1.13
Memorize a serial list of words of which you could recall about half when asked	2.31	.96
Solve a mechanical puzzle that you couldn't do in the time allowed	2.62	.98
Choose which of two other subjects you would rather work with when an extra subject shows up for the study	2.66	1.14
A psychology graduate student interviews you and allows you to see his comments about you. The comments are partially good, but it is obvious that he was not very impressed with your personality	2.86	1.08
Electrodes are attached to your scalp, and during the study the electronic device to which they are connected shorts out and begins to smoke	2.94	1.38
Give a 5-minute speech on a current topic to a group of other subjects	3.02	1.38
Your two-man team competes against another team for a $10 prize. Although your partner did well, your team loses due to your troubles with the game	3.06	.94
The experimenter tells you that a test you took in the experiment indicates that you have latent homosexual tendencies	3.38	1.20
When recalling a long list of words you were to learn, another subject received a painful shock for each mistake you made	3.51	1.16
Sit in a small room for 10 minutes with the thing you are most afraid of	4.09	1.05

Source: "Stress and discomfort in psychological research: Subjects' perceptions of experimental procedures," by J. L. Farr and W. B. Seaver. *American Psychologist*, 1975, **30**, 770–773. Copyright 1975 by the American Psychological Association. Reprinted by permission.

TABLE 15-5. Ratings of Perceived Invasion of Privacy for Various Experimental Procedures.

Procedure	$\bar{X}$	SD
Questionnaire about hometown, family size, and family mobility—sign name	1.16	.46
Occupational interest test—sign name	1.16	.57
Questionnaire about size of high school attended, athletic participation, and college major—sign name	1.23	.59
Wear nonpainful electrodes which measure physiological reactions to objects of different colors	1.29	.75
Questionnaire about opinion of economic policies—sign name	1.29	.65
Wear nonpainful electrodes which measure physiological reactions to statements about religious beliefs	1.36	.78
Attitude scale about political beliefs—sign name	1.40	.71
Wear nonpainful electrodes which measured physiological reactions to obscene words	1.50	.81
Attitude scale about racial integration in residential areas—sign name	1.52	.72
Special abilities tests including perceptual accuracy, mechanical ability, and verbal reasoning—sign name	1.64	.94
Intelligence test—sign name	1.65	.93
Personality inventory measuring self-esteem—sign name	1.67	.94
Personality inventory measuring masculine and feminine characteristics—sign name	1.74	.86
Questionnaire about personal usage of hard and soft drugs—sign name	1.83	1.20
Questionnaire about family income, religious beliefs, and ethnic/cultural background—sign name	2.04	1.38
Personality inventory measuring the presence of a number of personality abnormalities—sign name	2.05	1.08
Questionnaire about feelings toward parents, number of times arrested, and thoughts regarding suicide—sign name	2.07	1.20
Personality inventory measuring heterosexual/homosexual orientation—sign name	2.13	1.15
Wear nonpainful electrodes measuring physiological reactions to pictures of nude men and women	2.19	1.17
Questionnaire about past sexual experiences—sign name	2.93	1.33

Source: "Stress and discomfort in psychological research: Subjects' perceptions of experimental procedures," by J. L. Farr and W. B. Seaver, *American Psychologist*, 1975, **30**, 770–773. Copyright 1975 by the American Psychological Association. Reprinted by permission.

TABLE 15-6. Percent of Departments Using Various Ethical Policies and Procedures: 1967 vs. 1976. From Jung, 1977.

Screening of Projects	1967 (n = 52)	1976 (n = 45)	Feedback Procedure:	1967	1976
All	54%	80%	Immediate	33%	67%
Some, not all	21%	13%	Delayed	20%	0%
Laissez-faire	13%	4%	Both Immed/Delay	9%	4%
			No Reply	0%	9%
			Optional	38%	20%

Table 15-6 shows several changes since the 1967 survey (Jung, 1969). The percentage of departments requiring departmental level screening of all projects for ethical propriety increased from 54 to 80 by 1976. A laissez-faire or nonscreening policy dropped from 13 to 4 per cent over the same period. The use of a double standard in which some selected studies were screened but others were not dropped from 21 to 13 per cent.

A large change occurred in the use of the requirement that subjects be provided with immediate feedback or debriefing after experiments, increasing from 33 to 67 per cent as shown in Table 15-6. Delayed feedback as the primary policy, in contrast, dropped to 0 per cent. Similarly, the percentage of departments allowing the use of debriefing at the discretion of individual investigators dropped slightly.

No direct comparisons are possible about the rate of use of informed consent since information about this concept was not included in the original survey because the concept was only just being proposed about that time (Privacy and Behavioral Research, 1967). The level of use in 1976 was at 55 per cent, which is probably higher than it was 1967, but still rather low in view of the emphasis on its use by the APA Ethics Code.

One unexpected outcome from the practice of ethical conduct by experimenters may be reciprocation on the part of subjects. Jourard's classic flight of fantasy, "A letter from *S* to *E*" (Jourard, 1968) implies that the subject would be more than willing to cooperate with the experimenter, if given half a chance. Perhaps we might envision an emergence of an implicit code of ethics which would govern the ethical subject:

> I pledge to be responsible in my interaction with the experimenter by showing up—and on time—following instructions with care, and taking the whole matter seriously.
>
> I pledge to try my best.

I pledge not to deceive the experimenter.

I pledge not to unduly stress or harm the experimenter.

I pledge to debrief the experimenter at the end of the session, disclosing how I really thought and why I did what I did.

I pledge to maintain confidentiality of the purpose, procedures, etc., regarding the study from other potential subjects.

SUMMARY

A number of ethical issues exist regarding the conduct of psychological research. Problems arise in deciding appropriate methods for recruiting participants, the kinds of experiences they should be exposed to, the amount and type of feedback they should receive after the study, and the purposes to which research findings are applied. The practices that have developed generally call for informed consent of participants and the protection of their safety and well-being as prerequisites for any research. The widespread practice of deception is more controversial as well as more complicated since a number of different aspects of an experiment may involve deception such as the purpose, feedback about the subject's performance or that of others, or information about other aspects of the procedure.

Where deception is employed, it has generally been the policy to take extra measures to provide debriefing in which the nature of the deception was explained and justified to participants. However, inadequate attempts have been made to evaluate the effectiveness of such debriefing in alleviating any anxiety or lowered self-esteem, in some cases, among deceived subjects. Some evidence suggests that many subjects do not believe information received during debriefing but persist in thinking that their behavior while deception was operating was their true performance.

The American Psychological Association developed an Ethics Code for researchers in 1973 based on case incidents reported by members of the association. Some psychologists have objected to the code as being overly restrictive of researchers; furthermore, they object to the establishment of ethical principles not themselves based on systematic research. Thus, while there may be moral reasons for providing debriefing, we also need research proving that it is effective. Or while objections may be directed against the use of deception on moral grounds, is there empirical evidence to demonstrate its presumed adverse effects?

Some studies aimed at evaluating the ethics code have compared attitudes of researchers and subjects toward various practices employed in experiments and have found that the researchers were more conservative or cautious as a group than were the subjects. It appears that subjects are not as upset or disturbed by some of the procedures used in research as some members of the psychological-research community are. In any event, the widespread awareness and discussion of these issues may be beneficial in minimizing or preventing certain types of ethically-objectionable practices. A survey of actual policies used by major psychology departments in universities suggests a number of changes in the recruitment of subjects and practices regarding debriefing, and so forth, have occurred in recent years, which may be partly attributable to heightened sensitivity to these issues.

REFERENCES

Alumbaugh, R. B. Another "malleus maleficarum"? *American Psychologist,* 1972, *27,* 897-899.

American Psychological Association. Ethical standards of psychologists. *American Psychologist,* 1963, *18,* 56-60.

Aronson, E. Avoidance of inter-subject communication. *Psychological Reports,* 1966, *19,* 238.

Aronson, E., and Carlsmith, J. M. Performance expectancy as a determinant of actual performance. *Journal of Abnormal and Social Psychology,* 1962, *65,* 178-182.

Aronson, E., and Carlsmith, J. M. Experimentation in social psychology. In G. Lindzey and E. Aronson (Eds.), *Handbook of Social Psychology* (Vol. 2). Reading, Mass.: Addison-Wesley, 1968.

Aronson, E., and Mettee, D. R. Dishonest behavior as a function of differential levels of induced self-esteem. *Journal of Personality and Social Psychology,* 1968, *9,* 121-127.

Baumrind, D. Some thoughts on ethics of research: After reading Milgram's "Behavioral study of obedience." *American Psychologist,* 1964, *19,* 421-423.

Baumrind, D. Principles of ethical conduct in the treatment of subjects: Reaction to the draft report of the Committee on Ethical Standards in Psychological Research. *American Psychologist,* 1971, *26,* 887-896.

Bersheid, E., Baron, R. S., Dermer, M., and Libman, M. Anticipating informed consent: An empirical approach. *American Psychologist,* 1973, *28,* 913-925.

Britton, B. K., Ethical and educational aspects of participating as a subject in psychological experiments. *Teaching of Psychology,* 1979, *6,* 195-198.

Brock, T. C., and Becker, L. A. "Debriefing" and susceptibility to subsequent experimental manipulations. *Journal of Personality and Social Psychology,* 1966, *2,* 314-323.

Campbell, D. T. Artifact and control. In R. Rosenthal and R. Rosnow (Eds.), *Artifact in Behavioral Research.* New York: Academic Press, 1969.

Committee on Ethical Standards in Psychological Research. *Ethical Principles in the Conduct of Research with Human Participants.* Washington, D.C.: American Psychological Association, 1973.

Darley, J. M., and Latané, B. *The Unresponsive Bystander: Why Doesn't He Help?* New York: Appleton-Century-Crofts, 1968.

Davis, J. R., and Fernald, P. S. Laboratory experience versus subject pool. *American Psychologist,* 1975, *30*, 523-524.

Deci, E. Effects of externally mediated rewards on intrinsic motivation. *Journal of Personality and Social Psychology,* 1971, *18*, 105-115.

Diener, E., and Crandall, R. *Ethics in Social and Behavioral Research.* Chicago: University of Chicago Press, 1978.

Elms, A. C. The crisis of confidence in social psychology. *American Psychologist,* 1975, *30*, 967-976.

Epstein, Y. M., Suedfeld, P., and Silverstein, S. J. The experimental contract: Subjects' expectations of and reactions to some behaviors of experimenters. *American Psychologist,* 1973, *28*, 212-221.

Farr, J. L., and Seaver, W. B. Stress and discomfort in psychological research: Subjects' perceptions of experimental procedures. *American Psychologist,* 1975, *30*, 770-773.

Fillenbaum, S. Prior deception and subsequent experimental performance: The "faithful" subject. *Journal of Personality and Social Psychology,* 1966, *4*, 532-537.

Flotz, D. Proposed human subjects regs make progress, pose problems. *APA Monitor,* 1980, *22,* 1, 14.

Gergen, K. J. Social psychology as history. *Journal of Personality and Social Psychology,* 1973, *26*, 309-320. (a)

Gergen, K. J. The codification of research ethics: Views of a doubting Thomas. *American Psychologist,* 1973, *28*, 907-912. (b)

Hiroto, D. S., and Seligman, M. E. Generality of learned helplessness in man. *Journal of Personality and Social Psychology,* 1975, *32*, 311-327.

Hollingsworth, R. Effectiveness of debriefing. *American Psychologist,* 1977, *32*, 780-782.

Holmes, D. S. Effectiveness of debriefing after a stress-producing deception. *Journal of Research in Personality,* 1973, 7, 127-138.

Holmes, D. S. Debriefing after psychological experiments. I. Effectiveness of post-deception dehoaxing. *American Psychologist,* 1976, *31*(8), 858-867. (a)

Holmes, D. S. Debriefing after psychological experiments. II. Effectiveness of post-experimental desensitizing. *American Psychologist,* 1976, *31*, 868-875. (b)

Holmes, D. S., and Bennett, D. H. Experiments to answer questions raised by the use of deception in psychological research. I. Role playing as an alternative to deception; II. Effectiveness of debriefing after a deception; III. Effect of informed consent on deception. *Journal of Personality and Social Psychology,* 1974, *29*, 358-367.

Jourard, S. *Disclosing Man to Himself.* New York: Van Nostrand Reinhold, 1968.

Jung, J. Current practices and problems in the use of college students for psychological research. *Canadian Psychologist,* 1969, *10*, 280-290.

Jung, J. New trends in the sources of and policies for use of humans as psychological research subjects: 1967 vs. 1976. Unpublished manuscript, California State University, Long Beach,

Kelman, H. C. Human use of human subjects. *Psychological Bulletin,* 1967, *67,* 1-11.

Kelman, H. C. The rights of the subjects in social research: An analysis in terms of relative power and legitimacy. *American Psychologist,* 1972, *27,* 989-1016.

Kelman, H. C. Privacy and research with human beings. *Journal of Social Issues,* 1977, *33*(3), 169-195.

McGuire, W. J. Suspiciousness of experimenter's intent. In R. Rosenthal and R. L. Rosnow (Eds.), *Artifact in Behavioral Research.* New York: Academic Press, 1969.

Milgram, S. Behavioral study of obedience. *Journal of Abnormal and Social Psychology,* 1963, *67,* 371-378.

Milgram, S. Issues in the study of obedience: A reply to Baumrind. *American Psychologist,* 1964, *19,* 848-852.

Mills, J. A procedure for explaining experiments involving deception. *Personality and Social Psychology Bulletin,* 1976, *2,* 3-13.

Menges, R. J. Openness and honesty versus coercion and deception in psychological research. *American Psychologist,* 1973, *28,* 1030-1034.

Panel on Privacy and Behavioral Research. *Privacy and Behavioral Research.* Washington, D.C.: U.S. Office of Science and Technology, 1967.

Resnick, J. H., and Schwartz, T. Ethical standards as an independent variable in psychological research. *American Psychologist,* 1973, *28,* 134-139.

Ring, K., Wallston, K., and Corey, M. Mode of debriefing as a factor affecting subjective reaction to a Milgram-type obedience experiment: An ethical inquiry. *Representative Research in Social Psychology,* 1970, *1,* 67-86.

Rosenberg, M. J. The conditions and consequences of evaluation apprehension. In R. Rosenthal and R. L. Rosnow (Eds.), *Artifact in Behavioral Research.* New York: Academic Press, 1969.

Ross, L., Lepper, M. F., and Hubbard, M. Perseverance in self-perception and social perception: Biased attitudinal processes in the debriefing paradigm. *Journal of Personality and Social Psychology,* 1975, *32,* 880-892.

Rubin, Z. Designing honest experiments. *American Psychologist,* 1973, *28,* 445-448.

Schachter, S. Some replies to Schnur. *Journal of Experimental Psychology: General,* 1978, *107,* 235.

Schnur, P. Comments on "Studies of the interaction of psychological and pharmacological determinants of smoking, by Schachter, *et al. Journal of Experimental Psychology: General,* 1978, *107,* 232-234.

Smith, M. B. Protection of human subjects–ethics and politics. *American Psychological Association Monitor,* 1973, *4* (No. 12), 2.

Smith, M. B. Some perspectives on ethical/political issues in social science research. *Personality and Social Psychology Bulletin,* 1976, *2,* 445-453.

Smith, R. J. SUNY at Albany admits research violations. *Science,* 1977, *198,* 708.

Sullivan, D. S., and Deiker, T. E. Subject-experimenter perceptions of ethical issues in human research. *American Psychologist,* 1973, *28,* 587-591.

Tennen, H., and Gillen, R. The effect of debriefing on laboratory induced helplessness: An attributional analysis. *Journal of Personality,* 1979, *47,* 629-642.

Tesch, F. E. Debriefing research participants: Though this be method there is madness to it. *Journal of Personality and Social Psychology,* 1977, *35,* 217-224.

Valins, S. Cognitive effects of false heart-rate feedback. *Journal of Personality and Social Psychology,* 1966, *4*, 400–408.

Walster, E., Bersheid, E., Abrahams, D., and Aronson, V. Effectiveness of debriefing following deception experiments. *Journal of Personality and Social Psychology,* 1967, *6*, 371–380.

Weinberger, C. W. Protection of human subjects. *Federal Register,* 1974, 1975, 30 May 39(105): 18914–20 (45 CRF, Part 46).

West, S. G., and Gunn, S. P. Some issues of ethics and social psychology. *American Psychologist,* 1978, *33*, 30–38.

CHAPTER 16

What Alternatives Do We Have?

Chapter at a Glance

A number of problems that confront the experimenter in the course of doing research have been raised in the preceding chapters. Perhaps the most difficult ones to resolve are the problems of the use of deception and the reactive nature of experiments on human subjects. Other problems, such as lack of generalizability due to overreliance on college students as subjects, can, potentially at least, be eventually resolved by discovering new sources of participants. The problem of biases due to experimenter expectancy and experimenter-attribute effects can be controlled to some degree with the use of automated procedures and a wider sampling of experimenters.

The more troublesome aspects of deception are twofold, methodological and ethical, as noted in the preceding chapter. The present chapter will explore the alternative methods developed and tried in the effort to deal with these problems. First, a discussion of roleplaying methods as a solution to the ethical problems of deception will be presented.

Since many topics of psychological interest can not easily be studied with subjects who know the purpose of procedures of the study, how can scientific investigations on these topics be made? This question is the core issue underlying the inherent reactive nature of experiments when subjects must grant informed consent before they can be studied in an experiment. One solution that we will examine is the use of unobtrusive measures and naturalistic experiments outside the formal laboratory as a possible remedy to the problem of reactivity.

ROLEPLAYING ALTERNATIVES TO DECEPTION

One alternative to deception that seems to avoid ethical problems is roleplaying. Kelman (1967, 1972) has repeatedly championed the use of roleplaying in which the participants are treated honestly by the investigator almost as if they were co-investigators rather than subjects. In this paradigm, participants receive a description of the experimental procedures and try to imagine how they would respond to such a situation without actually undergoing the experimental procedures. Although this method might hold ethical advantages, critics have questioned its validity.

Aronson and Carlsmith (1968) pointed out that what people think they would do, even under the best of intentions, is not always what they will actually do when confronted by a situation. Roleplaying is simply lacking in realism and can not predict accurately what real-life behavior will be like. In cases of stressful situations, for example, a roleplayer may give a false show of bravado which may quickly dissipate if the person were actually placed in the real danger.

Direct Comparisons of Roleplaying vs. Deception

A number of investigators have conducted roleplaying versions of deception experiments previously conducted by other investigators. The logic is that if the roleplaying replication fails to demonstrate the same effect as the original deception experiment, then it would constitute evidence showing the inadequacy of roleplaying as a substitute for studies involving deception. On the other hand, if similar findings occur, the case is strengthened for using the roleplaying approach to avoid the ethical problems of the deception technique.

Most of these comparisons have shown some discrepancies in the results obtained between roleplaying and deception experiments, leading one reviewer (Miller, 1972) to conclude that roleplaying can not be accepted as a replacement for deception. For example, Darroch and Steiner (1970) found that while roleplayers could predict their own behavior, they were less successful in predicting what others would do. Willis and Willis (1970) found that roleplayers could show similar results to those of actual subjects in a study of conformity as a function of whether or not they previously received fake feedback that they were competent on a different prior task. However, the roleplayers could not predict a more complicated aspect of the study that showed a more subtle effect. A final example is the failure of Holmes and Bennett (1974) to obtain physiological arousal from roleplayers pretending to receive shock comparable to that made by subjects deceived to expect shock, although both groups were similar in their self-reported arousal.

Miller (1972) also pointed out that even if the data from a roleplaying version of an actual behavioral situation showed similarity, the actual processes leading to the results are quite different. He also noted that roleplaying is not an ethical alternative to deception since he argued that for every deception study one wished to replace with a roleplaying version, one would still have to conduct the deception version in order to prove the two methods were comparable.

Varieties of Roleplaying

Freedman (1969) felt that roleplaying can never be an adequate substitute for experiments since they are guesses about how people would behave in a situation rather than actual observations of behavior. At the same time, he recognized that a wide variety of procedures have been termed under the same label, roleplaying, ranging from situations where subjects are merely told to imagine some procedures to those in which the subject goes through the entire set of actual procedures *except* that the independent variable is withheld and the subject is told to pretend that it is received. The latter situation is more realistic, being similar to Orne's quasicontrol simulator method described in Chapter 10, and may enable the subject to do a better job of imagining, but it is still only a pretend situation, according to Freedman.

Role Enactment. Forward, Canter, and Kirsch (1976) preferred the term, *role enactment*, to contrast it from other forms of less involved roleplaying where subjects merely guess what would happen. Role enactment may also be useful in situations that do not involve the use of deception, such as simulation studies dealing with collaborative demonstrations of phenomena with the experimenter rather than the testing of hypotheses. Thus, Forward et al. argued that role enactment procedures differ from deception in that cooperation is needed to determine the meanings the subjects have in the situation, meanings ignored in deception studies. Finally, they suggested that the two approaches differ in their assumptions about human behavior and the methods for understanding it. Roleplaying, they insisted, is based on a broader conceptualization of human behavior and offers advantages over deception in identifying the underlying causes of behavior such as the meanings subjects form in various situations.

One demonstration of the usefulness of a roleplaying approach was reported by Mixon (1972) whose "all-or-none" method was used with Milgram's (1963) obedience paradigm. In order to determine what meanings the subjects in this situation ascribed to the task and their roles, Mixon developed a set of "scripts" through continuous interaction with subjects which could produce a wide range of obedience responses all the way from 0 to 100 per cent. It should be noted that in Milgram's (1963) study, full obedience in applying the highest shock to the victim was about 65 per cent. When the script implied that the investigator was trusted, Mixon was able to replicate this level of obedience, but more importantly, his results showed that a script requiring obedience even though the victim had a "heart condition" was ineffective and contrary to Milgram's findings, and led to a very low level of obedience.

Forward et al. suggested that the often-made criticism of roleplaying—that results obtained from it are not comparable to those obtained from the actual situation—ignores the fact that the meanings attributed to the behavior by roleplayers may be different from those held by subjects in the deception situation. Thus, Mixon's findings show that when roleplayers are given scripts that contain certain meanings, it is possible to replicate the original findings, whereas with scripts holding other meanings, results are not replicated.

By use of variations of roleplaying scripts, insight can be gained as to how the meanings of the situation held by subjects affect their behavior. In contrast, possible variations in meaning are not detectable in experiments with deception. Therefore, Forward et al. took the opposite position that roleplaying behaviors should be viewed as the true standard rather than the behavior in the deception experiments, as is usually the case whenever the two methods are compared. If the deception version of a study is not replicated in the roleplaying version, it is usually assumed that the latter method is invalid.

Cooper (1976), in criticizing the position of Forward et al., suggested that deception and roleplaying are not totally independent methods. In defense of deception, Cooper argued that there are situations such as Milgram's where the use of deception is actually *more* ethical than the lack of it, as if the subjects actually received the shocks.

However, this type of argument is rather like insisting that a robber who merely threatens to kill you, but does not, is more "ethical" than one who kills you without giving any advance warning! We should be looking at the absolute levels of stress, and if a situation exceeds whatever maximal level we think subjects should be exposed to, it should be rejected. If we look only at relative stress, we may justify some rather high absolute levels of stress simply because we can find something worse.

Involved Participation. Cooper regarded deception as necessary in some situations because it induces a higher degree of *involved participation* than is usually possible under roleplaying procedures. Such involved participation should lead to behavior that is more representative of real life than what subjects say they think they would do when asked to roleplay. Cooper allowed that a person's motivation to cooperate and make a good self-presentation is an important factor deserving further study. However, he insisted that this tendency, which plays a major factor in roleplaying behavior, is of less relevance to the study of certain forms of behavior, such as reactions to emergencies which can better be studied with real-life situations. Furthermore, Cooper pointed out that involved participation methods also can permit the study of these tendencies to please the experimenter or to put oneself in a good light.

A position held by Cooper is that both roleplaying and deception are valid in their own right, with roleplaying being more useful for the study of self-presentation while deception is necessary to examine behaviors requiring more "involved participation." In addition, while roleplaying can be highly productive for exploratory work, the formulation of hypotheses, and the construction of theories, Cooper insisted that the testing of the validity of these ideas at the behavioral level required involved participation, his term for deception paradigms. Thus, each method has its unique role in research and the methods complement one another.

However, Cooper's argument seems to assume that subjects who serve in deception or involved participation studies are truly deceived in the direction intended by the experimenter. We have already noted evidence that this assumption is not always tenable. Furthermore, many deception studies do not involve checks on the nature of the suspicions and perceptions of the subjects; even if checks were made, there is the added problem of whether or not to accept at face value what the subjects report.

Forward et al.'s positions assumed that role-enactment subjects are truly involved; otherwise their armchair predictions should not be successful in matching actual behavior. In one sense, Cooper's concept of involved participation and Forward et al.'s role-enactment methods are more alike than different, with the main difference being whether deception is considered necessary to create the adequate degree of involvement.

A demonstration of the successful use of roleplaying when subjects are involved with their participation was reported by Geller (1978). He used male subjects who simulated three different variations of the Milgram (1963, 1974) obedience-to-authority task. One condition involved vocal feedback from the victim that he had a heart ailment, another condition required the experimenter to have to leave during the session, and a third condition had a limited contract in which the victim was asked to sign a release form freeing the university from legal responsibility and gaining the right to be released from the study at any time he requests.

As a frame of reference, it should be noted that Milgram (1974) reported 65 per cent obedience in a condition comparable to the first one described above. However, when the experimenter was absent from the room in the Milgram (1974) study, obedience dropped to about 20 per cent and under the limited contract condition it dropped to about 40 per cent. Geller reasoned that if roleplaying is truly effective or involved, similar variations in obedience should be obtained in his replication. In contrast, uninvolved subjects who are merely roleplaying were predicted to show equally *high* levels of obedience in *all* three conditions.

Subjects later made ratings of their degree of involvement that were consistent with independent ratings of observers who viewed videotapes of the sessions. Comparisons of the percentages of obedient subjects in the different conditions showed very comparable results between Milgram's study and the highly-involved subjects in Geller's experiment. The least involved subjects, however, were more likely to be highly obedient across all three conditions, as predicted.

Geller concluded that roleplaying can be as effective as the use of deception while at the same time avoiding some of the ethical problems associated with deception. However, he pointed out that it should not be assumed that roleplaying is not stressful or free from some ethical risks when the subjects are truly involved. Roleplaying does have the advantage ethically over deception in that truly informed consent and honest relationships between the experimenter and subject is possible.

Hypothetical vs. Empirical Roleplaying. A distinction between *hypothetical* and *empirical* roleplaying was offered by Spencer (1978). Hypothetical roleplaying is probably more common and refers to those situations where there is no independent way of checking the extent to which subjects are involved or the degree to which different processes are used by different subjects. In contrast, empirical roleplaying is defined as the situation in which the experimenter can independently monitor the subject to determine if the script devised by the experimenter is accurately being played by the subject. A good example of this testability is the physiological recording of arousal used by Holmes and Bennett (1974) to see if subjects asked to role play a shock experiment did in fact get aroused.

Spencer felt that wider use of empirical roleplaying would lead to more agreement when comparisons are made between roleplaying and *in vivo* versions of the same experimental procedures. Since hypothetical roleplaying merely calls for the subject to imagine an experience, it is impossible for the experimenter to identify exactly what processes may have occurred. If differences are found between the role players and subjects who actually get tested in the experiment, it is not clear whether such disagreements are due to inadequate roleplaying on the part of the subjects or to some inherent weakness of the roleplaying method in general.

The use of empirical roleplaying also offers the advantage that improved procedures and instructions may be possible if one learns that the previous procedures are inadequate. There are still some benefits of hypothetical roleplaying such as the determination of the demand characteristics of a situation; roleplayers should behave in ways they think the situation calls for. Finally, Spencer pointed out that the issue of generalizability or the external validity of both types of roleplaying is a separate issue. We can not know if roleplayed behaviors in laboratory situations can extend to everyday ones anymore than we can assume that behavior in actual experiments will be valid in the real world.

NATURALISTIC METHODS AS ALTERNATIVES TO REACTIVITY

The problem posed by reactivity has led psychologists to turn to a variety of alternative methods unaffected by this process. The use of unobtrusive observation methods free of the participant's awareness has been described by Webb, Campbell, Schwartz, and Sechrest, 1966. These procedures range from the use of archival records and other indirect methods where direct observation of behavior is unnecessary to the use of surveillance of behavior without any interaction between the observer and the participant.

A study (Campbell, Kruskall, & Wallace, 1966) on racial attitudes illustrates how unobtrusive methods can provide data on a sensitive topic that might prove difficult or impossible to study with direct methods. Campbell et al. inferred racial attitudes in three different schools they assumed would vary by analyzing the seating patterns chosen by black and white students. Attitudes were not directly measured by methods such as questionnaires which rely on verbal report, but were inferred from seating preferences that presumably reflected attitudes and could be measured without affecting the students in any way.

Interventions or rearrangements of the environment may also be used in making unobtrusive observations. Thus, Milgram, Mann, and Harter (1965) determined political attitudes indirectly by use of a lost-letter technique. They "lost" letters addressed to either the "Friends of the Nazi Party" or to "Friends of the Communist Party" by distributing them in various locations where they would likely be found. A comparison of the return rates of the two types of addresses from different neighborhoods provided an indirect measure of their sympathies, assuming that people are more likely to drop a "lost letter" in a mailbox if they like the organization to which it is addressed.

These types of studies belong to the category called naturalistic or field studies, as distinguished from laboratory experiments that take place in less realistic circumstances. We further distinguish between naturalistic investigations where the investigator does not intervene with or manipulate the environment such as the Campbell et al. *naturalistic* or *field study* and those investigations in which a controlled experiment with manipulated independent variables is involved in a field or real-life situation. The Milgram et al. lost-letters study is an example of this latter type which we will refer to as *naturalistic* or a *field experiment*.

Field studies involve the examination of some naturally-occurring phenomenon with as little observer intervention as possible. Studies of stress such as reactions to natural disasters (Barton, 1970) or a study of rates of violation of car-license tax payments for cars bearing bumper stickers for presidential candidates with varying attitudes regarding "law and order" (Wrightsman, 1969) both illustrate this type of research. In some cases, the investigator becomes part of a group to avoid arousing the suspicions of the group under study. This participant observation approach was used by Festinger, Riecken, and Schachter (1956) to infiltrate the ranks of a religious sect so they could observe members' reactions as they gathered to observe one of the prophecies of their leader—the end of the world—a prediction that, needless to say, failed.

The field experiment falls in-between the field study and the laboratory experiment, combining the realism of field situations with the experimental control of laboratory studies. The problem of reactivity can sometimes be avoided if subjects do not know they are in an experiment, as in the Milgram et al. study, but in some field experiments the participants are informed that they are in an experiment in order to gain their informed consent, as in Feshbach and Singer's (1971) field experiment on television viewing and adolescent aggression which involved weeks of observation. Most of our discussion, however, will focus on field experiments on unsuspecting participants.

There is some disagreement as to the extent to which uncontrolled naturalistic field studies have increased (Higbee & Wells, 1972; Fried, Gumpper, & Allen, 1973), according to tabulations of published journal articles. The upsurge of interest in real-life situations may have been a passing fad, a reaction to the activism of the 1960s which called for more research in social problems and settings, or it may have stemmed from dissatisfaction with the shortcomings of laboratory settings. Future factors such as the relative ease of availability of sources of subjects from different settings may also influence if experiments are conducted in the laboratory or the field.

Experiments, laboratory or naturalistic, are preferred over correlational studies because they afford greater control and analytical power regarding causal factors. Instead of defending one method or another, however, in the long run it may be more fruitful to employ both laboratory and naturalistic studies. It is important to compare laboratory findings with the real-life situations we are trying to understand. Although most of the ideas and hypotheses tested in laboratory studies derive their inspiration from observations of naturally-occurring behaviors, many investigators fail to relate their findings back to the original phenomena. A "continuous interplay" between the two sources of evidence is needed as a means of generating new hypotheses and of solving problems of making generalizations between the two.

The challenge comes when discrepancies arise between the laboratory and natural-setting observations. How do we reconcile the differences? For example, Hovland (1959) observed that laboratory tests of the factors underlying attitude change showed greater changes than those obtained in real life persuasion campaigns. Whereas political attitudes have been resistant to mass media campaigns (Lazarsfeld, Berelson, & Gaudet, 1948), Hovland's experiments with college students in the laboratory showed large changes.

Hovland noted that audiences in natural settings are more selective in what they attend to, listening to those they already agree with while ignoring or avoiding the messages of those they already disagree with. It is not surprising then that attitudes are difficult to change under natural conditions. Why then does substantial attitude change occur in the laboratory? One reason is that in experiments, typically subjects are randomly assigned to different conditions so that all groups receiving different messages are equivalent, on the average, in their receptivity.

A final example of the discrepancy between some laboratory findings and conclusions based on natural observation comes from the study of the effects of crowding. Freedman (1975) has suggested from the evidence obtained in his laboratory experiments with human subjects that there is no overall negative effect of crowding. In fact, he concluded that there may be two opposing effects in that crowding seems to intensify the mood that prevailed just prior to the experience of crowding, so that both positive and negative moods can be increased by crowding.

It must be kept in mind that these experiments are very brief in duration, lasting generally from about 20 minutes to an hour. Are the findings under these conditions generalizable to those real-life situations such as the crowded conditions of life in big cities which involves periods of many years? The Kerner Commission (Report, 1968), which analyzed the widespread civil disorders in many of our cities during the 1960s, attributed part of the unrest to crowded living conditions, but this type of evidence is open to a number of alternative explanations naturalistic observations can not rule out. On the other hand, the controlled laboratory studies also provide evidence of questionable relevance to the real-world phenomena since the subjects knew they were being observed, received pay for their participation in some cases, performed innocuous memory and verbal tasks, and experienced very short periods of crowding they knew would end soon.

How could evidence obtained under these conditions bear on such issues regarding crowding as whether long-term confinement in jails has undesirable effects on behavior? Yet, as Sommer (1978) reported, such evidence was presented by Freedman in the case of Amrose v. Malcom in New York on behalf of the defense against a suit that the crowding in the Bronx House of detention was harmful. Since none of this evidence cited by Freedman actually involved study of any jail conditions, the judge was more persuaded by the testimony presented on behalf of the plaintiff by another psychologist, Susan Saegert, who did not cite laboratory studies but based her case on descriptions of the actual living conditions in the jail she obtained by making a personal tour of the facility. The judge ruled in favor of the plaintiff.

In this example we have the methodological, rigorous, experimental evidence pitted against the real-life evidence which holds greater validity but more ambiguous interpretability. But as Sommer (1978) pointed out, it would be ethically and practically impossible to perform a scientifically-sound laboratory experiment of crowding in the prison, complete with random assignment of prisoner-subjects to various degrees of crowding for varying periods of numerous years and with blind experimenters and inmates who did not know the purpose of the study to rule out expectancy biases.

Unless we check the findings from our controlled experiments with the conclusions derived from evidence obtained from the real-life phenomena we wish to understand, we are apt to fail in our goals, according to Tunnell (1977). The naturalistic studies, with all their warts and blemishes, to use Sommer's description, have the critical advantage of dealing with the phenomena of interest as they exist. Although controlled experiments provide analytical precision, they also introduce artificiality and oversimplification so the results obtained by these methods must always be compared against the more complex natural phenomena we are interested in understanding.

Ethical Issues Involved with Naturalistic Research

The methodological advantage afforded by naturalistic observations is obtained at the cost of some ethical price. In using unobtrusive observation to avoid reactivity, no attempt is made to obtain informed consent so that the risk of invasion of privacy exists. After observations are completed, no efforts are generally made to debrief participants who, after all, did not even know they were being studied. The seriousness of the lack of informed consent and debriefing varies with the specific procedures used in each study, becoming more and more objectionable as the degree of possible harm to participants increases.

Invasion of Privacy. What is privacy? And is there a right to privacy? If so, is there also a right to know or seek knowledge investigators are entitled to? Assuming that both rights exist, how does one determine which party's rights take precedence in case of a conflict? These types of important questions arise when naturalistic studies are undertaken, quite unlike the situation where subjects have granted informed consent and relinquished their claims to privacy to some extent.

The issue of freedom is closely tied to the concepts of an individual's right to privacy. A person may choose to disclose personal information or, alternatively, decide not to divulge certain information. When a subject gives informed consent to be in an experiment, he or she may not only be willing to share personal feelings and thoughts for the purposes of scientific study but may actually expect such intrusion and probing, provided the data will be kept confidential.

The same information, or even more innocuous data, may be carefully guarded from other strangers or even close acquaintances. Yet, naturalistic research often involves various forms of surveillance and misrepresentation aimed at inducing disclosure or certain behaviors from subjects who have not had an opportunity to decide whether or not they wish to be involved. In this sense, many forms of naturalistic research entail invasions of privacy.

In the case of some behaviors that occur in public and are not influenced at all by the observer, the charge of invasion of privacy is less valid. Thus a study (Schachter, Friedman & Handler, 1974) of the relationship between obesity and the use of chopsticks in a Chinese restaurant requires unobtrusive observation, which is hardly threatening to the subjects. It would make little sense to obtain informed consent or to provide debriefing; indeed, either process would create greater imposition and possible anxiety among those observed.

On the other hand, the same methodology used to study illicit behaviors such as observing characteristics of persons frequenting public toilets for purposes of making homosexual contacts (Humphries, 1970) creates some more considerable problems with regard to invasion of privacy. Even if the investigator has no interest in any legal aspects of the behavior and is conducting the study only for scientific goals, there is the threat that the data could be given to or subpoenaed by law-enforcement agencies.

Naturalistic experiments, as opposed to strictly observational studies with no intervention, also vary widely in the threats they pose to individual rights to privacy. In one experiment (Doob & Gross, 1968), confederates driving in cars of different status remained at intersections after the traffic light turns green. This study—which posed little threat to privacy—was done to see if motorists behind stalled cars of varying status would differ in how long it it would take them to honk their horns impatiently.

Naturalistic experiments conducted in public situations do at least only involve actions the participants are aware may be seen by other members of the public. When surreptitious observations are made of private behaviors, the most serious invasions of privacy occur. For example, although toilet facilities outside of homes are called "public," it is still generally felt that one's behavior in such locations is private and personal. A field experiment by Middlemist, Knowles, and Matter (1976), however, involved use of the men's room as a field laboratory to see if invasion of personal space would affect the duration and latency of urination. Personal space refers to the idea that each person prefers to have a certain territory or degree of privacy from others (Sommer, 1969). This concept has been demonstrated in a variety of settings, but prior to the Middlemist et al., not in the men's room.

Middlemist et al. used a men's room with a row of three urinals. Whenever a male approached the urinals, he had to use the far left urinal since a confederate of the experimenters occupied either the middle or extreme right-hand urinal and the remaining urinal was blocked for cleaning by a mop and pail. It was hypothesized that when the confederate used the urinal closer to the subject, there would be increased latency of urination but decreased duration due to the invasion of personal space.

In order to execute the study, it was necessary to have another member of the research team sit in a toilet booth, watching through a periscope-like device embedded in some books on the floor to see when the urine started and ceased to flow. As a sort of "ethical" considerations, Middlemist et al. made sure their observation technique did not enable them to view the faces of the subjects or otherwise identify them through the periscope.

Investigators have also invaded the home to find unsuspecting participants for their naturalistic experiments. Even when the actual experimental procedures are innocuous, all of these studies do involve some form of annoyance and inconvenience. For example, the use of the "wrong number" technique (Gaertner & Bickman, 1972) to assess racial attitudes begins to become, if not an invasion of privacy, then certainly a form of public nuisance. In this procedure, the experimenter makes a phony wrong number call to different predominantly black or white neighborhoods and pretends he has a disabled vehicle. It is late at night and he has allegedly used his last dime, so he asks the unsuspecting recipient of the call to do a small favor and call a number that is allegedly the garage's. His voice is disguised to sound "black" for some recipients of calls and "white" for the other half. An assistant answers the phone if the favor is made.

Stronger versions of this basic technique involve the experimenter trying to gain entry under false pretenses into the homes of participants to use their telephones (Milgram, 1970) or to do consumer research on the use of household products (Freedman & Fraser, 1966).

In varying degree, all of these studies could be seen as involving some form of invasion of privacy of unsuspecting participants not only in public but also in their own homes. Since the subjects never have a chance to decide *not* to cooperate because they do not know these encounters were inauthentic interactions, these studies involve ethical problems.

Although the value of research on private topics such as sex, death, and religion is substantial, the necessity of ethical procedures is even greater since these are very sensitive areas, as Kelman noted (1977). Research on such topics may involve invasion of privacy if methodological precision is imposed; conversely, protection of ethical rights of individuals may introduce methodological weaknesses into the research. For example, it would be an ethically-unsound procedure to use unobtrusive methods to study sexual behavior of a random sample of persons, however useful such data might be. It is possible, however, as Masters and Johnson (1966) have demonstrated, to find a select portion of the population that is willing to engage in sexual intercourse while being studied and observed under certain scientifically legitimate conditions. One need be careful, however, in making generalizations from this sample to the population in general.

Kelman (1977) also warned of the need to consider individual and group differences in attitudes toward and conceptions of privacy. It is vital to recognize that procedures agreeable to one ethnic group might prove highly objectionable to another. This advice is particularly important in view of highly sensitive feelings about ethnic rights in our contemporary society.

Participant observation in which the research joins a group to be inconspicuous while making field observations may also introduce threats to privacy. Groups or organizations that exclude outsiders from their activities may engage in behaviors that might occur only in the privacy of their own members. Such activities may be, but need not be, illegal, immoral, or objectionable; it may simply be embarrassing to be seen by outsiders. Since the investigators will have gained acceptance and trust by misrepresenting themselves, they can be considered to have invaded the privacy of others. Whyte (1979), a noted sociologist, argued that a collaborative arrangement is ethically desirable when participant observation is used so that the research is a joint effort between the investigator and key informants who are members of the group under study. There should be a responsibility to the targets of investigation in return for this observation.

Protection from Harm. Studies conducted in public field settings in which the investigator does not intervene probably raise little or no danger of harm to those being observed. The observer is unobtrusive and at some distance from the naturally-occurring behavior which anyone present can observe. For example, a study using observations at bus stops of the factors affecting tendencies for people to form queues or waiting lines is no great threat to those being observed (Mann & Taylor, 1969).

However, situations where the observed behavior is illegal, immoral, or in some manner threatening to the well-being of the observed persons are more complicated. First, if the observation records are not maintained to protect anonymity, the identities of participants may be discovered by persons or agencies with purposes other than research goals. Even when attempts are made to safeguard the confidentiality and safety of the records, they may fall into other hands accidentally or through legal means such as subpoenas. Secondly, in the case of illegal behavior, the investigator who started out with only research goals may find later that he or she may feel a responsibility to report some information to legal authorities.

Many field *experiments*, where some intervention is arranged, are relatively safe. For example, Milgram, Bickman, and Berkowitz (1969) used confederates to create different-sized crowds that gazed up toward the top of a tall, downtown building to see if this variable affects the reactions of passersby. This study involves only some mild disruption which would create little objection or foreseeable danger.

Other field experiments, however, introduce situaions that are more potentially dangerous or ethically objectionable for other reasons. Latané and Darley (1970) rigged a stolen-beer caper in a liquor store; confederates pretended to steal beer in the presence of a customer while the clerk had gone to the storeroom. The purpose of the study was to see what factors determined whether or not the customer would report the theft when the clerk returned. It takes little imagination to see that some customer may have gotten involved even more actively and taken after the confederates in vigilante fashion with a weapon. Fortunately, this response did not occur during the experiment.

What stress was imposed upon the customer by this procedure? Most people would be quite agitated and emotionally aroused by witnessing a crime. Was the benefit of this study worth the risk and stress suffered by the subjects? Since there was no debriefing, what guilt feelings would arise in the subjects who were too frightened to report the crime for fear of getting involved?

In a similar type of experiment conducted in the New York subway during times of light use, Piliavin, Rodin, and Piliavin (1969) had a male confederate apparently faint on the floor of an almost empty subway car to determine some of the factors affecting the extent to which bystanders would provide assistance to the victim. The status of the attire of the victim, whether he was black or white, and whether he was carrying a cane and apparently was blind or had the smell of alcohol on him, were some of the variables examined.

Again, we must ask whether the benefit in knowledge obtained from this study justified the stress and inconvenience this naturalistic experiment imposed upon participants who were not aware that they were subjects and received no debriefing. Did some of the subjects experience extreme fear or anxiety from this contrived encounter? Did others feel ashamed later for not intervening? There is no way to know for sure, but it is reasonable to assume that these types of reactions may have occurred for some subway passengers.

Piliavin et al. may have been concerned about these issues, but their report does not raise these problems, which should be brought to the attention of their readers. In a later article (Piliavin & Piliavin, 1972, p. 356), they primarily expressed annoyance at the unreasonableness of the transit authorities in disapproving of their activities, rather than expressing any concern about the rights of subway passengers. Curiously they also interpreted the "pulling of the emergency cord" by a few subjects as a form of irrational behavior that created problems for their study. Perhaps this action represented a genuine and more intelligent form of bystander intervention than rushing to the victim to render potentially incompetent aid.

Debriefing. The participant in a naturalistic experiment usually does not know that he or she is in an experiment so the issue of whether or not debriefing is necessary differs somewhat from the laboratory experiment where the subject has given informed consent. Campbell (1969, p. 372) took the position that it is not necessary because if we did generally debrief them, "we are doomed to wear out our laboratories." Another argument against debriefing is that this procedure may create more stress than the observation per se for many innocuous procedures. It may also prove inconvenient, boring, or embarrassing for participants when they are debriefed.

The exception to this advice would be naturalistic studies where possible harm, such as excessive anxiety or loss of self-esteem, may be involved. In cases where it is obvious that subjects are highly stressed, the experimenter can anticipate such risks and provide debriefing. Similarly, if it is obvious that a situation involves no risk to subjects, one might accept the policy of not debriefing. The problem, of course, is the large in-between category of "maybe." How does one know for sure whether a given situation involves undue stress for subjects unless there is some type of follow-up, directly or indirectly, of participants? In some situations it might be physically impossible to debrief participants, as when large numbers of subjects are observed simultaneously.

We will more fully describe several examples of field experiments where debriefing was needed. In the "Watergate" field experiment by West, Gunn and Chernicky (1975), a private investigator approached undergraduate majors in criminology and arranged to meet them at a business office in the community. At this meeting, subjects were asked to help break into the office to microfilm some documents. One group of subjects was offered $2,000 for their involvement in the crime that would aid a rival company. A control group was offered no reward and told nothing would actually be stolen, and that they just wanted to see if their burglary plans would work. Another group of subjects was told that this company had defrauded the Internal Revenue Service and that the data was needed to prove the case; half of the group was promised immunity from prosecution if they were caught but the other half was not.

West, et al. were interested in the factors affecting the decisions of students to commit the break-in; there was no actual burglary involved and both of the cover stories were total fabrications designed to provide plausible justifications for the contemplated crime. Although the actual results of the study are unimportant for the purposes of the present discussion, the reader will probably be curious. Only 4 of 20 subjects who were offered the $2,000 reward were willing to agree to attend a final planning session, whereas almost half of those asked to help the government agreed to attend, provided they would receive immunity from prosecution in case they were caught. Without such a promise, only one of 20 subjects offered to aid the government in getting the data.

Another example of a study in which ethical concern might call for debriefing—although the participants did not know they were being studied—is that of Gelfand, Hartmann, Walder, and Page (1973) which dealt with the reporting of shoplifting. The experiment was conducted in several variety-drug stores with the full cooperation of their staffs. A female confederate dressed either in hippie or conventional attire conspicuously took about $5 worth of small items and left the store without paying.

Videotapes were made of reactions of witnessing subjects, as well as their tendencies to report the crime or to ignore it. Since a large percentage (over 70 per cent) of subjects did fail to report the incidents, another confederate at the checkstand later confronted the subjects, asking if they had been aware that shoplifting had occurred.

Finally, in order to obtain a fuller insight into the reactions of subjects, Gelfand et al. told subjects that they had actually been in an experiment. During the interview, it was also possible to determine the extent to which subjects had realized shoplifting was occurring and the nature of their reactions and attitudes about that specific incident and to shoplifting in general.

In order to obtain these reactions, Gelfand et al. first had to inform subjects that they had been in an experiment. Thus, debriefing was provided as a methodological necessity rather than as an ethical consideration. In fact, the explanation of the study was given to subjects on a printed handout, which may have done little to reduce any negative or stressful reactions to the incident. For ethical reasons, debriefing was considered essential by Bickman and Rosenbaum (1977) in a highly similar study where subjects observed confederates who shoplifted in a supermarket. During debriefing the research deception was justified to subjects on the grounds that this research might help find solutions to the shoplifting problem. It was hoped that any stress or anxiety about their experiences would be reduced by debriefing. However, no specific details of the debriefing procedure were reported nor was any evidence presented regarding the effectiveness of the debriefing.

Conclusion. One defense made on behalf of naturalistic observations is that the behaviors observed are generally part of normal, everyday life that are freely performed in public places. In the case of unobtrusive observation where there is no intervention or contrived circumstances imposed by the investigator, this defense is more valid since the researcher is not much different from any other observer of the public scene. When the researcher turns to study more private behavior, even though no intervention is involved, more serious problems arise.

When rigged situations are contrived by experimenters outside the laboratory, as in the case of naturalistic *experiments*, the justification that these events are similar to those people ordinarily might encounter in real life becomes more questionable. While it is true that one does potentially encounter requests for charitable donations, cries of help during emergencies, liquor store or grocery store thefts, and so forth in daily, public situations, the likelihood of some of these situations is rather low. More seriously, some of these contrived events are potentially harmful or stressful to participants. The fact that they could actually occur in reality does not excuse the creation of additional instances, especially if the risk of harm to the participants can be great.

As an illustration, consider an example of a naturalistic study of aiding behavior by Bryan and Test (1967) in which a "lady in distress" stood by her car on the side of the road with a flat tire. The research question, which is not crucial to the issue, was whether the number of motorists who would stop to help varied depending on whether or not they had just passed a similar situation back along the same road where a male confederate was helping a similar female confederate motorist.

It is easy to imagine that just one out of hundreds of motorists passing by may have been distracted and produced a serious accident. The fact that the same type of accident could have stemmed from an authentic situation with a lady in distress is irrelevant. The question that the naturalistic experimenter must consider is whether he or she bears any legal or moral responsibility for the hypothetical accident, unintentional though it certainly was. Had the experimenter not imposed one additional traffic hazard in this example, the accident would not have occurred. Was the knowledge obtained from this study worth the imposition of risk to persons who did not know they were in an experiment? Were there less risky alternative procedures for obtaining the same type of information? What benefits are there to society to learn that helping of motorists per se may be affected by the presence or absence of a prior modeling of helping? In other words, could a test of the same question be conducted in a less hazardous condition to determine the effects of modelling in general rather than in the specific case of disabled motorists?

Another type of danger of naturalistic experiments taken collectively is that the distortion and misrepresentation of apparently real experiences—that are actually experimental manipulations—are fast becoming an imposition on the public. Aside from the serious matters of lack of informed consent, lack of debriefing, and threat of harm in some instances, naturalistic experiments are increasing at a rate that may pose an ethical problem in its own right. Just as one might tolerate an occasional "junk phone call," but become irritated when the rate increases, the public may not object to a rare field experiment but may find it annoying when they occur more frequently.

Certain techniques, such as the lost-letter technique (Milgram, 1969), wrong number phone call technique (Gaertner & Bickman, 1972), foot-in-the-door technique (Freedman & Fraser, 1966), and fake emergencies (e.g., Latané & Darley, 1970) have virtually become standard paradigms used by other investigators in one form or another to generate further studies with these procedures.

Not only is the public exposed to stressful staged events, such as shoplifting (Gelfand et al., 1973) and apparently bleeding, unconscious victims on subways (Piliavin & Piliavin, 1972), but also to contrived "good" experiences. Isen and Levin (1972) planted a dime in an airport telephone coin-return slot for half their subjects and left it empty for the other half to see if this prior good luck would lead the former group to be more helpful when a female confederate dropped a folder full of papers in front of them as they left the booth. Airport phone booths were also used by Benson, Karabenick, and Lerner (1976) as a setting to "lose" graduate-school applications in stamped and addressed envelopes to see if different return rates would occur as a function of the racial and physical attractiveness of the enclosed photographs of the applicant.

No activity or area of human experience seems to be free from the curiosity and inquisitiveness of the psychological researcher. As noted earlier, Middlemist et al. (1976) invaded the men's room to determine how proximity of another person affected the latency and duration of urination. Children who were out on Halloween were the unsuspecting participants in an experiment by Diener, Fraser, Beaman, and Kelem (1976) who used a type of entrapment situation by leaving the children to "help themselves" to candies and monies (pennies and nickels). They wanted to see if anonymity provided by Halloween masks led children to take more candies than they were allowed or to take the money (which was not offered to them).

Commuters in New York's Grand Central Station were stopped by confederates posing as deaf in a study by Thayer (1973). They handed written notes to passersby asking them to phone a number and ask the party to come pick up the deaf person. Motorists have been participants in a number of studies such as those already cited by Bryan and Test (1967) and Doob and Gross (1968). Ellsworth, Carlsmith, and Henson (1972) had confederates stand at intersections and stare directly at motorists stopped at red lights as a means of invading their personal space to see if they would drive off faster when the light changed.

From this brief list of varied settings, it should be obvious that the psychological candid camera is very active. As more people learn about these naturalistic experiments from popular accounts in newspapers, magazines, and other mass media, their sensitivities and awareness will increase, perhaps to the point that they may find themselves wondering whether the disabled car they passed or the hippie panhandler was genuine or in fact part of a field experiment.

In fact, a colleague who observed an "out of order" sign on the psychology-building elevator once mused that perhaps it was an experimental procedure to see if anyone would bother to push the button on the elevator. This objectionable type of uncertainty about the validity of everyday experiences is created by the proliferation of naturalistic studies in addition to any threats of harm or stress that might exist. Unlike the laboratory experiment where the participant realizes deception may occur, the person is entitled to expect or hope for authenticity in the real world even though disappointment may occur without the help of psychologists. Just because fraud, dishonesty, and misrepresentation abounds in the real world is no reason for psychologists to add unnecessarily to this situation.

In the long run, the continued growth and publicity of such experiments may be self-limiting. As Wiesenthal (1974, p. 339) observed, "What will psychologists do once the popular media reveals to the public our crafty techniques?" It is hoped, however, that researchers will examine the situation and realize the dangers of excessive intrusions into the public sphere, especially in proportion to the benefits of some of the knowledge obtained from many of the studies.

Legal Responsibility and Public Reactions

In addition to the ethical judgments researchers may make about nonreactive or naturalistic experiments, we should also consider legal responsibility for any adverse consequences of this research as well as the reactions and views of the general public. Since the participants in nonreactive studies do not know they are being studied, it is obvious that they can not object if they wished. And if they suffered injury or stress caused by the imposition of experimental procedures upon them which they did not realize was part of a study, how could they even press legal charges?

These types of issues become increasingly important as the number of naturalistic experiments increases year by year. An informal survey of two attorneys by Silverman (1975) provided some conflicting legal views about the legal obligations of investigators in a small set of specific published studies which were briefly summarized for them. Here are a few examples:

1. Persons selected at random are phoned. The caller pretends he has reached a wrong number, using his last piece of change, and that his car is disabled on a highway. The party is requested to phone the caller's garage and ask them to come for him. The garage number is actually the caller's phone

and another experimenter, standing by, pretends to take the message (Gaertner & Bickman, 1972).

2. A person walking with a cane pretends to collapse in a subway car. "Stage blood" trickles from his mouth. If someone approaches the victim, he allows the party to help him to his feet. If no one approaches before the train slows to a stop, another experimenter, posing as a passenger, pretends to do so and both leave the train (Piliavin & Piliavin, 1972).
3. Experimenters, walking singly or in pairs, ask politely for either 10¢ or 20¢ from passersby, sometimes offering an explanation for why they need the money (Latané, 1970).

Although only three examples are described here, the general flavor of the situations presented to the attorneys can be sensed. One attorney saw no legal problems in any of the examples, ruling out harassment, annoyance, or invasion of privacy, whereas the other attorney saw matters quite differently, suggesting the possibility that trespass may have been involved in one study where the experimenters gained entry into private homes on the false pretense of needing to use a phone. He also suggested that harassment was involved in all of the cases.

The opinion of a judge of a criminal court, however, tended to be benign. He recognized the nuisance and inconvenience that the studies might create but did not see any criminal negligence, if, for example, a subway rider with a weak heart suffered a fatal heart attack when confronted with the fake subway emergency described above. Civil action could not be taken against the psychologist either, in this judge's opinion, because of negligence given there was no legal duty existing between the researchers and the victim for the former to be guilty of negligence.

Although Silverman's survey was based on a very limited number of examples and experts on legal matters, it does present food for serious contemplation for the naturalistic researcher. Although the majority of these studies are innocuous, such as the one by Milgram et al. (1969) in which confederates stand on a busy corner and stare up at a building to see what passersby will do, there are others such as the Piliavin and Piliavin (1972) subway emergency, the rigged shoplifting studies to see who reports shoplifters (Gelfand et al., 1973), and the staged stolen beer incidents to test bystander intervention (Latané & Darley, 1970) that can very easily turn from a cute study into a tragedy if someone gets hurt or killed.

Wilson and Donnerstein (1976) conducted a followup and extension of Silverman's study using a larger sample of respondents obtained from customers in a shopping center. Respondents varied widely in age, represented both sexes, and were primarily middle class. Each subject received brief descriptions of four of the following eight studies which were among those used by Silverman (1975): Latané (1970)–subjects were approached and asked for money; Freedman and Fraser

(1966)–subjects were asked for a small, then for a large favor by an experimenter who misrepresented himself; Piliavin and Piliavin (1972)–subjects witnessed a staged emergency on a subway; Milgram (1969)–letters are "lost" in various locations where they can be found; Milgram (1970)–subjects are approached in their homes and asked for use of a phone; Zimbardo (1969)–subjects are passersby of abandoned automobiles; Schaps (1972)–shoe salesman shows the experimenter's accomplice a number of shoes, all of which are rejected; Abelson and Miller (1967)–subjects sitting on park benches are interviewed for a survey and a confederate pretending to be another interviewee ridicules the subject's answers.

Each respondent was asked a number of questions about the possibility that they found the studies to be ethically or legally objectionable. Issues of harassment, invasion of privacy, ethics, and morality were raised. They were also asked if they would object if they later learned they had been in such studies, whether they felt such studies were worthwhile, and whether they felt psychologists should do such studies, and so forth. Finally, they were asked questions about whether they thought the studies were legal, and if they thought not, whether they would press charges. Their opinions about the use of deception by psychologists, politicians, and the military were also collected.

The results are shown in Table 16-1, combined over sex, age, and size of city where the data was collected, since none of these factors produced differences. The percentage of "no," "not sure," and "yes" answers for each question are presented for each of the eight studies. Although the studies differ widely, it can be noted that a majority of respondents reported feelings of harassment for four studies, and in the case of the remaining four, a sizeable minority expressed similar feelings. Examination of answers to other issues shows a similar variability over the eight studies, but usually with sufficiently high percentages of respondents expressing some negative sentiments for at least some of the studies, especially the fake subway person-in-distress study of Piliavin and Piliavin (1972). Few subjects thought any studies were illegal; moreover, when asked if they knew of an illegal study, it was rare that a majority of the respondents felt like pressing charges.

Wilson and Donnerstein (1976) offer two extreme types of interpretations which may be made of their data. If one requires over 50 per cent (a majority) of respondents to object to a study before becoming concerned, it would appear that most of the issues are not serious for most of these studies. On the other hand, the percentage objecting on these issues is often substantial and close to 50 per cent, and if the "not sure" responses are viewed as less than positive support of experimental practices in these studies, then ethical problems are clearly associated with this research in the public's mind.

Inasmuch as decisions on ethical issues are not like political elections where the winner is the position with the most votes, it makes more sense to view the results in a negative light. Since a large minority feels concern and negative feelings, and another sizeable percentage feels "not sure," it appears that some of these studies pose problems ranging from harassment to trespasss to annoyance of unsuspecting "participants" of these research projects. Even less positive responses might have been obtained if the survey was conducted anonymously or by mail; the direct face-to-face interview with a researcher may have intimidated some respondents to give responses that may have been more favorable than their true opinions.

Studies of the reactions and perceptions of the general public to studies conducted in their midst are valuable ways of gaining much needed perspectives from other points of view. As Wilson and Donnerstein concluded, "we simply feel that potential subjects should have the opportunity to participate in this consulting process." (1976, p. 772). They go on to pose the problem of how much weight to give to the views of public consultants, a decision they recognize may depend upon the values of each individual researcher. The first step, however, is for investigators with methods that may be controversial to seek this sort of information *before* conducting the study to minimize any possible problems, independently of the question of legal liability.

SUMMARY

Roleplaying simulations have been proposed by some researchers as an alternative to the use of deception, which avoid ethical problems as well as methodological weaknesses of the latter method. Critics, however, question the ability of subjects to predict accurately how they would behave in an actual experiment. There is some variation in the procedures used that are termed "roleplaying," ranging from mere armchair speculation in response to a verbal description of the procedures to a more realistic simulation in which the subject actually undergoes all of the actual procedures, with the exception that the independent variable is withheld and the subject is instructed to imagine it was received. This latter variant, referred to as role enactment, offers the advantage that it is a collaborative situation between the subject and the experimenter and enables better determination of the meanings subjects form about the task and their behavior.

Replications of experiments that previously used deception have been conducted using roleplaying procedures. Most of these comparisons have failed to show comparable results under the two versions, leading some to conclude that roleplaying is inadequate to replicate the deception versions of the phenomena being studied.

TABLE 16–1. Subjects' Responses to Questions Asked About Each Nonreactive Method.

	Question									
Answer	*Feel Harassed?*	*Privacy Invaded?*	*Un-ethical?*	*Mind Being Subject?*	*Do Such Experi-ment?*	*Justified by Scientific Contribu-tion?*	*Lower Trust?*	*Against Law?*	*See Lawyer?*	*Trespassing Committed?*
Latané (1970)–Asking for Money										
No	40	56	46	38	54	48	62	57	64	–
Not sure	3	1	1	8	27	23	9	23	10	–
Yes	57	43	43	54	19	29	29	20	26	–
Piliavin & Piliavin (1972)–Blood Study										
No	55	81	43	42	50	38	59	60	58	–
Not sure	2	1	10	5	18	36	4	19	11	–
Yes	43	18	47	53	32	27	37	20	32	–
Milgram (1970)–Ask to Enter Home and Use Telephone										
No	51	46	48	46	46	41	64	55	60	48
Not sure	5	8	15	10	22	24	5	19	21	12
Yes	44	46	38	44	31	35	31	26	19	40
Freedman & Fraser (1966)–Foot-in-the-door Technique										
No	45	50	53	41	36	38	69	59	58	63
Not sure	1	3	12	6	30	30	10	24	13	4
Yes	54	47	35	53	34	32	22	17	29	33

Abelson & Miller (1967)–Personal Insult Study										
No	28	48	42	40	35	30	68	73	68	–
Not sure	9	7	16	9	28	27	7	12	19	–
Yes	63	44	42	52	37	43	25	15	14	–
Schaps (1972)–Shoe Store Study										
No	20	60	52	28	49	42	68	75	73	72
Not sure	8	14	16	8	20	16	11	18	16	14
Yes	72	26	31	65	31	41	21	8	10	14
Milgram (1969)–Lost Letter Technique										
No	70	87	68	54	34	37	70	75	69	–
Not sure	3	2	8	8	33	31	10	15	10	–
Yes	26	11	24	38	32	32	20	10	22	–
Zimbardo (1969)–Abandoned Automobiles Study										
No	72	74	65	65	22	18	78	75	72	–
Not sure	5	5	16	6	28	32	5	18	18	–
Yes	24	21	18	28	49	49	17	6	10	–

Note. All data are given as percentages. Number of subjects on which percentages are based ranged from 79 to 93. Construction of conservative 95% confidence intervals for these proportions (cf. Hays, 1973) showed that all proportions were within ± 10 or 11 percentage points of the true proportions.
Source: "Legal and ethical aspects of nonreactive social psychological research: An excursion into the public mind," by D. W. Wilson and E. Donnerste. *American Psychologist*, 1976, **31**, 765–73. Copyright by the American Psychological Association. Reprinted by permission.

However, some evidence exists to show that when subjects are more genuinely involved, role playing results are similar to those of deception procedures.

The problem of the reactive nature of experiments has been attacked by increased use of naturalistic experiments in which subjects never know they are participating in a study.

Field studies in which the researcher does not intervene by introducing any independent variables are also used as alternatives to laboratory experiments in some situations. These studies are correlational and permit weaker conclusions about causal relationships than controlled observations allow. It is not rare for findings from uncontrolled naturalistic studies and controlled experimental observations to disagree for a variety of reasons. Controlled studies can only examine a few variables at a time, whereas real life phenomena may involve numerous determinants. Uncontrolled observation can provide a rich source of hypotheses but is unable to permit sound conclusions about the influence of different factors; controlled observation, on the other hand, can provide more conclusive evidence about the role of such factors. Thus, a combined use of both methods offers a productive approach.

A number of ethical issues are involved with naturalistic research, such as lack of informed consent and the invasion of privacy, the exposure of participants to possible harm, and the overproliferation of the use of the public. Ordinarily debriefing is not provided to unsuspecting participants, but in cases where the nature of the experience may have created anxiety and stress, it could be argued that it would be unethical not to debrief.

The question of legal responsibility, if not ethical accountability, of investigators for any harm suffered by participants in naturalistic research has also been raised. There is not much agreement on this issue, but surveys of the public have shown that a sizeable minority indicated feelings that certain experiments were illegal and might lead them to seek legal redress if they had been in such studies.

REFERENCES

Abelson, R. P., and Miller, J. C. Negative persuasion via personal insult. *Journal of Experimental Social Psychology,* 1967, *3*, 321–333.

Aronson, E., and Carlsmith, J. M. Experimentation in social psychology. In G. Lindzey and E. Aronson (Eds.), *The handbook of social psychology* (Vol. 2). Reading, Mass.: Addison-Wesley, 1968.

Barton, A. H. *Communities in disaster.* New York: Doubleday, 1970.

Benson, P. L., Karabenick, S. A., and Lerner, R. M. Pretty pleases: Effect of physical attractiveness, race, and sex on receiving help. *Journal of Experimental Social Psychology,* 1976, *12*, 409–415.

Bickman, L., and Rosenbaum, D. P. Crime reporting as a function of bystander encouragement, surveillance, and credibility. *Journal of Personality and Social Psychology,* 1977, *35*, 577-586.

Bryan, J. H., and Test, M. A. Models and helping: Naturalistic studies in aiding behavior. *Journal of Personality and Social Psychology,* 1967, *6*, 400-407.

Campbell, D. T. Perspective: Artifact and control. In R. Rosenthal and R. L. Rosnow (Eds.), *Artifact in behavioral research.* New York: Academic Press, 1969.

Campbell. D. T., Kruskall, W. H., and Wallace, W. P. Seating aggregation as an index of attitude. *Sociometry,* 1966, *29*, 1-15.

Cooper, J. Deception and role playing: On telling the good guys from the bad guys. *American Psychologist,* 1976, *31*, 605-610.

Darroch, R. K., and Steiner, I. D. Roleplaying: An alternative to laboratory research. *Journal of Personality,* 1970, *38*, 302-311.

Diener, E., Fraser, S. C., Beaman, A. L., and Kelem, R. T. Effects of deindivuation variables on stealing among Halloween trick-or-treaters. *Journal of Personality and Social Psychology,* 1976, *33*, 178-183.

Doob, A. N., and Gross, A. E. Status of frustrator as an inhibitor of horn-honking responses. *Journal of Social Psychology,* 1968, *76*, 213-218.

Ellsworth, P. C., Carlsmith, J. H., and Henson, A. The stare as a stimulus to flight in human subjects. *Journal of Personality and Social Psychology,* 1972, *21*, 302-311.

Feshbach, S., and Singer, R. D. *Television and aggression: An experimental field study.* San Francisco: Jossey-Bass, 1971.

Festinger, L., Riecken, H. W., and Schachter, S. *When prophecy fails.* Minneapolis: University of Minnesota Press, 1956.

Forward, J., Canter, R., and Kirsch, N. Role-enactment and deception methodologies: Alternative paradigms? *American Psychologist,* 1976, *31*, 595-604.

Freedman, J. L. Role playing: Psychology by consensus. *Journal of Personality and Social Psychology*, 1969, *13*, 107-114.

Freedman, J. L. *Crowding and behavior.* San Francisco: Freeman, 1975.

Freedman, J. L., and Fraser, S. C. Compliance without pressure: The foot-in-the-door technique. *Journal of Personality and Social Psychology,* 1966, *4*, 195-202.

Fried, S. B., Gumpper, D. C., and Allen, J. C. Ten years of social psychology. Is there a growing commitment to field research? *American Psychologist,* 1973, *28*, 155-156.

Gaertner, S., and Bickman, L. A nonreactive indicator measure of racial discrimination; The wrong-number technique. In L. Bickman and T. Henchy (Eds.), *Beyond the laboratory: Field research in social psychology.* New York: McGraw-Hill, 1972.

Gelfand, D. M., Hartmann, D. P., Walder, P., and Page, B. Who reports shoplifters? A field-experimental study. *Journal of Personality and Social Psychology,* 1973, *25*, 276-285.

Geller, D. M. Involvement in role-playing simulations: A demonstration with studies on obedience. *Journal of Personality and Social Psychology,* 1978, *36*, 219-235.

Higbee, K. L., and Wells, M. G. Some research trends in social psychology during the 1960s. *American Psychologist,* 1972, *27*, 963-966.

Holmes, D. S., and Bennett, D. H. Experiments to answer questions raised by the use of deception in psychological research: I. Role playing as an alternative to deception; II. Effectiveness of debriefing after a deception; III. Effect of informed consent on deception. *Journal of Personality and Social Psychology,* 1974, *29*, 358-367.

Hovland, C. I. Reconciling conflicting results derived from experimental and survey studies on attitude change. *American Psychologist,* 1959, *14*, 8-17.

Humphries, L. *Tearoom trade: Impersonal sex in public places.* Chicago: Aldine, 1970.

Isen, A. M., and Levin, P. F. The effect of feeling good on helping: Cookies and kindness. *Journal of Personality and Social Psychology,* 1972, *21*, 384-388.

Kelman, H. C. Human use of human subjects: The problem of deception in social psychological experiments. *Psychological Bulletin,* 1967, *67*, 1-11.

Kelman, H. C. The rights of the subject in social research: An analysis in terms of relative legitimacy. *American Psychologist*, 1972, *27*, 989-1016.

Kelman, H. C. Privacy and research with human beings. *Journal of Social Issues,* 1977, *33*(3) 169-195.

Latané, B. Field studies of altruistic compliance. *Representative Research in Social Psychology,* 1970, *1*, 49-60.

Latané, B., and Darley, J. M. *The unresponsive bystander: Why doesn't he help?* New York: Appleton-Century-Crofts, 1970.

Lazarsfeld, P. F., Berelson, B., and Gaudet, H. *The People's Choice.* New York: Columbia University Press, 1948.

Mann, L., and Taylor, K. F. Queue counting: The effect of motives upon estimates of numbers in waiting lines. *Journal of Personality and Social Psychology,* 1969, *12*, 95-103.

Masters, W. H., and Johnson, V. E. *Human sexual response.* Boston: Little, Brown, 1966.

Middlemist, R. D., Knowles, E. S., and Matter, C. F. Personal space invasions in the lavatory: Suggestive evidence for arousal. *Journal of Personality and Social Psychology,* 1976, *33*, 541-546.

Milgram, S. Behavioral study of obedience. *Journal of Abnormal and Social Psychology*, 1963, *67*, 371-378.

Milgram, S. The lost-letter technique. *Psychology* Today. June, 1969, pp. 30-33; 66; 68.

Milgram, S. The experience of living in cities. Science, 1970, *167*, 1461-1468.

Milgram, S. *Obedience to authority.* New York: Harper & Row, 1974.

Milgram, S., Bickman, L., and Berkowitz, L. Note on the drawing power of crowds of different size. *Journal of Personality and Social Psychology,* 1969, *13*, 79-82.

Milgram, S., Mann, L., and Harter, S. The lost-letter technique: A tool of social research. *Public Opinion Quarterly,* 1965, *29*, 437-438.

Miller, A. G. Roleplaying: An alternative to deception?: A review of the evidence. *American Psychologist*, 1972, *27*, 623-636.

Mixon, D. Instead of deception. *Journal for the Theory of Social Behavior*, 1972, *2*, 145-177.

Piliavin, J. A., and Piliavin, I. M. Effect of blood on reactions to a victim. *Journal of Personality and Social Psychology,* 1972, *23*, 353-361.

Piliavin, I. M., Rodin, J., and Piliavin, J. A. Good samaritanism: An underground phenomenon? *Journal of Personality and Social Psychology,* 1969, *13,* 289-299.

Report of the National Advisory Commission on Civil Disorders. New York: Bantam, 1968.

Schachter, S., Friedman, L., and Handler, J. Who eats with chopsticks? In S. Schachter and J. Rodin (Eds.), *Obese humans and rats.* Potomac, Md.: Lawrence Erlbaum Associates, 1974.

Schaps, E. Cost, dependency, and helping. *Journal of Personality and Social Psychology,* 1972, *21*, 74-78.

Silverman, I. Nonreactive methods and the law. *American Psychologist,* 1975, *30*, 764-769.

Sommer, R. Personal space: *The behavioral basis of design.* Englewood Cliffs, N.J.: Prentice-Hall, 1969.

Sommer, R. Are crowded jails harmful? Field and laboratory on trial. Invited address, Western Psychological Association Meetings, San Francisco, 1978.

Spencer, C. D. Two types of role playing. Threats to internal and external validity. *American Psychologist,* 1978, *33*, 265-268.

Thayer, S. Lend me your ears: Racial and sexual factors in helping the deaf. *Journal of Personality and Social Psychology,* 1973, *28*, 8-11.

Tunnell, G. B. Three dimensions of naturalness: An expanded definition of field research. *Psychological Bulletin,* 1977, *84*, 426-437.

Webb, E. J., Campbell, D. T., Schwartz, R. D., and Sechrest, L. Unobtrusive measures. *Nonreactive research in the social sciences.* Chicago: Rand McNally, 1966.

West, S. G., Gunn, S. P., and Chernicky, P. Ubiquitous Watergate: An attributional analysis. *Journal of Personality and Social Psychology,* 1975, *32*, 55-65.

Whyte, W. F. On making the most of participant observation. *American Sociologist,* 1979, *14*, 56-66.

Wiesenthal, D. L. Reweaving deception's tangled web. *Canadian Psychologist,* 1974, *15*, 326-336.

Wilson, D. W., and Donnerstein, E. Legal and ethical aspects of nonreactive social psychological research: An excursion into the public mind. *American Psychologist,* 1976, *31*, 765-773.

Willis, R. H., and Willis, Y. A. Role playing vs. deception: An experimental comparison. *Journal of Personality and Social Psychology,* 1970, *16*, 472-477.

Wrightsman, L. Wallace supporters and adherence to "law and order." *Journal of Personality and Social Psychology,* 1969, *13*, 17-22.

Zimbardo, P. G. The human choice: Individuation, reason, and order versus deindividuation, impulse and chaos. In W. J. Arnold and D. Levine (Eds.), *Nebraska Symposium on Motivation* (Vol. 17). Lincoln: University of Nebraska Press, 1969.

CHAPTER 17

What Is the Social Responsibility of Experimenters?

Chapter at a Glance

One ideal view of science holds that it is a method for objective investigation. It is detached and impartial, free from the influence of politics and vested interests. Those who believe that psychology can and should be a scientific discipline emphasize this truth-seeking function of the field. In contrast, another perspective calls for psychology, and other social sciences, to work on relevant and important social concerns and issues. Solutions to psychological problems such as mental illness, learning disabilities, violence and aggression, and drug abuse are a few of these challenges. Finally, a third aspect of the influence of psychology is similar to iatrogenic effects in medicine, disorders or problems *caused* by the medical profession such as the adverse effects of excessive use of x-rays. Is it possible that there are similar unintended adverse byproducts of psychological research? Some critics believe that studies aimed at measuring psychological differences among groups, such as ethnic differences, sex differences, and age differences contribute to, if not directly create, undesirable stereotypes based often on methods and tests biased in favor of one group.

The present chapter will examine these issues concerning the impact of psychological science on society. A look at some of the views about the social responsibility of psychology will also be considered. The terms, experiment and experimenter, will be used in this chapter in a broader sense than usual to include less rigorous methods of research dealing with psychological aspects of large-scale social concerns by investigators with applied as well as theoretical goals.

IS AN OBJECTIVE SCIENCE OF PSYCHOLOGY POSSIBLE?

Values and the Choice of the Problem and Type of Explanation

How problems are defined or conceptualized may reflect different assumptions about the underlying causes. Although most major behaviors are probably caused by a combination of internal or dispositional aspects of the person and external or situational aspects of the environment, psychologists often tend to place the blame on the person or victim in cases where social problems exist. For example, we search for the "criminal personality" or attribute traits of laziness and lack of motivation to welfare recipients in trying to account for the origins of such problems.

Caplan and Nelson (1973) examined a number of studies on social problems and categorized the types of interpretations made. In research on blacks, the causes of these problems were predominately seen as stemming from some personal or group membership features rather than from the social system. They noted that the *Psychological Ab-*

stracts, the major indexing journal which publishes summaries of all important psychological research, does not even include social-system variables such as concentration of wealth, unequal educational opportunity, or unequal justice in relation to the psychological variables of interest. Most entries involving social problems are classified in terms of behavior disorders at the individual level.

Caplan and Nelson raised the question of how social problems are identified—why do we turn to a study of the poor, but ignore the rich, in searching for the causes of poverty? Why is the use of marijuana by our youth viewed as a drug problem while governmental involvement in the use of drugs for minimal brain dysfunction is not?

Although the study of social problems may be well intentioned, the emphasis on viewing the causes of the problems of the poor, the minorities, the handicapped, the aged, and so forth, has served several latent functions, according to Caplan and Nelson. First, its conception frees the government and society from blame and secondly, if they provide help, they can be praised for being humane—a sort of "reverse Catch 22." Third, it favors the use of person-change rather than system-change solutions. Fourth, the system is strengthened by the loyalty to it from all those who are employed to treat problems of the individuals. Finally, person-blame accounts are needed to bolster the self-worth of the middle class so they can feel good that they "made it on their own," adding to the apathy toward and neglect of those who did not "make it on their own."

The position of Caplan and Nelson questions the objective nature of psychology as a social science and draws attention to the strong influence of the values of the status quo. They imply that psychologists may just be servants of the establishment if they accept the traditional definitions of social problems which ignore political considerations.

Sampson (1977) has also warned that the values of social scientists can determine the kinds of problems they identify and the types of formulations they devise. The American ideal has been to emphasize the individual while downplaying the interdependence among individuals within a system or group. He examined influential concepts such as Sandra Bem's (1974) androgeny, Kohlberg's (1963) stages of moral development, and the prevailing views of mental health such as the emphasis on self-actualization and autonomy as examples of self-contained individualism.

Bem (1975) has championed the virtues of the androgynous person who presumably contains the best features or traits of both sexes and is unlike either the traditionally-defined male or female in our society. She has devised situational tests and reported that androgynous persons are more flexible in that they can deal with cross-sexed situations better than traditional sex-typed persons. Thus, when a male is required to be nurturant, it is the androgynous rather than the sex-typed male who is more able, and when a female is called on to be independent and resist group pressure to conform, the androgynous female rather than the sex-typed female succeeds.

Sampson maintained that this conception emphasizes individual self-containment. While we disagree with his interpretation that an androgynous person is "self-contained," there is merit to his argument that androgyny, or any other sex role for that matter, is not universal but rather a reflection of arbitrary conventions that vary across societies. As Favreau (1977) observed, the masculine sex role has traditionally been dominant in our society and the nature of psychological research on sex differences has been affected by that bias. For example, she concluded that research reviews of sex differences generally imply that areas where males are superior to females are complex and important whereas those where females are superior are relatively simple and unimportant.

Sampson criticizes the universal validity of Kohlberg's (1963) theory of moral development in which persons first judge right and wrong in terms of the social conventions they are taught and the consequences of their actions before they can achieve the highest stages of morality which transcend law and order and deal with ultimate or universal truths. Not everyone, however, is assumed to advance to these ideal stages. Sampson viewed this theory as another that might apply to our society which values individualism, but he did not feel it should be presented as universally valid.

Sampson's argument that our concepts are affected by our values can be seen in his *own* position, he feels that self-contained individualism, which may have once been desirable, now leads to destructive tendencies. Following Riegel's (1976) concept of dialectical processes which has its immediate philosophical roots in the views of Hegel, Sampson argued that individual freedom has become excessive and that its opposing force, interdependence, is needed to counteract it in order to preserve democracy.

He offered an analogy with the role of bureaucracy which he regarded as a valid force for freedom in the middle ages since it helped free individuals from restraining social forces; however, today he feels it no longer serves that purpose and acts instead to stifle democracy. In a similar manner, Sampson criticized concepts such as androgyny and Kohlberg's view of moral growth as views that overemphasized the need for the individual to transcend dependence on society and cultural background.

Whether one accepts the particulars of Sampson's argument, several general implications have also been noted by others. First, as times change, validity and usefulness of previous concepts and principles may also change. Gergen (1973) has written extensively on this issue, which we will consider in more detail in the next chapter. Secondly, the behavior of individuals depends to varying degrees on factors outside the control of individuals such as social norms and values. As we will also see in the next chapter, the dominant approach in psychology has generally failed to fully recognize this important fact (Pepitone, 1976). Thirdly, and most important in the present discussion, the values of the investigator or theorist affects the kinds of interpretations and evaluations made, as Caplan and Nelson (1973) and Sampson (1977) have argued. Sampson's advocacy of interdependence is precisely such a case of a value-laden view going far beyond a description of the interdependent nature of the determinants of behavior.

Kelman (1968) correctly pointed out the impossibility of excluding the operation of values of investigators in the research process. The opposing view that scientists can be strictly objective, however laudable, is a form of self-deception, since as Kelman observed (1968, p. 72), "Value preferences are inevitably built into the assumptions of the research design, which determine the questions that are to be asked, the events that are to be observed, the variables that are to be assessed, the categories in terms of which the data are to be organized."

The influence of our values, however, does not mean that the research can not be conducted objectively insofar as the methods are reliable, explicit, and replicable. When research is undertaken to reduce juvenile delinquency, to increase worker satisfaction, or to facilitate intergroup harmony, for example, certain values are implicitly guiding these choices.

What is necessary since we cannot avoid the intrusion of our values, according to Kelman, is awareness of these factors and the deliberate analysis of their effects on our research and theories. In fact, he argued that provided we are aware of these influences of values, there can be some advantages insofar as heightened motivation and insight on the part of the investigator. New or alternative research methods that do not assume a completely impersonal relationship between investigator and the individuals or groups under study may be required and accepted.

Can and Should Psychology Be Used to Improve Society?

The cry for relevance of the 1960s was heeded by many psycholgists who turned more effort toward the application of research to practical social problems such as the reduction of crime and delinquency, control of the birth rate, reduction of racism and sexism, and the development of a psychologically-healthier environment. Research aimed at the evaluation of large-scale social programs in the areas of education, work productivity, and mental health was undertaken. The objective methods of science were employed to hopefully provide a firm empirical basis for social policies and legislation by decision makers.

Advocating the improvement of society is clearly virtuous, just as advocating motherhood used to be. But values change over time and differ among various segments of the society as to which specific changes are "good for society." There may be agreement on goals but discord over the appropriate means. If poverty is undesirable, what is the "best" program or policy for eliminating it?

For example, concern over the growing size of world population has prompted researchers to seek ways to discourage large families, by such means as providing economic disincentives for children and by persuasive programs showing the undesirable aspects of having too many children. However, this goal ignored the perceptions of some members of minority groups and underpopulated nations that in order to gain more power, they felt they needed an increase in *their* population. As Buckout (1972) reported, the plans of many minority groups regarding family size are determined by other considerations such as traditions favoring large families rather than the threat of world overpopulation.

The increased recognition of biases against women has led to a major revolution in conceptions about sex roles. The attitudes toward working women, with or without families, has become more accepting. Psychological studies showing the negative attitudes of women as well as of men toward the stereotypical traditional female role (e.g. Broverman, Vogel, Broverman, Clarkson, & Rosenkrantz, 1972) have been used to support the social changes that are redefining sex roles and opportunities.

Without meaning to imply that these changes are not desirable for large segments of the population, it must be recognized that the total impact of changing sex roles extends far beyond the lives of women. We do not as yet know how this social revolution will affect the lives of men and children, but it should be apparent that changes in one part of the family hold implications for other parts. As more women with children go to work full-time, the upbringing of children depends more on alternative agents such as fathers, day-care centers, grandparents, or other relatives.

The point of this discussion is that it is too soon to know all of the effects of these changes. In all likelihood, there may be some positive as well as some negative consequences, either in the short run, long run, or both. The opponents of legislation, such as the Equal Rights Amendment which improves the condition of women fear that the home or the children will suffer. But there are also sound arguments to suggest just the opposite will occur. Future research will hopefully provide the answers. The important point to note is the complexity of the issue and the crucial role values play in determining acceptable courses of action. The use of psychological research to either support or oppose changing sex roles clearly reflects the operation of personal values and preferences rather than a purely objective stance by investigators.

DO PARTICIPANTS UNDERGO UNINTENDED NEGATIVE EFFECTS OF RESEARCH?

Victimizing Participants with Their Own Data

Knowledge is neutral in one sense, as many researchers feel that their studies are conducted "for curiosity's sake." But knowledge can also provide power to those who have it to use for good or evil purposes. One situation that raises ethical problems of the legitimate use of research is the very relationship between the participants and the investigator and/or sponsors.

Kelman (1972) pointed out the substantial amount of power the experimenter holds over the subject in social research since the data provided by the latter may be used against the subject at some time. A good example would be studies of black intelligence which have led to the controversial interpretations made by Jensen (1969) based on comparisons of scores made by whites and blacks. Although the findings have been challenged on a variety of grounds including the cultural bias of the tests, the fact remains that the evidence has been used to conclude that blacks are innately less intelligent. This "finding" has been accepted as proven by some who use it to justify various social policies and programs that are not in the best interests of blacks. It may also have the unfortunate potential of being a self-fulfilling prophecy for some blacks by creating negative expectations and lowered motivations.

Kelman (1972) extended his discussion to consider the implications of the preceding example. Does it mean that any study of a disadvantaged group—regardless of who sponsored or conducted it—should be prevented because it may be biased and because its findings may have adverse effects on the group under study? Kelman called for a more moderate position, noting that the probability of negative effects may not be unduly great, and that in some cases positive effects may develop. He suggested that it is also important to consider mechanisms for counteracting such biases and misinterpretations of findings rather than to make a wholesale indictment of social research. In Kelman's view, not only is it unreasonable to assume a monolithic conspiracy on the part of social scientists with their establishment sponsors, but one should not assume that all of the research findings work to the detriment of those studied. He argued in the instance of race relations that social science had done much to counteract some of the racist stereotypes held against blacks.

At the same time he recognized the charge that the power to define and sponsor research is unevenly distributed, with the disadvantaged groups having little or no control of the planning of research or access to the information obtained when they are the targets of investigations. One of the solutions proposed by Kelman to alleviate this problem is what he called "democratization of the research community." All segments of the population, according to this concept, should have the opportunity and capacity to do research and, furthermore, all segments of the population should participate in the role of subjects in research. The viewpoints of disadvantaged groups would be represented during all aspects of research, thereby reducing the chances that findings would provide advantages to some groups at the expense of others. Finally, democratization would ensure that all segments have equal access to data they provided. Furthermore, it should be expressed in a language the nonscientist could comprehend.

An example of a situation where a shift in the balance between the researcher and the group under study has been called for is the questioning of the validity of research obtained by white investigators in the black community (Clark, 1973). The same type of scrutiny may easily be extended to other situations where the advantaged group member is analyzing the problems of the disadvantaged groups. Clark suggested that the perspectives of black researchers may differ from those of white investigators in the kinds of issues considered relevant. Whereas white researchers might look for the causes of deviance, criminality, and aggression among the black population, they may lack the concerns blacks may have about issues like exploitation, racism, colonialism, and paternalism.

Brazziel (1973) expressed concern that the increasing numbers of investigators swarming to study the black community may actually become part of the problem itself. He charged that some of these investigators publish findings that put blacks in a negative light but fail to adequately include a consideration of how racism has contributed to such differences. He called for a number of steps to increase the participation of black laypersons and professionals in activities related to the funding and publication of research on blacks.

Gordon (1973) charged that while psychology had been unethical toward the black community, using it as a source of data to promote the research aspirations and careers of investigators and providing nothing in return to the participants as well as failing to promote and advocate the needs of the black community. He called for a black psychology that would be more action-oriented and committed to serving the real-life needs of the black community.

It should be readily apparent from this brief sampling of the reactions of some psychologists that the feeling is strong that the approaches, concepts, and methods of white psychologists are unsuitable for the needs of blacks. One should note, however, that some of the criticisms of psychology are not limited to the relationship of white researchers to minority communities but even of their ties to white communities as well.

Will the long-run solution call for as many "psychologies" as there are different vested interests? A chicano psychology? An Asian-American psychology? An American Indian psychology? A male psychology? A female psychology? A gay psychology? And will each of these subdisciplines be valid only if they are formulated by members of their own group because outsiders are unable or unwilling to understand what it means to be a member of each group of insiders?

This prospect of an endless proliferation of different psychologies is discouraging in one sense. If only group members can develop the valid picture of the psychology of that group, will a self-serving tendency to look only at the good features and ignore the weak ones develop? Despite this reservation, there is some advantage to having insiders become active in studying themselves, especially if no one else is providing a psychology meaningful to them. How can an older black female relate to a psychology based on white middle class values validated with mostly white middle-class college students?

Rival formulations of psychology may be confusing, but many may be more accurate than only one. Several perspectives also make more apparent how the biases and values of each group affect the psychology they formulate, whereas with only one point of view, it is easy to erroneously conclude that it was free from cultural prejudices.

Value Differences and the Acceptance of Research Findings

A different type of example also involving the suggestion that some types of views and evidence can be dangerous or undesirable deals with the effects of early experience on development. The dominant perspective in developmental psychology (Bell, 1968) has been that the parents, especially the mother, exert influence on the child's characteristics by shaping its environment. This conception implies that whenever child behavior problems arise, researchers tend to look for the parents' shortcomings. Either they were too permissive, too strict, or too inconsistent, depending somewhat on the historical era in which the study was done (Bronfrenbrenner, 1961).

Recently, however, influential researchers such as Jerome Kagan (1978) and Arlene Skolnick (1978) have written accounts of their research indicating that children are surprisingly resilient and adaptable. Despite impoverished and hostile environments, many children still survive to become "normal" individuals. Perhaps parents have worried too much about how they can affect the development of their children.

Since these authorities published their provocative views in widely read popular magazines, their views undoubtedly impacted on parent behavior to some degree. Research findings do not merely reflect the nature of existing causes of behavior but may also determine future behavior. The views of a respected science writer, Albert Rosenfeld, appeared in the influential magazine, *Saturday Review* (April 1, 1978). He expressed the concern that some parents might use the positions held by Kagan and Skolnick to rationalize child neglect. He defended these psychologists for their personal concern and involvement in promoting the welfare of children but questioned the wisdom of their conclusions, charging that they performed a disservice by prematurely publishing what were tentative conclusions—a charge more usually directed at journalists.

Rosenfeld then proceeded to cite the work of other investigators that suggested the traditional view that parents can profoundly affect the development of their children, especially in early years, which is quite valid. The issue here is not which of the two opposing views is more correct, but the social impact and influence of scientific findings. *If* it is true that Rosenfeld's assumption that the views of Kagan, Skolnick, and others will adversely affect some children, what is the social responsibility of investigators with such views? Should they, as Rosenfeld suggested, withhold their findings and conclusions? On the other hand, these views hold some benefits for at least some other children and their parents who are overly anxious and tend to "overparent"?

In this complex issue, our own values and biases may affect our reactions to research in ways that may stifle objectivity. Certainly the determinants of child development are enormously complicated, and no single theory can account for all of the factors. It is quite likely that both theories regarding the effects of parenting could be valid, although for a different set of circumstances in each case. If we allow or accept only those views that support our preconceptions and personal views, we may be limiting our understanding of the total picture. Research from different perspectives rather than just a narrow point of view will stimulate healthy cross-examination of rival theories and generate further research, which will hopefully provide a more complete and valid analysis.

Threats from Loss of Confidentiality and Anonymity

The ethical obligations of the experimenter do not end after the debriefing and dismissal of subjects. The protection of the anonymity of the subjects and the confidentiality of their data must be maintained, especially if the information might prove harmful to their interests if they fall into the wrong hands. Thus, when personality or intelligence tests scores are part of the data collected or if the investigation deals with behaviors such as sexual activity, drug use, antisocial tendencies, and so on, care must be taken to insure that the identities of the individuals are protected. Use of a code system to identify data without threatening anonymity may be necessary.

The American Psychological Association Ethics Code also recommends that participants be provided with explanations of the procedures to be used to protect confidentiality at the time informed consent is obtained, if it appears that others may obtain access to the data. It also notes the problems that arise when data is published identifying the group to which individuals belong such as race or sex, if it presented them in a negative light. Another dilemma that may confront the investigator is when certain information is obtained, sometimes by accident, that perhaps *should* be divulged in order to protect either the participants or others. Thus, is the investigator correct in maintaining confidentiality if it is learned that a participant has homicidal or suicidal intentions?

Even when the investigator intends to maintain confidentiality, records may be subpoenaed by court order if the data provides information about illegal activities (Nejelski, 1976). Subjects should be informed of this possibility before they participate. Methods of recording data that prevent any identification of individuals might also be used.

Kelman (1977) pointed out the special problems of ensuring anonymity when a special group or entire organization is studied and the identity of the group is hard to disguise even if its name is changed or deleted. This type of problem exists when ethnic minorities are compared with the majority population, especially in view of the possibility that the minorities appear in a negative light due to biased measurement tools and procedures.

Kelman feels certain safeguards can be developed that will enable these important studies to be conducted. First, group comparison studies should be done only if it appears likely that the obtained data will be valid and uncontaminated by methodological biases. In addition, when these groups are approached for their consent to participate, they should be fully informed about the purpose of the study, how the results will be disseminated, and the nature of the possible consequences. Findings should be reported accurately, after consultation with representatives of the groups, to ensure fairness.

One problem with this solution is that data, once published, is no longer under the control of the original investigators or the participants. Neither of these groups can really foresee all of the possible adverse consequences of the research. A different type of criticism is that pressure groups will politicize research even further by allowing the conduct and publication of research that presents them only in the best possible perspective. Psychology would lose whatever claims it has to objectivity and become a force for promoting and propagandizing of special interests. Perhaps an objective study of social problems is really a delusion!

Delayed Adverse Effects on Participants

A subtle problem for which investigators may feel some sense of responsibility is what happens to the participants after they have provided the data and the researcher discontinues the project. Often in longitudinal studies where participants are observed repeatedly over numerous occasions or in quasi-therapeutic settings, for example, the participants may develop positive interpersonal ties and attachments with members of the research team. For most participants, this will not be problematic, but in some cases—such as with groups of children or elderly populations—a greater dependence on these social ties may develop.

A study by Schulz and Hanusa (1978) vividly illustrates the kinds of problems that can occur after the experiment is concluded. First, we need to briefly summarize an earlier study (Schulz, 1976) with a group of institutionalized elderly subjects that tested the hypothesis that lack of control was a factor contributing to the adverse psychological adjustment to old age. This research involved the use of college students who visited regularly with one group of patients whereas other groups of patients received either no visitors or unpredictable visitations. Improvements in outlook and psychological reactions occurred for the group that received the regular visits.

A followup study two years later by Schulz and Hanusa (1978) examined the durability of these improvements. Ratings made by observers who did not know the nature of the original variations in treatment revealed that the benefits had not only vanished but that the originally-improved group was now actually slightly *inferior* to the control groups. This surprising finding would not have been discovered if Hanusa and Schulz had not bothered to conduct the follow-up. It is possible that these after-effects of the study developed from the sense of loss experienced by the patients when the experiment was completed, although Schulz and Hanusa did not believe it was a major factor. In any case, this example shows the ethical necessity, let alone the methodological value, of conducting follow-up studies to assess long-term or delayed effects of social interventions.

It should be noted that the patients had been informed at the outset of the project that the visiting students would have to leave when summer vacation began. Certainly, this procedure was a wise one and may have prevented some potential problems that might have arisen after the study was over.

MISUNDERSTANDINGS BETWEEN PROFESSIONALS AND THE PUBLIC

Problems arise whenever researchers overgeneralize their own findings or those of others or fail to clearly indicate the limitations of their study. Even if the original investigators are careful to qualify their findings, other researchers may read their reports but fail to remember the details. The net result is that a study showing, for example, that 12-year-old white middle-class males engage in more fighting than females with the same background may be encoded or remembered as "males are more aggressive than females." This sweeping overgeneralization ignores a number of other factors that might alter the nature of the results—factors such as social class, ethnicity, the kind of aggression, the type of test situation, and so forth.

The public may misinterpret popular and journalistic accounts of the more interesting or provocative findings. Methodological issues and technical terms will not be fully understood by the average layperson, who is even more likely than the professional reader to form overly-simplistic conclusions about the nature and meaning of a set of findings.

Does the investigator have any obligation or responsibility to try to anticipate the types of misconceptions professionals as well as members of the public might form so that corrective information can be provided? The fact that many social-science studies are misunderstood by the public and can lead to weakened acceptance and support of research is well illustrated by the publicity generated by Senator William Proxmire's Golden Fleece Awards (Shaffer, 1977), which he gives to studies funded by government grants that he thinks are a waste of taxpayer monies. The issue is not whether or not his judgment is valid, for he has erred seriously on a number of occasions, but how researchers can communicate accurately so that legislators and laypersons do not misunderstand about the value of projects.

Attempts should be made to educate the public that the laws formulated by psychologists are actuarial in nature, much like life-insurance company norms of life expectancy. General laws reflect group averages but are inadequate for the prediction of the behavior of individuals. Even the general laws are usually limited in that they deal with relatively simple phenomena where only one or two variables are studied at a given time. More complex situations involving multiple determinants are less readily explained by simple general principles.

It is unrealistic to expect the public to be interested or, in some cases, able to learn enough about the nature of the research process and its limitations. Many laypersons do not fully understand that no one study on any important behavior can consider all of the factors that may affect it. Many researchers, let alone members of the public, do not recognize that individual differences exist for many processes. That many conclusions from experiments are probabilistic and based on group averages rather than certainties that apply to all individuals is another shortcoming of the public conception of research.

While investigators can not educate the public completely about the methods of science, they can take greater strides in this direction which may help reduce misconceptions about findings. Perhaps a more effective, less abstract method is to confront laypersons with alternative interpretations of a given study whenever they exist so they can appreciate the uncertainty of the conclusions. In cases where conflicting evidence exists, it is useful to ensure that all positions are presented along with the supporting evidence for each side, much as a courtroom case is presented to a jury.

Freedom of individual investigators to choose the problems they wish to study, to present their findings and conclusions, and to critically discuss the work of others is important to preserve. The suppression of unpopular theories and controversial findings by fiat is incompatible with the spirit of scientific investigation. Just as psychologists judge competing evidence and theories on their scientific merit, it may be more sound to present rival findings and views openly and fairly before the public.

Research can not tell us what *should* be done in a given situation. These types of social-policy decisions are vested in the hands of politicians and other bases of social power and control. Such decisions may include consideration of psychological research findings but are not generally limited to this source of information. Other factors such as tradition, public opinion, economic considerations, and sometimes plain old-fashioned prejudices, often carry more weight than the findings and pronouncements of social scientists. What psychology can do is provide as much evidence as possible about all possible alternatives and the costs and benefits of each policy of action. The dominant values of society, along with economic and political considerations, will determine the practical decisions in the final analysis.

No amount of research showing that one type of reading program is best, that busing improves interracial harmony, that a particular therapy works best for alcoholics, or that crowded cities foster crime, mental illness, and stress will be sufficient to outweigh the prevailing values of a society in setting social policies in these areas. Thus, if education is not considered important, if interracial harmony is of low priority, if alcoholics are regarded as deserving of their own fate, or if crowded cities are accepted as inevitable, the research will have little impact on social policy. And, if hearts and minds of decision makers want to follow policies suggested by research findings, but the policies are economically or politically unfeasible, they will again fail to influence social policies. The role of the researcher on issues affecting society is that of advisor, not decision maker.

SUMMARY

The science of psychology, according to some should be objective and impartial in its quest for knowledge about psychological processes underlying behavior. However, others maintain that such an idealistic orientation is not possible or even desirable. They point out the role of values and political factors as influences on the choice of problems to be studied and the kind of explanations postulated in many areas of psychological research. Psychology, according to activists, should be used to improve society by the study of the causes and solutions for various socially relevant issues. Finally, it has been observed that some research may have unintended negative side effects, such as the creation or perpetuation of stereotypes and injustices.

Values held by the experimenter cannot be avoided entirely but awareness of this process can produce attempts to minimize its operation. Some balance may occur if researchers with different values undertake investigations of the same topic since opposing biases may offset each other by sensitizing us to the possible influence of these biases.

The enlistment of researchers holding a greater variety of values among researchers may also reduce the tendency for some groups, such as disadvantaged groups, from being unduly victimized by research conducted on them by individuals whose values conflict with their own. The democratization of the research enterprise should include not only the opportunity to conduct research but also involve equal access to the findings so that groups that may suffer from findings that put them in an unfavorable light have the opportunity to question and criticize the validity of these findings. There is the danger that groups conducting research on themselves may produce self-serving studies, but at least it will serve to counteract any more subtle biases underlying research done by "objective" investigators.

Another type of adverse effect of research might exist when the findings lead to implications regarded as undesirable. The researchers may not intentionally draw such implications themselves, but others may make such interpretations. Should the investigator who foresees such possible misuses of his or her findings suppress the results?

Other ethical issues facing the investigator involves protection of anonymity and confidentiality. Precautions must be taken when the dangers to participants are great if their identity is discovered or reported to others.

Some of the problems facing researchers are created by the lack of knowledge by the public about the nature of scientific method and theory. They may regard tentative generalizations as immutable truths and fail to learn or realize that for many phenomena, conflicting research evidence exists. Although it would not be feasible for researchers to try to educate the public about the nature of science, the experimenter has some social responsibility to try to correct or prevent misconceptions and erroneous interpretations of research findings. Exposure of the public to differing theories and evidence where such disagreement exists may help the public achieve a healthy attitude of critical skepticism. The application and utilization of research findings ultimately depends on persons in positions of power to formulate social policy who may be influenced partly by psychological research but also by other considerations such as economic and political concerns. In the final analysis, the values of those in power rather than the findings of psychological studies will play the major role in the extent to which research affects social action. The responsibility of the investigator is not that of decision maker, but rather one of providing the most valid evidence possible as a means of influencing those who do make social-policy decisions.

REFERENCES

Bell, R. Q. A reinterpretation of direction of effects in studies of socialization. *Psychological Review*, 1968, *75*, 81-95.

Bem, S. L. The measurement of psychological androgyny. *Journal of Clinical and Consulting Psychology*, 1974, *42*, 155-162.

Bem, S. L. Sex-role adaptability: One consequence of psychological androgyny. *Journal of Personality and Social Psychology*, 1975, *31*, 634-643.

Brazziel, W. F. White research in black communities: When solutions become part of the problem. *Journal of Social Issues*, 1973, *29*, 41-44.

Bronfrenbrenner, U. The changing American child: A speculative analysis. *Merrill-Palmer Quarterly*, 1961, 7, 73-84.

Broverman, I. K., Vogel, S. R., Broverman, D. M., Clarkson, F. E., and Rosenkrantz, P. S. Sex role stereotypes: A current appraisal. *Journal of Social Issues*, 1972, *28*, 59-78.

Buckout, R. Toward a two-child norm: Changing family planning attitudes. *American Psychologist*, 1972, *27*, 16-26.

Caplan, N., and Nelson, S. D. On being useful: The nature and consequences of psychological research on social problems. *American Psychologist*, 1973, *28*, 199-211.

Clark, C. X. The role of the white researcher in black society: A futuristic look. *Journal of Social Issues*, 1973, *29*, 109-118.

Favreau, O. Sex bias in psychological research. *Canadian Psychological Review*, 1977, *18*, 56-65.

Gergen, K. J. Social psychology as history. *Journal of Personality and Social Psychology*, 1973, *26*, 309-320.

Gordon, T. Notes on white and black psychology. *Journal of Social Issues*, 1973, *29*, 87-96.

Jensen, A. R. How much can we boost I.Q. and scholastic achievement? *Harvard Educational Review*, 1969, *39*, 1-123.

Kagan, J. The baby's elastic mind. *Human Nature*, 1978, *1*, *No. 1*, 66-73.

Kelman, H. C. *A Time to Speak*. San Francisco: Jossey-Bass, 1968.

Kelman, H. C. The rights of the subject in social research: An analysis in terms of relative legitimacy. *American Psychologist*, 1972, *27*, 989-1016.

Kelman, H. C. Privacy and research with human beings. *Journal of Social Issues*, 1977, *33*, *3*, 169-195.

Kohlberg, L. The development of children's orientations toward a moral order: 1. Sequence in the development of moral thought. *Vita Humana*, 1963, *6*, 11-33.

Nejelski, P. A. *Social research in conflict with law and ethics*. Cambridge, Mass.: Ballinger, 1976.

Pepitone, A. Toward a normative and comparative biocultural social psychology. *Journal of Personality and Social Psychology*, 1976, *34*, 641-653.

Riegel, K. The dialectics of human development. *American Psychologist*, 1976, *31*, 689-700.

Rosenfeld, A. The "elastic mind" movement: Rationalizing child neglect? *Saturday Review*, Apr 1, 1978, 26-28.

Sampson, E. E. Psychology and the American ideal. *Journal of Personality and Social Psychology*, 1977, *35*, 767-782.

Schulz, R. The effects of control and predictability on the psychological and physical well-being of the institutionalized aged. *Journal of Personality and Social Psychology*, 1976, *33*, 563-573.

Schulz, R. and Hanusa, B. H. Long-term effects of control and predictability-enhancing interventions: Findings and ethical issues. *Journal of Personality and Social Psychology*, 1978, *36*, 1194-1201.

Shaffer, L. S. The golden fleece: Anti-intellectualism and social science. *American Psychologist*, 1977, *32*, 814-823.

Silverman, I. Why social psychology fails. *Canadian Psychological Review*, 1977, *18*, 353-358.

Skolnick, A. The myth of the vulnerable child. *Psychology Today*, 1978, *11*, *No. 2*, 56, 58, 60, 65.

CHAPTER 18

Future Prospects: What Are Our Limits?

Chapter at a Glance

The belief that psychological science, given enough time and effort, will develop to the point that it can identify a set of general laws underlying human behavior, has been seriously called into question in recent years by increasing numbers of psychologists. Aside from the more specific problems of experimenter bias, reactivity, methodological problems, ethical issues, and the question of generalizability of findings, the ultimate question of the validity or appropriateness of the experimental method itself as a paradigm for investigating important aspects of human behavior has also been raised.

Some of the basic underlying aspects of the conceptual approach followed by experimentalists have also been criticized as being inadequate to deal with the complexities of human behavior. The failure to recognize the role of social norms and values as determinants of behavior has led to, in the opinion of some critics, an overemphasis on the study of the behavior of individuals. Another issue receiving much attention has been whether it is truly possible to formulate scientific laws that can retain validity over extended periods of time.

In this chapter we will examine these criticisms of the experimental method and approach in more detail. While there are no clearcut or easy solutions to this ultimate dilemma facing the experimenter, a discussion of views about the role of experimentation in the research enterprise will be presented in the light of the limitations of the experimental method which have been raised throughout this book.

SHORTCOMINGS OF THE EXPERIMENTAL METHOD

Too Much Control by the Experimenter?

The experiment is a rigorous method stressing control and manipulation of variables. In terms of the social-psychological relationship between the experimenter and the subject, the experiment also involves a high degree of control and manipulation. It is, however, a unidirectional influence for the most part, according to some observers such as Argyris (1968). In everyday life situations where one party holds such power over another, there may be reactance and resentment, although these feelings may be nicely hidden. Reactance refers to a stubborn and sometimes defiant attitude resulting from excessive control (Brehm, 1966). Other reactions typically found in this type of situation include anxiety, evaluation apprehension, suspicion, and distrust by persons who feel they are being manipulated or coerced.

Argyris (1975) has questioned the usefulness of this paradigm for psychological investigation. He suggested that when some social psychological phenomena involving trust and cooperation are studied with this technique, they may paradoxically yield behavior that differs from what occurs in real-life situations precisely because of these adverse consequences of the method of study. He speculated about the possibility of the development of an alternative approach, a Model 2 in his terms, which would be more open and collaborative and based on mutual trust and consent between the experimenter and the subject.

It is possible, however, that the other situations in real life that *do* involve controlled, interpersonal relationships and deceptions—such as some forms of persuasion, salesmanship, and politics—may be understood using the existing experimental paradigm where the experimenter unilaterally controls the situation. In any event, Argyris also held that its findings may aid in maintaining the status quo of manipulation, distrust, and suspicion in interpersonal relations. Argyris (1975) argued that a new paradigm based on openness and collaboration might also exert influence toward changing social reality rather than merely describing the existing situation.

Demonstrations of the Obvious?

A number of critics have insisted that experiments are not actually designed to test hypotheses but represent arranged demonstrations of obvious or trivial truths. McGuire (1973, p. 449) maintained that "what the experiment tests is not whether the hypothesis is true, but rather whether the experimenter is a sufficiently ingenious stage manager to produce in the laboratory conditions which demonstrate that an obviously true hypothesis is correct." Harré and Secord (1972) arrived at a similar conclusion based on the observation that many experiments simplify complex processes to such an extent in designing their studies that the results can only be confirmatory. Finally, in the words of Henri Tajfel (1972, p. 106–107), " . . . we start with a proposition culled from day-to-day intuitions and horsesense about, for example, the role played by the need for approval in determining conformity in small groups. We then devise complex experimental and statistical techniques to arrange and interpret an appropriate example, and we are able to show in the end that the proposition known to be true was indeed true."

While many experiments can be found that avoid these criticisms, it is also true that numerous studies are guilty as charged. Trivial or self-evident effects are examined with accuracy to the nearest second decimal point. If pilot studies fail to show significant differences, the determined experimenter can always find ways of revising the experimental design, changing the dependent variables, rewording the instructions, or increasing the sample size so as to obtain results that exceed the magical 5 per cent level of occurrence due to chance.

Neglect of Interacting Variables

The inability to find many general laws that transcend individual and situational differences can be traced to a large extent to the complex interactions between these factors and the independent variables or stimuli controlled by the experimenter. Cronbach (1957, 1975) has repeatedly stated the prime importance of examining interactions between individual difference factors and independent variables. In our zeal to find general laws that will hold for all persons, situations, and times, we combine data over variations on these latter factors to obtain group averages. When interactions exist, they obscure any effects of the independent variable so that small or no overall group differences are noted, leading to the erroneous conclusion sometimes that there is no effect. In actuality, these outcomes may just be cases of two opposite effects cancelling each other out.

The experimental paradigm typically used is the factorial or multifactor design with several, usually two or three, independent variables, each with several levels so that the effects of all possible combinations of these conditions can be examined. This paradigm is inadequate to deal with the complexities created by the operation of numerous interacting factors. No one study can deal with more than a handful of independent variables, so in order to assess the effects of other factors, additional factorial experiments are needed. The existence of interactions among variables, however, means that the observed effects of one variable in one study may conflict with the findings when it is studied in combination with a different set of factors in another experiment.

The consequence can be chaotic, with tremendous overload of information due to these complexities. Thorngate (1976, p. 134) noted that current social psychological research "appears to be characterized by a mad rush to explore every conceivable combination of two, three, and four independent, correlational, and dependent variables." He envisioned future studies coming forth such as, "The effect of authoritarianism, race, sex, and room size upon attributions of causality following a risky shift." Of course, we might add, the findings for first borns may differ from those for later borns, but that will take at least one other study.

As Cronbach (1975) observed, it is not that behavior is not lawfully determined, but that there are too many interacting variables to allow detection of the effects of factors unless they are of great magnitude. These interactions pose a strong threat to the dominant approach in experiments involving the examination of the influence of only one or a few variables at a time. However, one cannot easily assess the nature of interacting influences because they represent what Cronbach called "a hall of mirrors that extends to infinity."

Cronbach argued for a reversal of priorities to deal with this problem, suggesting that instead of looking for general laws first, we should focus on identifying limiting conditions of various outcomes, that is, exceptions to laws. In essence, this strategy involves testing findings for conditions that will show where they lack validity or generalizability due to the operation of possible interacting factors.

Neglect of Individual Differences

Experimental designs typically ignore individual differences and focus on differences between groups that receive variations in treatment. But as Triandis (1976, p. 226) maintained, "This is a very poor way to construct *social* psychology. We need theories that reflect differences in personality, ability, and cultural experiences." To which we might add, . . . and on other dimensions such as age, sex, socioeconomic level, religion, political persuasion, health, and on and on.

In her important book on individuality, Leona Tyler, (1978, p. 234) observed, "No matter how carefully we equate groups of subjects for age, sex, social class, education, and other characteristics, each of them has unique ways of handling situations, unique concepts, strategies, and values, and these are partial determinants of the behavior being studied. Psychologists must learn to look separately at what each individual does and says and to rest their conclusions and generalizations not just on group averages but on their own creative syntheses of what the individual responses show."

Tyler also distinguished between what she termed vertical and horizontal differences among individuals. The tradition in psychology starting with the mental tests and measurement concerns of the early 1900s could be described as vertical in that it aimed at grading people along a quantitative dimension, such as amount of intelligence. The vertical approach was useful for applied problems such as job selection and placement; it is a competitive enterprise in which everyone is pitted against one another for advancement.

In contrast to these concerns, Tyler called for a horizontal approach which considers the complementariness of different people in relation to each other by looking at all of the skills and abilities that go into making each person a unique individual. Thus everyone is not measured on the same criteria.

Short-term Duration of Effects

Despite the substantial amount of time, effort, and resources devoted to performing the typical experiment—whether conducted in the laboratory or in field settings—the kinds of processes and behaviors studied are usually of very brief duration. Laboratory studies, whether they deal with cognitive processes, conformity, attitude change, aggression, or cooperation, usually last from about 20 minutes to an hour. Even college students have limits to their patience and time for serving as subjects. In natural settings where subjects are often unwitting participants, it is possible to study a process for a more extended period, but it is still common for field experiments to entail relatively brief time periods. After all, the experimenter also has other duties to perform.

As Silverman (1977) noted, this restriction to short-term studies limits us to situations that may have low impact or significance to the subjects. The findings may be trivial since we may not be measuring behavior that reflects what occurs under longer time periods. Thus, do the short-term studies of the effects of viewing violence in the media provide evidence that accurately shows how chronic exposure to these materials affects people? Silverman expressed doubts just as he suggested that psychologists conducting laboratory experiments on the frustration-aggression hypothesis probably did not really think the behavior observed in these short-term studies "perservered beyond the moment of the experiment itself or had any cumulative effects on our subjects' general aggressive tendencies."

Limited Generalizability of Results

An often made indictment of experiments is that the results of one experiment have little or no generalizability to other experiments with other subject populations, tasks, dependent measures, and settings. In a literal sense this criticism is undoubtedly true. Just as the old adage goes that you can not step in the same river twice, it is a truism that you cannot repeat the same experiment or obtain the same results.

As Epstein (1980) has observed, a lack of prestige is associated with replications in which prior experiments are merely repeated since they do not involve much creativity. And, when two or more experiments on the same topic are compared, it is not unusual for them to conflict in their findings. This lack of generalizability or external validity is due in part to the fact that any two studies dealing with the same variables on the same topic may still differ in the setting, dependent measures, or types of tasks used and so forth. However, these factors are often overlooked as determinants of the low replicability of findings because, as Epstein pointed out, researchers rarely set out to deliberately vary these factors. Instead, they assume that one task or a given dependent variable is equivalent to another and that it is unnecessary to sample a variety of each. An ironic contrast is the practice used for subjects who are tested in experiments; in this case, it would be unthinkable for many psychologists to use only one or a few subjects since one might by chance end up with a biased sample. Epstein argued that just as we use a larger sample of subjects so that scores from extreme subjects can be offset by using a group average score, we should use aggregation of scores on other dimensions such as stimulus situations or settings, temporal occasions, and the measures of the dependent variable. By such an averaging procedure it is possible to cancel out incidental factors that differ over a group of experiments so that one can end up with more reliable and generalizable conclusions about the effects of our independent variables.

Epstein's analysis is well-founded but may prove quite difficult to implement or gain acceptance. Thus, an individual researcher might not be motivated to spend several years repeating the same experiment to demonstrate its reliability. What is more likely to happen is that the results of an experiment will be accepted as generalizable until evidence to the contrary is produced. Then further experiments will be done to add further fuel to the fires of controversy. A number of different researchers will choose up sides and get inspired to produce evidence to prove their views are correct. Psychologists, like other people, get ego-involved in their work! The net results of this collective research will eventually provide the aggregation of evidence called for by Epstein. It is then up to someone to synthesize all of the conflicting findings and distill the evidence to derive any stable and salient generalizations that might exist.

Thus, while generalizations from *individual* experiments may appear hopelessly weak at times, as a body of literature is built by a number of investigators it is potentially possible for more powerful generalizations to be discovered after sifting through a *group* of experiments dealing with the same phenomenon. Variables with reliable effects will show up more consistently while weaker variables will not show repeatable results over many experiments.

Low Generalizability Between Laboratory and Life

A somewhat different problem of generalizability concerns the question of the extent to which laboratory experiments can provide results generalizable to the real world. Since the laboratory experiment usually involves an artificial and oversimplified replica of some real-world counterpart, it is hardly surprising that generalizability is less than total. Yet, this very highly controlled nature of the experiment is at the same time its primary strength, since it enables us to draw sound conclusions about the effects of our independent variables. While we gain this analytical precision with the experimental method, we risk the loss of applicability of the results to real life analogs.

Another important characteristic of experiments with human subjects that may reduce lab–life generalizability is the reactive nature of the experimental situation. As we have already noted in earlier chapters, human subjects assume various roles in experiments, experimenters may unintentionally provide biasing cues, and the demand characteristics of experimental situations are quite different from those of naturalistic settings. All of these factors may jeopardize the generalizability of laboratory findings to the real world.

The overreliance on the use of college psychology students is not an inherent feature of the laboratory experiment but this practice may also restrict generalizability to other populations. Similar biases in the types of subjects preferred have even been found in field studies, so the problem is not unique. Thus, Dipboye and Flanagan (1979), after reviewing a large body of published research in the area of industrial and organizational psychology, concluded that in this area, " . . . field research can be described as having produced a psychology of self-report by male, professional, technical, and managerial personnel in productive-economic organizations" (p. 146).

One problem with discussions of generalizability, whether it be among different experimenters or between experiments in the laboratory and real-life counterparts, is that there is no clear notion of how much generalizability is enough. We all lament the presumably inadequate degree of generalizability; yet there is no objective and quantifiable measure of this relationship. Perhaps one reason for this lack is that a given laboratory experiment does not have only one real-life analog to which it may be compared, but potentially a very large number of them. The degree of generalizability of an experiment, then, is not a fixed value, but varies depending on which real-life situation it is evaluated against.

As the author (Jung, 1981) has observed elsewhere, the typical situation for questioning the generalizability between laboratory and life involves dubious evidence at best. A disparity is first noted between evidence from a laboratory experiment and evidence from a study in a real-life setting. Although the two studies may also differ in other factors other than the type of setting, the conclusion is asserted that the disparity is due entirely to the difference in settings. However, since the setting variable is confounded by the other simultaneously varying factors, no sound conclusions are possible.

Fortunately, this dilemma about assessing generalizability may not be as hopeless as it appears. If, instead of viewing the primary function of experiments as providing direct copies of real-life phenomena, we were to regard the experiment as a tool to test hypotheses about the effects of variables we think should be important, then there is less reason to despair. Under this approach, we would recognize that we need to test our theoretical assumptions and explanations of phenomena under rigorous and controlled circumstances. We would recognize that the experimental method, although it is artificial and can only examine a few variables at a time, can give us this precision but only at the possible price of reduced generalizability of any individual experiment to the real world.

However, when we combine and coordinate a series of interrelated experiments designed to test our theoretical formulations, we eventually achieve a better understanding of the real-life situation. We are then in a better position to make new predictions about the phenomenon due to this understanding. In the final analysis, then, the experiments are extremely useful but not in an immediate sense of direct correspondence of results of individual experiments. There is an indirect process instead so that the body of evidence gathered from a number of experiments that test our theories of the real-life situation is eventually useful.

CONCEPTUAL LIMITATIONS OF THE EXPERIMENTAL APPROACH

Overconcern with the Behavior of Individuals

Conceptual inadequacies of psychological theories and constructs that focus on the individual level of analysis have also been pointed out by Pepitone (1976) and Tajfel (1972). These analyses emphasized the need to examine social and cultural norms as important determinants and modifiers of individual behavior. The values and beliefs of a social or group unit must be considered if one is to understand and predict the behavior of individuals, even though we may still be interested in identifying the psychological processes that occur within each individual.

As an example, Pepitone discussed aggressive behavior by calling attention to the social norms or "rules" that govern this behavior. Men are expected not to be aggressive toward women, women are not expected to be aggressive toward either sex, adults are expected to refrain from aggression towards children, and so forth. Individuals may act aggressively and either be reinforced or punished for such behavior. It is possible to develop a set of principles about such behavior, based on learning theory. However, without considering the social context of the behavior and the customs, norms, and mores concerning aggression, the analysis would be incomplete. Prediction of real-life aggression would not be very accurate.

The importance of reciprocal influences among the components of a social system is also noted by Bandura (1974, 1978). Although much of his analysis of reciprocal determinism focuses on intraindividual relationships among various self-regulatory processes, Bandura also emphasized the applicability of the model to processes between individuals, groups, and organizations. Individual behavior cannot be viewed in isolation but must be analysed in terms of mutual influences on social units of an interacting system.

Unidirectional Model of Causation

McGuire (1973) as well as Bandura (1978), have criticized the tendency for our models and theories to be unidirectional, looking only at how A causes B, and suggested the value of bidirectional formulations. A good example of such a bidirectional model is Bell's (1968) conception of the interplay of influences between parents and children. Correlational evidence showing that some aspect of the parent's child-rearing method is associated with differences in the behavior of the children is usually interpreted to reflect the parent's influence on the child. Thus, father nurturance is positively linked with masculinity of sons (Mussen & Rutherford, 1963) but which factor is the cause and which the effect? In contrast to the tendency to assume that the father's behavior leads to the son's traits, Bell called attention to the opposite process by which the son's traits might be viewed as antecedents of the father's reactions. Numerous other studies also suggest that children's behaviors are as much the causes of the parent's behaviors as is the opposite sequence. Bell suggested that parents may start with low control methods of dealing with their children and that these methods are sufficient for some children. When these methods fail, it may become necessary for them to resort to strong forms of control. The net result would show a correlation between the type of parental control and the children's traits but instead of assuming that the parent's behavior caused the children's traits, it is more plausible in this example to interpret the causal sequence as being just the opposite–difficult-to-control children cause their parents to resort to stronger forms of discipline.

Method Restricts Content

Gadlin and Ingle (1975) criticized the experimental paradigm as being of limited value and argued that psychology needs a new paradigm or methodology. Following Kuhn's (1962) conception that the dominant paradigm in any science influences the way the scientist views the subject matter of the discipline, the kinds of methods used to answer questions, and the way for raising further questions, they concluded that only when a new paradigm is developed to replace the existing paradigm will major changes in the approaches of the field occur.

Gadlin and Ingle called for a new paradigm in which the content or phenomena of psychology would take precedence over the methodology. They felt that the study of psychology involves relationships with people which should be "reflexive," to use their term, in which the experimenter and subjects would cooperatively interact. Finally, this paradigm would also recognize the value of studying the behavior of psychologists in their capacities as scientists.

The criticism of experimentation raised by Gadlin and Ingle, however, could also be directed toward any other paradigm or method if it is the case that the choice of content is determined in part by the methods used. Rather than call for a new paradigm to *replace* the old, it would seem more productive to encourage a diversity of paradigms to ensure that no content is overlooked simply because there were no appropriate methods of investigation.

Psychology As History

Perhaps one of the most critical challenges to the future of psychological research modelled after the physical sciences has been raised by Gergen (1973). His argument that a science of psychology is not fully possible is similar to the same issue confronting other fields like sociology (Mills, 1959) since they both conceive of social sciences as historical in nature in that the discoveries are more or less unique and nonrepeatable events. As such, Gergen concluded that generalizations or universal principles will not be achieved. Whereas findings in the physical sciences can be repeated and possess transhistorical validity, the knowledge obtained in the social sciences may become less valid over time because dissemination of these theories among the populace may undermine or reduce the susceptibility of people to these processes. If selling technique A is developed to encourage people to buy what they do not need, publication of this method will perhaps enable the consumer to be on guard or develop counter resistance to prevent being persuaded to buy.

As social, economic, and political conditions change in a society over generations, the factors that led to one type of effect may no longer exist, so that repeatability of that effect is lessened. For example, Karlin, Coffman, and Walters (1969) assessed ethnic stereotypes and compared them to findings obtained a generation earlier by Katz and Braly (1933). Karlins, et al. found that large shifts had taken place over time and the earlier stereotypes were not confirmed. Ethnic groups previously viewed as extremely positive or negative were later seen in a more moderate light.

If Gergen's thesis is that theories are doomed to self-negation because of the "reactions to theory" when people become enlightened or informed about them, one might think that a theory of these "reactions to theory" could be formulated which would be universal and transhistorical. Gergen rejected this possibility on the same grounds by pointing out that people, once sensitized to the theory, would also resist and disconfirm it. As an example, he cited the approach of reverse psychology in which you try to trick someone into doing something they would not do if you asked directly. Tell a young child to clean up his or her room and you encounter resistance; however, if you forbid the child to clean up, the child may actually do it to prove self-control. However, before long the child realizes what you are doing and the technique will no longer work.

One of the main critics of Gergen's position, Barry Schlenker (1974), sees an inconsistency in Gergen's assumption that there is a universal tendency to resist being influenced, which is the basis of Gergen's argument for the lack of transhistorical validity of all other findings. Schlenker argued that at least this one universal process must be postulated if Gergen's position is tenable.

Schlenker attacked Gergen's position as unduly pessimistic and misleading because it is based on too narrow a conception of scientific laws. When one deals with a specific finding such as the effects of praise on reading in five-year-old boys using a phonics approach, it is likely that a different study with slightly different conditions will not produce the same results. But if one was using this study as evidence for a more general theory of the effects of reinforcement on learning, greater generalizability may exist. In other words, it is important to consider the level of analysis involved in determining whether or not a science of psychology is possible, according to Schlenker. Even though specific findings may vary from study to study, he maintained that some higher order principles can be extracted which will hold greater generality. In short, Schlenker does not agree with Gergen that the social and physical sciences have any fundamental differences.

There is probably no "right or wrong" answer on this issue and the position one adopts may depend on, as Schlenker implies, how optimistic or pessimistic one is. Either position has to be taken on faith since it is not possible to disprove the alternative view.

Those who concur with Schlenker will continue formulating theories and testing their predictions with empirical evidence. Proponents of Gergen's views may follow his advice to abandon the search for general laws and to focus more on integrating pure research methods with the solution of practical social problems. Instead of trying to predict and control behavior, Gergen saw the goal of research as that of sensitization and enlightenment by identifying the range of factors which might potentially affect behavior under various conditions. Research would be more directed toward descriptions of the nature of psychological processes as they exist in society rather than attempts to test hypotheses about the effects of variables. Finally, research would aspire more toward viewing phenomena within the historical context of events rather than as isolated short-term laboratory events.

Sampson (1978) has distinguished two paradigms of science, Paradigm I which is concerned with abstract and general laws, and Paradigm II which is similar to Gergen's view and recognizes the historically and culturally restricted aspect of the findings of science. Sampson argued that the dominance of Paradigm I has stemmed from generally unrecognized values such as Protestantism, puritanism, and a male-dominant society stressing individualistic goals which regard the positivistic approach based on the discovery of objective and universal facts as the most valid approach to truth.

Unfortunately the assumption that this approach can be value-free is incorrect, according to Sampson, and tends to promote and reflect the values of those in power and preserve the status quo. Sampson called for greater recognition and acceptance of Paradigm II, not as a substitute for Paradigm I, but rather as a complementary and equal status approach. Paradigm II, which acknowledges the influence of the values of a particular society on the findings obtained by science, provides a balanced perspective so that Paradigm I knowledge will not be represented as absolute and value-free.

A CASE EXAMPLE: SEX DIFFERENCES IN INFLUENCIBILITY

A number of issues raised about the limitations of the nature of research can be illustrated with the example of the study of sex differences in influencibility, which has been thoroughly reviewed by Alice Eagly (1978). She observed that although most textbooks dealing with this question offer the assertion that there is unequivocal evidence that females are more susceptible to persuasion and social influence due to social norms internalized during socialization, the evidence cited is meager. Her review of the research literature on conformity and attitude change portrayed a complicated set of relationships, which we will describe shortly. In the light of the research evidence failing to support the conclusion that females are more influencible over a variety of situations, Eagly raised the question of how it was possible for expert psychologists to overlook the existing research which contradicted their conclusions.

Perhaps this situation involves selective perception or bias on the part of psychologists, who noticed those studies that yielded results consistent with their preconceptions. Studies that showed no sex differences may have been dismissed as inconclusive rather than accepted as evidence of a genuine lack of difference. Thus, it is possible that the personal prejudices and expectations of authors may have led to their erroneous conclusions.

Turning now to Eagly's review of research, it should be first noted that many of the studies that provide evidence on sex differences in influencibility were primarily interested in assessing the effects of other variables. Secondary interest in sex differences may have been due to the assumption that task variables, such as communication content or style, have a stronger effect or that individual differences are relatively unimportant.

Most of the situations surveyed by Eagly deal with studies of persuasion and of conformity, either with or without the presence of other persons. The typical finding in these studies is that of *no* sex differences in persuasibility or conformity, unless there is group pressure where other members of the group hold opinions different from that of the subject and the group monitors the subject's responses. Under these latter conditions, females do appear to be more influencible in many studies.

A number of other factors exist, however, which complicate the picture. First, a breakdown of studies into two groups, pre- and post-1970, disclosed a dramatic difference toward a reduction in the percentage of studies showing greater female influencibility, even for the group pressure conformity studies. This historical effect may be an example of Gergen's (1973) view of the ahistoricality of psychological research results, the lack of generalizability over time. One possible explanation for this particular instance could be the impact of the women's movement, which has reduced the validity of traditional sex roles.

A third factor that may be important in determining the likelihood that greater female influencibility will be demonstrated is the content of the topic. Eagly noted that most previous studies chose topics such as economices and politics, areas where males have traditionally been encouraged to develop greater knowledge and involvement. Perhaps the findings of female influencibility occur primarily because of a more general tendency for persons to yield and conform on topics on which they knew the least amount. An implication of this argument is that males should be more influenced if the topics used are those where females are usually more expert, as Sistrunk and McDavid (1971) have demonstrated.

A fourth factor that may affect results is the sex of the person attempting to induce attitude change. Most studies have employed males to present persuasive communications to subjects, partly perhaps due to the aforementioned tendency to choose masculine topics and partly to the fact that evidence shows males are more persuasive because they are regarded as more knowledgeable. The net effect of this procedure is for male subjects to have a same-sex communicator whereas the female subjects have one of the opposite sex. Greater female influencibility might be due to the fact that they generally encounter communicators of the sex they regard as more competent.

In summary, it appears that the generalization that females are more influencible depends on a number of other interacting variables: historical period when the study was conducted, type of situation, topic content, and sex of the communicator. Cronbach's (1975) focus on the complexities of interacting variables emphasized individual difference variables such as age, personality, and intelligence, but the general argument applies equally well to this example. Influencibility is affected by numerous variables but any single investigation can attempt to study two or three of them. The conclusions one draws about the effects of the variables examined in that study may interact with additional variables that were not included.

The issue of the relationship between laboratory studies and real-life phenomena is also illustrated by the research on sex differences in influencibility. As already noted, the laboratory findings show much smaller sex differences than one might suppose from an examination of popular beliefs among the public. As Eagly observed, the stereotypical beliefs of laypersons can not be rejected simply on the basis of the laboratory studies. These stereotypes must have been formed in large measure from the everyday experiences and interactions we have with men and women, and although these beliefs may be exaggerated and biased, there probably is a reasonable degree of validity to them. Furthermore, whereas stereotypes are based on years of experience, laboratory findings deal with very brief events as Silverman (1977) pointed out.

How then do we reconcile the discrepancies between laboratory findings and real-life beliefs? Eagly suggested several factors that might contribute to the different conclusions: cultural lag, unrepresentative sampling, and the different roles which men and women play in real life as opposed to laboratory situations. Cultural lag simply refers to the possibility that the newer findings have not been assimilated and that conclusions are still being based on earlier pre-1970 studies which did show greater female influencibility. The possibility that college students who serve as subjects in most psychological studies may not share the more traditional sex roles leads to the argument that the smaller degree of female influencibility in laboratory studies stems from the fact that college students are not representative of the general population.

Perhaps the most important factor leading to differences between laboratory findings and popular stereotypes is the fact that the role of subject in a laboratory experiment is essentially identical for males and females whereas real-life roles for males and females vary widely from situation to situation. This fundamental difference could account for the reduced influencibility of females in experiments as compared to in everyday situations. In the latter social contexts, social and cultural norms are significant determinants of behavior, as Pepitone (1976) has argued, which must be examined in order to fully understand it. In our society, the traditional norms regarding sex roles place women in less powerful positions and social roles.

What, then, is the value of experiments and laboratory research if they fail to reflect the actual determinants of everyday life accurately? Eagly suggested that the experiment offers the advantage of greater analytical precision since it can isolate factors to rule out alternative explanations. In the case of real life sex role differences, the differences could be due to social norms, physiological differences, or possibly to a complex interplay between both factors. Biological and social causes of sex differences are confounded in everyday life, being inextricably interwoven processes. Eagly argued that the laboratory situation that offers the same role of "subject" to both sexes permits a better assessment of the other factors such as innate physiologically-based differences. She concluded that these latter factors are relatively unimportant since laboratory studies have shown negligible sex differences in influencibility. Therefore, it would seem plausible to attribute the larger sex differences in influencibility found in everyday situations to the types of social roles assigned to each sex, roles which will *not* be the same in all real-life situations.

The comparison of the findings of laboratory studies and real-life contexts regarding the nature of sex differences in influencibility suggests that it is important to obtain both sources of information wherever feasible because they may not yield the same conclusions. In such an outcome, the task then becomes a search for reasons why the two sets of findings conflict. Is there some critical element distinguishing the laboratory analogue from the real-life phenomenon that produced the discrepancy? The proof of the experimental evidence lies in whether it reveals valid information about the real phenomena. However, since experiments involve artificial conditions, reactivity, random sampling, and brief time periods, among other things, their findings may not match those of the real world. As Tunnell (1977) suggested, since we ultimately want to understand the real-world processes, we need to continually compare our laboratory findings with reality to make sure our experiments are on the right track.

WHERE DO WE GO FROM HERE?

The experiment, whether used in the laboratory or in naturalistic situations, has been found to hold a number of serious problems described throughout this book. Solutions to one type of shortcoming have opened the door to other weaknesses. Use of strategies such as deception to circumvent the lack of realism in the laboratory creates some ethical impasses. Some loss of control is the cost for the elimination of reactivity by doing naturalistic studies.

The solution to the dilemma is not to abandon the experimental method but rather to augment it by including other techniques which, taken alone, might be considered weaker than the experiment as a source of analysis. Individual case studies, autobiographies, surveys, interviews, field observations, archival data and other historical information such as trends, and clinical observations are among the types of evidence that can be used to complement experimental findings. These less controlled methods can provide data that may generate interesting questions which can then be examined experimentally, or they may serve as an alternative source of information against which the experimental results can be checked. To the extent that these converging methods yield consistent conclusions, greater confidence can be held since different methods do not share the same limitations as research tools. In contrast, when various methods lead to conflicting data it serves to alert us to be cautious in drawing conclusions until further research can identify the basis for the disagreement.

The usefulness of the experimental approach has been seriously examined and called into question for a variety of reasons. The problems of methodological precision, ethical propriety, and generalizability to the real world which confront the experimenter has presented the ultimate dilemma. Silverman (1977, p. 356) observed, "And social psychology can only begin to grow into an authentic discipline when we abandon the experiment as a modus operandi." He envisioned the future role of the experiment as a supplemental technique rather than as the cornerstone for developing knowledge about psychological phenomena and predicted a greater role for less rigorous methods of a more descriptive nature. This shift would permit more generalizability as it would focus more on naturalistic techniques, which are admittedly less precise.

Kelman (1968, p. 162) expressed a similar view in which he called for greater use of other techniques such as "population surveys and correlational research, participant observation and community studies, analysis of documents and of individual cases, historical studies and ethnographic reports."

The role of experiments, in Kelman's conception, is not to discover general laws, since the discrepancy between laboratory and the natural world is too great, at least at this stage of development of the discipline. Nonetheless, according to Kelman, experiments have a vital role to perform in facilitating systematic thinking about psychological processes in the following ways. First, it brings discipline to our thinking: "The necessity of devising an experiment forces us to commit ourselves—to state clearly what our concepts mean and to pin down precisely what relationships we expect" (p. 160). Secondly, experiments can help us identify what *can be* between two variables, which can help us determine the directions in which our conceptual thinking might best proceed. Thirdly, experiments, when used in combination with observations from real life, can offer insights to our thinking about psychological processes since the control afforded by this method enables us to study effects of specific variables of interest. Finally, when unexpected experimental findings occur we are forced to examine our theories and consider variables and processes that had previously gone unnoticed. In essence, those varied roles of experiments point out the fact than an experiment does not stand alone but must be related to other data from other experiments as well as from other sources so that our thinking can "narrow-in" on a more accurate conception of the phenomena we are investigating.

Similarly Gergen (1978) suggested some adjunct roles for experimentation to play even if it should be dethroned from the center of the stage. On one hand, experiments can be used to dramatize phenomena and help publicize them rather than serve only to test theoretical formulations. The respect with which science is held by the public attracts attention to its endeavors. The experimenter can create simplified paradigms that provide more dramatic or clearcut models of phenomena, such as Milgram (1963) did with his obedience-to-authority study or Haney, Banks, and Zimbardo (1973) did with their simulation of prison-guard interactions.

Although these studies are more aptly termed "demonstrations" rather than true experiments since they did not test hypotheses about the role of independent variables which might have some causal influence, they eventually lead to or generate a number of subsequent studies employing the experimental method. As Gergen observed, these studies serve a sensitizing effect so that the societal consciousness of certain phenomena is raised by them. This is one type of alternative function to which experiments can be usefully applied that avoids the limitations of the method Gergen saw as obstacles when experiments are used to test hypotheses and formulate general laws of behavior.

SUMMARY

Even if problems facing the experimenter, such as experimenter bias, reactivity, and ethical concerns, can be resolved, we are still confronted with some other serious issues about the usefulness of the experimental method. The inherent control of experiments in which the experimenter holds power over the subject may produce resentment and resistance, according to one view, which may jeopardize the validity of results obtained with experiments at least for some types of human behavior. An alternative research method involving more collaborative and equal status between the researcher and the persons under study has been proposed to deal with this concern.

Experiments have been criticized for often being demonstrations of the obvious which are staged or contrived to fulfill the predictions of the researcher. Experiments provide misleading, oversimplified answers because most important behavior is complex and involves a myriad of determinants. Since the experiment typically can handle only two or three variables at a time, it is unable to detect interactions among variables affecting the behavior under study. Apparent confusion due to numerous small-scale studies with conflicting or incompatible results often results. Experiments, due to the contraints of time, must necessarily deal with short-term effects for the most part. These findings have questionable validity in understanding real-life counterparts of laboratory phenomena because of the difference in the temporal duration between the two situations.

Experiments are often conceptualized in the vacuum of the laboratory and neglect the role of social, cultural, and historical factors influencing real-life behavior. Laboratory findings are accepted as universal principles whereas real-life counterparts of these phenomena vary widely in different social groups and cultures. The results of experiments tend to be viewed as timeless, but there is reason to believe that the historical era in which studies are done may yield different findings for some types of phenomena. Due to the changing historical context in which real-life behavior occurs, it should hardly be surprising that the kinds of behavior and the determinants of behavior may vary over time.

The experimental approach emphasizes a unidirectional model of causation in which the independent variable is presumed to produce differences on the dependent variable. However, many phenomena involve bidirectional influences in which two or more factors affect one another, as in the case of dyadic relationships such as parent–child, husband–wife, and student–teacher.

All of these problems pose quite a dilemma, for as one solution is devised for one problem, it often opens the door for a different type of problem. Instead of abandoning the experiment, however, it would appear that wider use of other forms of evidence such as surveys, archival data, interviews, field observations, case studies, autobiographies and other personal documents should be sought and used in combination with the controlled observations afforded by the experimental method. A continuous interplay between the rigorous methods and the less stringent sources of information is needed to provide the most complete analysis. Careful observation of less artifical real-life behavior may aid in formulating concepts and hypotheses which can then be subjected to better scrutiny by the more rigorous tools of controlled observation. To the extent that the evidence from most sources agree, we can have greater confidence in our conclusions. Discrepancies between controlled and naturalistic observations should make us more cautious and lead us to reexamine our concepts and theories, revise them, and seek additional evidence to further test our notions. Neither method—controlled and uncontrolled—used alone is likely to provide as much validity as the use of both approaches.

REFERENCES

Argyris, C. Some unintended effects of rigorous research. *Psychological Bulletin,* 1968, *70*, 185-197.

Argyris, C. Dangers in applying results from experimental social psychology. *American Psychologist,* 1975, *39*, 469-485.

Bandura, A. Behavior theory and the models of man. *American Psychologist,* 1974, *29*, 859-869.

Bandura, A. The self-system in reciprocal determinism. *American Psychologist,* 1978, *33*, 344-358.

Bell, R. Q. A reinterpretation of direction of effects in studies of socialization. *Psychological Review,* 1968, *75*, 81-95.

Bem, S. L. The measurement of psychological androgyny. *Journal of Clinical and Consulting Psychology,* 1974, *42*, 155-162.

Bem, S. L. Sex-role adaptability: One consequence of psychological androgyny. *Journal of Personality and Social Psychology,* 1975, *31*, 634-643.

Brehm, J. W. *A Theory of Psychological Reactance.* New York: Academic Press, 1966.

Cronbach, L. J. The two disciplines of scientific psychology. *American Psychologist,* 1957, *12*, 671-684.

Cronbach, L. J. Beyond the two disciplines in "scientific psychology." *American Psychologist,* 1975, *30*, 116-127.

Dipboye, R. L., and Flanagan, M. Research settings in industrial and organizational psychology: Are findings in the field more generalizable than in the laboratory? *American Psychologist,* 1979, *34*, 141-150.

Eagly, A. H. Sex differences in influencibility. *Psychological Bulletin,* 1978, *85*, 86-116.

Elms, A. C. The crisis of confidence in social psychology. *American Psychologist,* 1975, *30*, 967-976.

Epstein, S. The stability of behavior: II. Implications for psychological research. *American Psychologist,* 1980, *35*, 790-806.

Gadlin, H., and Ingle, G. Through the one-way mirror: The limits of experimental self-reflection. *American Psychologist,* 1975, *30*, 1003-1009.

Gergen, K. J. Social psychology as history. *Journal of Personality and Social Psychology,* 1973, *26*, 309-320.

Gergen, K. J. Experimentation in social psychology: A reappraisal. *European Journal of Social Psychology,* 1978, *8*, 507-527.

Gergen, K. J. Toward generative theory. *Journal of Personality and Social Psychology,* 1978, *36*, 1344-1360.

Haney, C., Banks, C., and Zimbardo, P. C. Interpersonal dynamics in a simulated prison. *International Journal of Criminology and Penology,* 1973, *1*, 69-97.

Harré, R., and Secord, P. F. *The explanation of social behavior.* Oxford: Blackwell, 1972.

Jung, J. Is it possible to measure generalizability of laboratory-life settings? And, is it really that important? In I. Silverman (Ed.), *New directions for methodology of social and behavioral science. Generalizing from laboratory to life.* San Francisco: Jossey-Bass, 1981.

Karlins, M., Coffman, T. L., and Walters, G. On the fading of social stereotypes: Studies in three generations of college students. *Journal of Personality and Social Psychology,* 1969, *13*, 1-16.

Katz, D., and Braly, K. W. Racial stereotypes of one hundred college students. *Journal of Abnormal and Social Psychology,* 1933, *28*, 282-290.

Kelman, H. C. *A time to speak.* San Francisco: Jossey-Bass, 1968.

Kuhn, T. S. *The structure of scientific revolutions.* Chicago: University of Chicago Press, 1962.

McGuire, W. The yin and yang of progress in social psychology: Seven koan. *Journal of Personality and Social Psychology,* 1973, *26*, 446-456.

Milgram, S. Behavioral study of obedience. *Journal of Abnormal and Social Psychology,* 1963, *67*, 371-378.

Mills, C. *The sociological imagination.* New York: Oxford University Press, 1959.

Mussen, P., and Rutherford, E. H. Parent-child relations and parental personality in relation to young children's sex role preferences. *Child Development,* 1963, *34*, 589-607.

Pepitone, A. Toward a normative and comparative biocultural social psychology. *Journal of Personality and Social Psychology,* 1976, *34*, 641-653.

Sampson, E. E. Psychology and the American ideal. *Journal of Personality and Social Psychology,* 1977, *35*, 767-782.

Sampson, E. E. Scientific paradigms and social values: Wanted—a scientific revolution. *Journal of Personality and Social Psychology,* 1978, *36*, 1332-1343.

Schlenker, B. R. Social psychology and science. *Journal of Personality and Social Psychology,* 1974, *19*, 1-15.

Silverman, I. Why social psychology fails. *Canadian Psychological Review,* 1977, *18*, 353-358.

Sistrunk, F., and McDavid, J. W. Sex variable in conforming behavior. *Journal of Personality and Social Psychology,* 1971, *17*, 200-207.

Tajfel, H. Experiments in a vacuum. In Isreal, J., and H. Trajfel (Eds.) *The context of social psychology*. New York: Academic Press, 1972.

Thorngate, W. Possible limits on a science of social behavior. In L. H. Strickland, F. E. Aboud, and K. J. Gergen (Eds.) *Social psychology in transition.* New York: Plenum, 1976.

Triandis, H. C. Social psychology and cultural analyses. In L. H. Strickland, F. E. Aboud, and K. J. Gergen (Eds.) *Social psychology in transition.* New York: Plenum, 1976.

Tunnell, G. B. Three dimensions of naturalness: An expanded definition of field research. *Psychological Bulletin,* 1977, *84*, 426-437.

Tyler, L. E. *Individuality.* San Francisco: Jossey Bass, 1978.

GLOSSARY

Abscissa: the horizontal axis in a graph; also known as the X axis

Artifact: a result which is not genuine due to methodological flaws

Between-groups variance: differences in the means of various differentially treated groups or conditions

Between-subjects design: a design which uses each subject in only one of the possible treatment conditions

Blind experimenter: an experimenter who is uninformed about the purpose of the study or the nature of the treatment which each subject receives

Confounding: the situation in which some unintended variable also covaries with the intended independent variable so that any results cannot be unequivocably attributed to the latter factor

Construct validity: the extent to which measurements actually reflect the assumed theoretical process that is intended

Control group: the group (or condition) in which the treatment of interest is deliberately withheld to provide a baseline performance against which the experimental group performance can be compared

Correlation: the degree to which two variables are related, expressed numerically by the correlation coefficient which can vary between values of + 1.0 and −1.0

Counterbalancing: procedure used in the within-subjects design to control for temporal and order effects by presenting the different treatments in varying sequences so as to evenly distribute these effects over all treatments

Debriefing: the procedure of explaining the general purpose of an experiment to subjects after the session is over in which any deceptions are revealed and any adverse effects are offset

Dehoaxing: the aspect of debriefing which focuses on the disclosure of deceptions

Demand characteristics: cues in experimental situation used by subjects to infer what behavior is expected or seems appropriate; can be a source of error as when its effects are confused due to the independent variable

Dependent variable: the aspect of the subject's behavior which varies with or is dependent upon the influence of variations in the independent variable

Descriptive statistics: measures such as the mean and standard deviation which summarize, condense, and describe a set of data from an experiment

Desensitization: the aspect of debriefing which focuses on attempts to reassure subjects who have been deceived and to restore their self-esteem if the experimental procedures had lowered these feelings

Evaluation apprehension: the anxiety of subjects concerning how adequately they performed and how well they were scored on their responses

Expectancy controls: conditions where experimenters are given different expectations about the outcomes in order to see if part or all of the results can be due to expectations alone

Experimental method: research technique in which one or more independent variables are controlled or manipulated in order to determine their effects on the dependent variable

Experimenter attribute bias: the extent to which physical and psychosocial attributes of experimenters influence the subject's behavior

Experimenter expectancy bias: the expectations of the experimenter about the outcome of an experiment leads to differential behavior of the experimenter towards different treatment groups which leads to the fulfillment of the expectancies

External validity: the extent to which the findings of a laboratory experiment are valid when applied to a real life counterpart of the situation

Factorial design: a design with more than one independent variable which employs all possible combinations of the different levels of all of the independent variables

Frequency distribution: an arrangement of a set of data which is ordered so as to indicate the frequency of occurrence of each subgroup or category of scores in increasing order of magnitude

Frequency polygon: a graphical presentation of a frequency distribution

Fudging: a form of cheating or fraud in which data is altered or invented

Generalizability: the extent to which we can apply the results of one experiment to other subjects, tasks, situations, or measures

Hawthorne effect: spurious effects due to the fact that the subjects realize they are being observed but which may be mistakenly attributed to the independent variable

History: threat to internal validity in which some events which occur concurrently with the independent variable may be responsible for observed changes

Human subject pool: the supply of human research participants which, in universities, generally consists of students enrolled in introductory psychology courses

Hypothesis: prediction based on theory about possible outcomes of an experiment

Independent variable: the factor which is manipulated or controlled in an experiment so that its influence on the dependent variable can be assessed

Individual differences: variation in characteristics and behavior among a set of different individuals

Informed consent: the ethical procedure calling for obtaining the permission of research participants in advance after provisions of sufficient background information so that they can reach an "informed" decision

Interaction: in factorial designs where the effects of one independent variable differ depending on the levels of the other independent variables

Internal validity: feature of a design which controls adequately all other factors than the one which the experimenter wishes to assess

Interval scale: measurement where the variable involves successive values which are equal in distance along a single underlying dimension

Invasion of privacy: threat to the rights of the subject to privacy created by the observations made by researchers

Involved participation: a form of roleplaying which is highly realistic or engaging to the subject

Inferential statistics: use of results obtained from samples to generalize to a larger population

Instrument decay: type of threat to internal validity where the measuring technique or apparatus may change during the experiment so that the true effects of the independent variable can not be measured accurately

Literature search: review and synthesis of research findings in a specific area of interest

Main effects: the overall influence of each of the independent variables in a factorial design

Manipulation check: procedure aimed to measure directly the extent to which the procedures designed to create different levels of the independent variable were in fact effective

Matching or *matched group design:* procedure used to form equivalent groups with respect to a specific variable assumed to be correlated with the type of behavior being studied; for each subject in one group at a given level on the matching variable, there is a matched counterpart assigned to each of the other groups

Maturation: type of threat to internal validity where growth and other age-related changes may occur over the course of the experiment and prevent the accurate assessment of the effect of the independent variable

Mean: the arithmetic average (sum of scores divided by the number of individual scores) for a set of scores

Median: the value of the score which is at the midpoint of a set of scores

Metaexperiment: experiment designed to test hypotheses about the nature of the experimental method itself

Mode: the score which occurs most frequently among a set of scores

Monotonic relationship: the relationship between an independent and dependent variable where the latter increases in magnitude as the former one is increased

Mortality: type of threat to internal validity in which the original sample of subjects is selectively reduced due to nonrandom loss of subjects over the course of the experiment so that it prevents accurate assessment of the effects of the independent variable

Naturalistic field experiment: a controlled experiment conducted outside the laboratory often without the awareness of subjects

Naturalistic field study: a correlational or uncontrolled study conducted outside the laboratory usually on subjects who are unaware they are being observed

Nominal scale: measurement where the variable involves qualitatively distinctive categories rather than a dimension which varies in quantity or amount

Nonexperiment (also called *preinquiry*)*:* a type of control procedure to measure demand characteristics in which the subjects do not actually perform the task but are given instructions in the test setting and asked to describe their perceptions

Normal distribution: a symmetrical or bell shaped frequency distribution with specific mathematical properties which allows the determination of the relative frequency or probability of different possible scores

Null hypothesis: the statistical hypothesis that assumes that there is no difference between different treatment groups caused by the independent variable and that any observed differences are small enough to have occurred by chance

Operational definition: concept in which the definition of a concept is a description of the operations or procedures used to measure it

Ordinal scale: measurement where the variable involves successive values which are ordered in relative size along a single dimension but the distances between different successive values are not necessarily equal

Ordinate: the vertical axis in a graph; also known as the Y axis

Pact of ignorance: concept that the subject is unlikely to disclose to the experimenter if he or she knows the true nature of the experiment and that the experimenter is unlikely to probe too deeply during the postexperimental inquiry for fear it will be learned that the subject will turn out to have seen through the deception

Pilot study: preliminary or exploratory trial test to refine and improve procedures

Placebo: a treatment condition which is assumed to have no genuine effect on the behavior under examination and is included as a control against factors such as expectancies which could affect results

Postexperimental inquiry: interview with subjects after session is completed to determine how they perceived the situation or what types of strategies they used

Preinquiry: interview with subjects before an experimental session in which subjects are asked for their perceptions of the situation to determine the demand characteristics; also called nonexperiment

Protection from harm: precautions to ensure the physical and/or psychological well-being of subjects in an experiment

Pseudo-volunteers: subjects who are coerced or pressured to participate rather than truly volunteer

Psychology as history: Gergen's concept that some findings in psychology cannot be generalized over different historical eras because they tend to be negated as greater dissimination of these findings occurs

Random assignment: procedure employed for creating different groups of subjects so that each subject has equal chance of being assigned to any specific group

Random sampling: procedure for insuring that each member of a population has an equal chance of being selected for inclusion in a sample

Randomization: procedure by which variables, subjects, or treatments are selected so that potential biases are controlled

Range: the difference between the highest and lowest score in a set which is an index of variability

Ratio scale: measurement where the variable involved has successive values which are equally distant from each other along a single dimension and there is an absolute zero value

Reactivity: the situation in which the subject is aware of being observed and may lead to a distortion of typical behavior

Reliability: the extent to which measurements are repeatable or consistent in outcome over two or more occasions or situations

Replication: repetition of a prior experiment, often conducted by other researchers, to determine if the same results can be repeated

Risk-benefit ratio: the concept that the ethical soundness of an experiment depends on the extent to which the risk of harm to the subjects is outweighed by the benefits of the knowledge to be obtained for others

Role enactment: a form of role playing where the subject is highly involved

Roleplaying: procedure in which the subject specifies how he or she thinks he or she would behave in a specific situation rather than requiring the actual conduct of the entire procedures

Rosenthal paradigm: the photo-rating task used in many of the experiments on experimenter expectancy bias

Sample: a subset selected from a larger population

Sampling error: variability of estimates obtained from different random samples taken from the same population

Sampling distribution of the mean: hypothetical frequency distribution of all possible sample means of random samples from a population

Self-quality task: where the correct responses are ambiguous and depend on the subject's own personality

Significance level: a conventional or arbitrary probability level such as 1 or 5 per cent used to decide if the size of the difference obtained between the experimental and control group justifies the rejection of the null hypothesis

Standard deviation: a measure of the variability of a set of scores which is based on the mean difference of deviations of all scores from the mean score for the set

Standard error of the mean: the standard deviation of the sampling distribution of the mean

Subject: a participant in an experiment

Subject variable: a factor such as age, sex, personality, or ability on which different subjects vary

Subject roles: the types of attitudes which subjects hold about the appropriate or desired behavior that subjects should display in a given experimental situation

Task ability tasks: where the correct response is clear and performance depends on ability

Theory: a formulation which interrelates several factors in order to explain a set of observations or phenomena; useful as integrator of different facts and leads to testable hypotheses for other experiments

Type I error: incorrect decision in which the null hypothesis is rejected when it is true

Type II error: incorrect decision in which the null hypothesis is accepted when it is false

Validity: the degree to which a measure is an accurate reflection of the construct which it is designed to assess

Variability: the degree of fluctation among a set of scores

Variable: a dimension which can assume different values

Within-subjects design: where each subject usually serves in all of several treatment conditions but in differing temporal sequences for different subsets of subjects; also known as repeated-measures design

NAME INDEX

SUBJECT INDEX